THE COLONIZATION

Translations from Latin America Series

Institute of Latin American Studies
University of Texas at Austin

THE COLONIZATION OF THE AMAZON

BY
ANNA LUIZA OZORIO DE ALMEIDA

University of Texas Press, Austin

First paperback printing, 2013
First Edition, 1992

Requests for permission to reproduce material from this work should be sent to Permissions, University of Texas Press, P.O. Box 7819, Austin, Texas 78713-7819
utpress.utexas.edu/index.php/rp-form

♾ The paper used in this publication meets the minimum requirements of American National Standard for Information Sciences—Permanence of Paper for Printed Library Materials, ANSI Z39.48–1984.

Library of Congress Cataloging-in-Publication Data

Almeida, Anna Luiza Ozorio de.
[Colonização dirigida na Amazônia. 1970–1980. English]
The Colonization of the Amazon / by Anna Luiza Ozorio de Almeida
p. cm. — (Translations from Latin America Series)
Translation of: A colonização dirigida na Amazônia, 1970–1980.
Includes bibliographical references and index.
ISBN 978-0-292-75598-7
1. Amazon River Region—Colonization. 2. Brazil—Colonization. 3. Land settlement—Amazon River Region. 4. Land settlement—Brazil. 5. Migration, Internal—Brazil. I. Title. II. Series.
HD499.A44A4413 1992 92-5938
333.3'1811—dc20 CIP

For my darlings:
Joana and Gabriel

CONTENTS

Part 4: The Colonists

Tables

Maps

Charts

Graphs

ACKNOWLEDGMENTS

This research project began in 1978 as a joint project of the Faculdade de Economia e Administração of the Universidade Federal do Rio de Janeiro (FEA/UFRJ) and the Instituto de Pesquisas of the Instituto de Planejamento Econômico e Social (INPES/IPEA). The research continued between 1980 and 1984 under an agreement between IPEA, the Instituto de Colonização e Reforma Agrária (INCRA), and the Coordenação de Programas de Pós-Graduação em Engenharia e Tecnologia (COPPETEC) with the title "Migrações internas e pequena produção agrícola na Amazônia: uma análise da política de colonização do INCRA," funded by INCRA, IPEA, and the Ford Foundation. In 1985, the project was partially financed by the Programa Nacional de Pesquisa Econômica (PNPE) with partial World Bank funding under the aegis of the Projeto de Crédito Agrícola e Desenvolvimento de Exportações. From 1986 to 1990, the project received funding from CNPq, the Sub-Reitoria de Pesquisas of UFRJ, the Fundação de Amparo à Pesquisa do Estado do Rio de Janeiro (FAPERJ), and the Associação Brasileira de Estudos Populacionais (ABEP).

During its peregrinations through various institutions, the research gathered coauthors, collaborators, and advisers, both formal and informal. Their involvement varied in duration and intensity ever since the proposal phase, which benefited from suggestions made by Fredericka Santos, Cristina Gladwin, and Leonarda Musumeci.

During the INCRA/IPEA phase, Maria Beatriz Albuquerque David was an inexhaustible collaborator and field researcher, collecting, organizing, and analyzing all of the primary and secondary data. Sarah Hawker Costa added a demographic and health component to the field survey; Brancolina Ferreira researched farmers' perceptions; Horácio

Martins Carvalho prepared the preliminary versions of the questionnaires and, along with Clovis A. Perez, developed a process of iterative sampling, given the absence of previous information about the universe to be studied. Avigdor Meroz prepared the empirical methodology for studying small farmers' accounts, translating detailed field data into precise balance sheets.

During the project's World Bank/IPEA phase, Carlos Henrique Guanziroli put together diverse information from the INCRA/IPEA agreement and conducted new complementary interviews. Angela Moulin Penalva Santos analyzed the field data concerning merchants on the frontier; Edgar Acosta Alvarez and Carlos Eduardo Gouveia began the analysis of farmers' accounts; and Pedro Luiz Vals Pereira organized data on agricultural productivity.

Generations of research assistants at IPEA contributed to the study, some of whom have since become well-known professionals: Inês Emília M. S. Patrício, Eliane Gottleib, José Luiz Viana da Cunha, Paulo Renato Muniz, Regina Botelho Villela, Eclair Mangaravite de Moraes, Nilva Maria Nobre, José Eduardo Carneiro de Mattos Pereira, Jones Castelar Júnior, and Gyorgy Varga. Graduate and undergraduate students at FEA and at the Instituto de Economia Industrial (IEI) also produced studies that were of use to this project: Mário Audifax Pinto Sobrinho, Maria Claudia Gutiérrez, Maria da Piedade Morais, Charley Francisconi Velloso dos Santos, Leonardo Rangel Tura, Alexandre Gheventer, and Ana Margarida Keidel da Cunha. Hans Henze was generously lent by the Banco Nacional de Desenvolvimento Econômico e Social (BNDES) for field research. Leonardo and Charley were responsible for editing, bibliographic updating, and organizing field data.

Carlos Ozorio de Almeida, Sérgio Gomes de Castro, and Antônio José Alves Júnior generated some of the most difficult and original findings in this research. Daniel Gleizer and Antônio Vinhas Catão helped to update the bibliography. Sônia Maria Vasconcelos was the most dedicated interviewer and reviser of field research data and became part of the "elite troop" of interviewers, along with Maria Lúcia Kitogaki, Francisco Barghigiani, and Leocarlos Marques Mundim. Other "field" colleagues—including Altamira, Romeu, Ana, Luiz, Beth, Washington, Patriarca, Wilson, Neide, Sivuca, among so many others—are part of the long history of this project and will always be affectionately remembered.

Institutionally, Luiz Carlos Rozemberg gave this project its first "green light," but Ibrahim Eris and Mikhal Gartenkraut suffered the consequences within INPES. Flávio Grinspan and Marlene Meireles facilitated COPPETEC support. Francisco Wollman provided solidarity and logistic coordination from INCRA. Guilherme Leite Silva Dias, David Goodman, and Antônio Dias Leite provided necessary supplemental resources from the IPEA/World Bank agreement, the Ford Foundation, and the José Bonifácio Foundation. Roberto Verschleisser lent his architectural offices for emergency preparation of tables and questionnaires. The Instituto Brasileiro de Geografia e Estatística (IBGE) prepared special tabulations of great interest. The Conselho Nacional de Pesquisas (CNPq) and the Fundação de Amparo à Pesquisa do Estado do Rio de Janeiro (FAPERJ) gave grants for field research follow-ups in 1988 and 1989.

The relatively unorthodox methods of this study demanded much from its supporting institutions:

At INPES, Luiz Carlos Dias prepared the maps, Antônio Brito edited numerous partial reports, and Carmem Argolo Falção ran countless alternative estimations. Arlete Diniz Braga, Alzira da Silva Souza, and Lillien Lenmertz were secretaries, collaborators, and friends. My colleagues at INPES will probably never forgive me for invading their rooms and hallways with piles of questionnaires, hoards of outside field researchers, and bouts of malaria brought in from the Amazon frontier.

At INCRA, the field research was made possible by José Luiz Spino, Antônio Lemos, Walter Cardoso, Mioshi Terada, the administrators of the visited projects and innumerable employees—radio operators and drivers, among others. At INCRA's headquarters in Brasília, Carlos Otto Schultz, George William Prescott, Edivado Souza Alves, Sjefried C. K. Steager, José Eloísio de Andrade Melo, Plínio Augusto de Meireles, Raimundo João Amorim Pereira, José Vaz Parente, José Vaz Lordelo and others provided access to and aided the interpretation of office-based information.

At FEA, Amara Silva de Souza Rocha was the project's administrative coordinator and Maria de Fátima Paiva Almeida provided bibliographic assistance. Raquel Pellizzeti and Marina Pellizzetti shared the typing of the first version of the text with Valeria Andrade Costa. Valeria was invaluable in her patience and skill in typing innumerable intermediate versions. Sergei Soares and William Savedoff shared with me the task of translating the text into English. Roberto das Chagas Campos typed the final version in English.

Margaret Hanson Costa, Vice-Director, and Américo Boscagli Reis, Assistant Director, took over the direction of FEA during my periods of writing and revising this text. My other FEA colleagues—professors, students, and employees—were tolerant of my absences, without which it would have been impossible to put together the ideas and pieces that constitute this interpretation of the Decade of Amazonian Colonization.

The committee that reviewed my promotion to full professor at FEA—Antônio Dias Leite, Ignácio Rangel, Hélio Schlitter, Guilherme L. S. Dias, and José Graziano da Silva—made valuable criticisms. I would especially like to thank Graziano for his many detailed comments and suggestions.

Parts of this material were presented at various congresses and meetings where commentators and the public helped clarify ideas: Associação Brasileira de Estudos Populacionais (Rio de Janeiro, 1981); Congresso Internacional de Geografia (Belo Horizonte, 1982); Discussão sobre Colonização e FINSOCIAL (IPLAN-Brasília, 1983); Encontro sobre a Fronteira Agrícola (INPES–Rio de Janeiro, 1984); Associação Nacional de Centros de Pós-Graduação em Economia (Salvador, 1985); Seminário sobre Tecnologia Agrícola Apropriada aos Trópicos Úmidos (CEPAL-Manaus, 1987); Encontro sobre as Cidades e a Fronteira (PUR/UFRJ–Rio de Janeiro, 1987); Encontro Anual da SOBER (Brasília, 1987) and International Economics Association (Athens, 1989). Chapters 3, 4, and 5 were extracted from an article published in *Pesquisa e Planejamento Econômico* (vol. 14, no. 2, August 1984).

Over the years, in addition to those already mentioned, various researchers discussed concepts, criticized drafts, suggested alternatives, and helped me to reflect upon the Amazon frontier: Marianne Schmink, Gervásio Castro de Rezende, George Martine, Otávio Velho, Túlio Barbosa, Carlos Minc Baumfeld, Lena Lavinas, Carlos Guanziroli, Ana Célia Castro, Maria Helena Henriques, Jean Hebette, Don Sawyer, Charles R. Clement, Sérgio Margulis, Ronaldo Seroa da Motta, Eustáquio Reis, and Donald Harris. The affection of many others stimulated me to persevere: Affonso, Myriam, Sônia, Inês, Gabarra, Takis, Álvaro, Maggie, Sandra, Maria Rosa, and my mother, Zelita. I have a special debt of gratitude to Avigdor Meroz, whose confidence and dedication were, surely, more than I deserved. Innumerable others, in town and in the field, gave of their time, information, criticism, opinions, and goodwill, teaching me how "to get things done" in Brazil.

Responsibility for all errors and omissions remaining in the text is mine alone. To all, many thanks.

THE COLONIZATION OF THE AMAZON

PART 1: THE DIMENSIONS OF THE FRONTIER

This part of the book provides an estimate of the magnitude of the Amazon frontier during the 1970s. The geographical area and population involved are shown in chapter 2; issues pertaining to availability and suitability of lands are addressed in chapters 3 through 5. Many different sources (INCRA, RADAM, BINAGRI, CENSES) are used; some are quite unknown to the public and require detailed explanation if they are to be adequately interpreted. Given the controversy over the Amazon, establishing a reliable base of information on the dimensions, direction, and conditions for agricultural occupation is of utmost importance, though perhaps tedious to the unspecialized reader.

Overview of Amazon forest and rivers from Belém to Altamira, in Pará

A colonist cutting a tree with a power saw in Monte Alegre, Pará

Recently cleared plot with stumps still on the ground in Alta Floresta, Mato Grosso

1. THE DECADE OF COLONIZATION

Large-scale occupation of the Amazon began during the 1970s. It was an ambitious decade. A military dictatorship hoping to solve land conflicts in the rest of the country by redirecting the landless toward the Amazon embarked upon an immense colonization program. What happened, though, was not what was expected, and the decade's results ended up as a surprise to everyone.

During the 1980s, the pace of road building and paving accelerated, appreciating land values and bringing into the Amazon violence, devastation, and international concern. The ideology of occupation weakened with the demise of the military dictatorship early in the decade. Criticism of colonization mounted from the ecological, anthropological, sociological, and even economic perspectives. Agriculture expanded into the *cerrados* (dry plains) of the Center-West region of the country, bypassing the Amazon altogether. News coverage of the failure of colonization projects convinced the public that they were uneconomic. What really happened in the Amazon during the 1980s, however, is not yet known, as reliable information is still insufficient and imprecise. Nor can any prediction be made for the current decade. Evaluating the state of the Amazon's occupation today requires establishing an initial starting point to serve as a basis for comparison.

This book proposes that the 1970s are such a benchmark. They are the "Decade of Colonization." The period began with hegemony of purpose and large-scale mobilization of governmental resources for "conquering" the Amazon. The Brazilian state built roads, fought guerrillas, brought in settlers, and carried through a xenophobic national program of Amazon occupation. Yet the decade ended on a sour note, as the migratory flow accelerated toward a frontier that was already closing.

Halfway through the 1970s priorities shifted. Public and private agricultural investments were increasingly redirected away from the Amazon and toward the Center-West. Two frontiers arose: one, the "social" frontier, which involves small farmer settlement; the other, the "productive" frontier, which involves large-scale agro-industrial operations. Since the 1970s, the "productive frontier" has expanded toward the Center-West *cerrado* regions of the country. Meanwhile, the "social frontier" has spread not only into, but also beyond, the Amazon. The demand for settlement is becoming increasingly militant all over the country.

This book is about the "social frontier" in the Amazon during the 1970s. More specifically, it is about "directed colonization," which is the settlement of small farmers on formerly public land by official or private projects. The book also refers, on occasion, to "spontaneous colonization," which is settlement by small farmers with no public or private tutelage. The objective of the book is, however, to analyze a deliberate large-scale national project of Amazon occupation, which was carried out by the Brazilian state during the 1970s.

Amazon colonization is generally considered to be a "failure." Yet settlers themselves say that settlement improved their lot in relation to alternatives in the rest of the country. Why did so many people go to the Amazon frontier? Why does a frontier shift so rapidly from place to place? Why does a frontier last so briefly in any one location? Why do frontier towns grow and vanish so rapidly? What are the real advantages a small farmer can reap from going to the frontier? What does colonization cost society? How much does it return to society? Who profits most from colonization: settlers, colonization firms, or merchants? How does colonization compare to agrarian reform? Did land distribution in colonization generate a lasting and significant redistribution in rural income? What was the price paid in terms of natural resources destroyed in the Amazon? Were there technological alternatives to the agriculture practiced by settlers? What is the Amazon's real population absorption capacity? What conclusions may we draw from the past to interpret what is happening in the Amazon today?

This book addresses all these issues.

The Amazon Issue

A frontier is a place very different from any other. It traditionally elicits strong emotional connotations: opportunity, liberty, and hope for a better future. The myth of free land does not die even with an adverse reality. Migrants see the frontier as an individual solution to their livelihood needs. Others envisage the frontier as a place that relieves social and economic restrictions imposed elsewhere. The political and cultural appeal of finding land of one's own on a distant frontier is strong and resists the passage of time.

Nowadays, nature is valued increasingly in developed nations, but it is still disregarded in poor countries, where the environment is simply a means to attain immediate objectives. If attitudes are to change in countries such as Brazil, then many changes must also occur in the social reality that motivates them. The dispossessed must be offered better alternatives to slash and burn agriculture; investments by the rich must be redirected away from speculative and predatory projects; a technocratic and still authoritarian government must become democratic and sensitive to public opinion. Without such real changes, the Amazon's present destruction will not be stopped. Without understanding underlying motives, no effective action can be taken to change such a broadly based and deeply rooted phenomenon.

The Amazon frontier's advance expanded land ownership in Brazil over areas much larger than ever before. Agrarian reform, therefore, has become a much more difficult task than it would have been in the 1960s. Frontier advance into the Amazon also extended the reach of southern industrial capitalism to the most remote corners of the country. Commodity and financial flows were thereby reoriented and regional cultures were integrated into the rest of the economy. The Amazon provided opportunities for some and frustration for others; it enriched and impoverished many, large and small.

Brazil has not yet fully taken upon itself to confront the conflicting interests and pressures involved in Amazon occupation. New social alternatives must be found in the process of political debate to reverse tendencies that are accelerating. Some conflicts are irreconcilable, such as those between small and large farmers, or between farmers in general and extractivists, whether rubber tappers (*seringueiros*), small prospectors (*garimpeiros*), or large mining companies. All of these, additionally, conflict with governmental projects, such as hydroelectric dams. Producers in general, public and private, are harmed by speculators. Developmentalists in general are opposed by conservationists, and so on and so forth. The list of antagonisms in the Amazon is endless. Without determined consciousness-raising efforts, as well as legitimate political mediation of conflict, the present upward spiral of violence, injustice, and depredation will only accelerate.

This book does not do justice to all these urgent Amazonian issues. It is directed only to one of them: small farmer settlement and its alternative, agrarian reform in the rest of the country. Other policies that seriously affect the Amazon will not be dealt with here, as they are too numerous to be analyzed in any one piece of work. The book's theme, therefore, is not the Amazon in general, but rather its colonization and its implications for land distribution.

Colonization and Agrarian Reform

During the 1970s, colonization was the antithesis of agrarian reform. It was supposedly a way to circumvent the land problem, taking the landless to frontier regions and leaving property structures in the rest of the country untouched. Today, the land problem has become so serious and so radical that it has already arrived at the frontier, where landed property is becoming even more concentrated than in established regions. Thus, the "colonization *versus* agrarian reform" conflict is now dead. Reality in the 1990s is much worse than it was in the 1960s. The occupied territory is much greater, as is the land distribution problem. With increasing social pressures for land in general, the demand for land in the Amazon is also much stronger.

The demand for land has always been greater than the supply coming from directed colonization. The great majority of migrants, therefore, settled "spontaneously," with no assured access to land. They were often expelled from the land they had cleared, or were forced into violent social clashes in trying to keep it. On the other hand, as this book attempts to show, directed colonization did benefit that minority of settlers to whom it supplied effective access to land. Incomes and accumulation rates obtained by settlers are compared to economic costs incurred, both public and private. The estimated final balance at the end of the decade is positive. Thus, directed colonization appears to have been an effective social policy, despite the many problems with its execution, to be discussed throughout this book.

One should perhaps note that colonization is the only large-scale land distribution policy undertaken in Brazil in one hundred years of Republican government. Its lessons are essential if one is to learn how to distribute land in the future. The findings in this book, therefore, will lend support to an agrarian reform that many still wish to carry out today.

The most original contribution of the book is a broad view of Amazon colonization as a whole, based on systematic presentation of quantitative data. The results are provocative, not because such was the intention, but because, in Brazil, small farmers are generally not expected to be successful, whether in the Amazon or anywhere else. The making of the 1988 Constitution showed that small farmers have little political power when confronted with other economic groups interested in the same land. In a democratic regime, their strengthening can result only from favorable public opinion. But the Brazilian public must still be convinced that the family farmer, in a sense, "deserves" the land he demands.

It is not easy to defend land distribution as social policy in Brazil today. There are many well-founded arguments against it. Anyone who knows Brazilian rural poverty cannot help but ask why an important productive asset, such as land, should be given to those who will apparently continue to be as miserable as ever, with it or without it. Many believe that progress requires increasing concentration into ever larger production units and consider "pulverization" into family-based units as a step backward. Those who believe in scale economies in agricultural production fear that reducing any rural establishment's size is economically wasteful. Finally, most consider land to be an asset like any other, and ask why the decision to distribute should fall on just this one, not on the remaining assets in the economy.

These, as well as many other opinions, tend to discredit the view of small farming as a social solution, even if partial, to the problems of poor income distribution and rural poverty. The findings here presented will, one hopes, strengthen the defense of land distribution, whether in the form of colonization or of agrarian reform, as an "efficient" social policy from the economic point of view.

Empirical and Theoretical Base

Amazon occupation is an increasingly emotional issue. At one extreme are the conservationists who disagree with any settlement in Amazon lands. At the other are the Brazilian xenophobes who demand that the international community respect Brazil's right to dispose of its own natural resources as it sees fit. The land distribution debate is also becoming increasingly heated. On one side, the numbers of the landless are growing, and they are becoming increasingly organized in their demands. On the opposite side, the "agro-industrial complex" demands ever larger areas for its expansion. As conflicts escalate, this book attempts to provide a quantitative, systematic, and, as far as possible, "neutral" description of the evidence. In this respect, it is very different from the existing literature on the Amazon.

Most of the data come from field research carried out by the Rio de Janeiro branch of the Institute of Economic and Social Planning (IPEA-Rio) of the Economics Ministry, in conjunction with the Colonization and Agrarian Reform Institute (INCRA) of the Ministry of Agriculture. Under the title of *Migrações internas e pequena produção agrícola na Amazônia: uma análise da política de colonização do INCRA* (vols. 1–

6) are to be found exhaustive citations of all the literature and careful descriptions of all the primary and secondary data used. They are summarized in the three appendixes to the thesis from which this book is extracted, whose title is "Colonização dirigida na Amazônia" (the thesis presented for the Full Professorship Chair in Microeconomics, Department of Economics of the School of Economics and Business Administration of the Federal University of Rio de Janeiro [FEA/UFRJ, 1977]. That work is being published in Brazil by IPEA, under the same Portuguese title, simultaneously with this book. Due to space limitations, such descriptions had to be excluded from the English version, though their Portuguese counterparts are referred to in the notes to each chapter.

As can be inferred from the summary of the book in the last section of this chapter, many different kinds of information were spliced together. Empirical methods are also quite varied, requiring detailed explanations in every chapter. Multiple sources and methods may, therefore, make the reading somewhat tedious. All monetary values were converted into U.S. dollars, as high Brazilian inflation rates have destroyed any meaning contemporary *cruzeiros* ever had.

This book makes use of widely differing theoretical bases: from neoclassical to neo-Marxist. Along the way, diverse theories are tapped, such as those of microeconomic modeling, market concentration, labor market segmentation, central place, and others. Viewing the expansion of the Amazon frontier from varied points of view may yield a rich idea of the process as a whole, but it certainly precludes theoretical purity.

Terminology is also eclectic. For example: "family farmers," "small agricultural producers," "peasants," "colonists," and "settlers" are referred to interchangeably. The terms "informal credit" and "usury-mercantile capital" are used synonymously, regardless of historical, theoretical, or ideological specificities. Likewise, "commercial agriculture" is equated with "capitalist agriculture," "capitalist expansion" with "market penetration," and so on.

The Amazon Frontier

One particular abuse of terminology must be mentioned. The term "frontier" is considered by some as improper for the Brazilian case. Yet it is used throughout, acquiring specific spatial and chronological connotations in different parts of the book. In the first part, it is the area that experienced rapid increase in population and land appropriation during the 1970s. In the second part, it is the area covered by the Brazilian state's colonization policies during that period. In the third part, it is any geographical boundary between "directly productive" and "usury-mercantile" capital and lasts as long as landed property does not consolidate. In the fourth part, it is the area delimited by directed colonization projects.

In the last analysis, however, a frontier is not any one fixed place. It is the all too brief transitional process whereby specific new territory is incorporated into an economy. It takes on different characteristics according to how each area becomes linked to the rest of the economy. In turn, a frontier changes the society it joins.

Due to its magnitude—vast area, large population, high value, and increasing social conflicts—the Brazilian Amazon frontier is changing Brazilian society. As the last tropical forest of vast proportions, however, the Amazon may also be changing the ecological equilibrium of the entire planet. Thus, the Brazilian frontier is special. Its advance concerns not only Brazil, but the whole world.

Summary of the Book

This book will not give final answers to criticisms of small farming or of the environmental hazards of Amazon occupation. Its objective is only to contribute to the debate on these issues by presenting a large amount of systematic information on directed colonization in the Amazon during the 1970s. Each part of the argument is necessarily short and schematic, and each issue discussed deserves better bibliographical and analytic treatment than has been possible here. However, the findings and their policy implications, taken jointly, are sufficiently important to warrant being brought together in one piece of work.

The book is divided into four parts, in addition to this introduction and the concluding chapters. The first part provides an estimate of the demographic magnitude of the frontier, delimits the total Amazon land area suitable for settlement, and measures how much of it was occupied during the 1970s. The second part describes the Brazilian state's involvement in the general advance of the Amazon frontier during the decade and estimates the total public cost of colonization. The third part analyzes the economic dynamics of the advancing frontier and of market penetration into the Amazon during the period. Finally, the fourth part analyzes the results obtained by the end of the decade among a sample of settlers in directed colonization projects in the Amazon.

The first part of the book, "The Dimensions of the Frontier," focuses on the physical and demographic characteristics of the frontier. It shows that Amazon occupation during the 1970s was a swift, predominantly urban, migratory wave of immense proportions. In general, each new area's occupation proceeded according to a sequence of phases: initially, small farmers settled and deforested each region; subsequently, landed property rapidly reconcentrated, causing massive rural exodus. Southern migration flowed predominantly toward the western Amazon; other migrants went mostly to the eastern Amazon (chap. 2). During the 1970s, practically all the land that is good for small farming became private property so that by decade's end the frontier was effectively closed. From the 1980s onward, occupation passed to lands increasingly inadequate for small farming. Thus, the economic benefit of clearing the forest diminished as the deforested area expanded (chaps. 3–5).

The second part of the book, "The Frontier and the State," describes the main public policies that created physical conditions and an institutional environment for Amazon colonization: territorial homogenization (chap. 7), private and public directed settlement (chap. 8), and institutional complementation (chap. 9). Physical access to the Amazon was redirected from river transportation, which runs toward the traditional northeastern economy, to road transport, running toward modern southern capitalist centers. Legal access to Amazon lands was changed from traditional, loosely defined rights to forestry extraction into registered private property, compatible with agro-industrial production. Settlement was redirected away from the outskirts of riverside towns, such as Marabá and Altamira, and toward faraway places, as along the Transamazon Highway and Rondônia.

The cost of directed colonization as a whole during the 1970s is estimated in chapter 10. The principal findings in this part are approximate estimates that the total cost of Amazon colonization during the 1970s was roughly $7.5 billion (all monetary values are for U.S. dollars). More than half of this sum was spent in road building, one-third in transplanting social and institutional infrastructure, and only 6 percent in actual settlement projects. Colonization was, thus, expensive in comparison to what agrarian reform would have cost for the same number of settlers in areas already served by local physical and social infrastructure. As it was, the institutional support that was provided to settlers—schooling, health care, communications, technology, rural extension, cooperatives, credit, transportation—was very meager in comparison to their basic needs.

The third part of the book, "The Frontier and the Market," analyzes how newly occupied territory was incorporated into the economy. During the early 1970s, Brazil was experiencing an upturn in the economic cycle. This boom extended financial and commodity flows between southern industrial capitalism and the advancing frontier, particularly in the western Amazon (chap. 11). Each area's incorporation into the market economy proceeded roughly according to the same phases as those of demographic occupation, described in chapter 2. During initial settlement, frontier merchants monitored small family labor in agriculture indirectly, through classic "crop-lien" mechanisms. During the subsequent concentration of landed property, "directly productive" capital penetrated into both agriculture and commerce (chap. 12).

Chapters 13 and 14 propose a typology and a formal model of the general process of economic incorporation of frontier territory. They predict that conditions in the initial (settlement) phases of a frontier lead to indebtedness, sharecropping, and low productivity. These then pave the way for rural proletarianization, exodus, and property reconcentration during subsequent phases. The final emergence of a wage labor force allows frontier merchants to switch from indirect appropriation of agricultural income, through small farmers' indebtedness, toward verticalization into direct agricultural production.

Chapter 15 tests some of these propositions empirically, based on field research on merchants. In private settlement, agricultural and land markets were highly concentrated from the outset and relative prices were least favorable to farmers. The most successful "merchants" were southern colonizing firms who sold land to settlers, and commercial intermediaries who bought agricultural products from settlers. In public settlement, where land was cheaper and product markets were more competitive from the beginning, relative prices were more favorable to farmers. The most successful merchants in this case were southern suppliers of industrial inputs for agriculture.

The first three parts of the book "set the stage," as it were, for the fourth part: an analysis of directed settlement in the Amazon during the 1970s. They describe the creation of the demographic, economic, and institutional environments in which agricultural incomes were generated and appropriated on the Amazon frontier. According to the evidence presented, the expansion of the frontier was always closely linked to the general process of urbanization and industrial growth, as well as to the structural and cyclical dynamics of the rest of the economy. The Brazilian state's role was mainly to reorganize commodity and financial flows into and out of the Amazon, thereby integrating the region into the sphere of influence of southern industrial capitalism.

Part 4 of the book, "The Colonists," considers evidence from a field survey of directed settlement projects in Pará and Mato Grosso. Colonization outcomes of various types are analyzed as reactions by settlers to the economic and institutional environments of the frontier.

Three distinct subgroups of settlers emerge from the findings. Those with the most initial assets were, on average, the southerners who settled in the private projects of Mato Grosso; however, they became the most indebted due to payment for "expensive" land. The southerners who settled in public projects in Pará had fewer initial assets than the first subgroup. Due to more favorable relative prices—cheaper lands and higher product prices—their borrowing was more productive; they obtained the highest incomes and the highest capital accumulation rates of all. The poorest migrants were those from other regions who settled in public projects in Pará; they arrived so poor that they borrowed regularly from local merchants to ensure family survival. Surprisingly, perhaps, some did prosper with the passage of time.

Indebtedness, therefore, was general among farmers on the frontier and was the main means of income appropriation by other agents (chap. 16). On average, the three groups above—southerners in private settlement, southerners in public settlement, and others in public settlement—achieved "good" income levels and accumulation rates when compared to contemporary alternatives in the financial and labor markets elsewhere in the economy. Average cost per job created was approximately $13.9 thousand, and rough estimates of benefits and costs yield favorable approximate figures. These imply that, during the 1970s, the returns to directed colonization had covered its costs. A notable finding, contrary to expectations, is that the highest accumulation rates during the 1970s were in official settlement and the lowest were in private settlement projects (chap. 17).

This outcome appears to be due to the aforementioned unfavorable relative prices in private settlement: high land prices and low product prices in comparison to public projects (chap. 18). In response to such prices, agricultural technology was more intensive in private settlement, where land was more expensive, and more extensive in public settlement, where land was cheaper (chap. 19).

It is disappointing to find that, even after becoming landowners, settlers retained itinerant agricultural practices that wasted recently deforested land and often led to its eventual abandonment. Settlers' incomes were thus obtained in exchange for the destruction of natural forest resources. The need for alternative agricultural technologies—more land intensive, more adequate to the humid tropical environment, and more compatible with settlers' low financial possibilities—were not foreseen. A deliberate wide-ranging policy of appropriate technology in Amazon farming, backed by consistent relative prices, was never attempted. Yet the price responsiveness actually observed in this book among settlers implies that they would probably have been sensitive to such a policy. Thus, the chance was missed to reduce the impact of colonization on the devastation of the Amazon.

Chapter 20 extends the study of settlers' response to frontier environments into an econometric analysis of three variables: current income, investment, and accumulated assets. The impact of the local environment on current income was found to be very strong, but not so for investment or accumulated assets. Investment responded little to local conditions in general and was found to be determined mainly by time on the plot. This is because, on the frontier, the main "investment" made is that of clearing away the forest.

Accumulation was found to respond to different influences according to time on the frontier. At first, accumulation depended mainly upon previous experience. Those who most accumulated in the early years had previously been itinerant elsewhere. In a path of "itinerant accumulation," they acquired knowledge and resources that were decisive during the first years on the frontier (chap. 20). However, the longer settlers remained on the same plot of land, the weaker the influence of previous experience and the stronger the influence of local stimuli. Thus, settlement policies that act on the local economy should become increasingly effective over time, though they may be slow to alter migrant behavior at first (chap. 21).

"Itinerant landowners," an important type of migrant identified in this book, are landowning farmers who migrate often, buying and selling land at a profit as they move along. They have a strange relation to the land and, thus, to nature. Ownership does not hold them to any one place. They use land and leave it without long-term concern for conserving natural resources. Deeply rooted technological practices thus formed, associated with a long history of successive rural migrations, take a long time to be altered.

Chapter 22 brings together the main findings in the book. The experience of colonization is brought to bear on today's debate on agrarian reform. A summary of current research into Amazon colonization during the 1980s is also provided. The main lesson drawn is that land distribution can be an effective policy of rural income redistribution, provided correct pricing and other economic conditions are met.

The appeal of the Amazon, however, is much stronger than that of a mere demand for land, no matter how pressing. Even if all of the landless were to be settled somewhere else in the country, many migrants would probably still risk going to the Amazon. The region will continue, for a long time yet, to exert its fascination over those adventurous spirits who try to "improve their lot in life" by moving to a frontier (chap. 23).

In sum, the use of Amazon land as an instrument for income redistribution involves much controversy. To reduce the devastation provoked during the 1970s, settlers should have had much better institutional support, while control mechanisms should have been much more effective. Specifically, adequate extension work would have sped up the adoption of appropriate small farming technology for the humid tropics and, hence, would have reduced deforestation; less concentrated land, credit, inputs, and product markets would have allowed for greater income appropriation by farmers and, hence, for higher accumulation rates; more social infrastructure should have provided for basic needs and, therefore, reduced turnover and exodus. The absence of such support even today implies that Amazon colonization is still as predatory as it was during the 1970s.

To avoid taking from some and giving to others, Brazil has been taking land and resources from nature. The political cost avoided by not undertaking agrarian reform is being paid by devastating the Amazon. By the time the first decade of colonization had ended, though, this alternative no longer existed: all suitable land had been appropriated. The conflict between distribution and conservation has grown worse ever since. Today, it can no longer be circumvented.

PART 2: THE FRONTIER AND THE STATE

This part of the book addresses how public investments during the 1970s inverted economic access to the Amazon. Chapter 6 discusses several of the Brazilian state's actions and omissions in the region. Chapter 7 shows how land titling and road building opened the Amazon to southern populations and capital and weakened traditional links to northern regional centers. Chapter 8 discusses the settlement projects themselves. Chapter 9 explores social institutions complementary to settlement. The final result of part 2 is an estimate, in chapter 10, of the total cost of Amazon colonization. This cost will be compared with the estimated benefits of colonization to be analyzed in part 4 of the book.

Various sources were used to compile the data analyzed in these chapters. Original research was done in all institutions analyzed, in their respective headquarters as well as in Amazon settlement locations. To avoid problems created by Brazilian inflation, all values are in U. S. dollars. Cost estimates refer to accumulated costs during the 1970–1980 period in the region that chapter 2 designates as the "Amazon frontier": Acre, Roraima, Rondônia, Amazonas, Mato Grosso, Pará, and Amapá.

Institutional presence on the frontier: the municipal government building at Pacajá, in Pará

Directed colonization: a colonist family in front of their house built by INCRA, in Pacal, Pará

2. RURAL FRONTIER AND URBAN FRONTIER

The advance of a frontier is a social movement that occurs over a geographic territory for a limited period of time. The rural population increases during an initial phase, due principally to settlement by small farmers. During a second phase, the population emigrates or urbanizes while landed property consolidates and concentrates. The process then moves to another geographical area where the same two phases are repeated. In this way, the agricultural frontier has "swept" the national territory, lately in the northwestern direction toward and into the Amazon. It has been a permanent phenomenon throughout Brazilian history, even though short-lived in each region.

This chapter presents demographic evidence at the national level about the advances of the Brazilian agricultural frontier during the 1960s and 1970s. Later chapters will interpret the phenomena described here and summarize the existing literature. IBGE's Demographic and Economic Censuses and INCRA's Registry of Rural Properties trace the Amazon frontier from its origins in the 1960s to its advance during the 1970s.

The data indicate that a large migratory wave into the Amazon burgeoned in the mid-1970s from the South and from São Paulo. It included native southerners as well as northeasterners "recycled" in southern states.[1] Penetrating the Amazon through the Center-West, this wave moved primarily to Rondônia and Mato Grosso and later on to Acre and Roraima. Another front, here prosaically called "other migrants," was composed predominantly of northeasterners, but also included people from Espírito Santo (*capixabas*) and Minas Gerais (*mineiros*), as well as from all other parts of the country. This other flow entered the Amazon through Pará and met the southern flow in the disputed region of eastern Mato Grosso and southeastern Pará. Finally, it will be seen that during the two decades from 1960 to 1980, the frontier was more an urban process than a rural one, as the pace of urbanization on the frontier increased over time.

The Rural Frontier

During the 1970s, the occupation of Brazil's agricultural frontier led to rural population growth that was slightly less than during the previous decade: an increase of 1,281,575 inhabitants versus 1,325,233 in the 1960s. The fronts of this occupation shifted geographically, as the areas that had been attracting migrants in the 1960s—such as Mato Grosso do Sul and Goiás—became areas of emigration in the following decade. Meanwhile, new areas of expansion intensified in the Northwest, such as in Rondônia. The agricultural frontier maintained approximately the same demographic dimension over the two decades, but it shifted spatially in moving toward the Amazon.

Tables 1 and 2 show that, from 1960 to 1970, the Southeast was the principal source of rural emigration in the country; however, in the next decade, the main source of migrants shifted to the South. This shift in the origin of rural exodus seems to result from multiple causes. One is the exhaustion of the old frontiers of São Paulo and later Paraná; another is the economic boom of the late 1960s and early 1970s. Widespread rural modernization, a process known as "capital penetration into agriculture," accompanied by large fiscal and credit incentives and increasing land values, allowed a large mass of former small farmers to sell their tiny plots in the South and buy larger units on the frontier.[2] These combined cyclical and regional processes provoked a rural exodus without precedent in Brazil's history, with absolute decline in the rural population—first in the Southeast, and later in the South. Even the Center-West began to expel more rural population in the 1970s than it absorbed, as a consequence of the exhaustion of the frontier in Mato Grosso do Sul and Goiás.

Between 1960 and 1970, Maranhão, Goiás, and Mato Grosso do Sul had been the frontier states with the greatest population growth; but in the 1970s, Pará, Maranhão, and Rondônia were those most rapidly growing. Thus, out-migration shifts were matched by a simultaneous forward shift of the frontier. Maps 1 and 2 show this large movement of the frontier toward the Northwest, subdividing states into IBGE's "Homogeneous Microregions."[3] Map 2 clearly shows that the frontier in the 1970s formed an inverted "L" bordering the Amazon. It stretched westward by way of Rondônia and the north of Mato Grosso and eastward by climbing through the state of Pará. Behind the frontier, extensive areas formed a belt of rural exodus in the states of Maranhão, Goiás, and Mato Grosso—exactly where the frontier of the 1960s had been (see map 1). The general phenomenon is one in which rapid exhaustion of the "old" frontier (i.e., from the 1960s) pushes settlement forward into the Amazon (i.e., during the 1970s). The key point is that the frontier's advance is of short duration in each area through which it "passes."

Due to sequential movements of rural population, the states on the outer band of the Amazon—Mato Grosso do Sul, Goiás, and Maranhão—will be called the "*cerrado* frontier," while those located to the Northwest—Acre, Rondônia, Roraima, Amazonas, Pará, Amapá, and Mato Grosso—will be referred to as the "Amazon frontier." These terms refer only to movement toward the Amazon, not to other old frontiers in Brazil, such as those of Paraná or of the South more generally. As seen in table 2, Maranhão was the state with the largest absolute increase in rural population during the 1970s, but it was expelling more rural population than it was absorbing. According to the sequence of frontier advance, therefore, Maranhão was already in the "second phase" (i.e., that in which landed property becomes concentrated). It was in this sense "old," in spite of a large absolute increase of rural population during the 1970s. For this reason, it will not be included in the "Amazon frontier" of the 1970s in the remainder of this book. The frontier of western Bahia may have received more people than Rondônia in the same period. As it is not in the path toward the Amazon, however, it was also excluded from the focus of this study.[4] Hence, the use of the term "Amazon frontier" applies strictly to the states specified above.

Data from IBGE's Agricultural Census and INCRA's property registry indicate areas of attraction and exodus similar to those shown in map 2. Map 3 is based on the Agricultural Census that refers to "establishments" (i.e., units of agricultural production). Given that bean cultivation is strongly associated with small farmers, a reduction in the area harvesting this crop, as indicated by the dark area of the map, implies a reduction in small farmers on the *cerrado* frontier during the 1970s. Map 4 is based on INCRA's registry and refers to "properties" (i.e., units of registered land ownership). The declining number of these titles, shown in shade 5 on the map, indicates an increase in the average size of these properties. Thus, there was increasing concentration of land ownership on the *cerrado* frontier during the 1970s.

The year 1970 is exactly midway in the period 1960–1980. At that time, almost half the migrants residing in rural areas of the frontier originated in the Northeast and more than one-quarter came from the

Center-West, as can be seen in tables 3 and 4. Table 5 shows that immigrants from the Northeast at the time were concentrated in Maranhão and Goiás, while Center-West immigrants moved within that same region, above all in Goiás. In 1970, migrants from the South and Southeast were barely one-fifth of the total, directing themselves primarily toward Goiás, Mato Grosso do Sul, and Mato Grosso. It is important to emphasize, as noted earlier, that a large number of these southern migrants were actually people born in the Northeast who had traveled first to the frontiers of Paraná and western São Paulo, and who later continued moving toward Goiás and Mato Grosso do Sul.

In sum, the Amazon frontier advanced along two large fronts, as can be seen in tables 1–5 and in maps 1–4. The eastern front, largely composed of northeasterners, extended the Maranhão frontier, crossing the border into Pará and entering Mato Grosso. The western front, an extension of the Goiás and Mato Grosso do Sul frontier, shifted to Rondônia and Mato Grosso, above all to the microregion of Aripuanã (shade 2 on map 2). This western front swelled with the rural exodus from the South and Southeast, beginning in the mid-1970s. It increased greatly until the mid-1980s, relative to the mere 20 percent it comprised in 1970. It can be supposed that the advance of the Amazon frontier during the 1980s was an extension and acceleration of what occurred in the 1960s and 1970s.

Table 1. Changes in Rural Population by Region, 1960–1980
(number of people)

Regions[a]	*1960–1970*	*1970–1980*
North	383,076	924,532
Northeast	1,945,981	957,853
Center-West	720,432	–178,430
Southeast	–1,224,574	–1,963,936
South	1,826,351	–2,023,200
Brazil	3,651,266	–2,283,181

[a]North: Acre, Rondônia, Amazonas, Roraima, Pará, Amapá.
Northeast: Maranhão, Piauí, Ceará, Rio Grande do Norte, Paraiba, Pernambuco, Sergipe, Alagoas, Bahia.
Center-West: Mato Grosso, Mato Grosso do Sul, Goiás, Distrito Federal.
South: Paraná, Santa Catarina, Rio Grande do Sul.

Table 2. Changes in Rural Population by State, 1960–1980
(number of people)

Area	*1960–1970*	*1970–1980*
Amazon Frontier:		
Rondônia	16,138	207,610
Acre	31,238	13,640
Amazonas	70,098	28,459
Roraima	6,937	8,687
Pará	239,469	645,177
Amapá	19,196	20,959
Mato Grosso	164,669	123,380
TOTAL	547,745	1,047,912
Cerrado Frontier:		
Maranhão	221,715	535,473
Mato Grosso do Sul	213,030	–88,953
Goiás	373,077	–229,831
Distrito Federal	–30,344	16,974
TOTAL	777,478	233,663
Total Frontier	1,325,223	1,281,575
Other States:		
Piauí	208,597	83,133
Ceará	467,361	–177,511
Rio Grande do Norte	138,473	–68,111
Paraiba	116,109	96,754
Pernambuco	111,201	–11,422
Alagoas	121,132	52,565
Sergipe	25,549	37,334
Bahia	535,844	409,638
Minas Gerais	517,478	–1,011,218
Espírito Santo	–131,786	–144,123
Rio de Janeiro	–311,995	–163,017
São Paulo	1,298,271	–645,578
Paraná	1,482,390	–1,267,786
Santa Catarina	212,140	–177,400
Rio Grande do Sul	131,821	–578,014
TOTAL	2,326,043	–3,564,756
Brazil	3,651,266	–2,283,181

Sources: IBGE, *Censos demográficos de 1980, 1970, 1960,* and *Migrações internas*, vol. 2, chap. 2.

Map 1. Rural Population: 1960–1970 (% variation)

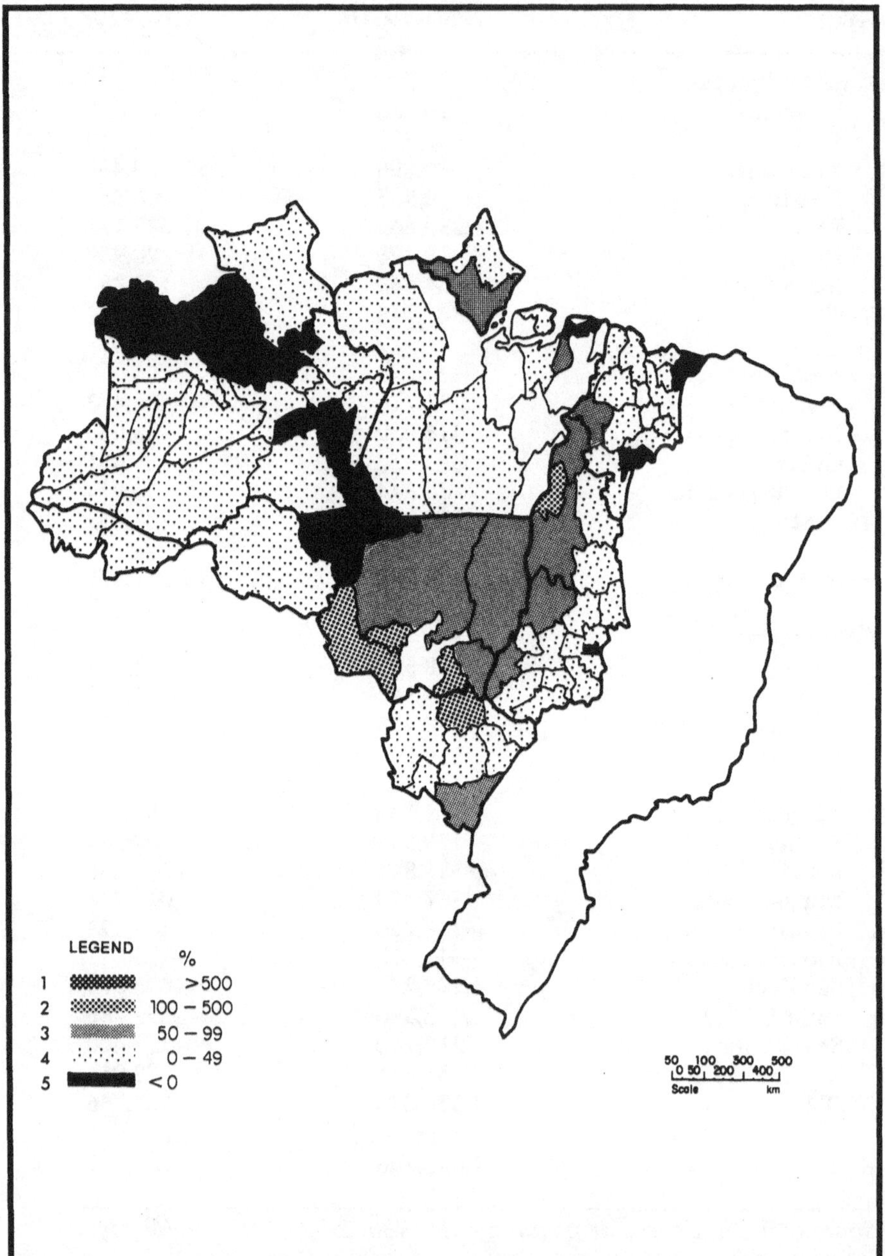

Map 2. Rural Population: 1970–1980 (% variation)

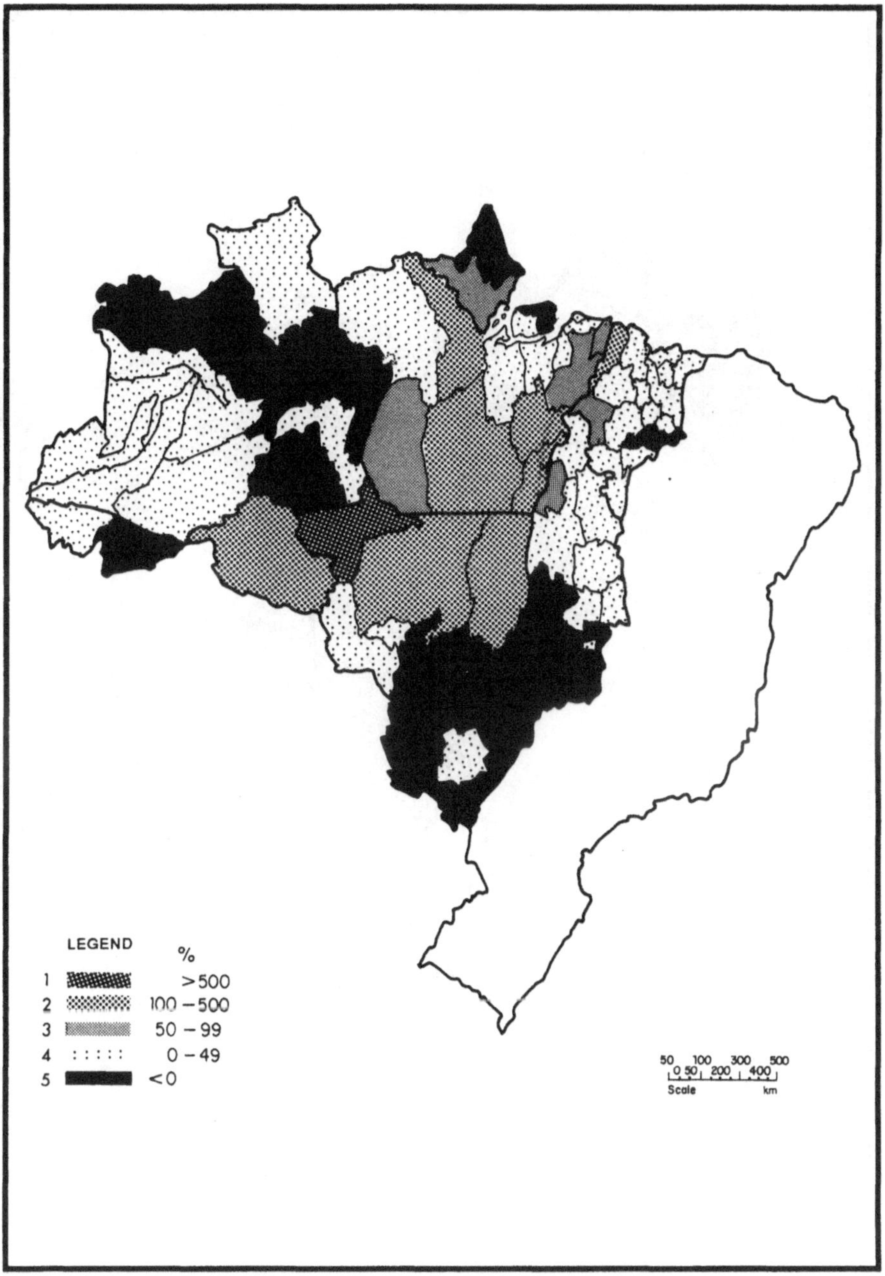

Map 3. Harvested Area—Beans: 1970–1975 (% variation)

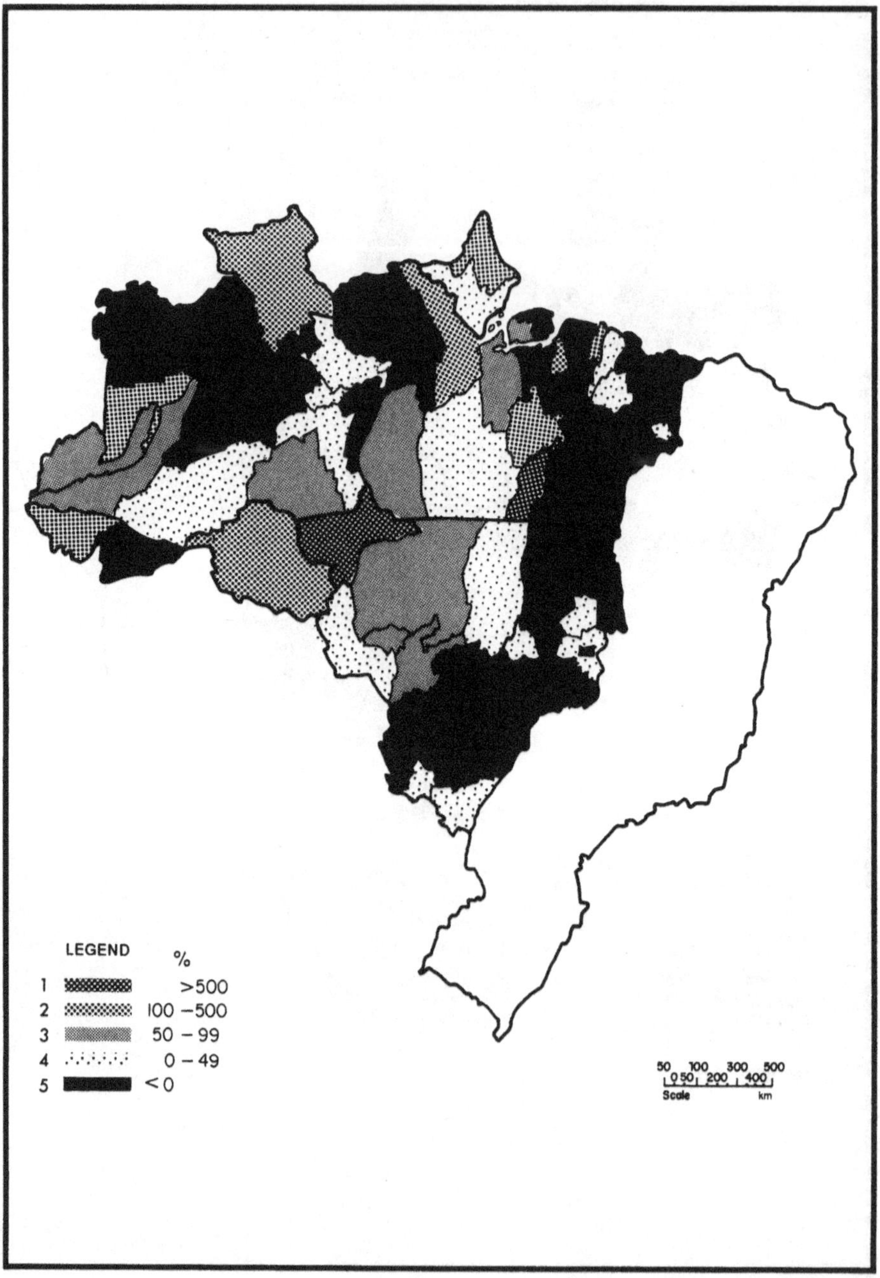

Map 4. Number of Rural Properties: 1972–1978 (% variation)

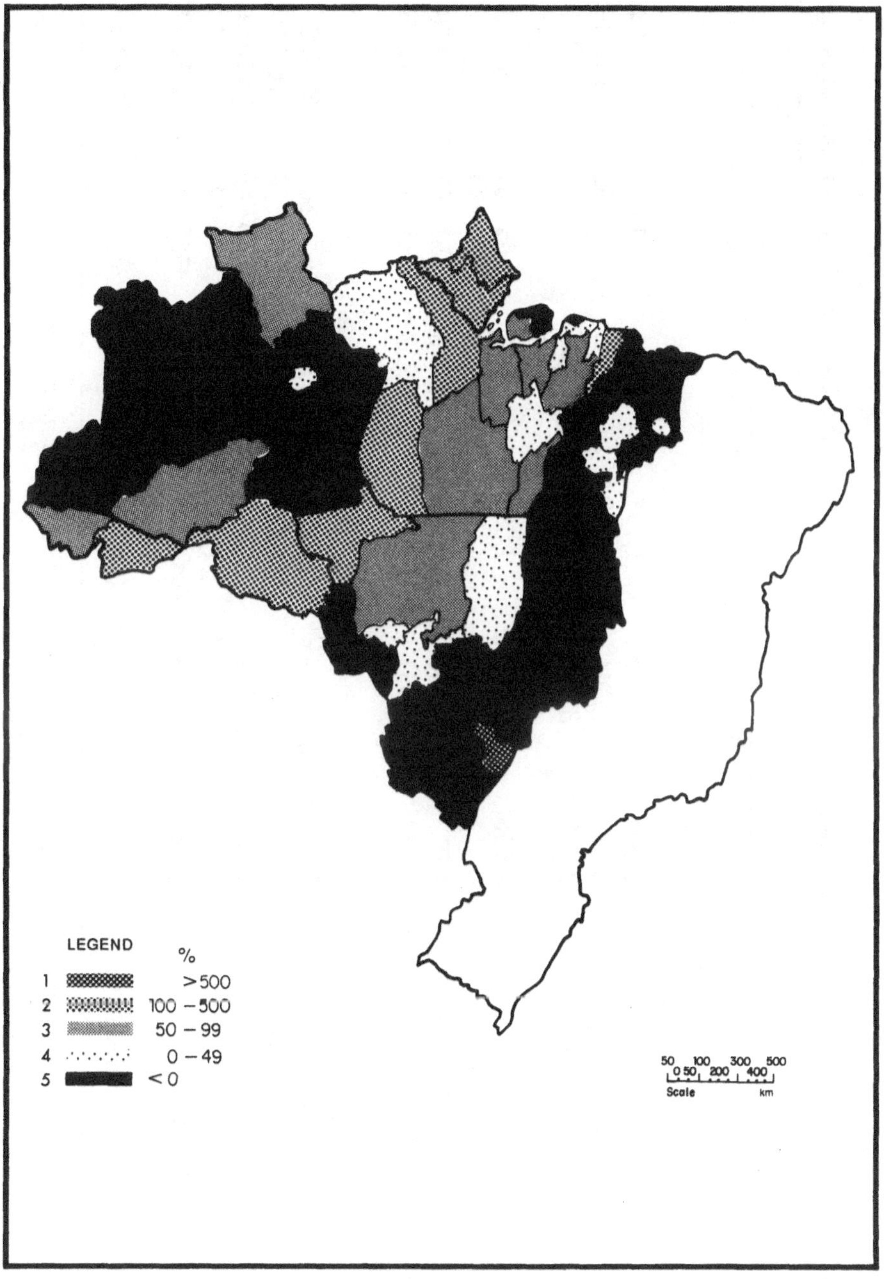

Table 3. Origin and Destination of Rural-Rural Migration to the Frontier, 1970 (number of people)

	Origin					
Destination	*North*	*Northeast*	*Southeast*	*South*	*Center-West*	*Total*
Amazon Frontier:						
Rondônia	8,007	5,347	1,191	1,170	1,079	16,794
Acre	6,793	6,244	29	0	40	13,106
Amazonas	27,878	3,675	105	23	91	31,772
Roraima	809	824	0	4	19	1,656
Pará	70,056	37,397	2,032	352	11,661	121,498
Amapá	9,911	276	0	0	4	10,191
Mato Grosso	1,023	12,288	50,786	8,378	52,203	124,678
TOTAL	124,477	66,051	54,143	9,927	65,097	319,695
Cerrado Frontier:						
Maranhão	2,175	516,867	1,654	230	2,300	523,226
Mato Grosso do Sul	47	22,619	101,602	23,485	57,802	205,555
Goiás	1,507	109,756	126,943	1,226	290,849	530,281
Distrito Federal	59	1,672	1,806	161	4,792	8,490
TOTAL	3,788	650,914	232,005	25,102	355,743	1,267,552
Total Frontier Area	128,265	716,965	286,148	35,029	420,840	1,587,247

Sources: IBGE, *Censo demográfico de 1970*, special tabulation; *Migrações internas*, vol. 2, chap. 2.

Table 4. Origin and Destination of Rural-Rural Migration to the Frontier, 1970 (percentage of destination)

	Origin					
Destination	*North*	*Northeast*	*Southeast*	*South*	*Center-West*	*Total*
Amazon Frontier:						
Rondônia	47.68	31.84	7.09	6.97	6.42	100.0
Acre	51.83	47.64	0.22	0.00	0.31	100.0
Amazonas	87.74	11.57	0.33	0.07	0.29	100.0
Roraima	48.85	49.76	0.00	0.24	1.15	100.0
Pará	57.66	30.78	1.67	0.29	9.60	100.0
Amapá	97.25	2.71	0.00	0.00	0.04	100.0
Mato Grosso	0.82	9.86	40.73	6.72	41.87	100.0
TOTAL	38.94	20.66	16.94	3.11	20.36	100.0
Cerrado Frontier:						
Maranhão	0.42	98.78	0.32	0.04	0.44	100.0
Mato Grosso do Sul	0.02	11.00	49.43	11.43	28.12	100.0
Goiás	0.28	20.70	23.94	0.23	54.85	100.0
Distrito Federal	0.69	19.69	21.27	1.90	56.44	100.0
TOTAL	0.20	51.30	18.30	1.90	28.00	100.0
Total Frontier Area	8.08	45.17	18.03	2.21	26.51	100.0

Sources: IBGE, *Censo demográfico de 1970*, special tabulation; *Migrações internas*, vol. 2, chap. 2.
Note: Because of rounding errors, some percentages do not add up to exactly 100.

Table 5. Origin and Destination of Rural-Rural Migration to the Frontier, 1970 (percentage of origin)

	Origin					
Destination	*North*	*Northeast*	*Southeast*	*South*	*Center-West*	*Total*
Amazon Frontier:						
Rondônia	6.24	0.75	0.42	3.34	0.26	1.06
Acre	5.30	0.87	0.01	0.00	0.01	0.83
Amazonas	21.73	0.51	0.04	0.07	0.02	2.00
Roraima	0.63	0.11	0.00	0.01	0	0.10
Pará	54.62	5.22	0.71	1.00	2.77	7.65
Amapá	7.73	0.04	0.00	0.00	0	0.64
Mato Grosso	0.80	1.71	17.75	23.92	12.40	7.85
TOTAL	97.05	9.21	18.92	28.34	15.50	20.13
Cerrado Frontier:						
Maranhão	1.70	72.09	0.58	0.66	0.55	32.96
Mato Grosso do Sul	0.04	3.15	35.51	67.04	13.73	12.95
Goiás	1.17	15.31	44.36	3.50	69.11	33.41
Distrito Federal	0.05	0.23	0.63	0.46	1.14	0.53
TOTAL	2.95	90.79	81.08	71.66	84.50	79.90
Total Frontier Area	100.00	100.00	100.00	100.00	100.00	100.00

Sources: IBGE, *Censo demográfico de 1970*, special tabulation; *Migrações internas*, vol. 2, chap. 2.

Urban Frontier

In order to evaluate the dimensions of the Amazon frontier, it is necessary to compare the movement of rural and urban populations during the same period of time. Table 6 shows that the absolute increase in Brazil's urban population was almost 30 percent greater in the 1970s (29.1 million people) thanit was in the 1960s (20.9 million). Meanwhile, in Brazil as a whole, total rural population declined in absolute terms (-2.3 million) in the 1970s, dampening the increase (3.6 million) of the previous decade. That is to say, an immense growth of cities (which increased by 50 million inhabitants from 1960 to 1980) occurred during the incorporation of vast new rural territories into the national economy.

There was a general tendency in Brazil, then, for urbanization and abandonment of the countryside. The call of the frontier acted in a direction opposite to the much stronger attraction exercised by cities. In this sense, one could say that urbanization "hindered" the advance of the frontier. Many potential colonists preferred to risk their luck on urban employment (or underemployment) than to venture into the Amazon forest. Although a detailed analysis of Brazilian urbanization is beyond the objectives of this study, its importance should be recognized since it acted across the entire national territory and, therefore, also upon the frontier.

Tables 2 and 7 show that urban population growth was greater than rural population growth during the entire period, even on the frontier. When the "*cerrado* frontier" was new (i.e., during the 1960s), rural popu-

Table 6. Changes in Urban Population by Region,* 1960–1980
(number of people)

Region	*1960–1970*	*1970–1980*
North	666,152	1,453,229
Northeast	4,300,334	5,978,672
Center-West	1,439,905	2,753,430
Southeast	11,528,521	14,203,494
South	2,965,093	4,716,775
Brazil	20,900,005	29,105,600

*See table 1.
Sources: IBGE, *Censos demográficos de 1980, 1970, 1960*, and *Migrações internas*, vol. 2, chap. 2.

Table 7. Changes in Urban Population by State, 1960–1980
(number of people)

Area	*1960–1970*	*1970–1980*
Amazon Frontier:		
Rondônia	29,699	178,895
Acre	26,559	75,197
Amazonas	169,619	459,742
Roraima	5,212	31,693
Pará	406,668	665,063
Amapá	28,395	42,639
Mato Grosso	117,608	433,545
TOTAL	783,760	1,886,774
Cerrado Frontier:		
Maranhão	323,281	524,623
Mato Grosso do Sul	218,049	479,373
Goiás	669,631	1,200,168
Distrito Federal	434,617	640,344
TOTAL	1,645,578	2,844,508
Total Frontier	2,429,338	4,731,282
Other States:		
Piauí	262,929	370,123
Ceará	686,373	1,066,353
Rio Grande do Norte	315,875	389,633
Paraíba	311,287	460,367
Pernambuco	1,004,489	1,001,765
Alagoas	213,980	353,136
Sergipe	125,429	208,057
Bahia	1,056,691	1,604,615
Minas Gerais	2,202,533	3,017,975
Espírito Santo	331,295	589,945
Rio de Janeiro	2,712,428	2,533,490
São Paulo	6,282,265	8,062,084
Paraná	1,218,917	2,019,856
Santa Catarina	571,362	934,641
Rio Grande do Sul	1,174,814	1,762,278
TOTAL	18,470,667	24,374,318
Brazil	20,900,005	29,105,600

Sources: IBGE, *Censos demográficos de 1980, 1970, 1960*, and *Migrações internas*, vol. 2, chap. 2.

lation growth was 47 percent of urban population growth. By the 1970s, however, rural population growth in the *cerrado* frontier had fallen to only 13 percent of urban growth. Urbanization had thus become very strong in areas that only ten years previously had been fronts of agricultural expansion. Within the "Amazon frontier," rural population growth was 70 percent of urban population growth in the 1960s and 56 percent in the 1970s. Even in the agricultural "front line," then, urbanization increased, although less than it did on the rest of the frontier or in the rest of the country. Therefore, the main population increase on the frontier was not in the countryside. It occurred in cities and was concentrated in the larger ones. In each of the two decades shown, the cities of the state of São Paulo had greater population increases than those of the whole frontier, a pattern that continued through at least two decades. Only the Census of 1991 will tell whether there was any change in this general pattern during the 1980s. "Frontier urbanization" is an important issue and deserves deeper treatment than can be done in this chapter.[5]

The Entire Frontier

In terms of population size, frontier expansion—both urban and rural—was not insignificant. From 1960 to 1980, in cities and the countryside, the frontier had a total growth of almost 10 million people. In the 1970s alone, the "Amazon frontier" absorbed almost 3 million people, one-third of these in rural areas.

The agricultural frontier is important, however, not merely because of the large number of people involved, but because of what it represented to Brazilian society as a whole. It was a broad process of regional, economic, and political transformation, but was perceived in fragments, not in its entirety.

Brazil's agricultural frontiers have been short-lived. Rural exodus followed quickly upon the opening of new fronts, enlarging local cities, whose populations always grew more rapidly than in the countryside. This frontier exodus is worrisome, as it indicates that the forces expelling people from the countryside were strong, rapid, and extensive, even on the frontier. These same forces would be a menace to policies of land redistribution, as they could eliminate the potential benefits of any program of colonization or agrarian reform. It is important to understand how they acted in the 1970s so as to investigate how they might be reversed today. This is a first step in securing the conditions required for small farmers anywhere to establish and maintain themselves on their own land.

With respect to Amazon colonization, this preoccupation implies studying not only farmers, but the whole frontier, including the (mostly urban) economic institutional and economic systems with which farmers interact. The institutional and economic systems established as the frontier advanced into Amazon territory are analyzed in parts 2 and 3 of this book. The next chapters in this part proceed to measure the physical dimensions of the Amazon frontier.

Notes

Measurement of immigration flows to frontier regions will not be done here, since it is available in other studies. This chapter refers to the total net intercensal population growth observed in the geographic regions defined in tables 1–4. All of the data, concepts, calculations, and sources used in making the tables and maps for this chapter are described in appendix 1 of vol. 1 of *Migrações internas*. Note that there are some white areas in map 1, caused by incompatibilities between the demographic censuses of 1960 and 1970. These and other methodological issues are described in detail in the cited sources. See note 3, below.

1. Many northeasterners who migrated to the South, above all to Paraná's coffee frontier, acquired agricultural expertise and techniques that are typical of these regions. They later took their knowledge to the Amazon, along with other migrants born in the South and Southeast. For this reason, these native-born northeasterners are here considered to be "southern migrants." This issue will be taken up again later.

2. Average Semester Rates of Increase in the Price of Land in the South (%)

State	*Period*			
	1966–1972	*1972–1975*	*1975–1980*	*1980–1983*
Paraná	2	18	5	<0
Santa Catarina	<0	16	<0	<0
Rio Grande do Sul	2	16	0	<0

Source: Approximations from Resende (1981).

3. *Migrações internas*, vol. 2, appendix 1, gives the name and numbering of each of the states and microregions indicated in maps 1–5, according to IBGE and a special methodology used in that study for bringing compatibility to the 1960 and later censuses.

4. The Bahian agricultural frontier is a little-researched local process not fueled by the general movement toward the Amazon, but rather by its own social and economic evolution. In Maranhão, however, the frontier is a well-researched topic, which has already been the object of various valuable works.

5. See Martine and Camargo (1983), A. Santos (1985), Lavinas (1987), and Rebello de Mendonça (1987).

3. OCCUPATION AND AVAILABILITY OF LAND IN THE AMAZON

This chapter examines the Amazon's role in absorbing small farmers during the 1970s. It also considers its potential, at the end of that decade, for sustaining a social policy of further land distribution.[1]

The principal finding of this and the following two chapters is that by the end of the 1970s some 313 to 393 million hectares of land were still available in the Amazon (70 percent to 89 percent of the total area,[2] depending on the source). These data refer to the 1970s and therefore cannot be compared with more recent information concerning the much-publicized acceleration of Amazon deforestation that occurred during the 1980s.

Chapter 4 will show that a mere 12 million hectares (3.3 percent of the region) were adequate for simple colonization; that is, they would not require modification of small farmers' agricultural techniques. Combining information from chapters 3 and 4 on both quality and availability, chapter 5 indicates that land occupation in the Amazon was selective in terms of soil quality. All of the good lands had already been appropriated by the early 1980s. Still, 45 percent of unoccupied territory could be considered "more or less" appropriate for colonization. These available lands, however, would not be colonizable unless investments were made in reorienting small farmers' technologies to the Amazon environment.

The issue of land "availability" is thus controversial. Brazilian government sources use concepts that are completely different from one another; this leads to diverse estimates concerning the area still available for colonization. Specifically, the public knows very little about INCRA's activity of "land titling" (*regularização fundiária*), which determines the rate at which large tracts come to be considered legally owned or free for occupation. Given the multiplicity of sources and criteria, much space must be devoted to methodological explanations necessary to the interpretation of the results.

The remainder of this chapter compares and analyzes the data on land occupation in the Amazon frontier. The following chapter discusses the quality of Amazon soils. Chapter 5 juxtaposes land availability and quality and measures how much land was both available and suitable for small farming in the Amazon by the end of the 1970s. Chapter 5 will also summarize the conclusions of part 1 as a whole.[3]

The Degree of Occupation

This section estimates the amount of land available in the Amazon at the end of the 1970s according to several criteria and different sources of information. Secondary data come from the Agricultural Census of 1980 (IBGE) and from the Land Property Registry of 1978 (INCRA). Primary data come from a direct survey of Land Titling Projects operated by INCRA. The main finding is that, by the end of the decade, 17.6 percent of the Amazon area was covered by agricultural establishments, 29.4 percent of it was registered, and 11.3 percent was legally titled. Thus, a high percentage of Amazon land was apparently still available.

The differences among the alternative estimates presented here are due to each source's specific problems of measurement and to the fact that they imply different definitions of land occupation. The Agricultural Census concerns agricultural establishments in effective production, whether or not those responsible own the land. The INCRA Real Estate Registry (Cadastro Geral de Imóveis) is concerned with recording rural land claims, for the purpose of potential taxation, independent of production or legal title. INCRA's Department of Land Resources runs its land titling projects. These, in turn, deal with legal titles, temporary or permanent, for possession or ownership, whether or not the areas are economically active or registered.

The sources employed vary not only in their concepts, but also in the geographical extent of their coverage. The census and the registry theoretically cover all of Brazil, although undercounting and underregistering are notorious in frontier regions. By contrast, land titling activity spreads gradually and contiguously; by the end of the period, only 55 percent of the Amazon area within INCRA's jurisdiction had been reached. This jurisdiction, in its turn, does not cover the entire Amazon territory, but only 73 percent: half within titling projects, half outside them, as can be seen in map 5. It includes land located within 150 kms of the country's international border, land up to 100 kms on each side of federal highways, built or projected, and all the area within

INCRA's titling projects (see map 5). Thus, by 1980 only 40 percent of the Amazon (55 x 73 percent) had yet been subjected to INCRA's land titling.

INCRA was the single federal-level entity responsible for occupying the Amazon during the 1970s and was the largest landowner in the region. It also concentrated the greatest quantity of data concerning land titling. Hence, all of the data on land titling in this chapter refer to the area under INCRA's jurisdiction. Budgetary and time restrictions precluded collecting information about other areas, dispersed among diverse state agencies and organizations.

INCRA considers "appropriated lands" to be those that fall into one of the following categories:

1. areas under the jurisdiction of federal government organs, such as FUNAI, IBDF, and SEMA, which include Indian and forest reserves, national parks and ecological stations, located within titling projects;
2. areas held by the armed forces and state and municipal governments—airports, landing fields, military posts and training grounds, urban areas, and other areas with some approved project or already defined use;
3. areas in private domain—occupied by squatters, holders of ownership titles, settlement licenses conceded by INCRA, large and small farms, and other properties with legal deeds or in the process of legalization according to criteria established during INCRA's surveying processes;
4. areas that INCRA considers to be under "social tension,"[4] including those that were under the administration of GETAT and GEBAM;[5] and
5. areas destined for colonization projects by INCRA and those destined for public sale.

All remaining areas are considered "available" after eliminating the appropriated areas according to criteria 1–5.

The geographic unit of land area within a titling project is called a "tract." This includes those tracts already absorbed into public domain as well as those still being evaluated. Appropriation is only recorded officially where tracts have already been delineated. No survey has been conducted of appropriation outside of these tracts. The set of delineated tracts occupied 55 percent of the area within titling projects. This in turn corresponded to 37 percent of the Amazon territory. That is, precise information on the appropriation of land existed only for about 20 percent of the Amazon area (55 percent x 37 percent). Because INCRA's land titling proceeds slowly by contiguous tracts, complete information about the degree of appropriation of Amazon lands will become available only when all of the region has been titled—which is not likely to occur even in the 1990s. Wherever such "tracts" had not yet been delineated,

Map 5. Area under the Jurisdiction of INCRA in the Amazon

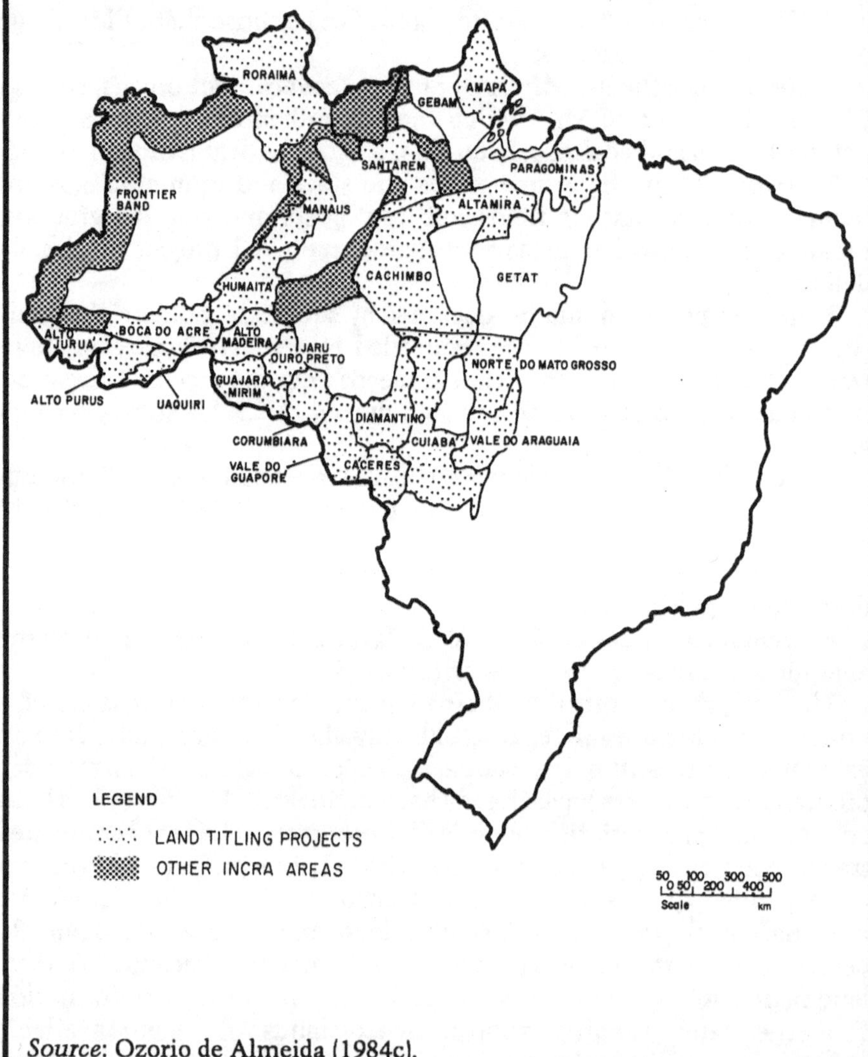

Source: Ozorio de Almeida (1984c).

the entire area is here considered available. Within such areas considered vacant, however, unrecorded occupation may have occurred.

There is no information about occupation outside titling projects, even in other areas under INCRA's jurisdiction. All of this unknown territory, then, was also considered entirely available. By ignoring unregistered occupation outside tracts and outside titling projects, the figures considerably overestimate the amount of land still available for settlement by the end of the 1970s.

Establishments, Registered Lands, and Titled Lands

Information about land tenure in the Amazon during the 1970s is so precarious that any use of it, even cautious and qualified, is questionable. Several factors motivate this attempt. In the first place, existing data from other sources (census and registry) do help to verify basic orders of magnitude on tenure, as will be seen below. Second, the attempt itself reveals the need for a rigorous survey of land tenure in the region. Such an undertaking, however, would require years of work and substantial resources. It must be justified on the basis of extremely grave preliminary results, as those that follow.

A survey of occupied and vacant areas was conducted for the tracts within each titling project. As explained above, all areas outside the boundaries of titling projects, even those within INCRA's jurisdiction, were considered entirely vacant. The data by state, presented in column 4 of table 8, refer to total area within tracts.[6] In column 1 of this table, two additional totals appear, corresponding to the total area within titling projects (Total B) and to total area under the jurisdiction of INCRA (Total C). These are the bases for the percentages calculated in table 9, as explained in the notes to the two tables. The aggregations of states in tables 8 and 9 into regions of the "*cerrado*" or "Amazon" frontiers were made in conformance with chapter 2. Table 10 presents the states in the conventional groupings based on the IBGE regions (North, Northeast, etc.). The "Amazon frontier" corresponds to the North region plus Mato Grosso, while the "*cerrado* frontier" corresponds to the Center-West plus Maranhão, which IBGE classifies with the Northeast.

In sum, the census, registry, and titling data referring to different geographical bases imply distinct conceptions of what constitutes land "occupation." These data are presented in table 8 (in absolute numbers) and in table 9 (in percentages) merely to furnish an approximate order of magnitude of the degree of occupation or availability of land in the Amazon at the end of the 1970s. Table 11 compares these data across the entire country, aggregated by conventional macroregions.

As can be seen in tables 9 and 10, at the beginning of the 1980s, titled

Table 8. Land Occupation on the Frontier (according to different sources of information) (1,000s hectares)

States	*Total Geographic Area*[a] (1)	*Area in Agricultural Establishments*[b] (2)	*Registered Area*[c] (3)	*Titled Area*[d] (4)
Amazonian Frontier:				
Rondônia	24,304.0	5,688.3	5,791.3	14,236.7
Acre	15,258.9	5,851.1	10,463.5	2,694.2
Amazonas	155,898.7	7,220.5	25,536.8	1,596.2
Roraima	23,010.4	2,478.8	1,846.7	9,191.2
Pará	122,753.0	20,571.9	29,397.7	19,938.8
Amapá	13,906.8	735.5	2,008.9	1,112.2
Mato Grosso	88,100.1	35,683.9	55,517.5	1,332.8
Total A: Amazonian Frontier	443,232.3	78,299.9	130,382.2	50,102.1
Total B: Titling Projects	163,412.7[d]	—	—	—
Total C: Under INCRA Jurisdiction	224,973.7[d]	—	—	—

States	*Total Geographic Area*[a] (1)	*Area in Agricultural Establishments*[b] (2)	*Registered Area*[c] (3)	*Titled Area*[d] (4)
Cerrado Frontier:				
Maranhão	32,461.6	15,177.9	18,088.6	—
Mato Grosso do Sul	35,054.8	30,660.9	28,413.7	—
Goiás	64,209.2	48,703.5	39,036.6	—
Distrito Federal	577.1	279.6	106.4	—
Cerrado Frontier Total	132,302.7	94,821.9	85,645.3	—
Frontier Area Total	575,535.0	173,051.8	216,027.4	—

[a]IBGE (1971) and INCRA (1982).
[b]IBGE (1980).
[c]INCRA (1978).
[d]INCRA (1982a), referring only to the area of the Amazon frontier indicated in map 5, excluding therefore all the lands on the "*cerrado* frontier."
Source: Ozorio de Almeida (1984c)

Table 9. Percentage of Occupied Land on the Frontier (%)
(according to different sources of information)

States	*Area in Agricultural Establishments* (1)	*Registered Area* (2)	*Titled Area* (3)
Amazonian Frontier:			
Rondônia	23.4	23.8	58.6
Acre	38.4	68.6	17.7
Amazonas	4.6	16.3	1.0
Roraima	10.8	8.0	39.9
Pará	16.8	23.9	16.2
Amapá	5.3	14.4	8.0
Mato Grosso	40.5	63.0	1.5
Total A: Amazonian Frontier	17.6	29.4	11.3
Total B: Titling Projects	—	—	30.7
Total C: Under INCRA Jurisdiction	—	—	22.2
Cerrado Frontier:			
Maranhão	46.8	55.7	—
Mato Grosso do Sul	87.5	81.0	—
Goiás	75.9	60.8	—
Distrito Federal	48.5	18.4	—
Total: *Cerrado* Frontier	77.7	64.8	—
Total: Frontier Area	30.1	37.5	—

Source: Derived from table 8 as follows:

(Cols. of table 9)	(Cols. of table 8)
col. (1)	= col. (2) / col.(1) x 100
col. (2)	= col. (3) / col. (1) x 100
col. (3):A	= col. (4) / col. (1) x 100
col. (3):B	= col. (4) A/col. (1) B x 100
col. (3):C	= col. (4) A/col. (1) C x 100

Table 10. Percentage of Land Available on the Frontier (%)
(according to different sources of information)

States	*Area in Agricultural Establishments (1)*	*Registered Area (2)*	*Titled Area (3)*
Amazonian Frontier:			
Rondônia	76.6	76.2	41.4
Acre	61.6	31.4	82.3
Amazonas	95.4	83.7	99.0
Roraima	89.2	92.0	60.1
Pará	83.2	76.1	83.8
Amapá	94.7	85.6	92.0
Mato Grosso	59.5	37.0	98.5
Total A: Amazonian Frontier	82.4	70.6	88.7
Total B: Settlement Projects	—	—	69.3
Total C: Under INCRA Jurisdiction	—	—	77.8
Cerrado Frontier:			
Maranhão	53.2	44.3	—
Mato Grosso do Sul	12.5	19.0	—
Goiás	24.1	39.2	—
Distrito Federal	51.5	81.6	—
Total: *Cerrado* Frontier	28.3	35.2	—
Total: Frontier Area	69.9	62.5	—

Source: Derived from table 8 as follows:

(Cols. of table 9)	(Cols. of table 8)
col. (1)	= [1 - col. (2) / col.(1)] x 100
col. (2)	= [1 - col. (3) / col. (1)] x 100
col. (3):A	= [1 - col. (4) / col. (1)] x 100
col. (3):B	= [1 - col. (4) A/col. (1) B] x 100
col. (3):C	= [1 - col. (4) A/col. (1) C] x 100

Table 11. Percentage of Land Available in Brazil, 1980
(according to the agricultural census)

Regions[a]	*Total Geographic Area*[b] *(1,000 ha.)*	*Area in Agricultural Establishments*[c] *(1,000 ha.)*	*Degree of Availability*[d] *(%)*	*Occupation*[e] *(%)*
North	355,132.2	42,546.0	88.0	12.0
Northeast	153,640.2	89,555.1	41.7	58.3
Center-West	1,187,941.2	115,327.9	90.3	9.7
Southeast	91,880.8	73,973.8	19.5	80.5
South	56,207.1	48,185.0	14.3	85.7
Brazil	1,844,801.5	369,587.9	56.3	43.7

[a]This table presents data only from the Agricultural Census of 1980, since it was impossible to collect the corresponding information in INCRA's Real Estate Registry or in its Department of Land Resources, due to limitations of this research.

[b]IBGE (1968).

[c]IBGE (1980).

[d][1 – (2)/(1)] x 100.

[e](2)/(1) x 100.

lands included only 30.7 percent of the area within titling projects. Of the lands within these projects, 69.3 percent were still available (table 10, col. 3, total B). Compared to the other two criteria used in these tables—establishment area (col. 1) and registered area (col. 2)—titling (col. 3) indicates the smallest degree of apparent occupation and therefore the greatest degree of apparent availability. The single exception is Rondônia, where both settlement and titling were particularly intense.

Registration criteria indicate the highest degree of occupation (table 10, col. 2); 70.6 percent of the total Amazon frontier was unregistered at the beginning of the 1980s. Mato Grosso and Acre were the most registered states, with only 37 percent and 31 percent of their lands available, respectively. Criteria based on establishments in operation yield intermediate estimates (col. 1), according to which 82 percent of Amazonian lands were not in economic use at the end of the 1970s (col. 1). Mato Grosso and Acre were the most occupied states in the region; only 59 percent and 61 percent of their territory remained available for occupation, respectively.

It is interesting to note that the difference between columns 1 and 2 in tables 9 and 10 is surprisingly small. That is, it is generally supposed that large expanses of land in the Amazon had already been unproductively registered during the 1970s. This does not appear to be the case from these data.

The explanation perhaps lies in the fact that, for census purposes, the definition of an establishment "in operation" is excessively broad. Any area with a minimum of exploitation is recorded as an establishment in operation over its entire declared extent. This includes forested areas, natural pasture, and idle lands. Such intraestablishment differentiation, available in the census, cannot be explored here, given the limitations of this chapter.[7]

The *cerrado* frontier had a much higher degree of occupation than the Amazon frontier, as would be expected. Of the *cerrado* frontier, 77 percent was covered by agricultural establishments, and 65 percent was registered. Surprisingly, states that until recently were frontiers, such as Mato Grosso do Sul, had a higher degree of occupation than those of the country's South and Southeast regions, as can be seen in tables 9 and 11. That is, frontier advance was becoming an ever more rapid process. Consequently, the consolidation and concentration of the settlement pattern in Mato Grosso do Sul was much quicker than had been that of Maranhão or Paraná. Thus, new frontiers rapidly reached occupation indices much higher than did old frontiers.[8] In general, by 1980 the degree of occupation in the Center-West was already much higher than in the Northeast.

The High Apparent Availability of Land

In sum, it is estimated that between 50 and 130 million hectares of Amazon land were occupied (11 percent to 30 percent of the total), and that 313 to 393 million hectares (70 percent to 89 percent) remained available at the end of the 1970s. Apparent availability, however, is much greater than the effective availability of land, in terms of adequacy for agricultural exploitation. Agriculturability depends on fertility, slope, rockiness, natural irrigation, depth, and other factors that, together, determine the suitability of land for occupation by farmers operating at different levels of technology. This issue is examined in the next chapter, which addresses the agricultural suitability of Amazon lands.

Notes

This chapter and the following two chapters are extracted from an article originally written jointly with Maria Beatriz de Albuquerque David (1981), and later published as Ozorio de Almeida (1984c).

1. The terms "small farmers" or "family farmers" are used interchangeably here to denote low income, predominance of family labor, little mechanization, and few purchased inputs. Such farmers therefore constitute the target group for the policy of directed colonization. Although there are cases of small farmers using advanced agricultural techniques, it is more typical to find low productivity and rudimentary techniques in official colonization projects, as is shown in various sources and in the field research reported in this book (chap. 19). For this reason, small farmers will be assumed to practice low level or primitive techniques. The term "primitive" will be defined in chapter 4, with reference to soil surveys on agricultural suitability.

2. The Amazon is a region whose limits are defined in different ways, depending upon the focus of analysis. The Amazon Basin, in geographic terms, does not coincide with the Legal Amazon, and neither of these coincides with the perimeter of the states that compose the North region of Brazil. In this chapter, the area under study does not correspond to any of the usual classifications. Rather, it is determined by the availability of INCRA data on land titling, as seen in map 5.

3. The full methodology utilized in this work is detailed in Ozorio de Almeida (1984c) and is not repeated here for reasons of space.

4. These include areas of potential or actual conflict over land between landowners and squatters, or even free lands where conflicts exist among large-scale occupants, "land grabbers" (*grileiros*), and small settlers. These disputes over land are often carried out through violence, rather than settled by judicial means.

5. Although there may be large expanses of land available for colonization in the areas under the jurisdiction of these agencies, they were not taken into consideration in this study for lack of access to pertinent information.

6. The tables in this chapter contain data only at the state level. Two appendixes that are not presented here contain information about the availability of Amazon land by state and administrative units of INCRA. They can be found in Ozorio de Almeida (1984c).

7. This is partially done in chapter 19, with field data showing the degree of idle land within establishments. Even among small producers in colonization projects, this level is high: from 60 to 75 percent.

8. In this respect, see Mueller (1983b) and G. Müller (1987).

4. AGRICULTURAL SUITABILITY OF AMAZON SOILS

As was seen in the previous chapter, there were large extensions of land in the Amazon still legally available for occupation at the end of the 1970s. In light of this, the issue of whether these soils were also technically suitable for occupation becomes relevant. Is the technology used by small farmers compatible with Amazon soil quality? This is a relevant question as there is a vast bibliography on the subject that has already affected public opinion in this regard. It generally considers Amazon soils as being, in large part, unsuitable for agricultural exploitation, particularly by small farmers.[1] This opinion would logically lead to another: that any adequate soils in the Amazon be reserved for large farmers, whose use of modern practices and inputs would ensure long-term fertility

Several recent studies, however, contradict established opinion and suggest that family farming, especially *caboclo* agriculture, is technologically adequate to Amazon soils.[2] Indeed, some of these studies show that inadequate use of mechanization and of technologies that are appropriate for other regions of Brazil are detrimental to the tropical environment and speed up soil degradation after deforestation.[3] The result is that, instead of increasing Amazonian agricultural productivity, these so-called modern practices reduce it.

Due to the controversy on what agricultural technology is adequate for the region, it is no easy task to determine the size of the land area suitable for occupation by small producers. The problem is aggravated by the fact that all surveys on the subject use the same methodology for classification of agricultural suitability.[4] This methodology presupposes wrongly that "primitive" producers cultivate the soil continuously for many years, as more modern producers do.[5] Thus, it expects "primitive" agricultural techniques will promote soil degradation, unless under exceptional circumstances regarding fertility, slope, water supply, and so on.[6]

Brazilian small farmers, however, and especially "primitive" farmers, use "traditional-extensive" land rotation technology. In order to recover fertility, they leave the soil fallow for many years after using it for only one or two. Although the new undergrowth is different from the original vegetation, it grows rapidly enough to prevent erosion; even artificial pastures protect soil fertility.[7] To improve income levels and maintain soil fertility using "modern extensive" technology would lead farmers to pass old lots to new uses in varied combinations of pastures, permanent crops, and forestry.[8] Given the great variety of ecosystems in the Amazon, the best plant "mosaic" for each subarea would vary from place to place.

Unfortunately, existing information about Amazon soils is not based on knowledge of traditional extensive technologies, such as area rotation, or of modern extensive practices, such as interplanting and rotation of annual and permanent crops. Prevailing methods of soil classification assume wrongly that intensive use of machinery and chemical inputs is the sole means of maintaining soil fertility. The result is that many areas that are adequate for proper use by small producers are not so classified. This leads to a gross underestimate of the total Amazon area which could, technically, be made available to colonization. This chapter reinterprets such data, so as to obtain an approximate estimate of the real extension of Amazon lands suitable for family farming.[9]

At the end of the 1970s, the most complete source of information on Amazon soils was the RADAMBRASIL survey, which used remote sensing and photo-interpretation techniques. Information regarding the area covered by RADAM is not very precise, however, and a good part of the Amazon was still unknown ten years after large-scale settlement had begun. The Amazon was thus occupied without any knowledge of its agricultural capacity. In fact, the mapping of much of the region in any detail began only *after* the roads had been built! Major projects and plans were initiated with no idea of soil quality. It is hardly surprising, then, that results were as perverse as those to be seen in the next chapter.

Although several institutions use RADAM data in different ways, BINAGRI is the best published source on agricultural soil quality.[10] BINAGRI's precision regarding the Amazon is not much greater than RADAM's, however, because it used few additional sources and little complementary field research in that area; its soil classification methodology is also the same as RADAM's. The main difference between RADAM and BINAGRI involves classification of permanent crops (coffee, cocoa, pepper, and others).[11] This is no small difference, since it leads to divergent conclusions as to Amazon soil quality, as will be seen in the following sections.

Distinguishing between long- and short-cycle crops is fundamental in deciding whether an area can be occupied by small farmers. This is because, on the frontier, permanent crops are crucial to the fixation and economic viability of these farmers. Success depends a good deal on whether the initial annual crops are followed by pasture, permanent crops, or planted tree species.[12] Even if land is cultivated with extensive techniques, permanent crops allow accumulation to occur. As newly deforested areas enter annual crop cultivation, the area planted with permanent crops can expand over areas previously devoted to annual crops, which are thus not abandoned. After a few investment years, permanent crop yields begin to rise and so do profits as a whole. The farmer is then in a position to improve agricultural technology, progressing, it is hoped, from "low" to "medium" or even "high" tech levels.[13]

The objective of this chapter is to measure, based on RADAM data, the amount of land in the Amazon that can sustain such a path of small farmer fixation and accumulation, starting from a low technological level. The next section describes the soil classification methodology employed; the third section presents main results; the fourth section discusses conclusions. As will be seen, only 1 to 3 percent of the Amazon is found to be adequate for colonization.

Classification of Soil Quality

Map 6 shows that the RADAM soil quality survey covers a smaller perimeter than that indicated on map 5. For the state of Mato Grosso, the survey covered only the region to the north of parallel 12° S and to the west of meridian 54° W, accounting for only 29.6 percent of that state. The state of Pará was not covered east of meridian 48° W, which omits its easternmost portions. These limitations are due to several changes introduced in the methodology employed by RADAMBRASIL in these peripheral Amazon areas, making the data from them incompatible with those from the rest of the region.

Soils considered here as adequate for small farmers were those classified as "good" and "regular" for annual and permanent crops at "low" and "medium" technological levels. All other soils, including those of unknown suitability, were considered "poor." This classification generated many different soil subgroups that were ordered according to decreasing soil quality and were regrouped into four large categories:

Group 1: "good" soils. These are those classified by the sources as being good *and* regular for annual *and* permanent crops at low *and* medium technological levels. On this kind of land, the farmer can begin with annual crops and rudimentary techniques and evolve, in time, into permanent crops and improved techniques, remaining on the same soil for many years.

Group 2: land that is good for low technology only. These are soils classified as being good *and* regular for annual *and* permanent crops at a low technological level, but not at a medium level. This kind of land permits the farmer to become established, but prevents any improvement of technological level, thus barring capital accumulation.

Group 3: lands that are good for medium technology only. These are soils classified as being unsuitable for annual and permanent crops at a low level but are considered good and regular at a medium level of technology. These soils permit accumulation, but only starting from already medium level technology.

Group 4: "poor" soils. These soils are classified as being unsuitable, or of unknown quality, for both low and medium technological levels. They offer the typical small farmer no chance of improvement. Only that small minority of farmers who arrive with "high" level technology can become established or accumulate capital.

As must be the case with any classification, this one imposes an artificial discontinuity on a continuous phenomenon. In this case, the phenomenon is determined by a combination of many variables associated with soil quality. The soils in group 4 (poor), for example, can be cultivated with primitive technology, but with far lower productivity than soils in other groups. Boundaries between groups, therefore, are not sharply defined. Findings are shown in tables 12 and 13.

Amazon Soil Quality

Table 12 shows that 3.3 percent of the land in the Amazon was classified as being good, that is, capable of sustaining a path beginning at a low technology level and progressing to medium or high levels. Group 2 covered 14.6 percent of the Amazon area. These were lands considered good for low level technology, but were considered inadequate for technical improvement because of depth, slope, stoniness, or other reasons. Group 3 soils comprised 23.8 percent of the region. These lands are good for medium level technologies, as they permit good productivity for cultivation of annual and permanent crops, but only starting from an already medium technical level. More than half of the total Amazon land area, 58.3 percent, was considered poor (group 4).

Map 6. Area on Which RADAM Has Compatible Information on Amazon Soil Quality

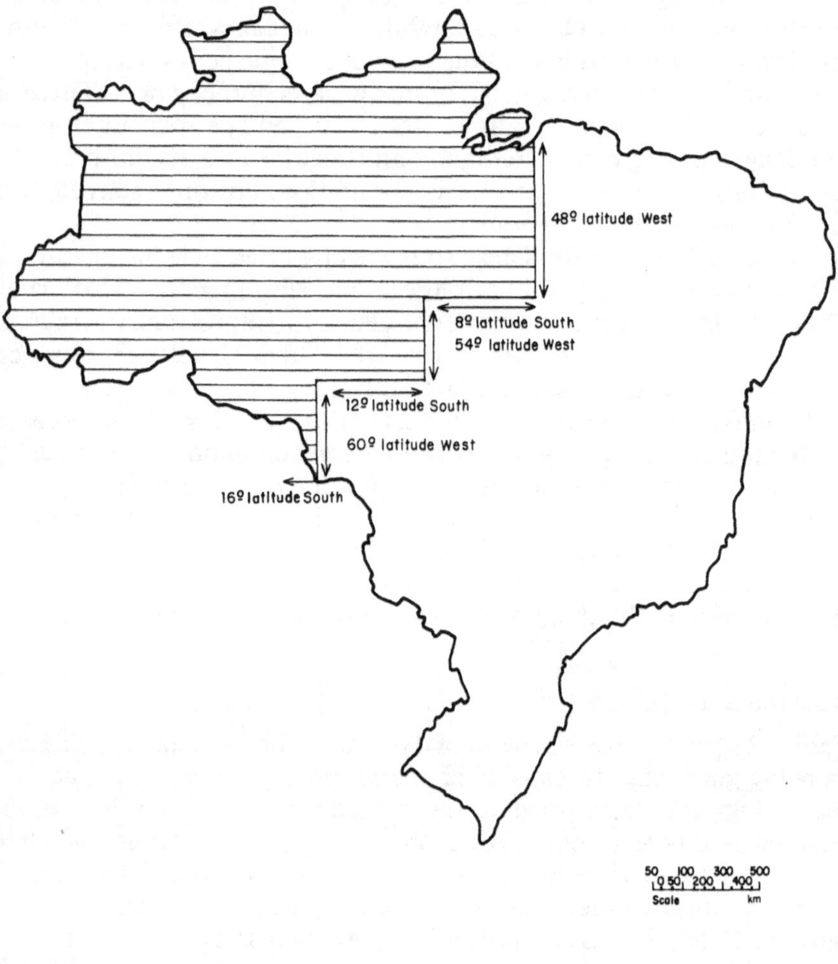

Source: Ozorio de Almeida (1984c).

These data indicate, according to the restrictive criteria discussed previously, that the soil area considered good for small producers at a low level of technology (group 1) was small (only 12 million hectares—3.3 percent of the total). However, from a less restrictive standpoint, there were far greater land areas appropriate for small producers, even though without prospects for future technical improvement (group 2), or requiring some start-up technology (group 3). In all (groups 1, 2, and 3), there were 156 million hectares (42 percent of the total) of soils that could be considered adequate for small agricultural producers: one part for low level migrants and the other for those with medium technology.

To compare these results with those published by BINAGRI, table 13 was converted into the terms used by that source. For low technology farming, four soil groups emerge: (1) soils considered good for annual crops, (2) soils that are good for permanent crops, (3) soils that are regular for annual crops, and (4) soils considered regular for permanent crops. Each of these soil types was summed separately. The same was done for medium level farming, generating the data presented in table 13. A specific land area may appear in two different columns, there being double counting each time this happens. The procedure used in compiling BINAGRI data was the same; lands considered adequate for low and medium levels appear twice: once on the left side of the table and once on the right side. The column for annual *and* permanent crops refers only to those lands adequate for both crops simultaneously. This joint (BINAGRI) result corresponds to an area much smaller than that of the individual aptitudes considered separately (RADAM).

At a low technological level, RADAM data indicate that there are

Table 12. Soil Quality in the Amazon

Soil Groups	*Area (in 1,000 ha.)*	%
Group 1: Good soils	11,982.0	3.3
Group 2: Good soils for low level technology	54,679.0	14.6
Group 3: Good soils for medium level technology	88,908.7	23.8
Group 4: Poor soils	217,899.3	58.3
TOTAL*	373,469.0	100.0

Source: Ozorio de Almeida (1984c)
*Total area indicated on map 1.

Table 13. RADAM versus BINAGRI: Comparison of Good Lands in the Amazon (in 1,000 ha.)

Source	*Annual*	*Permanent*	*Both*
	Low Level Technology		
RADAM	15,068.0	12,355.5	3,439.0
BINAGRI	—	—	2,803.7
	Medium Level Technology		
RADAM	11,244.0	93,232.7	11,149.0
BINAGRI	—	—	10,912.6

about 15 million hectares suitable for annual crops and 12.3 million suitable for permanent crops, but only 3.4 million suitable for both simultaneously. This last sum is comparable to the 2.8 million that BINAGRI considers appropriate for both kinds of crops at this technological level. Thus, it is evident that the criterion of simultaneity is extremely exclusive, as it means only 1 percent of the Amazon is suitable for small farmers. Four to five times this number of hectares are good for each type of crop separately.

At the medium level, the data from RADAM (11.1 million hectares) are comparable to those offered by BINAGRI (10.9 million hectares) for those lands classified as good for annual and permanent crops simultaneously. Once again, RADAM considers 11.2 million hectares as good for annual crops and 93.2 million for permanent crops—almost nine times the amount of land good for both crops at once.[14]

These results about Amazon soils can be compared to those pertaining to Brazil as a whole. Since, at the time, RADAM's survey of the entire national territory had not yet been completed, the comparison had to use previous surveys. They indicate that only 2 percent of Brazilian soils were good for annual crops at low level technology.[15] Values for the North and Center-West regions of Brazil were much inferior to those found by RADAM and BINAGRI.[16] Evidently, the fertile lands of the South were much better known than those of the Amazon. In fact, the fertile areas in Acre and Rondônia were entirely unknown then.[17] Even today, the Amazon still contains immense areas of unknown soils. Since good soils tend to occur in relatively small tracts dispersed inside large areas of low-quality land, it is probable that further field research will considerably increase the Amazon area considered good for small farmers. Even now, soil surveys in the Amazon are still mostly exploratory.

The Amazon's Low Absorption Capacity for Small Farmers

In conclusion, under quite restrictive criteria, the data indicate the existence of great extensions of adequate land for low and medium technology farming in the Amazon. Given the huge size of the region, however, these areas represent small proportions of the total. According to RADAM, only 3.3 percent of the region (12 million hectares), and according to BINAGRI, less than 1 percent of the region (2.8 million hectares) can sustain small farmers' capital accumulation starting from low and medium technology levels. The existence of these lands, however, does not mean that they were available for agricultural occupation by small producers. It is now necessary to cross-classify the data from this chapter (about suitability) with those from the previous one (about availability) to estimate the extent to which land in the Amazon was, at the same time, free and adequate for occupation by small farmers.

Notes

1. See, for example, Goodland and Irwin (1975), Gouru (1961), Klinge (1965, 1971), and Stark (1978).
2. Moran (1981, esp. chap. 7) and Cochrane and Sánchez (1982).
3. Cochrane and Sánchez (1982), esp. 172–176.
4. In 1947 the Soil Commission, a part of the National Agronomic Teaching and Research Center of the Ministry of Agriculture (which after successive mutations was transformed into EMBRAPA's National Soil Surveying and Conservation Service), carried out the first survey of Brazil's soils. The systematic work of interpreting the data began with Bennema, Beek, and Camargo (1964). This work guided the surveys begun in 1965 with USAID financing, imported material, and specialists from the United States and FAO. The final result was the soil map of the North, Middle-North, and Center-West regions (see Ministério da Agricultura 1975a), published on a scale of 1:5,000,000. The methodology established since then for the interpretation of these data was published in the USDA *Soil Survey Manual* (FAO 1975). It was used in the exploratory survey by SUDENE/EMBRAPA (1973/1979) and other regional surveys undertaken in Brazil. This same methodology is adopted by the RADAMBRASIL project of the Ministry of Mines and Energy, the only source on agricultural suitability of Amazon soils as a whole during the period studied. As the only complete base of information at the time, it transferred to all other studies on Amazon soils the same "vices of origin," independent of how hard each tried to reinterpret the data.
5. Cochrane and Sánchez (1982, 190).
6. "Good soils for low technology levels: . . . good earnings for a period of approximately 20 years, with production gradually declining"; "regular soils for low technology levels: . . . good earnings for the first ten years, declining to intermediate earnings during the following ten years"; "poor soils for low technology levels: . . . intermediate earnings for the first ten years, decreasing to

low earnings during the following ten years"; "inadequate soils for low technology levels: . . . earnings low to very low even in the initial production stages." See Ministério das Minas e Energia (1974, vol. 20, 289) for a complete description of the classification, extensive to "medium" and "high" level technologies.

7. Cochrane and Sánchez (1982, 191–192) and Sánchez et al. (1982).

8. Experiments show that it is possible to cultivate from eight to ten years of annual crops in Amazon soils with no loss of fertility. This, however, demands intensive use of fertilizers and therefore corresponds to medium level technology, and not to low level technology, as defined in this book. See Sánchez et al. (1982).

9. Dias and Castro (1976, esp. 9–14) describe the conditions for implantation and accumulation based on the "traditional technology" of the family farmer.

10. Menezes (1980).

11. Ministério da Agricultura (1979).

12. As will be seen in chapter 19, the most successful settlers were those who invested in permanent crops, thereby fixing themselves and accumulating as time went by.

13. This terminology, "low," "medium," and "high" technology, differs from that used by RADAM and BINAGRI, "primitive," "semideveloped," and "developed" producers. The implications, however, are the same: increasing use of purchased industrial inputs, chemicals, and machinery. Due to space limitations, the complex typology used by these sources cannot be detailed in this chapter. This information is in Ozorio de Almeida (1984c).

14. Comparison between the two sources, BINAGRI and RADAM, of soils considered "regular" for low and medium technology levels is even more difficult than for those considered "good" due to greater disagreement on classification and aggregation criteria. For this reason, no such comparison is made here. For the Amazon as a whole, BINAGRI admits that 175 million hectares may be considered regular (in this case, they include "good" soils too) for low and medium technology levels (sum of soils considered regular at the medium level). This area is much larger, though still within the same rough order of magnitude, than that obtained via RADAM: 156 million hectares.

15. Ministério da Agricultura (1975b, tables 1 to 6, 79–94). See also Paiva (1979, table III.2, 65).

16. See also Ministério da Agricultura (1975a, table II, 540), where good and regular soils for low technology are 11.68 percent and 1.09 percent, respectively, of the whole region (600 million hectares)

17. See Ministério da Agricultura (1981).

5. THE CLOSING FRONTIER

The greater the land area in the Amazon that is good for agricultural use, especially for low technology farmers, the stronger is the case for distributing Amazon land to small producers via settlement projects. However, the greater the area of good land that is already occupied, the stronger the case for preventing any further Amazon occupation, as neither large nor small farmers would benefit from deforestation of poor soils. Distributionist or conservationist policies in the Amazon, therefore, should be based on measuring the area that is both good for small farmers and still open for occupation. This chapter measures the extent of Amazon land that was suitable and available for colonization at the end of the 1970s.

The data about availability from chapter 3 and about suitability from chapter 4 are compared in this chapter by a method of overlapping maps. Availability data are based on INCRA land titling projects; suitability data come from RADAMBRASIL. These sources were chosen as both sets of maps are on a scale of 1:100,000, which makes cartographic manipulation possible. Evidently, the joint use of two sources escalates each source's independent imprecision, already discussed in their respective chapters, and also gives rise to new limitations arising from the comparison itself.

Areas considered good or regular at low or medium technology levels were measured over areas that were still available at the beginning of the decade. The measurement of each kind of soil was done by different methods on the different geographical units of observation already described. Within the delineated land tracts of INCRA's land titling projects, occupied areas were already mapped and could be measured directly. In this case, it was possible to use planimeters for direct measurement. In the remaining areas of INCRA's land titling projects (45 percent of their total area), and in other areas under INCRA's jurisdiction, occupied areas have not yet been identified on maps, even though their size is known. It was then necessary to make approximations. Areas already under private ownership, and which could not be located on maps, were considered to be endowed with the same soil quality mix as nonoccupied areas. This approximation means that soil quality in available areas was overestimated, since the best soils tend to be the first to be settled, as will be seen below. As pointed out previously, this text aims to raise an alarm about the lack of knowledge regarding occupation of Amazon lands and to motivate more precise surveys on this issue.

Unfortunately, it is not possible to present in this chapter a map comparable to the two previous ones, containing the overlapped information on land availability (map 5) and soil quality (map 6) in the Amazon. The areas that are both good and available constitute a large number of patches too small and discontinuous to be effectively visualized on the scale used in this book.

Availability and Quality of Amazon Lands

Table 14 shows the percentage and total area of each soil group in each state: within INCRA's land titling projects, in areas outside them, and in the total Amazon area under INCRA jurisdiction.[1]

It can be seen that good soils for low and medium technology small producers (table 12, groups 1, 2, and 3) contained almost 36 percent of land still available in the Amazon at the end of the 1970s. This proportion is similar to the 42 percent obtained for the region as a whole in table 12. However, only 838,000 hectares, or 7 percent, of the 12 million hectares previously classified as being good for low technology cultivation were still available at the beginning of the 1980s. Occupation was thus extremely selective of the best lands. It was also so fast that all the good lands (group 1) in Rondônia seen in table 14 were no longer available by the mid-1980s.[2] The once-available lands in Mato Grosso and Acre have also "vanished" since then.

The situation was different for group 2 soils (27 million hectares), 16 percent of the land under INCRA jurisdiction, which yield good returns at a low technology level, particularly for annual crops. These were concentrated mainly in Acre or in areas outside INCRA's land titling projects, which means they were located in areas with little or no infrastructure at that time. Rondônia, Acre, and Mato Grosso were thus the regions most suitable for settlement of low technology farmers. However, this is exactly the area that was occupied by medium technology farmers who were capable of using land of lesser quality.[3] Low technology farmers settled in Pará, where all the best land had already been appropriated by the beginning of the 1980s, and in the Northeast of Mato Grosso, an area that could not be analyzed due to RADAM's changes in methodology, as explained in chapter 4.

Group 3 soils covered 18.9 percent of the available land under INCRA jurisdiction. These soils are suitable only for migrants who use fertilizers and equipment and who have sufficient knowledge and resources to operate at the medium technology level. Such was the case of the southern migratory wave of the mid- to late 1970s.[4] The majority of these soils were in the state of Amazonas, or in areas outside INCRA's land titling projects, where, until then, there had been relatively little settlement of small producers.

Keeping in mind how restrictive this classification of good Amazon soils is, it is possible that much more available land is "good" for small producers than the data indicate. The term "availability" is also used in a restrictive sense that underestimates the amount of good land in the Amazon to which small farmers could still gain access. Idle but already appropriated lands are not considered "available" according to current legislation. Since the best lands were occupied first, they could become available again by rigorous land redistribution policy, carried out either by agrarian reform or rural taxation.

The overlay presented here is just a first approximation, aiming to see what conclusions can be taken from the available data referring to the period under study. One hopes that these results will stimulate more precise studies that will overcome this preliminary effort's inevitable limitations. Until this happens, the results here presented are the only existing ones for the Amazon as a whole.

Technological and Social Issues of Amazon Colonization

The express motive for surveying natural resources in the Amazon is to "rationalize" their use. Such rationality depends on ordering priorities among conservation and alternative modes of exploitation. If occupation by small producers has any priority as a social land distribution policy, one should give to these settlers lands suited to their technology level. The data presented here suggest that, as of 1980, this was no longer possible. The best land for settlement had already been almost entirely appropriated. Either contemporary information on natural resources had been insufficient to assure a "social" rationality of occupation, or settlers had less priority than other demanders of the region's lands.

The same data indicate that large areas of "reasonably good" lands remained available for small producer occupation, much larger than an

Table 14. Agricultural Suitability of Available Land under INCRA Jurisdiction in the Amazon[a]

Geographical Location	Area Available for Occupation		Soil Suitability: Group 1 (Good soils)		Group 2 (Good for low technology)		Group 3 (Good for medium technology)		Group 4 (Poor soils)	
	1,000 ha.	(%)	1,000 ha.	(%)	1,000 ha.	(%)	1,000 ha.	(%)	1,000 ha.	(%)
Land Titling Projects:										
Rondônia	5,896	100	544	9.2	12	0.2	3,649	61.9	1,689	28.7
Acre	12,553	100	29	0.2	10,201	81.3	1,218	9.7	1,104	8.8
Amazonas	29,670	100	0	0.0	1,191	6.7	11,887	40.1	15,790	53.2
Pará	27,674	100	0	0.0	3,503	12.7	0	0.0	24,171	87.3
Amapá	12,436	100	0	0.0	0	0.0	0	0.0	12,436	100
Roraima	13,819	100	0	0.0	0	0.0	0	0.0	13,819	100
Mato Grosso[b]	4,252	100	264	0.0	2,883	67.8	2,883	67.8	1,105	26.6
Total in Land Titling Projects	106,303	100	838	0.8	15,707	14.8	19,639	18.5	70,117	65.9

Geographical Location	Area Available for Occupation		Group 1 (Good soils)		Group 2 (Good for low technology)		Group 3 (Good for medium technology)		Group 4 (Poor soils)	
	1,000 ha.	*(%)*	*1,000 ha.*	*(%)*	*1,000 ha.*	*(%)*	*1,000 ha.*	*(%)*	*1,000 ha.*	*(%)*
Total Outside Land Titling Projects	61,561	100	0	0.0	11,478	18.7	12,012	19.5	38,06	61.8
Grand Total under INCRA Jurisdiction	167,864	100	838	0.0	27,186	16.2	31,652	18.9	108,187	64.4

[a]Overlapping of the areas on maps 5 and 6.
[b]Only in the area indicated on map 6.

Source: Ozorio de Almeida (1984c).

uncritical reading of the BINAGRI data suggests. Had settlers been accompanied by a good rural extension service, four to five times more land would have been adequate for low technology small farmers; as much as nine times more land would have been adequate for medium technology small farmers. But this large absorption potential could only have been attained in the presence of the deficient technical support necessary to adapt small producers to the available soils.

The soil quality of lands still available by the end of the 1970s was in contradiction to migrants' technological characteristics. High or medium technology colonists, particularly those from the South of Brazil, directed themselves to the western Amazon where the land was most adequate for low technology settlers. The low technology settlers, on the other hand, moved into the eastern Amazon where the only lands left demanded medium technology agriculture. Lack of information on the Amazon's natural resources contributed to an irrational distribution of land among small farmers from the technological point of view.

At the time, it would have been practically impossible to reverse migratory flows into the Amazon. These were determined by the simultaneous expansion of great zones of economic and institutional influence.[5] Since migrants could not be brought to the right land, the solution should have been to adapt migrant technology to the quality of the soil they settled on. In other words, the Amazon's colonization policy should have incorporated, as a fundamental component, rural extension and technical orientation to settlers. Without it, the economic viability of settlers, and of colonization itself, was undermined. In numerous cases low, medium, or even high technology settlers quit and left their plots, due greatly to technological inadequacy of local soils.

Evidently, the causes of these failures not only were technical, but also involved various other factors. Violence over land, marketing difficulties, insufficient physical and social infrastructure all played their roles.[6] The data presented in the two preceding chapters, however, suggest that technological adequacy needs attention. Choosing the right variety of seeds, making adequate use of machinery and inputs, spacing, intercropping, and rotation are all tasks in which settlers needed aid. As will be seen in part 4, especially chapters 19 and 21, without adequate technology, earnings fall rapidly. As small farmers left their lots, rural exodus and concentration of land property increased in settlement projects themselves. Social objectives were frustrated and natural resources were wasted.

Technology and Ecology in Amazon Colonization

The technological issue is especially complex because rural extension services were in a sense "contaminated" by agronomic information about other regions of the country. Agricultural modernization in Brazil, as elsewhere, involved a technological "package" in which seed productivity depends on the joint action of fertilizers, pesticides, and equipment. Agriculture thus became progressively integrated into the industrial production process as a purchaser of manufactured inputs and a supplier of agricultural raw materials for industrial processing.[7] The Amazon environment, however, provoked innumerable setbacks for this technology that was "imported" from abroad and adapted to conditions in the South. Notwithstanding, this is still the technological model learned by those who orient the region's farmers as rural extensionists.[8] Success in any Amazon settlement policy requires increasing field research on technologies suitable to the humid tropics and accelerating the incorporation of research results into rural extension services.

The magnitude of the task, however, was not foreseen. It involved no less than a total technical reorientation of an immense wave of migrants in a very short period of time. Farmers notoriously resist extensionists' advice;[9] they take many years to relinquish habits brought from their regions of origin and to begin responding to local stimuli, as will be seen in chapter 21. Resources allocated were grossly insufficient not only in financial terms, but also in terms of institutional competence or even political will. It was soon seen to be easier to expand the frontier through large-scale agro-industrial occupation of the Center-West *cerrado* than to adapt small farmers to the Amazon. As the *cerrado* alternative gained preference from the mid-seventies on, colonization of the Amazon was progressively abandoned as a policy priority. Existing projects continued to expand due to migratory pressure, but they did so within a technical orientation vacuum. Agricultural technology in colonization was truly primitive, and resulted in "excess" deforestation, as will be seen in chapter 19.

Through such national agencies as EMBRAPA and CNPAF, the institutional apparatus for research was relatively well developed, but not the necessary diffusion methods to reach small producers. Rural extension services, the now extinct EMATERS, operated at the state level and did not absorb the technological innovations developed in federal research institutions. However, as will be seen in part 4 of this book, whenever extension did effectively reach farmers, it made a significant difference in their income levels (chap. 20). The lack of technical assistance, therefore, depressed income levels and, over time, hampered settlers' performance (chap. 21).

The main problem for agricultural use of Amazon land by small farmers is not physical but chemical. Only 3 percent of the Amazon is covered by infertile or sandy soil and only 4 percent tends toward laterization.[10] On the other hand, 92 percent of the area has soils with little tendency to erode, due mainly to small slopes, and 75 percent of the basin is dominated by soils that are deep enough, well irrigated, yellow or red, and have good physical characteristics. They are, however, very acidic and poor in natural nutrients.[11] According to today's "modern" agriculture, they require a good deal of chemical correction. This makes agriculture much more expensive, particularly when one considers the prohibitive costs of transporting fertilizers all the way to the frontier.

In view of this, reorientation of agricultural research itself is fundamental to break the vicious cycle of the inadequate technological package now in use. It makes no sense to impose on the Amazon plants whose seeds require complex combinations of chemical compounds that recreate environmental conditions typical of other regions. Rather than change soils to suit foreign plants, one must use plant varieties that are compatible with these soils. This new orientation would open the door to some of the most recent advances in agricultural technology, such as plague prevention through "escape" mechanisms that involve bringing in plants from other regions of the globe (such as the African and Asian humid tropics), or the double grafting of tree trunks and tree tops. Additionally, there is ample room for application of different new forms of biotechnology.[12]

As was stated above, technological inadequacy is not the only, and perhaps not even the dominant, ecological issue in the Amazon. Soils that are "good" for small farmer occupation from a purely agricultural point of view might be located in areas contaminated by disease, or so far from the main roads that they become uneconomic. They might already have been appropriated by large farmers or other claimants, or they may suffer from many other evils, thus becoming unfit for occupation. Even if none of these problems occur, however, it is certainly true that good soils are misused by the adoption of technology inappropriate for the Amazon environment.

The Closing Amazon Frontier

The main conclusion to be extracted from chapters 3, 4, and 5 is that, by the end of the 1970s, given the existing physical infrastructure and prevailing technologies, the Amazon frontier was already closed. The best lands had already been occupied, and those remaining demanded heavy investments in generation and diffusion of technologies more adequate to the Amazonian environment. By the late 1970s, an increase in the availability of good lands for small farmers already required settling on occupied land. Expropriation could have been highly effective at that time, particularly since, in the recently occupied regions, land property had not yet been legally or historically consolidated. Many of the Amazon's great landowners acquired land in the speculative surge of the mid-1970s, but the subsequent recession reduced their expectations of deriving returns from the region. Government, then, had the possibility of reducing unproductive appropriation of good land. In other words, during the 1970s, agrarian reform became a necessary complement to colonization, no longer its alternative.

Unfortunately, the 1980s did not meet the challenge left behind by the 1970s. With the "New Republic" (1984–1989), political will for agrarian reform seemed at first to strengthen with the creation of a Ministry of Agrarian Reform. But its legal base was removed by the 1988 Constitution and the Ministry itself was extinguished in 1989. Land property disputes, and their attendant social problems, grew ever worse, preparing a legacy for the 1990s of growing social conflict in rural areas. Since the early 1980s, the occupation of land in the Amazon occurred in ever poorer soils. The social benefit of deforestation, in terms of agricultural product per hectare, must, therefore, diminish with time.

This chapter has attempted to give an approximate order of magnitude to these problems. As it is only an exploratory effort, it suffers from insufficient data and, consequently, imprecise methods and imperfect results. Adequate surveys are urgently needed, not only of the amount, but also of the location, of land suitable for settlement by small farmers. Only then can the geographical selectivity of Amazon occupation be improved.

The next part of the book will analyze how the occupation of the Amazon was institutionalized by the Brazilian state and by other agents that organized the social and economic activity of the incoming population.

Notes

1. Other tables, more detailed than those in this chapter, present the same data per land titling project in each state. To save space, they could not be shown here. See Ozorio de Almeida (1984c, 385).

2. Verbal communication by INCRA's technicians in a debate on the theme in a seminar, on 20 July 1983, at IPLAN, in Brasília.

3. See part 4 of this book, especially chapter 16, further on.

4. See chapter 2, above.

5. Parts 2 and 3 of this book are a description of the formation of the institutional and economic environments of the Amazon frontier.

6. Part 4 of this book is dedicated to an analysis of the influence of various of these factors over settlers' performance in directed settlement projects in the Amazon.

7. This process of growing "industrialization of agriculture" has been

described by various authors. Among the most important are Castro (1983), who emphasizes the interconnected character of modern agricultural practices adopted in Brazil in imitation of North American technology, and Graziano da Silva et al. (1982), who stress the technical and institutional aspects of the predominant technology "package." The growing role of agro-industry in the technological orientation of Brazilian agriculture has also merited the attention of many authors such as G. Müller (1982) and Coradini and Fredericq (1982), among others.

8. EMATER's extension services reach only 16 percent of the country's farmers. In the Amazon, this proportion is even smaller. These services tend not only to have technological biases, but also to be very bureaucratic, involving mainly inspection of rural credit and insurance. See Graziano da Silva et al. (1982, 31) and Musumeci (1987).

9. See Musumeci (1987), who shows that representatives of industrial, chemical, and mechanical input firms have much more success in influencing the small farmer than do formal extensionists.

10. See Sánchez et al. (1982).

11. Ibid.

12. See Ozorio de Almeida et al. (1984).

6. THE ROLE OF THE BRAZILIAN STATE ON THE AMAZON FRONTIER

The advance of the frontier across the Amazon is more than merely an ecological or demographic phenomenon. It is a transformation in that region's role in the national and international economy. One of the main agents in this change is the Brazilian state, which provides the newly occupied areas with physical and institutional infrastructure. Its role, active or neglectful with respect to different issues, leaves profound and irreversible marks in each area that is occupied.

This chapter and the four following it study the principal actions of the Brazilian state with respect to colonization of the Amazon during the 1970s. The objective is to give an overview of the institutional and political context in which migrants came in search of their own land in the Amazon and of the constraints imposed on them by the way local institutional environments were arranged. The findings are based on detailed measurement of the costs of colonization during the 1970s. The numbers represent outlays effectively incurred and not what should have been spent for less devastation and deprivation on the frontier.

An agricultural frontier advances across an area that the state prepares by building roads, demarcating and mapping territory, regularizing land ownership, and providing the physical and institutional infrastructure for social and economic activity. The results obtained by a small settler on a plot depend very much upon how these broad obligations of the state are performed and on the resources invested in the settler's environment as a whole. In spite of much criticism of the Brazilian state's omission during frontier occupation, one must bear in mind that it did indeed make an immense effort to direct the colonization of the Amazon frontier during the 1970s.

Amazon colonization consumed an estimated total of about $7.5 billion in public funds during the 1970s. More than half of this cost went to road building, one-third was spent by complementing institutions, and only 6 percent was spent on the settlement projects themselves. Thus, the greatest cost in colonization was not land distribution per se but the transportation of all the physical, economic, and legal infrastructure necessary for agriculture in the frontier. At the time, an agrarian reform would have been a much cheaper solution to the land distribution problem for the same number of people. The infrastructure provided by colonization increased the value of land on the frontier, and attracted new interest groups to the area in addition to settlers. This has made any redistributive proposal from now on, even in the Amazon itself, much more difficult.

Omissions of the Brazilian State

One of the scars left by the advancing frontier, and certainly the one that has received the most international attention, is the destruction of the natural environment by invading agents: governmental and private, large and small, agricultural and nonagricultural. As discussed in part 1, in the humid tropics, the forest is heterogeneous and much of the soil has serious chemical imbalances that make it largely unsuitable for conventional agricultural use. Solar radiation is intense and rainfall is highly concentrated, so the best productive use for these soils is based on trees and roots. Invading farmers, however, come linked to outside markets for grains. They use intensive monoculture technology that not only increases plants' vulnerability to pests but also demands expensive chemical correction in order to attain the level of productivity that justifies mechanization. Clearing away the rain forest extinguishes known and unknown native species, some of which may be more valuable than what replaces them.

Thus, agricultural expansion in the Amazon is destructive to the environment due to the species that are taken from the earth, to the species that replace them, and to the manner in which all this is done. With no social control, these substitutions spread ever faster. Due to the lack of a "rational" occupation policy, or of "adequate" technological policies, the harm to the environment caused by the advancing frontier becomes increasingly serious.

Another of the Brazilian state's omissions, which leaves irreversible scars behind the advancing frontier, is the destruction of Amerindian societies. Private projects, both large and small, involving agriculture, mining, and ranching, encroach upon Indian territories. Public projects involving settlement, hydroelectricity, and other enterprises do the same. Whether public or private, all projects do so with governmental consent and even encouragement. In spite of recent gestures, effective political will to legalize Indian territories and to preserve their societies is lacking. One would have to confront powerful interests that have much to gain from the appropriation of Indian lands.

Yet another of the Brazilian state's omissions during frontier expansion is health care. Infected populations from one region bring their diseases and carriers to other regions, contaminating vast territories. Traditional control methods, such as spraying against malaria, work well only in established areas where houses have walls, and where doors and windows can be shut. They are, however, entirely ineffective in pioneer areas where a large part of the population lives camped in makeshift shacks or even open tents and bowers. Without a public scientific research program specifically addressing the Amazonian population's health problems, health on the frontier will continue to deteriorate even further below its present disastrous level.

Finally, any economic activity presupposes legal, social, and commercial structures consistent with itself. In the Amazon, the structures existing before the agricultural frontier's advance are dismantled as new producers arrive. Extraction systems, such as rubber tapping and nut gathering, in which property of the soil is less important than access to the trees upon it, are destroyed. Collective grazing on floodlands during the dry season is repressed. Cities subsisting on extraction economies wither away when the economic system redirects itself to agro-industrial production. Serious new social imbalances are created as previous economic activity becomes incompatible with new private appropriation of the land, as is required by agriculture.

Perhaps the most serious of all the state's omissions is its lack of control over the occupation process itself. As was seen in chapter 5, by the beginning of the 1980s all the land suitable for settlement, as far as soil quality is concerned, had already been occupied. For the remaining areas to be exploited, without great harm to the environment, the techniques used by settlers would have to be considerably modified. This is a huge endeavor and a slow and difficult process. Brazilian technological research and diffusion institutions were not prepared for it. Given the notorious underexploitation of the land held in huge private properties, redistributive policies within the Amazon itself became increasingly urgent. The Brazilian state, however, has been not only neglectful of, but even contrary to such measures. Thus, the state's negligence affected the advancing frontier in various ways, resulting in serious consequences for the Amazon region and for the rest of society.

The State in Action: Homogenizing, Settling, and Complementing

In many senses, the state was very active and its presence on the frontier grew considerably during the 1970s. First of all, the Amazon was profoundly affected by the general agricultural policy reorientation of the beginning of the decade. This has been called the policy of "conservative modernization" in agriculture, whereby a huge framework of agricultural research, technological development, credit expansion, and financial and tax rebates promoted the adoption of a technological "package" based on machinery and chemical inputs.[1] Huge projects, both national and multinational, governmental and private, were stimulated. These projects began to occupy gigantic stretches of land and generated a greatly concentrated land ownership structure during, and even before, the arrival of migrant populations.[2]

As new latifundia were formed, increasing parts of the frontier became inaccessible to small farmers. Landholding concentrated through mechanisms analogous to those that had expelled migrants from their areas of origin. The frontier "closed from within and without."[3] Social tensions over land grew, and the Amazon came to harbor the same problems that it had been hoped it would solve.[4] In this sense, then, the state was very active in the 1970s, homogenizing landed property throughout Brazil. The fact that today the rural population must fight for land on the frontier, as well as in long-established regions of the country, is due not only to the omissions, but also to the active engagement of the Brazilian state.

Constructing roads, mapping, legalizing, and titling the land are activities that create the conditions for colonization, even if they often come after it chronologically. Schools, health care, and public security are part of citizens' basic rights; they should accompany populational shifts, although in fact they tend to do so only with a lag. Technical assistance, credit, cooperatives, unions, notary registries, consumer and product markets, and other services, public as well as private, are all essential to agricultural success. Ensuring access to all of these activities is the responsibility of the state throughout the nation, not only on the frontier.

In addition to these activities, a frontier places upon the state the demand for directed settlement. A directed settlement project identifies a specific area, demarcates individual plots, builds roads, sells the land, and transfers property deeds. It may also provide settlers with some social infrastructure, but such additional functions are not well defined. It is an administrative instance that speeds and unifies the various institutional tasks necessary for the occupation of a certain geographical area.

This chapter is a brief introduction to the broad issue of the role of the state in Amazon colonization, to be pursued in the following three chapters. Each will delve deeper into homogenizing, settling, and institutional complementing activities on the frontier. The cost of each one of these activities will then be calculated and summed in chapter 10, yielding an estimate of the total cost of Amazon colonization during the 1970s.

Notes

1. Graziano da Silva (1980a, 1981) discusses Brazilian agriculture's "painful modernization" process.
2. R. Carvalho (1979) and Mahar (1978) show the extent of land appropriations along the frontier. G. Müller (1987) shows that agricultural technological intensity has been growing more quickly in frontier areas, particularly Mato Grosso, than in the rest of the country.
3. Osório (1978, 1979).
4. Martine (1980) and Pacheco (1979).

7. SPATIAL HOMOGENIZATION OF THE AMAZON

During the expansion of the agricultural frontier into the Amazon, new productive activities penetrated a space where economic activity preexisted. The types of production that were already there were compatible with legal systems and ways of using the physical environment that were very different from those introduced during the 1970s.[1] Many examples can be listed in this regard.

One example is the case of Indian tribes who use each part of their territory for a specific function: hunting, farming, extraction, ceremonies, and migration. Another is rubber tapping, where land is not necessarily held in property; what matters is not so much ownership of the land where rubber trees are, as the right to exploit a path that winds through the forest from rubber tree to rubber tree. In Brazil nut or in *babaçu* extraction, gatherers do not own the forest either, as they use it only during the harvest period and leave it for the rest of the year. In the collective grazing on floodplains, small producers take their cattle to the riverside during the dry season and return to their highland properties when the rains begin. In all these examples, as in many other cases, prefrontier economic activity in the Amazon did not require private property. Informal types of right to access to extractive products were common.

In promoting the entry of farmers onto the Amazon frontier, it behooved the Brazilian state to physically and legally prepare the region to receive a larger population than before, with a new type of productive activity: agro-ranching. With this increase in population came more and different equipment, buildings, and new ties to the national economy. The state was also obliged to prepare a new legal land property structure to permit the land's appropriation by the incoming economic agents. This includes demarcation of areas to become farms and ranches, as well as ecological and Indian reserves, forest extraction areas (including lumbering), mineral extraction projects (including prospecting), and land devoted to other uses (including military). The legal basis for the use of land was to be changed. From an informal right to exploit a resource, consistent with extraction and collective economic activities, it was to become formal property, of the land and of all that is on it, consistent with agricultural production. Typically, however, state action was slow and one preparation task lagged behind another, such as when roads were opened before land regularization was complete, or when both fell behind migration. Such delays and contradictions contributed to the notorious conflicts and violence of the Amazon frontier of the 1970s, as they do to this day.

This chapter's objective is to make an approximate estimate of the contribution of homogenizing costs to the total cost of frontier expansion during the 1970s. The two preparation tasks most essential to the frontier's integration into the national economy were road building and land titling, both of which will be studied in this chapter, at the federal level.[2]

In spite of their important role in construction and social control of the region, the cost of the armed forces' presence on the frontier will not be taken into account. In the beginning of the period, guerrilla warfare in the Araguaia region intensely engaged the army. At the end of the decade, the region's social conflicts impelled the National Security Council to take direct command of much of the region's administration. The council created organisms, such as the GETAT and the GEBAM, that became responsible for vast areas about which there is still insufficient information.

The costs of other governmental programs in the region, such as the Ministry of Mines and Energy's RADAM project, are also omitted due to lack of information. The costs of localized operations, such as individual states' titling projects, were omitted for the same reason. Operations whose impact affected only a part of the total area studied, such as the SUDAM projects, were also omitted, as again there was no time to obtain information on them. The results, therefore, are an underestimate of total public investment in the Amazon frontier. They do, however, cover those programs most closely related to settlement: the provision of physical and legal access to land.

Land Titling Projects

INCRA's land titling projects (or *projetos fundiários*) involved vast areas of Brazilian territory—more than 300 million hectares, as can be seen in map 7. Their functions included: identification and discrimination of "vacant" land, incorporation of it into federal land, land titling, discriminated land regularization, expropriation in the name of social interest, and auctioning of federal land. Many of these are essential tasks for any social policy involving land distribution, both for settlement and agrarian reform.[3]

During the 1970s, land titling became increasingly important within INCRA. By the beginning of the 1980s, the program was absorbing almost the whole "agrarian reform" budget. In spite of its name, the program was used to auction huge tracts of land to large agro-industrial and cattle ranching projects and private settlement companies, which contributed a great deal to land property concentration on the frontier. Although states are also involved in land titling, the data here refer only to INCRA's federal level activities.

INCRA's land titling projects were, in general, implemented during the mid-1970s, with an average 10 million hectares each and an accumulated average cost of about $5.4 million from creation until the end of 1981. Of the more than thirty projects in the Amazon region, there is compatible information for only twenty-one, for which data on total and percentage costs are displayed in tables 15 and 16, respectively.[4] Each of these twenty-one projects employed seventy-five people per year on average and spent high percentages in mapping and surveying ("topography") costs, which were essential to their functions. The costs were proportional to titling intensity: they were most efficient in Pará, where 26 percent of the resources resulted in 38 percent of titling; in second place came Rondônia, with similar resources and 28 percent of titling.

In calculating the total cost of land titling during the decade, the mean cost ($5.4 million) was multiplied by the thirty-three projects, obtaining a total of $182 million. Given the large variation among projects, the use of the mean is certainly questionable and a confidence interval may have been preferable. But this would be impractical for every subitem in each table. The objective here, therefore, is merely to offer a rough order of magnitude on the main costs of Amazon colonization.

With due caution, then, $182 million will be transported to table 26 in chapter 10, to be added to other cost subtotals of Amazon colonization. The result obtained there is larger than the total on table 15, as it estimates the total for all thirty-three projects, not only for the twenty-one for which compatible data exist. In spite of this difference, $182 million is still an underestimate of INCRA's total land titling cost, as it takes into consideration only on-location outlays and does not incorporate central office costs for program administration in Brasília. It is, at least, a lower bound figure to be added to other frontier costs later.

Map 7. Land Titling Projects

Source: INCRA (1982c).

Table 15. Total Cost of Land Titling Projects

	Cost Items (in U.S. $1,000)				
State	*Capital*	*Personnel*	*Operational*	*Topography*	*Total*
Rondônia	973.62	11,996.90	4,261.77	17,724.78	34,957.07
Acre	943.30	12,407.66	5,397.83	400.41	19,149.20
Pará	1,919.30	16,493.53	8,100.36	3,590.27	30,103.46
Amazonas	499.74	6,858.77	3,187.79	987.07	11,533.37
Amapá	335.23	3,396.79	1,229.18	1,375.06	6,336.26
Roraima	164.51	2,560.79	1,072.94	1,878.94	5,677.18
Mato Grosso	761.51	1,130.88	3,769.27	930.16	6,591.82
TOTAL	5,597.21	54,845.32	27,019.14	26,886.69	114,348.36

Source: Guanziroli (1985) and my adjustments.
Note: The grand total is less than the value carried over to table 26, as explained in the text.

Table 16. Percentage Cost of Land Titling Projects

	Cost Items (in %)				
State	*Capital*	*Personnel*	*Operational*	*Topography*	*Total*
Rondônia	2.79	34.20	12.19	50.70	100.0
Acre	4.93	64.79	28.19	2.09	100.0
Pará	6.38	54.79	26.91	11.92	100.0
Amazonas	4.35	59.80	27.25	8.60	100.0
Amapá	5.29	53.61	19.40	21.70	100.0
Roraima	2.89	45.11	18.09	33.10	100.0
Mato Grosso	11.55	17.16	57.18	14.11	100.0
TOTAL	4.89	47.96	23.64	23.51	100.0

Source: Table 15.

Road Building

Roads have been the driving force of Brazilian frontier expansion policy. This is true not only of their presence in national and international headlines, but also of the costs involved. Events involving their construction and paving have attracted heated national and international debate: the Belém-Brasília Highway, the Transamazon Highway, the construction of the Cuiabá–Porto Velho Highway (and the consequent demographic explosion in Rondônia), the Cuiabá-Santarém Highway, the Porto Velho–Manaus–Rio Branco Highway. The interconnections among the main roads, the construction of road access to the Pacific, and the abandonment of the ambitious Perimetral Norte project are increasingly controversial issues.

Ecologists, anthropologists, and the church warned that roads would cause environmental destruction in the Amazon. Economists warned that the benefit of expensive constructions undertaken in areas of low demographic and economic density would not cover costs. For the former group, the occupation would be too fast and extensive; for the latter, it would be too slow and restricted. Yet all agreed that resources, natural for one and economic for the other, would be better used without the roads than with them.

In spite of all this opposition, the state did build the roads. The "opening of the Amazon" to road traffic during the 1970s can be seen in maps 8–11 and table 17.[5] Construction was greatest first in Pará and later in Mato Grosso, precisely the states in which there was the most directed settlement during the 1970s. In Acre and Rondônia, occupation and road building intensified later, in the 1980s. Thus, although the roads did not benefit settlers exclusively, they were consistent with the directed settlement policy of the time.

During the 1970s, the greatest "shortening" of distances between southeastern industrial centers and the frontier occurred during the first half of the decade. Comparing map 8 to map 11, one can see that, from 1970 to 1975, the whole of the Transamazon and of the Cuiabá-Santarém highways were built and the Belém-Brasília was paved. From 1975 to 1980 the density of highways on the frontier itself increased, with the construction of local feeder roads, as can be seen in table 19. It is important to note that, in both periods, road density increased more in Pará than in Mato Grosso. This is an important point, and its consequences will be analyzed in part 4 of this book.

To estimate total cost of road building on the Amazon frontier during the decade, average costs of national road construction and paving during the 1970s were multiplied by mileage increases. Central administration costs in Brasília were not included, as little information on them was

Map 8. Main Roadways of Access to the Amazon in 1960
(Federal and state roads according to the DNER)

Source: *Migrações internas*, vol. 2, appendix 1.

Map 9. Main Roadways of Access to the Amazon in 1970
(Federal and state roads according to the DNER)

Source: *Migrações internas*, vol. 2, appendix 1.

Map 10. Main Roadways of Access to the Amazon in 1975
(Federal and state roads according to the DNER)

Source: *Migrações internas,* vol. 2, appendix 1.

Map 11. Main Roadways of Access to the Amazon in 1980
(Federal and state roads according to the DNER)

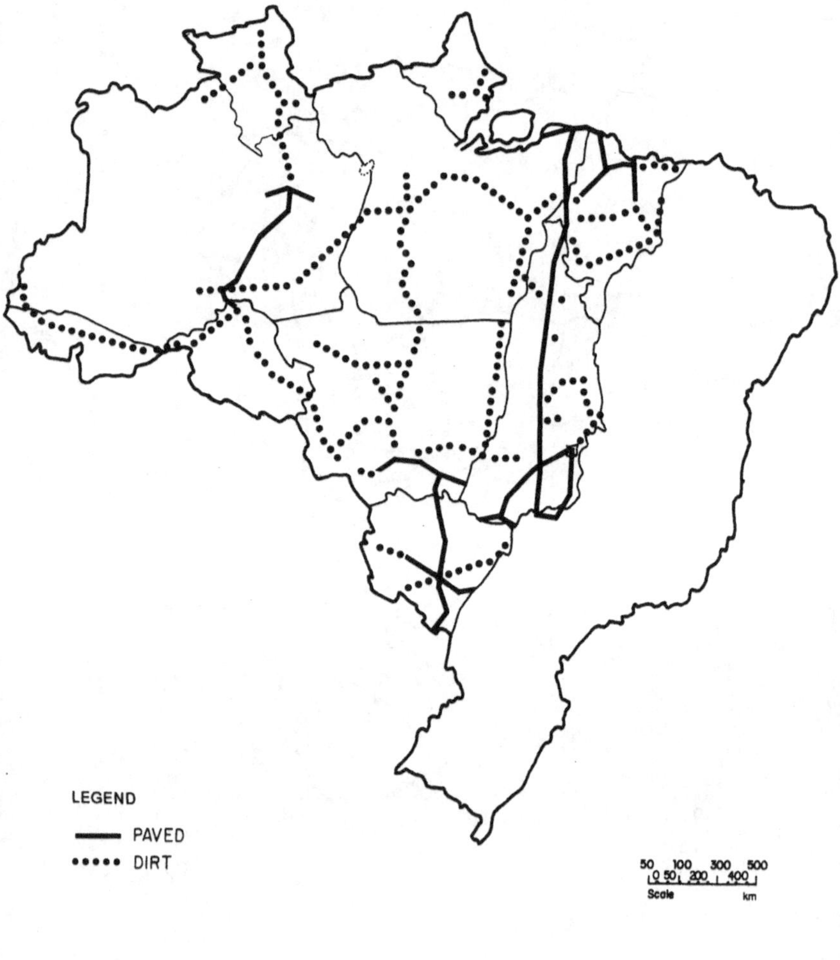

Source: *Migrações internas*, vol. 2, appendix 1.

Table 17. Road Construction on the Amazon Frontier: 1960–1980

	Roads (in kilometers)			
	1960–1970		*1970–1980*	
States	*Unpaved*	*Paved*	*Unpaved*	*Paved*
Rondônia	439.0	—	319.0	86.0
Acre	563.5	—	555.0	198.5
Amazonas	1,121.0	51.5	368.5	1,216.5
Roraima	194.0	—	1,080.5	62.5
Pará	895.0	363.0	9,322.5	1,277.5
Amapá	32.5	—	528.0	94.5
Mato Grosso	1,723.0	86.0	7,300.5	829.0
TOTAL	4,968.0	500.5	19,474.5	3,764.5

Source: Migrações internas, vol. 2, appendix 1.
Note: Totals are not exact due to rounding errors.

Table 18. Cost of Roads on the Amazon Frontier: 1970–1980

	Costs (in U.S. $1,000)		
States	*Construction*	*Paving*	*Total*
Rondônia	47,850	25,800	73,800
Acre	83,250	59,550	142,800
Amazonas	55,275	364,950	450,225
Roraima	162,075	18,750	180,825
Pará	1,398,375	383,250	1,781,625
Amapá	79,200	28,350	107,550
Mato Grosso	1,095,075	248,700	1,343,775
TOTAL	2,921,175	1,129,350	4,050,525

Source: *Migrações internas*, vol. 2, appendix 1, and Guanziroli (1985).
Note: Sums are not exact due to rounding errors.

Table 19. Evolution of Road Density: 1960–1980 (%)[a]

State	*Period*	*Degree of Accessibility[b] Divided by Total Area (in 1,000 ha.)*	*Total Mileage (in km) Divided by Total Area (in 1,000 ha.)*
	1960–1970	4,150.0	100.0
Pará	1970–1975	134.1	150.0
	1975–1980	1,529.6	1,720.0
	1960–1970	49.0	50.0
Mato Grosso	1970–1975	47.3	50.0
	1975–1980	78.3	66.7
TOTAL	1960–1970	40.7	25.0
Frontier	1970–1975	79.5	60.0
Area[c]	1975–1980	239.3	287.5

Source: *Migrações internas*, vol. 2, appendix 1.
[a]([Year 2 – Year 1] / Year 1) x 100.
[b]Mileage weighted by mean velocity that the roads can take, as explained in the source.
[c]Area covered in maps 1–4 and 8–11 pertaining to the Amazon frontier—Rondônia, Acre, Amazonas, Roraima, Pará, Amapá, Mato Grosso—plus the *cerrado* frontier—Maranhão, Mato Grosso do Sul, Goiás, Distrito Federal.

available. Another omitted factor is that road construction in Pará, where most roads were built, is more costly than in other states due to terrain difficulties. For these reasons, net highway expansion costs during the decade are underestimated. Keeping this in mind, the value carried over to table 26 was $4.05 billion.

Spatial Homogenizing Costs

Comparing road-building costs—around $4 billion—with land titling costs—roughly $182 million—one can see that roads cost over twenty times more than titling during the decade! Physical access to the frontier was thus much more expensive to the state than legal access. Given the huge investment in physical access, a part of it could have been spent in better legalizing the property of land on the frontier. Both types of access, physical and legal, are preconditions, at least conceptually if not chronologically, for settlement, the subject of the next chapter.

Notes

1. Otávio Velho (1985) reminds us that the Brazilian frontier is different from the American one in that the region was already integrated into the international economy prior to the arrival of new inhabitants. It involved not the occupation of "empty spaces" but the transformation of one mode of production into another. This difference would even invalidate the use of the word "frontier" were it not for the absence of a better one to express the increasing occupation of land by agricultural producers.

2. All the data, sources, and concepts in this chapter are given in detail in volume 2, appendix 1 of *Migrações internas* and in Guanziroli (1985–1986).

3. See Ozorio de Almeida (1984c) for a detailed description of INCRA's *projetos fundiários*. Map 7 differs from map 5 as it does not include areas close to federal roadways, international frontiers, and so on.

4. The projects in table 15 are: Rondônia: Guarajá-Mirim, Jarú, Ouro Preto, Corumbiara, Alto Madeira; Acre: Alto Juruá, Alto Purus, Uaiquiri; Pará: Paragominas, Cachimbo, Altamira, Conceição do Araguaia, Santarém, Marabá; Amazonas: Manaus, Boca do Acre; Amapá: Amapá; Roraima: Roraima; and Mato Grosso: Vale do Araguaia, Cáceres, Diamantino.

5. The definitions, data descriptions, and concepts on which the tables and maps of this section are based are in *Migrações internas*, vol. 2, appendix 1. The sources used were *CNT* (1974), *DNER* (1962, 1971, 1975, 1980), *Guia Turístico 4 Rodas* (1966, 1975, 1980), Lacorte (1976), and A. Cunha (1978). As in chapter 2, the geographical subdivisions in the maps correspond to IBGE's homogeneous microregions.

8. DIRECTED SETTLEMENT

Until the 1930s, directed settlement in Brazil was mainly the settlement of frontier regions by foreigners. Since then, the frontier's administration has passed through various state and federal organs, discontinuous in their actions and uncoordinated among themselves.[1] From 1970 to 1984, INCRA became responsible for all agrarian reform and settlement activities at the federal level.

This chapter describes public (or "official") and private settlement projects, and calculates their costs during the decade.

Official Settlement and Private Settlement

With the building of the Transamazon Highway in the beginning of the 1970s, INCRA tried to implant a complex type of colonization project, the Integrated Colonization Project (PIC). The PIC had a complex and idealized spatial organization, excessively lengthy bureaucratic procedures, and ambitious objectives. In Pará, this type of project was incapable of absorbing the great migratory influx, giving rise to violent land conflict situations. As a result, the administration of large areas was transferred to the National Security Council's direct authority, as already mentioned. In Rondônia, the migratory flux increased considerably during the 1970s and the beginning of the 1980s. The result was that existing projects became overcrowded and land values increased considerably in the settlement sites themselves.[2]

In an attempt to overcome the difficulties faced by official settlement during the decade, many different models were tried, although on a small scale. INCRA experimented with Directed Settlement Projects (PADs) and Rapid Settlement Projects (PARs), which were the most speedy. It tried coordinating settlement and cooperatives in Joint Settlement Projects (PACs). Other models included the Special Colonization Projects (PECs) and Special Settlement Projects (PEAs).[3] As no settlement scheme was sufficient to contain the overwhelming migratory flow of the time, land titling projects were also intensified. In 1980, their resources were three times greater than those of settlement itself.[4]

During the 1970s, the supposed "failure" of official settlement paved the way for projects by private companies. They were favored by PROTERRA's subsidized credit in the purchase of huge tracts of land. Since firms had the legal obligation to colonize only 20 percent of the land they acquired, these subsidies contributed deliberately to concentrating land property structures on the frontier. Private settlement had its peak in the 1978–1980 period but, with the end of PROTERRA and its subsidized 12 percent per year nominal interest rates, the rhythm of settlement fell drastically.

Each private settlement company developed its own type of project. This gave rise to great diversity among the more than eighty projects implanted in the 1970s. Settlers, on the other hand, were quite homogeneous, coming basically from the South. Whole small farmer communities sold their land in Paraná, or Rio Grande do Sul, and moved to the frontier. They often brought with them the social and economic infrastructure from their place of origin, such as cooperatives and even urban transport companies. Private colonization is also geographically more homogeneous than official, as it is highly concentrated in Mato Grosso. Maps 12, 13, and 14 show the distribution of official and private projects on the Amazon frontier .[5]

Map 15 shows the geographical distribution of those case studies known when this study began. It is striking that virtually no knowledge on private settlements was available at the time. In spite of the almost total absence of evaluation of its results, private settlement was frequently suggested as an alternative to official settlement. One of the initial objectives of this book was to test this very hypothesis. Thus, private and official settlement are given equal importance in allocation of research resources, in spite of the much smaller presence of private settlements on the frontier. Map 15 also shows many studies of "spontaneous settlement" in the eastern Amazon. No such study was made here, since this book's scope is limited to directed settlement.

This chapter has no intention covering the vast bibliography on directed settlement in the 1970s. Its objective is merely to present quantitative information on INCRA's role in the process. As it was the only federal colonization agency at the time, INCRA had regulatory authority over all private settlement projects and an executive role in official ones. Information refers to the twelve official projects and the forty-two private ones for which compatible cost figures were available for the 1970s.

In general, private and public projects had extreme variations within each group. Standard deviations were frequently twice the mean, which in turn differed considerably from the median. Such deviations would normally make averages useless, but this is not the case here. The two groups had an enormous difference in magnitude: public projects were, typically, ten times larger than private ones! One can see in table 20 that this is so in terms of number of settlers, area covered, and resources invested. Such between-group gaps were so much greater than within-group variations that one can safely accept that there was a difference between official and private settlement projects.

The Costs of Directed Colonization

Table 20 shows the dimensions of directed colonization in terms of total resources invested, total number of families settled, and total project area (including area not distributed) for those projects on which information was available.[6] It also estimates cost per settler. One can see that the total spent on official settlement was more than five times the total spent on private settlement. In terms of cost per settler, official settlements cost slightly over half of what private settlements cost. The greatest volumes, absolute and per settled family, were spent in Pará.

The total value in table 20 underestimates the real cost of directed settlement during the decade, due to the large number of excluded projects. To compute the frontier's total cost during this period, the average costs in table 21 were calculated, resulting in an average of $14 million for official projects and of $836 thousand for private ones. Multiplying these average costs by the total twenty-seven official and seventy-five private projects, respectively, yields estimates of $380 million for official and $63 million for private settlement, or $443 million spent on directed settlement during the 1970s.

Nothing ensures that the projects excluded from this calculation had the same dimensions as those included. There were small and large projects in both groups. In the absence of information on excluded projects, they are assigned the same average observed for those included, in spite of the statistical problems, mentioned above, involving large variances.

These values may continue to be an underestimate, as INCRA's central administration costs, 40 percent of its total budget, were left out of the estimate.[7] Again, due to insufficient information, no correction for this omission was made. The estimated total was carried over to chapter

Map 12. Location of INCRA Colonization Projects

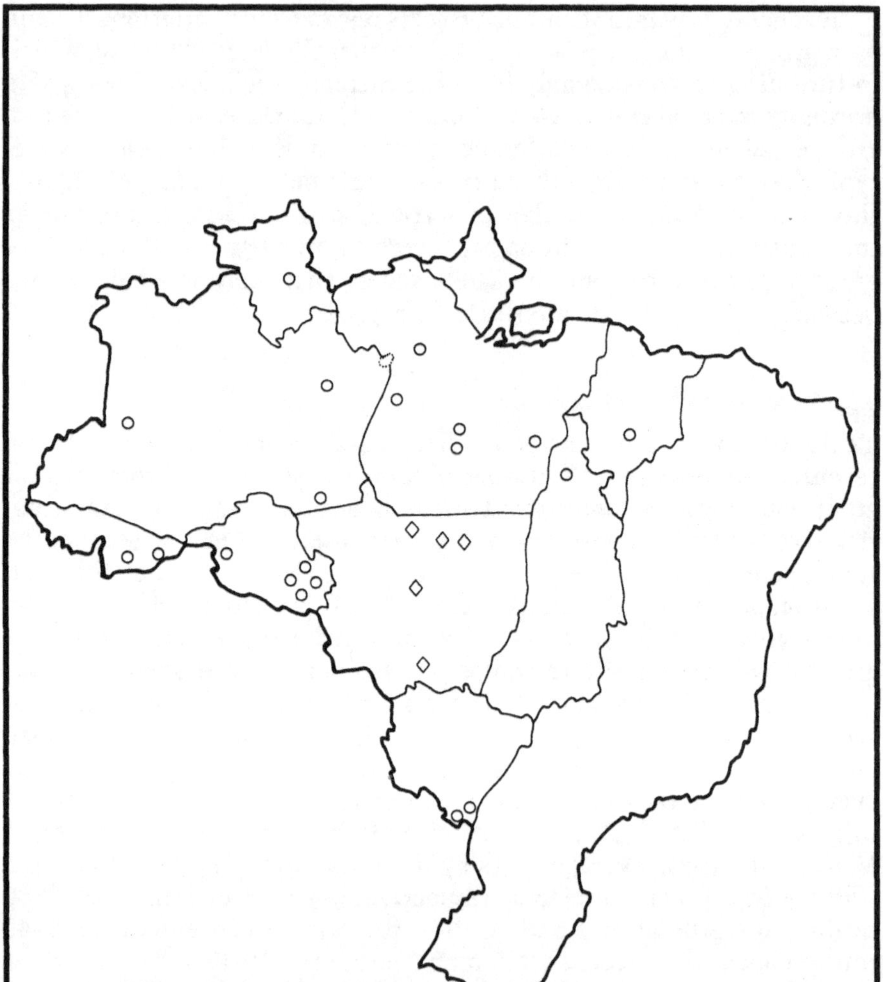

Map 13. Location of Private Colonization Projects

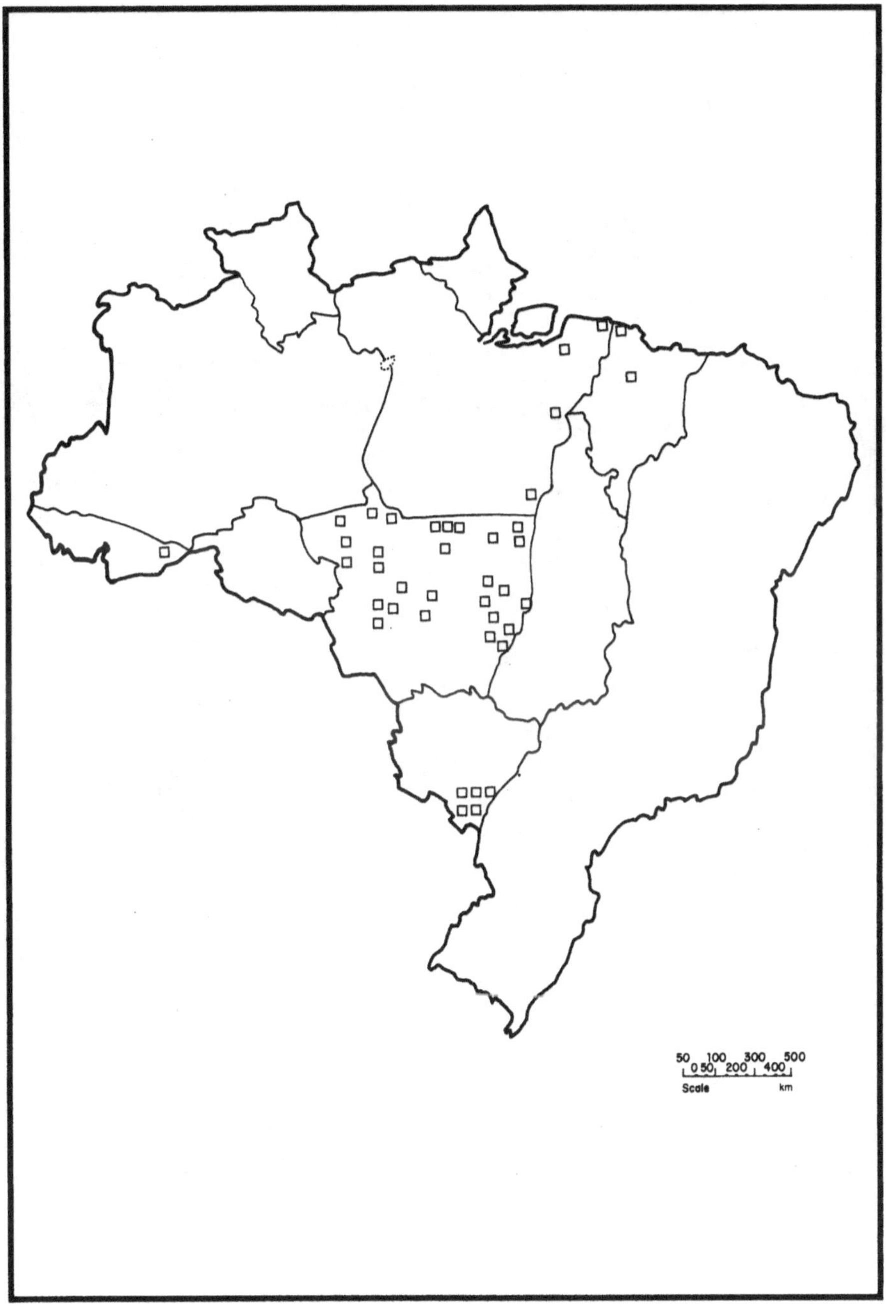

Map 14. Private Colonization in Mato Grosso

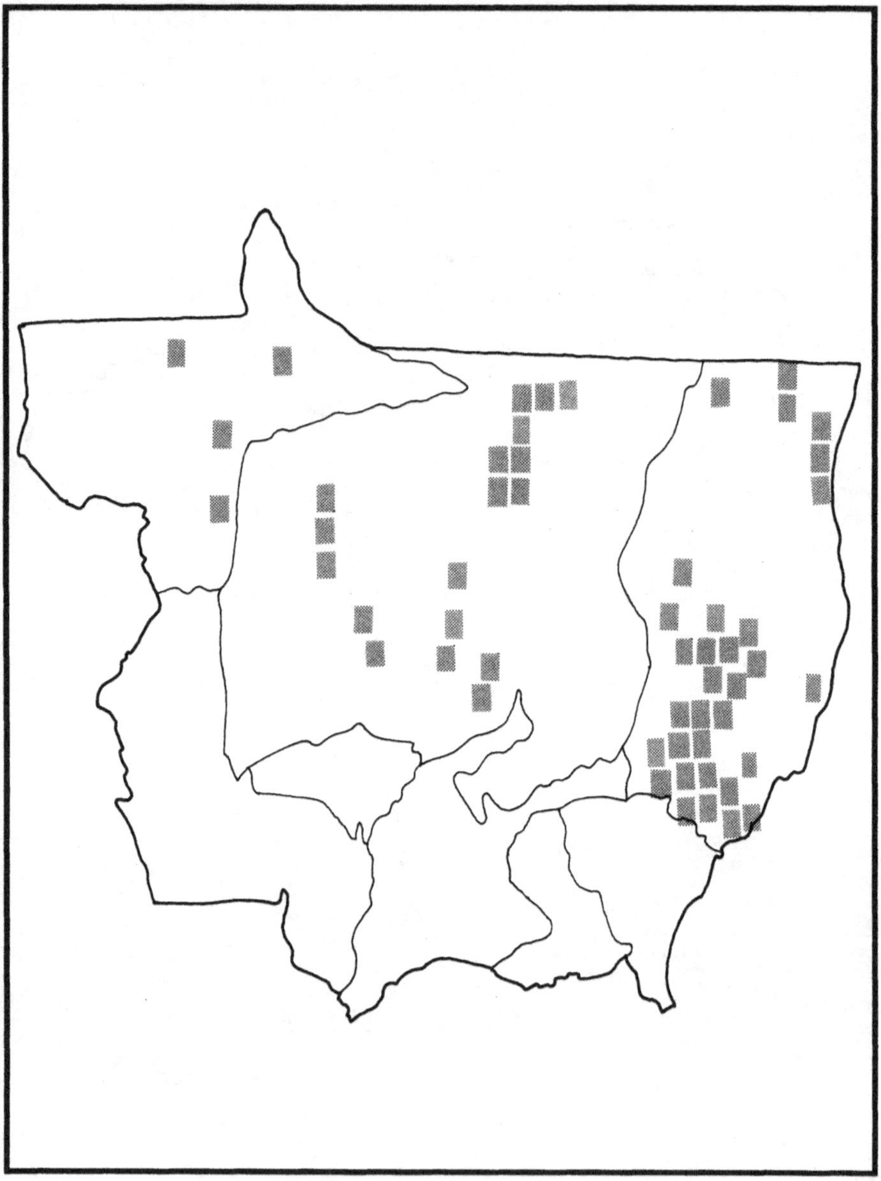

Map 15. Location of Case Studies on Colonization

10, table 26, to contribute to an estimate of the total cost of frontier expansion during the 1970s.

This total cost estimate, $443 million, is 2.32 times larger than the total cost figure from table 20 ($193.9 million). Multiplying the total area in settlement projects by the same factor used above for total cost (2.32), one estimates that 27 million hectares were settled by directed colonization. This represents 6 percent of the 443 million hectare area defined as the "Amazon frontier" in chapter 3. It corresponds, however, to twice the best Amazon land for settlement in table 15: 12 million hectares. The area INCRA devoted to settlement (27 million hectares), however, was less than 10 percent of the area in its land titling projects (over 300 million hectares), as seen in chapter 9.

The number of settlers shown in table 20, less than 70,000, is very small and does not correspond to the total number of families who benefited by the projects, only to those formally registered in them. Applying to this figure the same correction already applied above to total cost and total area (i.e., multiplication by a factor of 2.32) yields a total of 159,000 families. This falls far short of the one million deeds touted at the time. Surely, the majority of the deeds transferred to the public were conferred by land titling projects, not by settlement projects. The number of families settled certainly could never have been greater than the 159,000 estimated here. Field data indicate an average of seven family members per plot,[8] implying a population in directed settlement projects of more than 1.1 million people. This is about the same as the total increase in the whole rural population that occurred on the Amazon frontier during the decade, which was 1.05 million (table 2). The true number of settled families, therefore, is somewhere between 70,000 and 159,000.

According to INCRA data, the average price of land in public settlement was $2/ha., one hundred times lower than the average of $200/ha. charged by private settlement projects. The true price differential may have been even larger, as many settlers in public projects occupied the land as squatters for years[9] before having their deeds legalized by INCRA. When they finally began to pay, it was over a twenty-year period, with highly subsidized interest rates. Private settlers, on the other hand, had to pay for their land in cash, or, in the best of cases, 50 percent down with two years of installments on the remainder at high real rates of interest.[10] Such price differences suggest that official settlement was a "mass" measure and private settlement an "elite" solution to the settlement problem.

There may have been large differences in settlement quality offered in each case. Such quality can be measured indirectly by comparing average resources invested by the projects per settled plot. This comparison does not take into consideration many factors, such as soil quality differences, geographical advantages, or other complementing and homogenizing advantages supplementary to settlement itself. But it does at least yield an estimate of much of the investment made by settling agents.

The average cost per benefited settler during the period was calculated by other authors at $3,870.97 in official settlement, which is considerably higher than the $2,600 finding in the last column of table 20,[11] and $5,182.22 in private settlement, which is exactly the value given in that table.[12] Thus, there was a two-to-one difference in cost per settler between public and private projects.[13] Even though this difference is in the expected direction, it is too small to justify a one-hundred-to-one difference in the price of land. Perhaps the South's richer settlers preferred private settlement, in spite of the higher land cost, because of services unaccounted for in the above calculations. This possibility will be referred to in chapter 10, when all colonization costs are compiled.

Settlements projects executed internal homogenizing and complementing tasks supplementary to settlement itself. They built roads and demarcated plots. They created schools, health clinics, and other services, providing settlers with social infrastructure. When the Transamazon Highway was begun, INCRA built houses, cleared the forest over many plots, provided food and equipment, and still paid migrants a year's wages. INCRA also built urban nuclei of various types: *agrovilas*, *agrópoli*, and *rurópoli*. Private settlement companies frequently provided such services as well, bringing merchants and other services complementary to agriculture into projects, in addition to the settlers themselves.

Although it was not possible to include every kind of cost, tables 21 and 22 do compile all available information on the specific costs of colonization at the time.[14] The first column refers to outlays by projects on some homogenization costs. The next to last column refers to social complementing costs also incurred by projects. In both cases one can see that, contrary to expectation, public, not private, projects were those that internalized the greatest proportion of costs supplementary to settlement itself. In all, 71.3 percent of official projects' costs were for activities other than settlement in the strict sense. The majority, 64.8 percent, was spent on homogenizing activities. Only 6.5 percent of official settlement costs were for complementing activities. Settlement activities were responsible for only 28.7 percent of the official cost, coming under the headings of infrastructure, operational, and personnel costs.

Among private projects, 42 percent of total cost was for settlement in the strict sense. Complementing costs were mostly left to local public administration and were inexpressive. At times, this led to serious problems, particularly concerning the lack of health services. The main cost was land purchasing, despite the credit subsidy embedded in the PROTERRA program, which is not controlled for here. Among the operational costs, one category is called "business profits," on average 4.1 percent of total cost. Note that this item is independent of future income or profits, to be derived from resale of the land. So a return was ensured for participant enterprises. There is also a 5.1 percent advertising cost, generally spent in southern communities.[15] The proportion spent on roads and topography was very small when compared to public projects.

In sum, official colonization internalized ample social costs that benefited settlers as well as the surrounding region. The investments in roads and topography increased the value not only of settler lands but also of those nearby, incorporating them into the national land market. The schools and health posts installed extended the local public administration's reach. In contrast, private projects minimized social complementing and its cost, and concentrated on the entrepreneurial task of administering their capital. This capital consisted primarily of land, the acquisition of which was subsidized by the state.

Homogenizing and complementing costs for private and public projects were carried over to table 26 in chapter 10 using the percentages in table 22. Applying these percentages to the $443 million total cost calculated in this chapter, it is estimated that $283 million was spent on homogenizing and $25 million on complementing activities, leaving only $135 million for settlement in the strict sense. These figures are included in the total settlement cost in chapter 10.

Official and Private Projects: Some Additional Comparisons

During the 1970s, on average, each private settlement project spent less in all than public settlement spent just on schools—the largest item in complementing costs! In the case of official colonization, the bulk of costs include social expenditure as well as physically clearing the region; in the private case, costs were mostly in subsidized land purchase and in project execution itself. If profits and expenditures with advertising are subtracted out, the direct cost of private project execution falls from 41.7 percent to 32 percent of total private cost. This is roughly comparable to official colonization's 28.7 percent for settlement in the strict sense.

Thus, one cannot, based on available cost information, infer that the services offered by private projects were better than official ones. On the contrary, the greater percentage spent on homogenizing and complementing by public projects suggests that their "quality" was perhaps

Table 20. The Total Dimension of Settlement Projects

States	*Total Financial Resources (1) (U.S. $1,000)*	*Total Number of Families (2)*	*Total Area (3) (1,000 ha.)*	*Resources per Family Settled (4)= (1)/(2)*
Public Settlement:				
Pará	84,021	22,675	5,667.7	3,705
Rondônia	67,598	35,595	2,231.2	1,899
Amazonas	1,454	724	184.4	2,008
Roraima	1,055	476	210.0	2,216
Acre	6,388	2,268	542.0	2,817
Mato Grosso	[a]	[a]	1,604.1[b]	[a]
TOTAL	160,516	61,738	10,439.4	2,600
Private Settlement:				
Mato Grosso	33,434	6,452	1,200.0	5,182
GRAND TOTAL	193,950	68,190	11,639.4	2,844

Source: Guanziroli (1985) and author's adjustments.
[a]Information not available.
[b]Not added to total.

Table 21. Settlement Costs—Averages (in U.S. $1,000)

Item	*Homogenizing*	*Execution*			*Comple-menting*	*Grand Total*
		Infra-structure	*Personnel*	*Operational*		
Public settlement in Pará:						
Roads	5,946					
Topography	3,181					
Infrastructure		1,872				
Personnel			734			
Operational				1,435		
Schools					847	
Health					71	
TOTAL	9,127		4,041		918	14,087

Item	Homogenizing	Execution			Comple-menting	Grand Total
		Infra-structure	Personnel	Operational		
Private settlement in Mato Grosso:						
Land acquisition	384					
Roads	71					
Topography	29					
Infrastructure		144				
Administration[a]			69			
Operational[b]				138		
TOTAL	485		351		—	836
GRAND TOTAL	2,563		1,342		918	4,823

Source: Guanziroli (1985) and my adjustments.
[a]Constructions, vehicles, airports, infrastructure.
[b]Project, urbanization, land clearing, titling, promotion, miscellaneous, business profits.

Table 22. Settlement Costs—Percentages (%)

Item	*Homogenizing*	*Execution*			*Comple-menting*	*Grand Total*
		Infra-structure	*Personnel*	*Operational*		
Public settlement in Pará:						
Roads	42.2					
Topography	22.6					
Infrastructure		13.3				
Personnel			5.2			
Operational				10.2		
Schools					6.0	
Health					0.5	
TOTAL	64.8		28.7		6.5	100

Item	Homogenizing	Execution			Comple-menting	Grand Total
		Infra-structure	Personnel	Operational		
Private settlement in Mato Grosso:						
Land acquisition	46.0					
Roads	8.5					
Topography	3.5					
Infrastructure		17.2				
Administration[a]			8.3			
Operational[b]				16.5		
TOTAL	58.0		42.0			100
GRAND TOTAL	53.2		27.8		19.0	100

Source: Table 21.
Note: Percentages do not add up exactly to 100 due to conversion and rounding errors.
[a]Constructions, vehicles, airports, infrastructure.
[b]Project, urbanization, land clearing, titling, promotion, miscellaneous, business profits.

superior. Why, then, were some settlers willing to pay so much more for plots in private projects than they would have paid in public ones?

Perhaps the estimated cost differences are themselves exaggerated. For one, public settlement is much older than private. This may account for a wider variety and greater quantity of expenditure per plot. Another part may also be explained by public administration's well-known tendency to swell in personnel. With the passing of time, this creates a heavy administrative bureaucracy, which adds to the cost per plot in a settlement project. One might speculate that part of the cost incurred would not be for quality improvement, but rather for expenditures resulting from the public sector's typical inefficiency. Finally, there is a resistance to deactivating any public sector activity whatsoever, once installed. This retains in public cost items that could have been privatized sooner, which, in turn, increases cost per plot. An example of this was the difficulty in passing to the private sector the Abraham Lincoln alcohol distillery in the Pacal Colonization Project along the Transamazon Highway in Pará. Even after the project was "emancipated," and the plant had been passed to private hands, settlers continuously appealed to prolong INCRA's intervention.

In spite of such considerations on official settlement's inflated costs, the difference between public and private projects in investment per plot is still small and does not explain why some settlers were willing to pay so much more for private project land instead of acquiring it much more cheaply in public projects. If the reason is not superior quality in private projects, others must be found.

One possibility is that public settlement was overloaded and that there simply was not room for everyone. At the turn of the decade, more than ten thousand settler families were crowded onto irregular plots at the ends of the Transamazon's feeder roads. They were finally settled hurriedly during 1983–1984 with FINSOCIAL resources.[16] On the other hand, INCRA land prices were paid only by "primary" settlers—those directly settled by the institute. Many of those who installed themselves later bought land from previous owners at prices considerably higher than the official figure. Thus, public plots were, in practice, more expensive than low official prices suggest. Finally, more than half of the plots offered on private projects remained unoccupied at the end of the decade.[17] That is, private plots were priced above the market, and many decided against such expensive settlement. A growing return migratory flux from these projects during the 1980s indicates that many of those who did pay such high prices for private project land could not really afford to do so.[18]

Perhaps it is possible to open up a frontier only if land is cheap. This issue, and many of its implications, will be further discussed throughout this book. The next chapter deals with institutions complementary to settlement.

Notes

1. There is extensive literature on directed settlement in Brazil. Tavares (1972) is a classic piece written in the beginning of the period under study. Also Velho (1973), Osório (1978), Sawyer (1979b), M. Moura (1979), and Martins (1975) are important, among those attempting to give an overall perspective. Calvente (1980), Pacheco (1980), NAEA (1981), Henriques (1984, 1985, 1986), CEDEPLAR (1979b), M. Ribeiro (1986), Baumfeld (1985), and Rondônia (1980) concentrate on the western frontier.

2. Dias (1976) and Goodman (1978) comment that many different kinds of projects were tried, with no communication among them, and that many were not even effectively implemented. Martine (1978) and Bunker (1980) comment that official settlements' bureaucracy and paternalism obstructed settlement unnecessarily and made it excessively expensive, making impossible its effective large-scale application. Velho (1972) comments that a less ambitious mass solution should have been tried: one should not have attempted to cater to all of the settlers' needs; official projects should have been limited to providing minimum conditions for settlement, such as land property titles, and should have left more leeway for each project to evolve in its own way. Henriques (1984) and Martine (1980) comment on the poor living conditions, the lack of public assistance, and the many contradictions of Rondônia's agrarian development.

3. See Ozorio de Almeida (1984c) on all the different types of INCRA settlement projects.

4. David in *Migrações internas* (1981–1984, vol. 5, chap. 3, p. 18) estimates this differential based on INCRA's budget for 1980. The costs accumulated during the decade, however, suggest a lower relative share of land titling in total INCRA expenditures, with intensification mostly at the end of the period.

5. All information and sources on which these maps are based are in *Migrações internas* (vol. 3 and appendix), and in Guanziroli (1985–1986).

6. The following projects were studied:

In official settlement, 25 projects: Pará: Monte Alegre, Altamira, Itaituba, Marabá, Pacal; Rondônia: Sidney Girão, Gy-Paraná, Cacoal, Paulo Ribeiro, Adolpho Rohl, Mal. Dutra, Ouro Preto, Burareiro; Amazonas: Bela Vista, Tabatinga, Antonieta, Ataíde; Roraima: Anauá; Acre: Pedro Peixoto, Boa Esperança; Mato Grosso: Peixoto de Azevedo, Carlinda, Ranchão, Prata, Braço Sul.

In private settlement, 42 projects: Mato Grosso: Santa Cruz, Boa Esperança, Juína, Pacoval, Tapiraguaia I, Maika I, Itaaguara, Noidori, Mutum, Tauguru, Agua Boa, Garapu, Canarana, Xavantina, Serra Dourada, Vilas Rurais, Aracaty, Alto Turi, Pioneiro, Santa Felicidade, Colniza, Vale do Verde, Areões, Tabaju, Curua, Beleza, São Manuel, Cidade Gaúcho do Norte, Vale do Rio Sangue, Serra Azul, São Marcos, Guirai, Bariri, Tapurah I, Promissão, Santana, Campo Alegre, Alta Floresta, Paranaita, Núcleo Rural, Vitória, Gleba Azul.

Projects excluded due to difficulties in comparing cost figures are listed in note 14 below.

7. David in *Migrações internas* (vol. 5, chap. 2, p. 18).

8. See table 35, below.

9. B. Ferreira (1984, pp. 124–130) shows that, for a large percentage of settlers in Pará's official projects, squatting was a necessary preliminary stage to legitimate settlement later by INCRA.

10. David in *Migrações internas* (vol. 5, chap. 2, p. 4).

11. David, Subproject 2 of *Migrações internas*, vol. 5, data cited in Guanziroli (1985–1986).

12. Guanziroli (1985–1986), report no. 5, p. 8.

13. Chapter 17 will use the weighted average estimate of U.S. $4,000 average cost per family.

14. Table 21 refers to the same projects as table 20, listed in note 6 above, except for thirteen public ones: Itaituba, Pacal, Guamá, Bela Vista, Tabatinga, Antonieta, Ataíde, Anauá, Peixoto de Azevedo, Carlinda, Ranchão, Prata, and Braço Sul.

15. B. Ferreira (1984) shows that many of those in private settlement projects were informed of their existence by settlement companies' advertising and recruiting agents operating in the South.

16. David in *Migrações internas* (vol. 5, chap. 2, pp. 33–34).

17. Guanziroli (1985–1986), report no. 5.

18. J. Santos (1985b).

9. COMPLEMENTING INSTITUTIONS

In addition to settlement itself, colonizing a certain area includes providing the social infrastructure needed by the population for its day-to-day living. Access to public services, even if occasionally provided by private firms, should be an important factor in the economic results settlers will obtain.

One of the most criticized aspects of colonization as opposed to agrarian reform is precisely the high cost of this complementary infrastructure on the frontier. Whenever settlement takes place in long-occupied areas, farmers may benefit from preexisting institutions, thereby reducing the social cost of land access. Yet, when lands recently occupied are settled, these institutions must also be transported to the frontier, increasing the social cost of land access. The lack of complementing institutions on the Amazon frontier may have seriously hampered farmers and jeopardized the whole colonization program of the 1970s.

This impact must also be true of homogenizing costs in new areas. Without roads, there is not even a frontier. In Brazil today, getting to new areas is impossible without overland transport. The argument of institutional insufficiency, however, is most frequently invoked to explain the problems of already settled colonists. It holds with respect to marketing problems, as discussed in part 3, and with respect to farmers' access to various institutions such as technical assistance, health, education, religion, social integration, and others.

As the 1970s proceeded, governmental priorities shifted toward the "productive agricultural frontier" of the Center-West, which became more and more integrated into southern agro-industrial expansion. The "social frontier" of the Amazon, involving settlement projects, was progressively abandoned, and complementing resources essential to settlement were drastically reduced. Those involving technical assistance, in particular, were sorely insufficient. Without them, settlers' technological inadequacy to deal with the Amazon environment became ever more patent.[1] Much of the resulting environmental destruction could have been avoided if the role of complementing institutions had been understood from the outset as essential to colonization.

The objective of this chapter is to present field research findings with respect to institutions in various settlement locations. To this end, interviews were held in sixty-eight institutions although coverage was unequal among locations. The lack of literature on the role of social infrastructure on the frontier hampered both data gathering and analysis. What is offered here is merely a descriptive consolidation of gathered information, aimed at contributing to a more general discussion on the subject.[2] In long-established areas, outlays for complementing institutions are regularly incurred and should not be considered as part of settlement costs. On a frontier, however, social institutions come as a direct result of settlement. For this reason, this chapter considers them as part of the total cost of colonization.

Costs of Complementing Institutions

This survey's main conceptual difficulty comes from the poorly specified relation between institutions and farmers. With no design to remedy this problem, tables 23 and 24 show the total and percentage annual costs of each activity studied, by budget item and by type of institution. Among the "public service" institutions, there are institutions related to health (SESP Hospital and SUCAM's offices), technical assistance (EMATER, CEPLAC, CENAR), schools, banks (Banco do Brasil and BASA), and unions. Private sector institutions include notary registries, private health posts, and private hospitals. The only "joint" institutions identified are cooperatives. There is no information on religious or other institutions. These figures are thus an underestimate of what was effectively spent on frontier settlement complementing institutions during the 1970s.

In table 24 one can see that, in relative terms, operational costs were highest for cooperatives, fixed costs for private firms, and personnel costs for public institutions. Although this structure is consistent with their respective functions, it also suggests that in public institutions there was some typical swelling of personnel. Technical assistance (EMATER and SENAR) was very cheap, taking up only 2.8 percent of total cost, while health services (SESP Hospital, SUCAM, Health Posts,

Private Hospital) were very expensive—71 percent of total cost. Public services accounted for 64 percent of total cost, private ones for 27 percent, and joint services (cooperatives), for 9.3 percent.

In spite of its high cost, public service presence on the frontier was seriously deficient. According to INCRA criteria, it was very far from "reasonable," as can be seen in chart 1. In addition to the three types of public institutions shown in chart 1, many others were seriously deficient on the frontier. Rural extension (EMATER and SENAR) and unions, for different reasons, reached only a fraction of farmers. Banks and local governments reached an even smaller fraction of those in need. Much of the local credit was therefore offered by frontier merchants, as will be seen in part 3. As for police authority, it was insufficient in every way. Violence, disrespect for the law, and impunity were and still are everyday facts of life in the Amazon. The Transamazon Highway, where a large part of public settlement was located, runs parallel and far to the south of the Amazon River. Yet county seats were established in the heyday of river transport during the rubber boom at the turn of the century. They are therefore located along the Amazon River's margins, sometimes even on the north side. As a result, there was no contact at all between county level government and settlers. In Mato Grosso, private settlement projects were set up in tracts far from county seats and were subject to little or no control, particularly in their initial phases.

These considerations lead to the conclusion that public outlays for complementing institutions on the frontier were a fraction of what they should have been. Using health and education as a basis for calculating the deficiency in complementing institutions, multiplication by six would appear to be an initial estimate for the "ideal" cost of colonization. The lack of any such adjustment here is a further cause of downward bias in the estimate of social complementing costs.

One of the problems in consolidating the data to be presented here was that the costs (homogenization and settlement) analyzed in previous chapters referred to the whole Amazon frontier area during all of the 1970s. The data in tables 23 and 24, however, refer to annual operational and personnel costs in a "standard" frontier location during 1980–1981. In order to compare these with the other two types of costs, they had to be multiplied by the average age of the institutions analyzed, truncated at ten years, to cover only the 1970s. Since each institution probably grew over time, end of decade values surely overestimate the decade-long average. This adjustment, therefore, is probably an overestimate that may compensate for the general downward bias in other approximations. The result is table 25—an approximate estimate of accumulated average cost for each type of institution during the whole decade. This procedure was not applied to fixed costs, which are already adjusted for

Table 23. Complementing Costs: Annual Averages per Institution and Budget Item

Institution	*Cost Item (U.S. $1,000)* *Fixed*	*Personnel*	*Operational*	*Total*
Public				
EMATER	72	116	12	200
CEPLAC	223	190	12	425
SENAR	99	5	9	113
SUCAM	85	140	27	252
Hospital (SESP)	2,618	373	1,123	4,114
School	219	45	18	282
County seat	142	179	103	424
Bank	151	171	43	365
Union	23	3	*	26
TOTAL	3,632	1,222	1,347	6,201
Private				
Notary registry	32	21	7	60
Health post	421	15	75	511
Private hospital	1,599	85	299	1,983
TOTAL	2,052	121	381	2,554
Joint				
TOTAL	464	141	290	895
GRAND TOTAL	6,148	1,484	2,018	9,650

Source: Guanziroli (1985–1986) and my adjustments.
*Not available

inflation, as the updated 1981 value of physical infrastructure, accumulated during the 1970s: constructions, equipment, vehicles, furniture, and other permanent materials.

Observe that, on average, each set of "standard" complementing institutions is almost twice as expensive ($27.8 million, table 25) as an "average" public settlement project ($14 million, table 21) and more than thirty times an "average" private settlement project ($836,000, table 21). The estimates in table 25 were in turn multiplied by the same number of projects studied in the previous chapter: 27 public + 75 private

Table 24. Complementing Costs: Annual Percentages per Institution and Budget Item (%)

Institution	Fixed	Cost Item Personnel	Operational	Total
Public				
EMATER	36	58	6	100
CEPLAC	52	45	3	100
SENAR	88	4	8	100
SUCAM	33	56	11	100
Hospital (SESP)	64	8	28	100
School	78	16	6	100
County seat	33	42	25	100
Bank	41	47	12	100
Union	86	11	*	100
TOTAL	59	20	21	100
Private				
Notary registry	53	35	12	100
Health post	82	3	15	100
Private hospital	81	4	15	100
TOTAL	80	9	11	100
Joint				
TOTAL	52	16	32	100
GRAND TOTAL	63	15	21	100

Source: Table 23.
*Not available.

= 102 projects in all. This means that each project included in the previous chapter's calculations would have every one of the institutions listed in table 23.

On the one hand, this adjustment may be considered an exaggeration. Many of the projects had neither county seat, nor hospital, nor a great part of the services listed here. In some cases, however, projects that did not have all these services used those of neighboring towns. This happened with the Monte Alegre project, in relation to the city with the same name, and with the Pacal and Anapú projects, in relation to

Chart 1. Average Complementation Ratios on the Frontier

	User Ratios	
Institution	*Existing*	*"Reasonable"*
Schools	1/500	1/80
Health posts	1/600	1/1,000
Hospitals	—	1/2,000

Source: INCRA; Field research.

Altamira. Therefore, the institutional cost of the Amazon frontier's expansion was paid somewhere, even though the institutions concerned may have been in neighboring towns and not in the projects themselves. On the other hand, the estimated value can be considered too low. For example, it implies one school per project when, in general, there were more. Many projects were also omitted from this calculation, the result probably underestimating total outlays effectively incurred in social complementing of colonization during the 1970s, even at its ridiculously low levels. The total estimated figure, $2.84 billion until 1981, was carried over to table 26 in the next chapter. Thus, a "standard" set of complementing institutions would cost more than twenty times an "average" settlement project.

The High Cost of a Social Transplant

The total estimated cost of complementing institutions during the 1970s, $2.84 billion, is more than six times the estimated total cost of settlement projects. Transplanting society to the frontier was expensive, even at its well-known levels of deprivation. The greatest cost of directed colonization was not the settlers, but everything else they needed to operate on the frontier.

Technical assistance, the most important item in terms of environmental preservation, was the most neglected item of complementing institutions. This was the origin of colonization's notorious ecological incompetence and of the devastation it caused and continues to cause.[3]

This part of the calculation of the cost of colonization is the least rigorous of the three undertaken in this part of the book. Unlike the earlier calculations regarding homogenization and directed settlement, the complementing costs referred to here are "standard" rather than actually incurred outlays. In any long established area, these costs must be paid regardless of settlement; so maybe they should not have been added to the other two outlay types. But, in dealing with a frontier, these

Table 25. Complementing Costs: Accumulated Averages per Institution and Budget Item

	Cost Item (U.S. $1,000)			
Institution	*Fixed*	*Personnel*	*Operational*	*Total*
Public				
EMATER	72	779	83	934
CEPLAC	223	626	40	889
SENAR	99	5	9	113
SUCAM	85	601	117	803
Hospital (SESP)	2,618	3,731	11,228	17,577
School	219	174	71	464
County seat	142	717	414	1,273
Bank	151	768	195	1,114
Union	23	25	*	48
TOTAL	3,632	7,426	12,157	23,215
Private				
Notary registry	32	97	34	163
Health post	421	15	75	510
Private hospital	1,599	170	599	2,368
TOTAL	2,052	282	708	3,041
Joint				
TOTAL	464	352	724	1,541
GRAND TOTAL	6,148	8,060	13,589	27,797

Source: Table 23 and adjustments explained in the text.
*Not available.

costs do respond to settlement and must be taken into account. Since there is no better criterion, and total omission would have been unacceptable, the calculations made here will remain as they are. The objective is only to establish an approximate order of magnitude concerning costs of complementing institutions in Amazon settlement during the 1970s. In spite of obvious lack of precision, they at least contribute to constructing an approximate global estimate of the cost of Amazon colonization during the decade. This consolidation will be made in chapter 10.

Notes

1. See chapters 4 and 5 above, on the technological inadequacy of small farmer settlements in the Amazon

2. According to Guanziroli (1985–1986) sixty-eight "institutional interviews" were used from among the almost one hundred actually made in field research. They were complemented by data gathered at each institution's central administration. As in the preceding cases, however, only local costs, not those incurred by respective central administrations, were computed.

3. See note 1.

10. THE COST OF DIRECTED COLONIZATION

This chapter gathers together the findings made in the three previous ones on the costs of homogenization, settlement, and complementing institutions in Amazon colonization.[1] The data and sources used previously, subject to all the limitations already mentioned, yield a global estimate for the cost of Amazon directed colonization during the 1970s. This cost and some of its policy implications are discussed here.

Tables 26 and 27 show that, as measured, colonization of the Amazon frontier cost about $7.5 billion during the 1970s. More than half of this sum was spent on roads and more than one-third on complementing institutions, leaving only 6 percent of the total for settlement projects. Due to internalization of homogenizing and complementing functions by settlement projects, settlement in the strict sense cost only $53 million, or 1.8 percent of the decade's total cost of colonization.

According to these calculations, settlement projects studied in detail by many authors cost but a sixth of what complementing institutions did. The presence of these other institutions receives little attention in the literature on the Amazon, although they carried out very expensive tasks. The efforts by settlement projects to internalize these functions were almost in vain, as all their effort contributed to barely 1 percent of the total value of complementing services from 1970 to 1980.

Dividing total cost (table 26: $7.5 billion) by the increase in rural population during the decade on the Amazon frontier (table 2: 1,047,912 people) yields a per capita cost of $7,168. This value is an overestimate, as it assigns the total cost to only the rural population. Yet roads and institutions served the urban population as much as the rural. Adding to the rural population increase an even greater urban population increase

Table 26. Total Cost of Directed Colonization (in U.S. $1,000,000)

Activities	*Homogenization*	*Settlement*	*Complementation*	*Total*
Road building	4,050	—	—	4,050
Land titling projects	182	—	—	182
Settlement projects	283	135	25	443
Other institutions	—	—	2,836	2,836
TOTAL	4,515	135	2,861	7,511

Source: Tables 15, 18, 21, and 25 plus adjustments explained in the text

Table 27. Total Cost of Directed Colonization: Percentages (%)

Activities	*Homogenization*	*Settlement*	*Complementation*	*Total*
Road building	26	—	—	54
Land titling projects	30	—	—	2
Settlement projects	45	100	1	6
Other institutions	—	—	99	38
TOTAL	100	100	100	100

Source: Table 26.

(table 7: 1,886,774 people), one obtains a total population increase of 2,934,686 people. Using this figure yields a per capita cost of $2,559. This, on the other hand, is an underestimate, as it does not assign to the urban population its own specific additional costs, such as urban infrastructure and administration. Nor does it take into consideration the greater intensity of services in urban areas. Thus, per capita cost of directed colonization during the 1970s was somewhere between $2,500 and $7,200, with a weighted mean of $5,578.

These figures are "per person" and include men and women, children and the aged, whose rates of labor force participation are very different. They cannot yet be considered to be the cost of job creation in Amazon colonization nor can they be compared to that in the rest of the economy. This calculation will be done in chapter 17, based on field research. The remainder of this chapter qualifies the figures presented here, criticizes the criteria employed, and draws some policy implications from them.

Direct Outlays versus Social Costs

Several omissions render the figure in table 26 an underestimate of the cost of Amazon colonization. Regional costs not specifically related to directed colonization were omitted, as were those incurred by local agencies (e.g., SUCAM). Tax incentives to immense unproductive ranching projects, many of which were purely speculative, involved a considerable social cost. These were also left out. The migrant flow into the Amazon was also much greater than that which benefited from directed colonization. The incapacity of settlement projects to absorb this pressure added to the growing mass of "spontaneous" settlers. From a social point of view, this was surely one of colonization's highest costs.

On the other hand, there are some senses in which this simple direct cost calculation is an overestimate of the cost of Amazon colonization. In the first place, the costs that were avoided in the rest of the country because of Amazon colonization should be discounted from the total cost estimate. Populations who migrated out of the South did not demand at home the social and physical infrastructure that they would otherwise have required in their regions of origin. Second, roads served geopolitical and national security objectives, in addition to bringing goods and migrants to and from the frontier; their cost should not be assigned exclusively to colonization as was done here. Furthermore, the southern exodus to the western frontier favored modernization, increasing productivity, agro-industrialization, and internationalization of southern agriculture. The additional income generated thereby should be compared to the alternative income that would have been generated in settlers' home regions had frontier occupation not advanced. All of these social benefits should be partially deducted from the Amazon frontier's total cost estimated above.

Other more indirect benefits should also be discounted from the total national social cost of the advancing frontier. Agricultural, commercial, and industrial income increased in the rest of the nation, partly because of the advancing Amazon frontier. The market for agricultural inputs benefited from frontier expansion. Agro-industrial income also increased partly due to the advancing frontier.

Finally, one must remember that the cost of Amazon colonization is being paid for not only by Brazilian society but also, in broader terms, by all those who consider the Amazon a global heritage. Independent of whether the Brazilian government and society recognize such claims, a growing number of groups, organizations, and governments consider themselves injured by the destruction of the Amazonian environment. For them, the frontier's cost includes the irreversible loss of unique ecological reserves. As consciousness of the earth's finitude grows steadily in developed countries, ecological preservation is gaining priority all over the world, and the environmental cost of Amazon colonization adds to the cost measured up to now.

Such views about the Amazon were already present at the beginning of the 1970s. Their impact then, however, was to provoke a xenophobic reaction by the Brazilian state, which accelerated the occupation process. During the 1980s, the international press greatly increased its coverage of Amazonian deforestation and violence. In this sense, the cost of Amazon colonization to the "world at large" is sure to grow over the next years, though this international component is impossible to quantify.

The Cost of What Was Done and of What Was Not

Directed colonization should have been seen as an integrated task of urban and rural planning from the outset. Complementing services, provided by many different types of (generally) urban institutions, were administered in a particularly independent and uncoordinated fashion. A country that spent so much on the Amazon frontier should have given better treatment to the migrants it attracted there. The state opened the way and the population followed it, but then found no support. With the resources available, abandonment, isolation, disease, and poverty could have been much reduced. Though there were some "successes" in the colonization effort, as will be seen in the chapters ahead, their social cost could have been much lower.

INCRA's "integrated settlement" model did foresee and plan for the physical and social infrastructure necessary for colonization. But resource allocation and coordination with other institutions that should have been involved in the joint effort were lacking. It is true that INCRA attempted to cover the central planning failure with its own resources by internalizing functions of homogenization and complementing institutions, but in doing so it spread itself out too thinly and hampered its own settlement mission.

A frontier is a spatial expansion of the whole of society. It is, essentially, everybody's business. It can neither be undertaken in an authoritarian and militaristic way, by a few executive ministries, nor decided in a centralized manner in a few government offices. Though colonization was a redistributive social policy, it was created in an authoritarian regime, undertaken with no political legitimacy, and drew no support from public opinion. Thus, it did not resist the pressures of concentrated economic power. During the mid-1970s, when roads were already rapidly increasing the market value of Amazon lands, interest groups perceived the advantages of large-scale speculative land appropriation. They pressed their interests forward and aggravated the frontier's "enclosure from within and without," undermining the colonization program.

In the early 1970s, the Brazilian state avoided the political cost of redistributing already appropriated lands in the rest of the country. The option of frontier expansion, however, had high costs of its own. The decade of the 1970s was the peak of the colonization effort. It followed upon the implanting of a military dictatorship during the 1960s, and took place at a time when political expression was abruptly curtailed. With the "New Republic" of the 1980s, political debate reopened. Given the experience that accumulated during the 1970s, the costs of not having undertaken agrarian reform in Brazil can now be evaluated.

During those ten years, and ever since, many things changed in the nation. Huge populations followed, or even anticipated, the roads built by the state in an unprecedented northwesterly migratory flux. New social and physical infrastructure sharply increased land values on the frontier. Industrial and financial groups that previously had not been involved with land were attracted. A vast territory was added to the sphere of influence of the southern economy. Resources mobilized by the state were small compared to those demanded of Amazon occupation and were insufficient to control the transformation process that was started. Not only were governmental resources insufficient for the Amazon frontier, but they suffered increasing competition from the Center-West's agro-industrial frontier, which gained importance throughout the decade.

Since the 1970s, landownership has spread over a much larger area than ever before. This considerably raises the cost of agrarian reform for the 1990s. Land titling, auctioning of huge tracts, registration, and the whole institutional apparatus created in the name of frontier colonization generated faits accomplis on a large scale. The public sector transformed what were formerly loose rights of access to land into what is now legal ownership. This change can no longer be reversed. Meanwhile, agricultural production became increasingly "industrialized" all over the country, even on the frontier. Official credit for manufactured agricultural inputs increased, land property concentrated, and the work force was expelled from the countryside and turned into wage labor. Many of the "landless" workers, who today unionize and struggle for better working conditions in the field, were never independent small farmers.

The cost of Amazon colonization, therefore, is the cost of what was done and of what was not done as the decade of the 1970s passed. The country is no longer the same; its political alternatives have changed. Thus, the issue of how to implement a social land redistribution policy in Brazil is drastically different today from what it was in the 1960s.

In discussing the feasibility of agrarian reform in Brazil today, one should remember that the issue is reappearing after years of imposed silence during which reality did not remain static. Southern capitalism penetrates today into the Amazon much deeper than it ever did in the past. It brings in industrialized products, on which agriculture has come to depend more than ever before. Expensive roads appreciated the value of lands that today can no longer be disappropriated, whether because resources are lacking or political will. The high cost of Amazon colonization was paid, and it raised the cost of policy alternatives. As the geographical base of landownership was greatly expanded, the future financial and political costs of agrarian reform also increased. This topic will be taken up again in chapter 22.

The institutional incorporation of a vast new geographical area rearranged not only social relations but also economic relations. Roads attracted city dwellers and markets as well as settlers. The following chapters deal with the process of incorporation of new territories into the market economy.

Note

1. No sources are cited here, as all data and literature used in this chapter come from the previous three chapters

Market expansion: trucks transporting rice in Mutum, Mato Grosso

Birosca: small rural store in São Miguel (near Mutum) in Mato Grosso

PART 3: THE FRONTIER AND THE MARKET

This part of the book establishes the analytical groundwork for interpreting colonization data to be examined in part 4. The analysis presupposes that an evaluation of colonization must not be limited to settlers' economic performance but must also take into account the whole income appropriation system that is created on a frontier together with settlement projects. The greater the responsiveness of settlers to their economic environment, the greater the possibility for influencing their behavior through economic policies. The greater, then, would be the probability of successful colonization in the future. Correcting past failures can pave the way to future successes. The policy implications of this analysis are therefore very important to the construction of a new posture on Amazon colonization.

The following chapters interpret settlement during the 1970s as the incorporation of new geographical spaces into the national market. Chapter 11 shows the expansion of southern capitalism toward the Amazon and its competition with previous regional activity. Chapter 12 examines two great fronts of capital penetration into the Amazon, the western and eastern frontiers. Chapter 12 also postulates two distinct phases of a frontier: a settlement phase, in which usury-mercantile capital predominates, and a consolidation phase, in which productive capital predominates. Chapter 13 analyzes the market systems that appropriate settlers' agricultural income and transmit it to the rest of the economy. Chapter 14 presents a model of settlers' reaction to relative prices in frontier markets. Chapter 15 furnishes empirical evidence that frontier merchants transmit the appropriated income from the Amazon frontier to southern industrial capitalism.

The theoretical issues and the literature cited cover the entire ideological spectrum of economic analysis: from Marxist views of the phases of the subordination of labor to capital, through standard neoclassical microeconomic modeling. The terminology employed is equally eclectic. "Market economy" and "capitalist economy" are used interchangeably, as are "informal credit," "usury-mercantile capital," and other expressions. The intention is neither theoretical purity nor ideological rigidity, but the use of all possible analytical resources in the interpretation of a phenomenon as complex as that of Amazon colonization. In this sense, the analysis is conducted by a "neoclassical mind" and a "classical heart."

Colonist's accumulation: tractors and equipment in Monte Alegre, Pará

11. THE EXPANSION OF THE MARKET

The first two parts of this book described how population advanced and state presence increased in the Amazon during the 1970s. This part will analyze how colonization contributed to the economic incorporation of frontier territory during that period.[1] In the present chapter, maps are used to illustrate a general process of market penetration into the Amazon, whereby central-southern capitalism expanded its influence throughout the region.

The economic incorporation of Amazon territory entailed interlinked changes closely tied to the overall transformation of relations between agriculture and the rest of the Brazilian economy.[2] This process, generally called "capital penetration into agriculture," began well before, in the 1960s, and intensified during the 1970s. Its importance grew considerably during the 1980s.[3] It brought about changes in the organization of economic activity, work relations, agricultural technology, productivity, product composition, and land tenure all over the country. In the South-Southeast, where agriculture had been long established, all of these modifications had a common consequence: they expelled the rural work force from the land. Small holdings consolidated into larger ones and land values increased.[4] Another consequence, less well known, was a strong impulse toward the advancing Amazon frontier of the 1970s.

A frontier's economic significance is not limited to what it contributes currently to national product *while it is still a frontier*. A frontier matters according to what it will produce when it ceases to be so, and in how it will then be linked to the general market economy. A frontier's agricultural product increases slowly over time: planted area expands, permanent crops come to fruition, productivity rises, and technology intensifies. Thus, in the beginning, frontier supply is necessarily a small percentage of total national supply.

According to the economic and demographic censuses of 1980, the "Amazon frontier" still contributed very little to agricultural supply and employment—6.1 percent of employment and 3.3 percent of total agricultural product—after a whole decade of colonization. Such a supply-lag occurred during the 1970s with respect to the "*cerrado* frontier."[5] Yet, by 1980, this area was already accounting for 13 percent of employment and 11 percent of agricultural production. Recent data show an even more accelerated growth of the "*cerrado* frontier," particularly in the Center-West.[6]

The economic incorporation of the Amazon frontier is therefore taking time. As it advances, it determines the agrarian structure of a vast territory and the income distribution of a large number of people. As was seen in chapter 2, ten million people were living in the Amazon at the end of the 1970s; a still undetermined number arrived during the 1980s. The social opportunities they found depend a great deal upon how agricultural production entered new spaces and became linked to southern-southeastern capitalism.[7]

Thus, the economy of the Amazon frontier is not evolving alone. It depends on the spatial expansion of industry. At the time, industry was spreading out spatially: not in the sphere of production, which was ever more concentrated, but in that of circulation. During the 1970s, southern manufactured products began to reach the most remote corners of the national territory. They intensified the industrial component in farmers' final and intermediary consumption all over the country. In exchange, farmers increased marketed supply and became less subsistence oriented, even in the Amazon.[8] The mediators of these two product flows—agricultural and industrial—between the frontier and the rest of the economy were "merchants." These agents formed chains of intermediation that linked all areas of the Amazon into well-structured zones of influence, dominated by centers outside the region.[9]

The expansion of the market made the frontier economically viable and created the conditions by which new agricultural fronts could be incorporated into the general economy. This chapter discusses this process in the Amazon during the 1970s.

The Expanding Influence of Center-South Capitalism

Migrants into the Amazon come mostly from areas of the country where the consumption of manufactured goods is widespread. No matter how poor, a farmer must at least buy cloth, kerosene, soap, watches, oil, and a host of basic consumption items and social services (e.g., health) that the family does not produce for itself. Even if a small farmer can forgo a market for his product, he cannot do without a market for his inputs or for his consumption. Therefore, a farmer's decision to establish himself in a certain place depends on there being someone to bring him the manufactured goods he needs. As his income increases, probably so do the industrial components of consumption and production. Payment for these necessities comes mainly from the sale of agricultural products; partial or total outhiring by family members, or other remunerative activities, may also help "foot the bill." The consequent flow of marketed products requires that there be buyers and sellers for farmers. These are the merchants, whose role is to link agriculture to industry and the final market.

The *bodequeiros* and *biroscas* spread throughout rural areas in Brazil gather small quantities of agricultural products and sell small quantities of industrial goods to local farmers. They pass agricultural products on from smaller to larger intermediaries, who will exchange them further on, and so on, until they reach their final destination. Industrialized products are sold to the farmers mostly by small merchants, who buy them from larger merchants in an inverse succession that begins with original industrial producers. Government agencies, cooperatives, and large and medium farmers enter into the intermediation chain at different points. Small farmers are usually at the end of the line.

When agricultural regions are geographically distant from urban centers, merchants become increasingly important in many different ways. They begin to pass on to farmers not only goods, but also vital information, such as the state of the market for different products. They become the main influence on agricultural production, on technology, and on consumption patterns. Merchant intermediation turns the advancing frontier into a means for spatial advance not only of agricultural supply, but also of industrial demand.

Commercial intermediation, however, requires transport. From this standpoint, the Amazon has a basic problem in the positioning of its natural "avenues" of penetration: the immense river system that drains the basin. Amazon rivers do not run toward the centers of capitalist accumulation (i.e., the South of the country), where the final processors of agricultural products and the original suppliers of manufactured inputs are located. Instead, these natural throughways link the frontier to the North and Northeast (i.e., the poorest parts of the nation). To link the frontier to the dynamic centers of the economy, river transport has to be replaced. In the 1970s, this replacement was done by road transport, whence the gigantic road-building program already described in chapter 7. The result of linking the frontier to the South was immediate, as shall now be seen.

Maps 16 and 17 trace the expansion toward the Amazon of "economic zones of influence" of the principal urban centers in Brazil.[10] One can see that from the mid-1960s to the late 1970s by far the largest zone of influence, and the one that grew the most, was centered in São Paulo. It linked the whole western frontier, penetrating into Mato Grosso do Sul, Mato Grosso, Acre, Rondônia, and Amazonas. Next came Belém, in competition with other northern centers, for the eastern frontier: Pará, Maranhão, and Amapá. Centers such as Goiânia, São Luiz, and Manaus, which also had their respective zones of economic influence in the Amazon, competed mostly among themselves.[11]

Road expansion, therefore, strengthened southern influence over the frontier. It is interesting to note that, according to the data analyzed, this influence was apparently not weakened by the emergence of intermediary urban centers. Apart from methodological biases that tend to underestimate their influence,[12] the growth of frontier towns does not appear to have offered São Paulo and Goiânia much serious competition. The supply of industrial products to the frontier, at least during the 1970s, came mainly from the South, not from local cities.

This is an important point, as it appears to contradict what was seen earlier in chapter 2. That chapter showed that there was a surge of urbanization on the frontier during the 1970s, which could imply a correspondingly large increase in local production. Yet this chapter indicates that urban population increase may not have been caused by the economic pull of frontier towns. Since industry from the Center-South competed with regional manufacturing, big cities such as Marabá, Altamira, Imperatriz, Santarém, Porto Velho, and Cuiabá may have acted increasingly as commercial outposts rather than as manufacturing centers. Though local production must have grown, their demographic growth during the period was seemingly more than would have been justified by their economic influence. This, at least, is the impression one gets from these data on market transactions among cities during the 1970s.

Many simultaneous and still not well-known processes competed in urbanizing the Amazon frontier during the 1970s. Agriculture "industrialized" and began to demand more and more manufactured goods and services, whose producers were already concentrated in the South. The agrarian frontier became less "spontaneous," and the state, which "lives in cities," began to exert a more important role in the occupation process. Directed settlement and the implanting of physical and social infrastructure were conducted at a distance, from offices based in towns. Many migrants who had come in search of land, and who had not found it, swarmed into local towns for lack of economic alternatives. Without sufficient production of their own to absorb this migratory flow, frontier cities began to swell. Marginality, tertiary growth, unemployment, underemployment, and misery rose. They were no longer typical only of

Map 16. Areas Subordinated to Urban Influence, 1966

Map 17. Areas Subordinated to Urban Influence, 1978

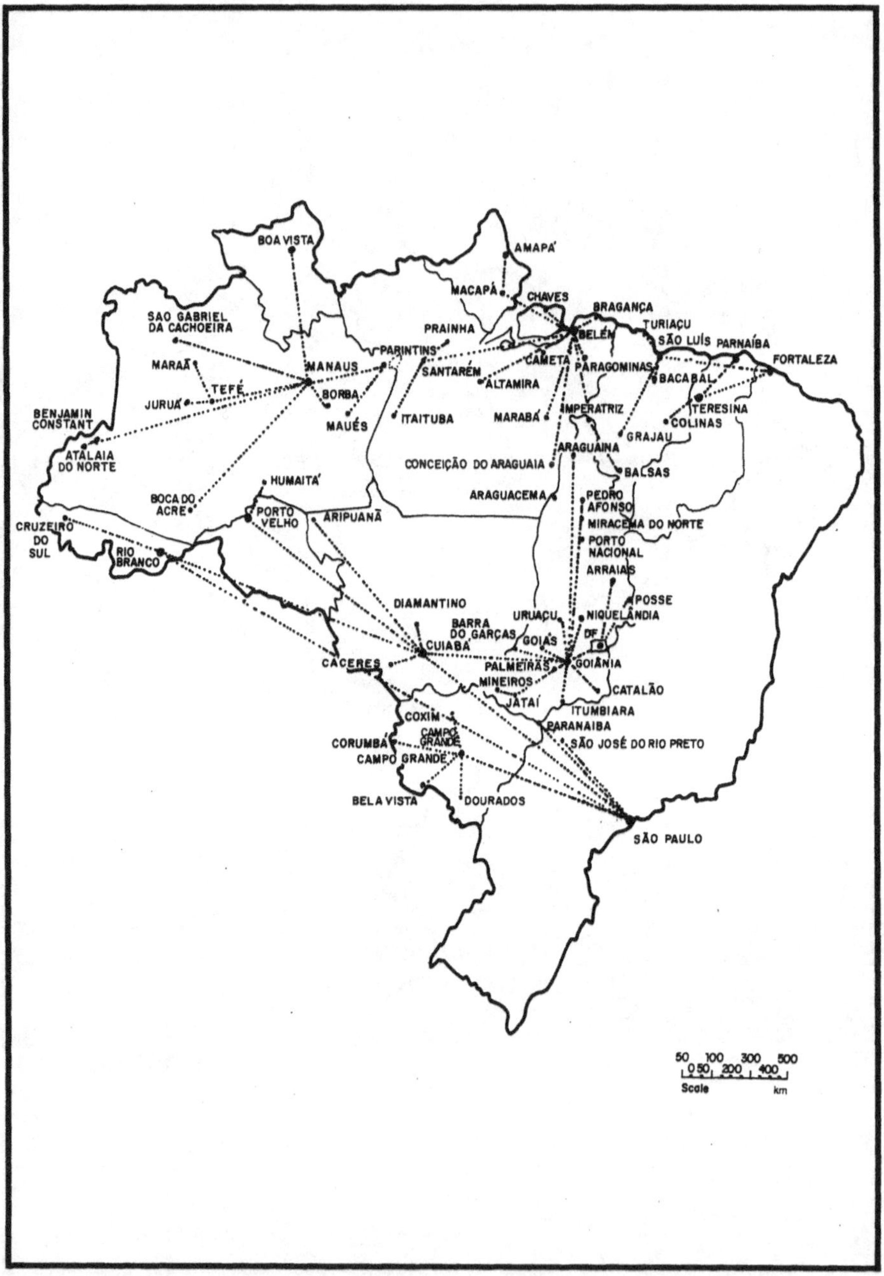

cities in older established regions.

Rural exodus in the Amazon created cities that were "born overnight," impelled by the growing unemployed work force.[13] Some had been forced off the land by larger farmers, or by other powerful groups. Some were victims of their own itinerant technology.[14] Many went to local cities as a transitory stage before leaving for other frontiers farther on. They swelled each town in succession with a temporarily urbanized population.[15] Once again, however, a profound analysis of urban issues on the frontier is beyond the scope of this book.[16]

Economic Reorientation of the Amazonian Space

In sum, market transactions linked the Amazon frontier to the rest of the country, according to a specific spatial reorientation. Great roads strengthened this spatial-functional link between southern industry and frontier farmers. As southern capitalism reached farther and farther into the frontier, especially into the western Amazon, its commercial intermediaries played an increasingly important role. The next chapters proceed to analyze the spatial expansion of industrial and commercial capitalism into the Amazon during the 1970s.

Notes

1. Important components of economic incorporation of the Amazon, which will not be discussed here, are the large-scale mining, hydroelectric, and ranching projects established in the region at and since that time. Many were direct investments of companies from the Center-South. They obtained SUDAM subsidies and vast tracts of land through public auctions, mostly held by INCRA. Such policies directly transformed much of the Amazon into private property belonging to central-southern capitalism. This phenomenon was of utmost importance in establishing the pace and the extent of Amazon occupation, and it decisively contributed to the "closing of the frontier" to small farmers during the 1970s. It will not be studied here, however, as the subject of this book is colonization, not large-scale farming or other agents of Amazon occupation. In the remainder of this book, therefore, the word "frontier" will be used synonymously with the "pioneer frontier" or the "social frontier," as described in chapter 1.

2. See Brandt (1977), S. Silva (1981), and Cardoso and Müller (1977).

3. More recently, economic incorporation of new territory has turned to the *cerrados* of the Center-West, and the notion of an "agricultural frontier" has come to refer to agro-industrial expansion there, not to Amazon colonization. For example, in Mato Grosso do Sul and Goiás, technological and biotechnological advances have paved the way for soy bean cultivation on a grand scale. But the *cerrado* frontier came after the period studied here, since it became significant only during the 1980s. Therefore it will not be discussed in this book. See

Agro-analysis (1986), IBGE (1982), INTERIOR (1977), Kageyama and Graziano da Silva (n.d.), Ozorio de Almeida et al. (1986), Planejamento e Desenvolvimento (1975)

4. See Rezende (1981), and chapter 2, note 3, above.

5. According to chapter 2, the "Amazon frontier" corresponds to the states of Pará, Mato Grosso, Amazonas, Rondônia, Acre, Roraima, and Amapá. The "*cerrado* frontier" corresponds to Maranhão, Goiás, and Mato Grosso do Sul.

6. Dias (1988).

7. Musumeci (1988), chapter 5, describes in detail commercial intermediation chains linking small farming in Maranhão's frontier to the rest of the market. She also provides a vast bibliography on the subject.

8. See chapter 16 on the small share of subsistence production in colonists' "income" and "expenditures" in Pará and Mato Grosso.

9. The capitalist "center" of Brazil is in the Center-South-Southeast regions of the country. The text, at times, will refer to these regions as being the "South" or the "Southeast" in a geographic sense, or the "Center" in a spatial-economic sense. In either case, of course, the words "South" and "Center" will not refer to a strict use of IBGE's definition of geographical regions. They mean that the southern part of the country is the "center of economic influence" over the frontier.

10. Definitions of terms such as "zone of influence" and others used in this chapter, as well as description of data and methodology for maps 16 and 17 are in *Migrações internas*, vol. 3. Sources were IBGE (1972a and 1980) and ICOTI (1976), inspired on the "central place theory" of Cristaller (1966) and Loesch (1967). The empirical basis for these studies is observations of the origins of suppliers and clients in market transactions for a specified set of basic products in large and small urban centers all over the country.

11. The expansion of São Paulo's and Goiânia's zones of influence during the 1970s was considerably greater than is shown in maps 16 and 17. Due to methodological limitations, these maps display only the greatest influence on each Amazonian region. However, several centers "compete" for each region and exert their influence in differing degrees. Thus, in much of the Amazon by the late 1970s, what was still a "secondary" penetration of Goiânia and São Paulo relative to the then still predominant influence of Manaus and Belém, remained camouflaged on the maps. The competition that southern centers put up vis-à-vis northern centers in the Amazon has certainly increased during the 1980s.

Despite this problem, the maps presented here do have the merit of providing a broad overview of the general direction in which southern influence grew during the 1970s.

12. See note 11.

13. See Gall (1977) and Hébette and Marin (1977).

14. See chapters 19 and 21 on field evidence on the itinerant technology of Amazon settlers. The next chapter (12) reviews the literature on the social causes of itinerant farming in Brazil. Chapters 4 and 5 discussed the environmental consequences of technological inadequacy by itinerant Amazon farmers.

15. A. Santos (1985) supplies the relevant bibliography in this respect.

16. See chapter 2 for some additional discussion of the urban frontier.

12. THE ECONOMIC DYNAMIC OF COLONIZATION

Different parts of the Amazon received different kinds of migrant farmers. The eastern front received a flow of mostly itinerant and poor migrants, many of whom were northeasterners. The western front initially received northeasterners as well, but these later competed with a migratory wave of richer southerners. The northernmost front was a later extension of Rondônia's expansion in terms of the type of immigrant it received.

Such geographic selectivity of migration to the Amazon, by origin and destination, is clearly not rigid. Nevertheless, the existing literature on the Brazilian frontier indicates that these two Amazonian fronts—eastern and western—correspond to distinct historical and institutional processes. The advance of these fronts into the Amazon represents a meeting of the "two Brazils"—the northeastern and the southern—in a process of economic and cultural integration in the Amazon that is new to the nation's experience.

This chapter examines hypotheses in the existing literature about the Amazon frontier, regarding migrant origins and destinations. Following this discussion of the literature, the chapter will identify distinct phases of frontier advance in terms of how farmers relate to the market and interact with merchants. It proposes that, during the initial settlement phase of a frontier, merchants manipulate family labor indirectly and appropriate colonists' agricultural surplus through "usury-mercantile" operations. This phase seems to be more persistent in the eastern Amazon, which is subordinated to northern and northeastern markets, than in the western Amazon, which is subordinated to the markets of the Center-South. As landed property consolidates in the subsequent phase, "productive capital" should increase—whether it belongs to colonists or to those merchants who vertically integrate their operations toward agricultural activities. This phase seems to be more advanced in the western than in the eastern Amazon.

These propositions are analytical simplifications intended to explain a diverse and complex reality. Along with chapters 13 and 14, this chapter constitutes the book's theoretical core and original contribution to the analysis of the Amazon frontier. As with any model, however, it "stereotypes" the agents involved. To sharpen the focus on the relationship between colonist and market, the model even abstracts from the type of colonization involved ("directed official," "directed private," "spontaneous"). As with any model, also, the goal here is to organize and evaluate empirical observations, which are to be presented in the next part of the book. The main point is that, to understand how colonists responded to the economic environment in which they were inserted, it is first necessary to understand how such economic environments formed and operated on the Amazon frontier.

The Western Amazon Frontier

The transformations that occurred in Brazilian agriculture during the 1970s are well known. The expansion of ranching accelerated in old labor-intensive farming areas, where such crops as coffee, cotton, beans, and corn used to be grown. In other areas, new crops such as soy, sugarcane, and peanuts were introduced and produced with highly mechanized techniques. The "productive" agricultural frontier shifted to the Center-West and became ever more highly capital intensive.[1] The areas closest to the main consuming urban centers underwent such real estate appreciation that they were no longer consistent with traditional farming. They came to produce high unit value products, and also adopted greater capital intensity and modern inputs. The northernmost region of the Amazon, still distant from the agricultural frontier, experienced declining extractive activities and extreme rural exodus.[2]

In the South, increasing capital intensity in agriculture was accompanied by real estate appreciation during the peak of the general economic cycle[3] in the early 1970s. Many small farmers sold their lands at high prices and bought larger areas of cheap land on the frontier, especially on the western front, which was opening at that time. Nevertheless, with the subsequent cyclical downturn of the early 1980s, the advance of the western frontier weakened. The exodus of former landowners in the South declined and was even partially reversed, as return migration increased. Within the decade of the 1970s, then, a large migratory wave from the South swelled and ebbed, responding to the cyclical stimuli of

Map 18. Brazilian States on the Frontier

general economic activity in Brazil.

There are many contemporary studies of the social transformations in the Brazilian countryside during the 1970s, including the formation of a wage-based labor force (*bóias-frias*), rural unionization, and social unrest.[4] However, their relationships to Amazon frontier expansion at the time, especially on the western front, were not apparent to all.

In effect, the western Amazon frontier can be considered an extension of the much older Paraná frontier. The latter had been impelled since the 1940s by São Paulo coffee growers and by various private colonization companies who, with official support, had an important role in establishing a farming plantation structure where previously small and medium properties had predominated. In a little over two decades, however, this frontier was "exhausted," coming to expel more laborers than it absorbed. In the 1960s, Paraná coffee cultivation began to be replaced by other expanding agricultural waves from São Paulo: cereals, soy, wheat, rice, and ranching. As a consequence, property concentration and emigration from Paraná reached unprecedented magnitudes during the 1970s.

The subsequent advance of the Paraná frontier swept into Goiás, Mato Grosso do Sul, Mato Grosso, and Rondônia during the 1970s. Later it extended into Acre, Roraima, and Amazonas. The occupation of Mato Grosso do Sul was done by large properties and both official and private colonization. Migrants to these areas were largely from Rio Grande do Sul (*gaúchos*) and Paraná, who planted coffee, rice, and pastures. In order to clear the forest and plant new fields, they utilized northeastern laborers, called *peões de trecho* (road peons) coming from São Paulo and Paraná. Other migrant groups comprised small landowners from Mato Grosso do Sul itself, as well as natives from Rio Grande do Sul and Paraná. Those from Paraná, however, remained the majority, due to recruiting by various private and official colonizing agents established in Mato Grosso do Sul. Later, the states of Paraná and Rio Grande do Sul came to provide the largest share of migrants to private colonization projects in Mato Grosso.

Goiás, in spite of its location farther eastward, also experienced intense rural population growth impelled from the South. With the opening of the Belém-Brasília and Brasília-Acre highways, areas contiguous to these roads were occupied by large agricultural firms stimulated by fiscal incentives, as well as by small farmers taking part in official, private, and spontaneous colonization. Spontaneous southern settlement concentrated in the extreme north of Goiás, where it came into contact with the expanding northeastern agricultural frontier, especially the front from Maranhão.[5]

Rondônia's occupation began with the exploitation of cassiterite and intensified as overland access increased, mainly due to the construction of the Cuiabá–Porto Velho Highway (BR-364) at the end of the 1950s, its later improvement in 1970, and its paving in the early to mid-1980s. INCRA's colonization projects—Ouro Preto, Ji-Paraná, Sidney Girão, Burareiro, Paulo de Assis Ribeiro, Padre Adolfo Rohl, and Marechal Dutra—and the opening of new highways, generated more intense migratory flows than ever observed in the country's history, with the population increasing almost fivefold during the 1970s. During the following decade, Rondônia became, without a doubt, the most important area of Amazon agricultural frontier expansion.

Initially, the majority of migrants to Rondônia came from the North and Northeast. Over time, however, the flow originating in the Southeast and Center-South grew in importance.[6] Small farmers arrived from Paraná, São Paulo, Mato Grosso do Sul, and Rio Grande do Sul—especially from areas where wheat, rice, and soy cultivation had experienced intense mechanization, or where coffee cultivation was being replaced by soy. Later, migration came from the "old frontier" itself, not from the more distant traditional agricultural areas. Many of these migrants were familiar with modern production techniques, since they had either been landowners themselves or were children of landowners from regions of capital-intensive agriculture.

Migration to Rondônia became significant from 1970 on and became intense after 1974. Its peak occurred in 1976, and then decelerated in 1977 due to a government campaign to slow migration along highways and to prevent it from beginning in areas of origin. But the flow was soon renewed, and the turn of the decade showed greater movement than hitherto registered. Each year during the dry season, between June and September, when overland access is easiest and it is time for planting, the pace of migration increased. At this time, Rondônia attracted increasing numbers not only of migrants, but also of researchers![7]

As shown in chapter 2, the Rondônia frontier spread northward to Roraima and eastward to Aripuanã, in Mato Grosso. The flow toward Roraima followed the Porto Velho–Manaus (BR-319) and Manaus–Rio Branco (BR-174) highways, while migrants to Aripuanã arrived as much from Rondônia as from the South, directly by the Cuiabá-Santarém Highway (BR-163).

The western front in all its dynamism, however, was not the largest part of the advancing agricultural frontier during the 1970s. The bulk of migration was still located in the eastern Amazon and responded to distinct impulses, which will be described in the following section.

The Eastern Amazon Frontier

Since the 1920s, northeasterners have practiced seasonal spontaneous migration to Pará's Southeast to take part in the harvest of Brazil nuts.

Initially, Pará absorbed few small farmers. Nevertheless, they began to increase in numbers by the beginning of the 1950s, basically as an overflow of the Maranhão frontier. The migratory flow, then, formed a link between the towns of Imperatriz (Maranhão), Estreito (Goiás), and Marabá (Pará), deepening the penetration of small farmers into the Amazon jungle. This type of "mobile" frontier, or itinerant agriculture, has been studied by various authors.[8]

Maranhão's agricultural frontier apparently reached "exhaustion" (i.e., came to release more migrants than it absorbed) by the end of the 1960s. Since then, a large part of the northeastern migrant flow was absorbed into southeastern Pará and, more recently, into northeastern Mato Grosso. These regions have also received part of the flow originating from the highways that link Barra do Garças to Marabá (BR-158), and especially the Belém-Brasília Highway (BR-153), which has generated more out-migration than in-migration since its construction.[9]

During the 1970s, an important change occurred in the attitudes previously rooted in the migrants of the eastern front. Their prior experience of successive expulsions, and the results of official colonization, taught these migrants that what they previously considered a natural right, access to a "land which is for working on"[10] remained secure only for those who acquired legal title to the land, according to the criteria set by the dominant institutional system.[11] By the 1970s, given the frontier's closure from within and without, many migrants began to avoid becoming occupants on others' lands. The waiting lists for settlement projects grew, and candidates even occupied and demarcated plots themselves, hoping to "regularize" them later as projects expanded into adjoining areas. Many became sharecroppers on plots that had already been distributed to others, while they waited to receive their own.

This rapid change in the perception of the power associated with private landed property was not accompanied by changes as rapid in the agricultural technology of small family farming. The vicious circle of low technology, subsistence agriculture, and itinerancy continued to reproduce itself even within colonization projects. Land ownership, then, did not hinder the advance of the moving frontier. This problem, which was especially apparent in the eastern Amazon, reflected a gap in time between, on the one hand, recent comprehension of the concept and advantages of land ownership and, on the other hand, the adoption of productive and technological behavior consistent with that ownership.

According to this interpretation, effectively settling itinerant migrant flows requires a profound modification of small farmers' agricultural practices. Itinerancy is a set of practices that are consistent among themselves and that do not change overnight. It is a complex reality, generating a set of demands upon directed colonization policies that are much broader and encompassing than was perceived during the 1970s.

Classic Itinerancy

Itinerant agriculture contains within itself complex motivations for continued movement, many of which are endogenous and independent of the causes that set the migrant in motion at the start.[12] In the eastern Amazon, one of the sources impelling itinerancy in small farm agriculture apparently results from interrelationships between family-based agricultural production and the family unit itself. These two levels of behavior—economic and demographic—interact and respond to external economic stimuli. Such interactions and responses determine how a small farmer behaves on the frontier and how initial settlement occurs, as well as the length of stay in each location. Even if wider transformations of surrounding agriculture were not taking place, or even if there were no general process of capital penetration into the countryside, the family unit's life cycle may lead a family to leave plot after plot and move ever onward. The mechanism underlying this itinerancy recreates vicious circles inherent to penury and low technology.

Upon arriving on new land, a family must first of all secure its own survival, which depends on clearing the forest and planting food crops. The less the financial resources, the technical knowledge, and the equipment available, the greater will be dependence on family labor. The size of cleared and planted area will then be a direct function of the number of available workers in the family. The quantity of marketed surplus will also be a function of the total number of family members. The larger the family labor force and the more favorable its age composition for farming, the more labor is available for expanding cleared land, planting commercial crops, establishing permanent crops, and building. The size of the family and its age composition, in a sense, constitute the family farms' "working capital," that is, resources available to form and accumulate fixed capital. Family size and age composition, thus, are important determinants of the agricultural unit's rate of accumulation. Given the level of other resources, only those families who have already reached a certain degree of maturity in the cycle of family formation have the size and age composition adequate for success on the frontier.

Families that are either too young or too old to produce the surplus necessary for accumulation are constrained to a subsistence economy. Such farmers rapidly exhaust the land and allow their fallow plots (*capoeiras*) to be invaded by weeds, which they are unable to control at their low technological level. Thus, the family is quickly driven to a kind of "catastrophe point," at which the decision must be taken to face the high cost of starting all over again in order to survive. They move on, financed by the meager earnings of the last harvest, abandoning their plots or selling them at a pittance. Clearing a new plot is financed by temporary wage labor or brute exploitation of own family labor. Being confined to subsistence, therefore, also means being confined to itinerancy.

The cycle of family formation is evidently not the only determinant of itinerancy for small farming on the frontier. This factor operates most strongly within the poorest strata of the population, who lack access to financial intermediation or to any additional resources. They have no other types of working capital, beyond the simple use of family labor, by which to promote accumulation and permanent settlement. The mechanism that moves the itinerant frontier forward is, therefore, not independent of the original social forces that expelled migrants in the first place. It is poor farmers' original status at the fringes of the market economy which forces them into reliance upon the family as the mainstay of their economic resources. The less they have to start with, the more vulnerable they are to climatic reversals, pests, and diseases, as well as other natural risks typical of recently occupied regions. Not the least of such threats are more powerful local competitors for the same land, which set off the violence that is typical of lawless frontiers. Thus, there is continuity in how social relations from the rest of the economy are recreated on the frontier.

An additional cause of itinerancy is the frontier's precarious marketing structure. The more concentrated the market, the greater the share of agricultural surplus that merchants appropriate, and the more they contribute to recreating small farmers' original low income position. Low income, in turn, hinders farmers' technological improvements and capital accumulation, thereby reproducing conditions for their itinerancy.[13]

Itinerant frontier farmers are, therefore, simultaneously dependent on family labor and inserted into mercantile relations. Their behavior often resembles that of classical "peasants," that is, motivated primarily by personal intra- and extrafamilial relations.[14] They are also comparable to the so-called informal sector—they choose independent production rather than subordinating to wage labor.[15] Some may be considered "small entrepreneurs," whose objective is capital accumulation.[16] Probably they combine varying proportions of all these attitudes toward productive activity. Regardless of their initial objectives, however, migrants who remain on a frontier after its phase of rural exodus and property concentration must surely adapt to the changes that occur in their economic environment. In so doing, they become economic agents distinct from what they were upon arrival.

A particular territory is usually "opened" to low-income migratory flows soon after road construction or improvement. It is "closed" when original migrants are expelled, whether by the frontier's own violence or by the vicious circle of itinerancy. After exhausting their plots, farmers leave the territory that they had cleared, and, if nearby lands are not available for occupation, must emigrate. In the areas of rural exodus, then, land ownership becomes concentrated and the countryside is drained of family farmers.

Summary: Origins and Destinations

Southerners in the Amazon may have been different from "itinerant" northeastern migrants in that they brought with them more resources from the proceeds of selling previous lands. They had learned how to manage small properties and had more experience of stable agriculture. Since they were once active in the country's most developed areas, they were probably closely linked to the market economy. They may also have had more experience with institutional transactions, such as financial agents and cooperatives. Southerners, therefore, probably used more purchased inputs (e.g., fertilizers and equipment) and may have had greater knowledge of agricultural technologies that retard soil erosion. Consequently, the vicious circle of subsistence and itinerancy may have had less of a hold upon migrants from the South.[17] This suggests the additional hypothesis that duration on the land and the rate of capital accumulation were higher on the western frontier than on the eastern frontier, since the former is an extension of the richer southern front, while the latter represents an expansion of the itinerant northeastern front.[18]

Regardless of farmers' origins, however, upon arriving on a frontier they must adapt to specific local conditions, which are, in turn, undergoing dynamic transformations of social, institutional, ecological, and marketing natures. These transformations are reviewed in the next section.

The Frontier and Capital Penetration into the Countryside

The transformation of capital in Brazilian agriculture has been rapid in the last decades.[19] Institutional/financial capital accounted for barely 18 percent of agricultural credit in the 1950s, while usury-mercantile capital accounted for most of the rest.[20] Since then, these positions have been reversed. Usury-mercantile credit declined, having shifted mostly to frontier regions; institutional/financial capital increased rapidly, generally in established regions. Meanwhile, directly productive capital has expanded greatly in Brazilian agriculture.

In addition to acting in the spheres of commerce and agriculture, both national and foreign, productive capital has penetrated agriculture through the manufacturing of inputs and equipment, in a process frequently called the "industrialization of agriculture."[21] Productive capital takes on a wide range of forms in direct agricultural production: verticalized agro-industry, commercially oriented landowners, commercially oriented tenants, independent small farmers, small farmers contracted by agro-industries, and others.[22] The first three employ wage labor, while the latter two use family labor.

The general process called "capital penetration into the countryside" (i.e., the "agrarian transition") involves growth of all of these different kinds of agricultural capital in varying proportions, depending on the region and the moment. In Brazil, this process accelerated during the 1970s. The more advanced regions experienced a strong increase in the proportion of wage labor at the beginning of the decade. Surprisingly, however, that increase was almost offset by the large shift of small farmers from the South to the North. Only during the second half of the decade did wage labor increase throughout Brazil, including frontier areas, as can be seen in table 28.

According to this table, the proportion of wage laborers in the total agricultural labor force in the North, which corresponds to the "Amazon frontier," doubled from 5 percent to 10 percent from 1975–1980. In the Northeast, which includes the state of Maranhão, it more than doubled, from 12 percent to 25 percent. The increase in both regions was concentrated in the second half of the decade, which shows how recent wage labor is to these areas. In the Center-West, which corresponds to

Table 28. Introduction of Wage Labor in Agriculture, 1970–1980: Permanent and Temporary Employees as a Share of Total Personnel Employed in Agriculture (%)

		Year	
Region	*1970*	*1975*	*1980*
North	6	5	10
Center-West	18	23	32
Northeast	12	12	25
South-Southeast	19	24	28
Brazil	15	16	24

Source: *Censos agropecuários* of 1970, 1975, and 1980 as tabulated in Ozorio de Almeida (1982), p. 960, and G. Müller (1987), table 7, p. 12.

the *cerrado* frontier except for Maranhão, labor's share of agricultural employment increased by 78 percent (from 18 percent to 32 percent). This growth accelerated over the decade from 28 percent between 1970 and 1975 (from 18 percent to 23 percent) to 39 percent between 1975 and 1980 (from 23 percent to 32 percent). In the South-Southeast, wage labor's share of employment for the whole decade grew by 47 percent (from 19 percent to 28 percent). In this case, the rate of increase slowed over time. During the first half of the decade, the share increased by 26 percent (from 19 percent to 24 percent); during the second half, the increase was only 16 percent (from 24 percent to 28 percent). By 1980, then, wage labor in Brazil as a whole barely accounted for one-fourth of total agricultural employment. Although the agricultural census underestimates the proportion of wage laborers, this form of hiring was certainly still far from being dominant in Brazilian agriculture by the end of the 1970s.

It thus appears that the agrarian transition was still an incomplete process in the 1970s, in spite of its acceleration during the decade. It was certainly occurring differently in each region. On the Amazon frontier, the transition toward wage-based agriculture was the farthest behind. On the "*cerrado* frontier" this process was the most advanced, due to the rapid penetration of new agro-industrial capital into the Center-West. The relation of agriculture to capitalism, then, changed very rapidly on the frontier, as is shown by contrasting the two first lines of table 28—"Amazon frontier" versus "*cerrado* frontier."[23]

A frontier has one particular characteristic that distinguishes it from the rest of the whole economy: the real or imagined availability of land for appropriation. This characteristic gives rural workers a unique subsistence option in addition to wage labor. In such circumstances, even those without capital, who cannot purchase their own means of production, can at least occupy some land and produce their own income, thereby avoiding working for others.[24] The "enclosure" of the Amazon frontier was practically complete during the 1970s, as was seen in chapters 2 through 5. Yet, at least in the aspirations of migrants, the Amazon frontier was still a place where they could work for themselves[25] on land that they considered still to be free.[26]

As long as these aspirations persisted, and some land existed on which to realize them, small family farming continued to reproduce itself on the Amazon frontier in spite of capitalism's penetration into the countryside in remaining regions. The two processes already described—the "proletarianization" of agriculture in the Center-South and the recreation of the "peasantry" in the North—can be considered effectively as aspects of the same general phenomenon: capital penetration into agriculture in an economy where land had not yet been completely transformed into private property.[27]

The same issue can be expressed in other terminology. In Brazilian agriculture, "the knot of the problem is how to characterize the dynamic of small producers when their submission . . . to capital is incomplete."[28] Classically, proletarianization of labor, or "formal submission of labor to capital,"[29] is concluded only when workers lose possession of their means of production and subsistence. Without other means to assure their reproduction, they are forced to submit to employment as wage laborers. Only after the generalization of wage labor should the technical intensification of productive processes be possible, that is, the "real submission of labor to capital."[30]

In Brazilian agriculture, however, "real submission" was already accelerating on the *cerrado* frontier [31] before "formal submission" had been completed on the Amazon frontier. Capitalist penetration into the countryside in the 1970s, then, has a complex temporal-spatial dimension in a country with an extensive agricultural frontier.

The general issue of "capital penetration into the countryside," or "agrarian transition," or "rural proletarianization," or "formal submission" of labor to capital is old and complex. It has been studied in many countries under different perspectives. It would be impossible to do justice to this long-standing debate in the space available in this work.[32] From Marx's works to the theories of articulation of modes of production, there is fascination with the complexities of the theme. It raises important questions, such as: Why, in general, has family-based production persisted in agriculture, even in wealthy countries? Why, in particular, is it being continually recreated on the Amazon frontier? In order better to understand this latter question, it is necessary to examine directly who frontier producers are—farmers and merchants—and how they interact during each phase of economic incorporation of new territory.

The Phases of a Frontier: A Schematic Interpretation

This section proposes a model of the process of incorporation of a frontier into the market economy. It breaks down a continuous movement with many variations into only two phases—settlement and exodus—and reduces the multiplicity of agents involved to only two types—farmers and merchants. As with any simplification, its objective is to facilitate data interpretation. It identifies some systematic tendencies that underlie the apparently chaotic diversity of frontiers in general and emphasizes the issue of their economic incorporation into the existing market economy.

Initially, when a frontier is first settled, small family farmers typically arrive before anyone else. Whatever capitalists are present mostly fulfill the role of merchants who finance farmers throughout the agricultural year. These merchants supply consumer goods and inputs on credit in return for advance purchase of the harvest. Compared to "free market" transactions, prices paid for agricultural produce may or may not be low, and prices of industrial products, as well as rates of interest charged, may or may not be high. Such prices are apparently not relevant in themselves; they merely belong to a set of interlinked transactions that attach the farmer to the merchant. In the same way, the sale of consumer goods to the farmer may not be, in itself, the merchant's key objective: it apparently serves principally as a way to ensure the merchant's own participation in the market of highest priority to him, which is the agricultural product market.[33] Consumer goods sold in this type of retail commerce tend to be of primary necessity, typical of the needs of low-income farmers who are attached to commerce in a vicious circle of indebtedness and dependency.

The key farmer-merchant transaction in this initial phase of occupation is the requirement that consumer repayment be made not in money but in kind—necessarily in agricultural produce. This mechanism of *nonmonetary* "interlinked transactions" directs agricultural produce flows to creditor-merchants, whose further intermediation with respect to the "outside" economy allows them to realize their main profits. It is merchants' commanding position in the outside product market that gives them an advantage vis-à-vis the farmer and allows them to extract farmers' surplus via interlinked credit operations.

Typically, town-based commercial firms advance funds to selected agents, often farmers themselves, dispersed in several different rural communities. These agents then capture local produce and transmit it to their own creditors, the town merchant. This combination "siphons" agricultural production from the frontier to the rest of the economy, through the chain of commercial intermediation.[34] Ironically, the way merchants are inserted into the outside market leads to a "repressed monetization" of the frontier economy. "Subsistence" farming on the frontier, therefore, does not precede market penetration, but constitutes a result of the way in which this penetration takes place.[35]

Small farmers, thus, become indebted when their own working capital is insufficient to finance family consumption over the course of a complete agricultural year. The credit they need, however, is not furnished by the formal financial system. This is because of various factors that are negative from a banking perspective, namely: (1) credit is oriented more toward consumption than production, (2) debtors' family incomes are low, (3) collateral is low, especially if the farmer is not a landowner, and (4) banks do not accept agricultural product as loan guarantee, only real estate and durable goods.

By accepting the future harvest as payment for consumer loans made between harvests, the merchant provides some of the necessary conditions for low-income family farming. By so doing, he also monitors and directs agricultural labor toward commercial production. When indebtedness and repayment in kind become extreme, marketed output may predominate and subsistence production may become a small part of total product. But restricting debtors' self-sufficiency reinforces their dependence upon merchants who become, in this way, virtual if not de facto employers of agricultural labor. Instead of managing labor directly by varying wages, as in the case of wage labor, merchants act indirectly, compelling work through managing farmers' debts. In both ways—wage labor and indebtedness—family labor can be directed toward commercial production.[36]

As long as family farmers remain subject to the various risks of a frontier, income variations will be great and farmers will tend to fall into indebtedness. Given their low productivity, once caught in debt they tend to appropriate little surplus and to remain indebted year after year. When land is cheap, subsistence production has low "opportunity costs,"[37] that is, it makes sense to use land on low unit value, low productivity crops. The merchant, then, may save on fixed costs by financing only the working capital necessary for agricultural production, not its total cost. Under these conditions, merchants would tend to remain merchants and not to enter into direct agricultural production. This relationship between low-income family farmers and the merchants who deal with them is called a "usury-mercantile" relationship. Although it is a centuries-old form of production and exchange, it reappears on the Amazon frontier today due to geographic factors that reproduce historical conditions.[38]

A new frontier has certain characteristics that are particularly favorable for the reproduction of usury-mercantile capital. Distance increases merchants' degree of monopoly power and, hence, their bargaining power as well. Uncertainty increases risk and therefore weakens farmers' bargaining power. Land is cheap in comparison with highly valued property in older occupied regions, and cheap land lowers the opportunity cost of subsistence (i.e., low productivity) agriculture. Formal financial institutions—banks and cooperatives—take time to become established in new areas, so that credit is initially scarce. As long as this economic space remains relatively empty, usury-mercantile capital can move in to occupy it.

As a particular frontier region becomes consolidated, however, these conditions change. Knowledge of the area increases, uncertainty diminishes, and farmers' risks decline. Competitors arrive, reducing merchants' degree of monopoly power in bidding for merchandise. Formal credit institutions begin to operate, breaking the "usurious" function of local commerce. Land prices rise, elevating the opportunity cost of subsistence cultivation and expelling family farmers from local agriculture. Agricultural labor, then, comes to be salaried or organized in some other directly remunerated manner.

At this point, the practice of indirectly managing agricultural production through controlling farmers' debts becomes more costly for merchants. From now on, given the demise of subsistence farming, they will need to finance the total cost of labor and not just its working capital. Indirect labor management loses its advantage, and merchants turn to direct production. Over time, then, some merchants become commercial farmers, while others consolidate their commercial businesses. They lose their old clientele of pioneering small producers, and, with the rural exodus, the usury-mercantile relations are dismantled.

In sum, two specific kinds of agricultural producers and also two specific kinds of merchants correspond to each of the successive two phases of frontier advance. In agriculture, the pioneering phase introduces small family farmers, while in commerce it introduces usury-mercantile capital. The phase of rural exodus transforms farmers and merchants alike into directly productive capitalists. Outside capitalists also move in at this point, once institutional, physical, and market conditions—private property of land, a wage labor market, formal credit institutions, adequate roads—are ready for them. The proportions of former pioneers, former merchants, and new capitalist farmers who constitute an "old frontier economy" will probably depend on conditions and policies effective when the frontier was new.[39]

This second phase of a frontier permits the establishment of wage labor, and, from that point on, technical intensification of production can proceed. Capital's penetration into the countryside, therefore, has its own specific evolution on the frontier. It also interacts with developments in the rest of the economy, as will be seen in the next section.

Capital Penetration and Itinerant Agriculture

The discussion presented in this chapter may now be summarized. In Brazil, distinct historical phases in the formation of capital coexist in different regions of the territory and respond to one another. The advance of the western Amazon frontier can be seen as the unfolding of southern capital's penetration into agriculture. The advance of the eastern Amazon frontier, by contrast, would be an extension of the northeastern itinerant "peasant" agriculture. In outline, though reality is much more complex, colonists in the western Amazon deal with the extension of the industrial economy of the South-Southeast, while colonists in the eastern Amazon deal with the traditional usury-mercantile capital of the North-Northeast.

The result of directed colonization on the frontier will depend, then, upon how colonists respond to the economic dynamic in which they are inserted. Colonists' incomes will depend upon how the surrounding system of markets operate and which mechanisms of surplus appropriation are utilized in their part of the frontier. The next chapter makes explicit how different market systems realize the appropriation of agricultural income on the Amazon frontier.

Notes

The sections "The Western Amazon Frontier" and "The Eastern Amazon Frontier" of this chapter are extracted from Ozorio de Almeida and David (1981). See map 18 for the location of Brazilian states mentioned in the text.

1. Sawyer (1981) and Martine (1987a).

2. See, among others, R. Carvalho (1979), Loureiro (1981), IBGE (1979c), and Dias (1979).

3. Resende (1981). See also the table presented in chapter 2, note 3.

4. See, among others, d'Incao e Melo (1975), Goodman (1986), J. Lopes (1973), Brandt (1977), and Bastos (1977).

5. The movement of the frontier in the South and Center-West was analyzed in various important works, such as Osório (1978), IBGE (1979c), and Velho (1973).

6. Martine (1978 and 1980) and IBGE (1979).

7. In addition to those already cited, see also Calvente (1980), Pacheco (1980), NAEA (1981), Henriques (1984, 1985, 1986), CEDEPLAR (1979b), I. Ribeiro (1981), Baumfeld (1985), Rondônia (1980).

8. Among many, the following works stand out: Velho (1973), Osório (1978), Sawyer (1979a), Moura (1979), and, more generally, Martins (1975).

9. Hébette and Marin (1977).

10. See, for example, Sá (1975), T. Cunha (1977), and Garcia Júnior (1975).

11. Musumeci (1980).

12. The summary in this section is adapted from Dias (1976).

13. The link between family agriculture and commerce on the frontier will be considered more deeply in subsequent sections of this chapter, as well as in later chapters.

14. Chayanov (1966) is the founder of the literature on the "peasant" economy. In Brazil, this literature has delved into the polemic over whether small farmers are oriented toward market relations or subsistence relations. Nevertheless, as Janvry and Deere (1978) state, subsistence is not an objective of small producers, but a result of how they are inserted into the economy as a whole. This book adopts this interpretation and raises empirical evidence in part 4 regarding how farmers' insertion into the market determines their income level and their greater or lesser utilization of family labor power on the agricultural frontier.

15. Part of the literature on the informal sector largely uses this interpretation of small producers. Independent producers are seen as workers whose objective

is to attain a level of remuneration that covers their opportunity cost in the labor market (i.e., the market wage). They are not expected to behave as entrepreneurs seeking to maximize a return on their capital. P. Cunha (1979), Schmitz (1983), and Souza (1980) have presented the classic statements in this literature for Brazil. They derive from an ILO (1972) perspective, updated by Tokman (1985). See, also, the evidence and works cited in chapters 17, 18, and 19 concerning labor market segmentation on the Amazon frontier.

16. There is also an extensive literature on an "entrepreneurial rationality" of small farmers, derived from neoclassical models of microeconomic decisions. Its empirical applications are generally oriented toward analyzing "price sensitivity" of supply (output or labor), demand (for inputs or credit), and technology. See, for example, Geertz (1963), Wharton (1969), Southworth and Johnston (1967), Nerlove (1958), and Schultz (1964). Chapter 14 presents bibliographical references and a simplified model within this perspective for interpreting small farmer behavior under frontier conditions.

17. This hypothesis was upheld by field survey evidence comparing southerners with other migrants under official directed settlement projects, as will be seen in part 4.

18. This hypothesis was not upheld by field survey evidence, however, as will also be seen in part 4.

19. Given lack of space, this text will not attempt to define or debate terms for different types of capital (e.g., "usury-mercantile," "productive," or "institutional-financial"), or such terms as "peasants," "modes of production," "agrarian transition," "articulation," and "proletarianization," which are discussed in depth in innumerable works. Consider the reviews by Goodman and Redclift (1981) and, with respect to the Brazilian agricultural frontier, Musumeci (1980). The terms appear here as used in the cited works.

20. Goodman and Redclift (1981), chapter 5.

21. See, for example, G. Müller (1981, 1982, 1987), Graziano da Silva (1981), and Graziano da Silva et al. (1982, 1983) on the formation of the Brazilian agro-industrial complex, in terms of both industrialization of agricultural inputs and of industrial demand for agricultural products.

22. The term "contractor" refers to "outgrower" farm families under an exclusive contract with one firm. This system is similar to the "putting out" system of the beginning of the industrial revolution, and to the "subcontracting" still practiced in the urban informal sector today, whereby workers labor at home although working for capitalist firms. See Ozorio de Almeida (1975).

23. See Mueller (1983b) and G. Müller (1987).

24. In an analysis influenced by Domar (1970), J. M. Camargo (1981) demonstrates that wage labor is only possible when access to the means of production (land, in this case) is denied to a substantial part of the working population. See also Katzman (1977).

25. B. Ferreira (1984) reports that one of the principal motivations for migrants in going to the frontier is to avoid working for others.

26. Musumeci (1987) discusses the "myth of free land" among colonists in Maranhão.

27. Ozorio de Almeida (1982).

28. Goodman and Redclift (1981), p. 97.

29. Marx (1975), pp. 73–77 and 79–89.

30. Ibid., p. 79.

31. G. Müller (1987) shows that agricultural capital intensity is increasing more rapidly in the Center-West than in the South-Southeast.

32. Marx (1975), Frank (1969), Laclau (1971), Wallerstein (1974–1980), Lenin (1964), Shanin (1971), Kautsky (1974), and innumerable other authors deal with this issue.

33. Using data from the Brazilian Northeast, Ozorio de Almeida (1977a) shows that prices conceded to sharecroppers by their landowners were frequently higher, and interest rates charged were often lower, than was the case for squatters or small landowners who had to rely on merchant transactions. These favorable relative prices served to channel sharecroppers' production to landowners, who thereby secured a larger volume of agricultural produce to transact further on than they would have obtained on their own. In the case of squatters or small landowners, produce was routed toward local merchants at relatively low prices and relatively high interest rates. Analogous mechanisms of appropriation on the frontier will be described below.

34. In addition to evidence already cited above, Musumeci (1987) presents a variety of other evidence and distinguishes various types of "tied transactions" that are associated with "usury-mercantile" capital on the frontier. Chapter 15 here presents evidence on the operations of merchants on the Amazon frontier.

35. Other forms of commercialization of agriculture can result in "repressed monetization" of labor relations, such as in a plantation economy (Harris 1988) in which conditions of credit shortage also play a crucial role.

36. Ozorio de Almeida (1977a) shows how, in different parts of the Northeast, merchants practically "extort" agricultural produce from farmers using indebtedness incurred through credit retailing subject to the advance purchase of harvests. Almost identical circumstances were observed in field surveys in the Amazon, as will noted later, in part 4.

37. "Opportunity cost" is a basic term in economics, whereby the highest alternative income that could be derived from a resource (in this case, land) is considered to be part of the cost of any one use of that resource.

38. Indebtedness through advance purchase of crops is well known in Asia. The case of India, for example, is analyzed in Thorner and Thorner (1962), Thorner (1965), Bhaduri (1973), Bardhan (1984), and Bardhan and Rudera (1978). This mechanism was also common in the last century in Eastern Europe and in the U.S. South, where it was called "debt-peonage" via the mechanism of "crop-lien." In the period after the U.S. Civil War, the mechanism was recreated among retailers who became merchants in the agricultural product market. See, for example, Ransom and Sutch (1972, 1975). In all cases, however, the linking of retail, credit, and product transactions repeats itself, always in monopolized or oligopolized markets. In the Amazon, many of the agents who act in these markets also follow the same usury-mercantile relations. This was directly verified in field survey data, to be reported in chapter 15, below, by examining the "accounts" of local retailers who registered consumer goods "advances" in exchange for farmers' future harvests.

39. Follow-up research on the Amazon frontier during 1991 will shed light on the composition of surviving agricultural and nonagricultural producers.

13. THE APPROPRIATION OF AGRICULTURAL SURPLUS

This chapter and the next one propose a formal analysis of the frontier economy on various levels. This chapter analyzes market structures established alongside agriculture in colonized areas and the way these markets appropriate agricultural surplus. The next chapter analyzes the influence on farmers' performance of the relative prices that are established in rural markets. Empirical evidence on interactions between farmers' productive behavior and rural markets will be examined in part 4, especially chapters 18 and 19. Various other influences will also be shown to act upon farmers' reactions to markets; their contributions will be tested econometrically in chapters 20 and 21. This part of the analysis abstracts from the concrete institutional characteristics of colonization in order to focus on general conditions of exchange and surplus appropriation.

One qualification must be made from the start. The terms "market structure" and "market systems" are employed in a rather distinct manner from what is usual in the literature. They will not refer to market concentration for a given product—monopoly, oligopoly, and so on—as in standard microeconomic analysis.[1] Nor will they refer to locational or hierarchical factors of market behavior, as in regional economic analysis.[2] Neither will they imply tracing the many links in the chain of intermediation and articulation established in the marketing of agricultural products.[3]

Rather, in considering rural market systems, this chapter seeks to characterize only those market transactions that determine the direct appropriation of farmers' surplus. It refers merely to the fundamental transactions made by *farmers* regarding land, credit, labor, agricultural output, inputs, services, and official or private transfers. This set of transactions is the primary connection between farmers and the rest of the economy, and the first level of appropriation of their surplus.

The objective of this chapter, then, is to present a static accounting framework for analyzing how rural markets channel the appropriation of agricultural surplus on the Amazon frontier. The next chapter presents a microeconomic analysis of how relative prices influence the behavior and performance of colonists. Each of these two chapters refers to a different level of analysis: the economic environment (market) in this chapter, and the individual farmer's reaction (to the market) in the next chapter. Together they constitute a single model for the generation and appropriation of agricultural surplus on the frontier. The model's empirical implications will be checked against evidence presented in the fourth part of the book.

Market Structure and Appropriation of Agricultural Surplus: General Framework

This section puts forward an accounting framework for analyzing how markets link frontier agriculture to the wider economy. The fundamental idea is very simple. In a market economy, every expenditure by farmers becomes someone else's income, and every income received by farmers is somebody's expenditure. Putting together all of farmers' incomes and expenditures yields the set of transactions that link farmers to the market.

A transaction always involves an exchange: of products for products (nonmonetized transactions) or of products for money (monetized transactions). Transfers involve only one side, that is, something is received without anything being paid "in exchange" or someone is paid without turning over anything else "in exchange." Farmers' incomes and expenditures, then, come not only from transactions, but also from transfers that they make or receive with respect to other economic agents, private or public. The set of farmers' incomes and expenditures determines the division of agricultural surplus among farmers themselves and between them and other participants in the economy.

Farmer's incomes and expenditures can be ordered as in chart 2. Each line refers to one market—for land, labor, inputs, credit, product, land—and registers what colonists earn or pay from/to each agent, whether private ("merchants") or public ("institutions"). The end of each line, on the right side of chart 2, shows the total value of payments made by colonists as transacted in each of these markets—wages, costs of production, interest, agricultural sales, rents, and taxes. The first line refers to the nonmonetized or "subsistence" economy, that is, own-production of consumption goods and of agricultural inputs. It also incorporates all transactions and transfers in kind, generally between colonists, which make up part of a farmer's total expenditure. The next lines refer to transactions for land, credit, labor, agricultural products, and agricultural inputs. An additional line shows the "official economy," where transfers predominate: taxes, tariffs, social assistance (e.g., health), pensions (e.g., FUNRURAL), and other payments and benefits. It is proposed here that different relative proportions of all of these flows help explain the different economic results that colonists attain on the Amazon frontier.

Each column refers to a type of economic agent: farmers, merchants, institutions. Each subcolumn shows what these agents receive from/pay to colonists. What they pay becomes colonists' receipts (W); what they receive becomes colonists' expenditures (E). These subcolumns are not filled in in chart 2 to facilitate exposition. They are used in chapter 16, where this framework serves to analyze farmers' income appropriation in directed colonization projects in the Amazon.

At the foot of the table is the total each type of agent pays to colonists (W). The column "farmers" refers to transactions and transfers among farmers only. These include not only market transactions, but also exchanges in kind, as in the case of sharecropping, crop-lien, labor swaps, or other transactions discussed in the previous chapter. It also includes what farmers consume from their own production, as own-consumption.

Among those called "merchants" are various types of buyers and sellers. Those who sell to farmers deal mainly with manufactured products and services—including transportation, maintenance, warehousing, rents, credit—and correspond to colonists' current costs of production. Those who buy from farmers mainly deal with agricultural products and labor hiring.[4] Among "institutions" are the colonizing entities (private or official), assistance entities (technological, health, social security, education, etc.), public services (land registries, justice, civil and police authorities, etc.), and associations (cults, unions, community organizations, cooperatives, etc.).[5] In directed colonization, one of the most important of these institutions is the colonizing agency or firm; in spontaneous colonization, this kind of agent does not exist. Although the foot of the column is labeled "transfers," the relationships it refers to may be mercantile, as in the case of payments for the purchase of land (to a colonizing firm) or health services (to a private hospital). In practice, the boundary between columns, according to the "public" versus "private" nature of the agent ("merchants" versus "institutions"), is somewhat imprecise.

The right margin of each row sums all expenditures registered in each

Chart 2. General System of Rural Markets

Type of Economy	Agents			Farmers' Total Expenditures (E)
	Farmers	Merchants	Institutions	
Subsistence				Subsistence Production
Market				
Labor				Wages
Goods and services				Commercial margins
Credit				Interest
Land				Rents/installments
Agric. products				Commercial margins
Official				Taxes
Farmers' total income (W)	Barter/ production/ consumption	Sales	Transfers	E = W =

Surplus appropriated by farmers: Y = W – E.
Surplus appropriated by the rest of the frontier economy: E.

market, resulting in farmers' total payments of each type. The foot of each column sums the payments made to each type of agent by farmers. The total at the farthest right column (E) represents total payments made by colonists. The difference between total income (W) and total expenditure (E) is net income (Y = W – E) appropriated by farmers during the observation period—one agricultural year. The income appropriated by other agents (i.e., by the surrounding market system) is E. During any given year, if W > E (Y > O), farmer net income is left over to be subsequently used for increased family consumption or agricultural investment. If W < E (Y < O), farmers become indebted and will eventually have to dissave, increase labor input, or reduce consumption or investment. It is in this sense that the structure of transactions within the frontier economy determines farmer behavior.

The variables E and W do not have exactly the same meaning here as they will in chapter 14. In this chapter, credit transactions are a part of current income and expenditures (E). Thus, the specific impact of indebtedness on surplus appropriation is not brought out at the foot of charts 2–7. The analysis of debt, emphasized in chapter 12, will be delayed until chapter 14. There, credit transactions will be considered separately, so as to focus on the impact of indebtedness on colonization outcomes: labor supply, deforestation, accumulation.

The more distant a frontier, the greater the cost of transportation for all merchandise exchanged by farmers with the rest of the economy. Transportation costs are added to the cost of purchases and deducted from the prices of goods sold by farmers, increasing E, reducing prices, and thereby reducing Y. In this sense, then, frontier distance imposes adverse terms of trade upon colonists, increasing apparent "commercial" margins and compressing farmers' incomes. This process is of extreme importance and will appear again in chapters 15 and 18.

Merchants and institutions gain income from their transactions with farmers through rents, loans, interest, commercial margins, taxes, tariffs, annuities, tithes, and so on. They also spend on farmers in the form of salaries, produce purchases, or assistance. Merchants have costs in the rest of the economy and derive income from the rest of the economy as well. How their incomes and expenditures are divided among the local and the outside markets determines whether the frontier is a net exporter or net importer in relation to the wider economy. This issue will be taken up in chapter 15.

Chart 2 refers to an individual farmer. Summing individual panels for all farmers in a particular location yields a portrait of the market structure that links that group of colonists to the frontier economy. As said before, this involves only the first link in the marketing chain—that which directly involves farmers' transactions, neglecting the rest of the existing chain of commercial intermediation. This framework emphasizes frontier farmers' positions with respect to other local economic agents according to a static accounting approach. All else is held constant: labor input, productivity, product composition, and so forth. The objective here is merely to identify the principal forms of appropriating and channeling surplus from frontier farmers to the rest of the economy. Some numerical examples will facilitate the exposition. Each one illustrates one type of "frontier economy," where farmers, merchants, and institutions interact through a specific set of transactions, within a given market system.

Interlinked Rural Markets: Numerical Examples

Pure Subsistence

Chart 3 illustrates a simple case of "pure subsistence," in which farmers squat on the land and use their own resources and family labor to clear the forest and plant crops. They consume all they produce and only what they produce: PQ = 100 percent, part (80 percent) goes to own-consumption (e.g., food) and part (20 percent) to own-production (e.g., seeds). Net income (Y) is therefore 80 percent of total income. In this case, no value

Chart 3. A Pure Subsistence System (%)

Type of Economy	Agents Farmers	Merchants	Institutions	Farmers' Total Expenditures (E)
Subsistence				Subsistence Production 20
Expenditures				
Market				
Labor				
Goods and services				
Credit				
Land				
Agric. products				
Official				
Farmers' total income (W)	Production =100		W=100	E=20

Surplus appropriated by farmers: Y = W − E = 100 − 20 = 80.
Surplus appropriated by the rest of the frontier economy: 80.

is registered in the market or official economies, since all of the income generated by farmers is in the subsistence economy. There are no transactions with merchants or institutions in the local economy, nor do those agents appropriate anything to transact with the "external" economy.[6] A "pure subsistence" economy does not necessarily imply low or stationary levels of consumption or production; it merely entails the absence of monetized transactions.

Usury-Mercantile Capital

As described in chapter 12, it is common for farmers to have insufficient resources of their own to finance an entire agricultural year—especially during the first year on a frontier during which they must also clear land and establish themselves in addition to producing. They enter the "credit market" in search of advances on consumption goods, pledging their future harvest as payment guarantee ("crop lien"). The creditor in this case tends to be the agent selling consumer goods. By virtue of interlinking credit and product markets, the seller then becomes a "usury-mercantile" operator as well, as shown in chart 4. Income appropriated by farmers will equal the value of production minus

Chart 4. A Usury-Mercantile System (%)

Type of Economy	Agents: Farmers	Agents: Merchants	Agents: Institutions	Farmers' Total Expenditures (E)
Subsistence				
Market				
Labor				
Goods and services				Debt repayment +
Credit				Interest = 60
Land				
Agric. products				
Official				
Farmers' total income (W)		Sales=100	W=100	E=60

Surplus appropriated by farmers: Y = W – E = 100 – 60 = 40.
Surplus appropriated by the rest of the frontier economy: E = 60.
Merchants: 30.
Outside economy: 60 – 30 = 30.

commercial margins on consumption goods and agricultural products and minus the interest corresponding to credit advances extended. Merchants' income will include: (1) profit margins on consumption goods sold to farmers and on agricultural products sold outside, and (2) interest received on advances that were made before the harvest.[7]

As a numerical example, consider that a farmer's production and consumption levels are equal and stable. After settling postharvest accounts, resources cover only half of subsistence needs for the year, as is not uncommon in high-risk frontier areas subject to extreme output fluctuations. Offering 100 percent of future production as a guarantee, the 50 percent needed is obtained in consumption advances during the second half of the year. Let the real annual interest rate be 20 percent; it will take up 10 percent of total production. At harvest time, production is, of course, 100 percent. After paying the 50 percent that was previously loaned for consumption, and 10 percent of total production in interest, farmers begin the next year with 40 percent of their subsistence needs. Since constant and equal levels of production and consumption are assumed, next year 60 percent will be borrowed under the same conditions as the year before, and so on, increasing indebtedness.

Keeping within the same numerical example, merchants' income is as follows. Let the charge be 10 percent on commercial margins on all (production and consumption) goods and the interest rate be the same as before (20 percent). During the first year, merchants get 10 percent of farmers' production in commercial margins on the sale of consumer goods all year long (consumption = production = 100 percent) plus 10 percent of farmers' production in interest on consumer advances (50 percent on credit, at 20 percent a year), plus 10 percent of farmers' production in commercial margins on the resale of the whole harvest to the outside economy. The merchant thereby appropriates 30 percent of the total value of agricultural production during the first year. During the following years, increasing shares are appropriated, and so on.

In chart 4, squatters or landowners appropriate 40 percent of agricultural income and transact with only one type of usury-mercantile agent, who is simultaneously buyer, seller, and creditor. This agent appropriates 30 percent of the value of farmers' product through transactions involving credit, purchase of agricultural output, and the sale of consumption goods. The remaining 30 percent (100 – 40 – 30) is appropriated by the outside economy. As can be seen with even a simple numerical example, such a system of transactions would lead to increasing indebtedness.

In reality, indebtedness would not increase as rapidly as in the idealized case above. Farmers would respond by altering other variables besides indebtedness, such as labor input or productivity, held constant here, to be taken into account only in the next chapter. The objective now is merely to focus on how different market systems influence agricultural income appropriation. Usury-mercantile systems, widespread on the frontier, thus contribute to the indebtedness that is a chronic feature among small frontier farmers, as will be seen in part 4 of this book.

Sharecropping

In the above example, no transactions were introduced involving access to land. A flat purchase implies only one payment, all of it in the first year. Its impact, however, may be prolonged to subsequent years if the farmer borrows to purchase the land. In the case of installment buying, a transaction appears every year during the payment period; in the case of sharecropping or rental, a land-related transaction appears every year, permanently.

Consider examples of sharecropping that are very common on the frontier. In one, the land owning colonist pays for the land and not enough remains to finance production. He then takes on share tenants and charges them with planting and caring for permanent crops (e.g., coffee) during a fixed number of years in return for a share in the proceeds.

During the contract period, tenants also plant temporary crops for own-consumption. That is, the sharecropper indirectly produces his own wage on the land of the landowning colonist, whose working capital is insufficient to finance wage labor directly. When permanent crops mature, the partnership is terminated. The sharecropper leaves the property and moves on with the frontier. The landowning colonist thus obtains the assets he needs—mature permanent crops—as bank loan guarantees for future credit to finance further production.

Another example is when sharecropping involves only temporary crops, in which case it generally has no fixed period of duration. The sharecropper may give half of all production to the landowning colonist, for example. If levels of productivity, commercial margins, and interest rates were similar to those already discussed in chart 4, then the typical half-and-half type of tenancy would be impossible. Repeating the calculation above, with a production level of 100 percent at harvest time, sharecroppers would have to pay not only 10 percent in interest and 50 percent to cover last year's debt, but also the 50 percent share to the landowner. They would then begin the following year with minus 10 percent!

Obviously, no such outcome is reasonable. The market system for sharecroppers cannot be the same as for farmers, landowners, and squatters. Commercial margins and rates of interest should be lower for sharecroppers than for other small farmers, as landowners already have an efficient mechanism for appropriating agricultural surplus, which is sharecropping itself. They thus probably renounce all or part of "market" commercial margins and interest rates that, if added to the payment for land, would make tenancy impossible. Landed property in itself is thus a sufficient mechanism for appropriating agricultural surplus through sharecropping.

On the other hand, interest and commercial margins compose the only appropriation system available to merchants. For this very reason, merchants tend to charge more for their interharvest advances to farmers in general than do landowners to their tenants. Many well-known mechanisms, such as letters of reference to local merchants, warehouses (*barracões*) on the property, and others, serve to reduce costs for sharecroppers relative to those prevailing in the market.[8]

This point is controversial, since there are many different types of sharecropping in Brazil and in some of them such mechanisms (letters of reference, *barracões*, etc.) increase sharecroppers' costs rather than reduce them. Data collected in some parts of the northeastern region of Brazil, however, show clear evidence that landowners do pay higher agricultural product prices and do charge lower interest rates to their sharecroppers than do merchants to squatters and their small landowner clients. This is because relative prices in themselves do not appear to be as important to large landowners as is their claim over sharecropper production via tenancy. This appropriation mechanism gives large landowners the means by which to expand their participation in the agricultural product market when wage labor (and their own direct production) are not possible.

The higher the profit to be had in the product market, vis-à-vis other markets, the more "rational" it will be for landowners to reduce the commercial margins and interest rates they charge to tenants. Rather, they will try to maximize the volume of tenants' agricultural product that they get to market directly. This can be done by increasing the total value of farmer debt to be paid in product. Thus, one would expect more sharecropping where commercial margins in agricultural product markets are highest. This hypothesis is supported by the data, as will be seen in part 4.[9] Chart 5 illustrates a case in which sharecroppers appropriate 50 percent of agricultural income and interact with only one other type of agent: landowners. This latter agent appropriates the other 50 percent of production solely through transactions involving access to land.

Land Purchase

Indebtedness and sharecropping are classic forms of appropriation via usury-mercantile transactions through interlinked rural markets: for credit, agricultural products, consumption goods, and land.[10] But other forms of appropriation are specific to the frontier. One, typical of private colonization, occurs especially in the early years, when the area still lacks a market for agricultural output. The colonizing firm then frequently becomes the main purchaser for colonists' output, setting monopsony prices. Since it is also a monopolist in land sales to colonists, land prices are typically higher than those paid by the colonizing firm to the state. In this case, interlinked land and product prices constitute a corresponding transfer mechanism of agricultural surplus to the colonizing firm. One would then expect lower product prices, higher land prices, and a higher share of colonists' income devoted to land payment in private than in public colonization. This hypothesis is supported by the data presented in part 4.[11]

In chart 6, appropriation of agricultural product is achieved through access to land (in this case, a purchase) from a colonizing firm. It is formally identical to the sharecropping situation portrayed in chart 5. In fact, as will be seen in part 4, it was quite common for colonists in private colonization to pay too much for the land and to then become financially incapable of initiating their own operation. By taking on tenants, they effectively turned over to them the burden of paying for the land.

Another system of appropriation of agricultural surplus in coloniza-

Chart 5. A Sharecropping System (%)

Type of Economy	Agents: Farmers	Agents: Merchants	Agents: Institutions	Farmers' Total Expenditures (E)
Subsistence				
Market				
Labor				
Goods and services				
Credit				
Land				Rent = 50
Agric. products				
Official				
Farmers' total income (W)	Production =100			W=100 E=50

Surplus appropriated by farmers: Y = W – E = 100 – 50 = 50.
Surplus appropriated by the rest of the frontier economy: E = 50.

tion appears throughout the Amazon frontier. Due to the high cost of transportation and the distance between frontier farmers and industrial and consumption centers, the figure of the "trucker" emerges. This is an agent whose services are needed by one and all: merchants, institutions, and colonists. If the region has been opened recently, there is little competition in the area, and the trucker will be able to charge a relatively high rate to colonists who sell their output directly "on the roadside," compared to prices in nearby urban centers.

The less the local physical and commercial infrastructure, and the more distant a frontier from "central" markets, the greater will be the monopsonistic/monopolistic power of local merchants and institutions, whether in providing services (such as freight, processing, financial intermediation, health, insurance, technical assistance, etc.) or in buying and selling (agricultural products, inputs, consumption articles, etc.). The greater the market power of these agents, the greater the degree to which they can appropriate agricultural surplus. Concentrated frontier markets, therefore, increase the vulnerability of farmers to appropriation by other agents.

Diversified Agriculture

As farmers' consumption and technology become more complex, their commercial and institutional transactions also become more varied.

Chart 6. A Land Purchase System (%)

Type of Economy	Agents: Farmers	Merchants	Institutions	Farmers' Total Expenditures (E)
Subsistence				
Market				
Labor				
Goods and services				
Credit				
Land				Installments = 50
Agric. products				
Official				
Farmers' total income (W)	Production =100			E=50 W=100

Surplus appropriated by farmers: Y = W – E = 100 – 50 = 50.
Surplus appropriated by the rest of the frontier economy: E = 50.

Chart 7 presents an example in which farmers sell 100 percent of production in a diversified system where 10 percent is charged on all commercial margins and another 10 percent in interest rates. After selling the entire harvest, they are left with 90 percent to spend. If purchased consumer goods take up 50 percent of the value of production, and the commercial margin on consumer goods is also 10 percent (taking 5 percent of the total value of production), they will be left with 35 percent for inputs and all services (90–55 percent). In the absence of borrowing, this must cover all other current transactions such as interest rates (10 percent), land amortizations (10 percent), taxes (10 percent), and wages (5 percent). Ceteris paribus, reducing merchants' monopsonistic/monopolistic margins would diminish the costs entailed in each type of payment and liberate the corresponding surplus for investment.[12] Conversely, an increase in these margins would force the farmer to forego investment, to reduce the level of operation, and/or to increase indebtedness.[13]

The numerical examples in charts 2–7 are intentionally very simple. No farmer adjustment to relative prices was allowed for, aside from varying surplus appropriation. Analysis of other responses is left for the next chapter. The main point here is: the more distant a frontier and the more concentrated and interlinked its markets, the greater the control local merchants and institutions will have over local prices, the greater

Chart 7. A Diversified System of Rural Markets (%)

Type of Economy	Agents: Farmers	Agents: Merchants	Agents: Institutions	Farmers' Total Expenditures (E)
Subsistence				
Market				
Labor				Wages: 5
Goods and services				Commercial margins: 5
Credit				Interest: 10
Land				Rent/installment: 10
Agric. products				Commercial margins: 10
Official				Taxes: 10
Farmers' total income (W)		Sales=100		E=50 W=100

Surplus appropriated by farmers: Y = W – E = 100 – 50 = 50.
Surplus appropriated by the rest of the frontier economy: E = 50.

the share of farmers' income these other agents will appropriate. If colonization performance is to be evaluated by small farmer income and accumulation levels, then the lower the share of farmer income appropriated by colonists, the less successful colonization will be.

Chapters 15 and, especially, 16 will show evidence of the complex and varied range of real transactions actually observed on the Amazon frontier and the structure of receipts and expenditures of merchants and farmers in both private and official colonization. It will be seen how incomes and investment of small farmers in Amazon colonization projects are affected by their transactions with merchants and institutions linking them to the rest of the economy.

Different transaction structures imply different relative prices and different divisions of income in each location. A low-income frontier may be accumulating very little and simultaneously be an "exporter" of agricultural surplus. An area where there is heavy investment may yield little to the national market for agricultural products, yet be expanding the national market for industrial goods by "importing" inputs and machines. Evaluating colonization requires an understanding not only of colonists' performance but also of how local markets function to channel income flows between the frontier economy and the rest of the economy.

In terms of the two-stage sequence of frontier advance proposed in chapter 12, one may predict that market concentration should be greatest during the initial phase (settlement) of a frontier when land ownership is less concentrated. The subsequent phase (consolidation), however, does not necessarily imply greater competition in rural markets. It is a phase when land ownership becomes more concentrated, and when ties between the local economy and outside markets are strengthened. In the Brazilian economy, where markets are generally so concentrated, stronger ties to the main industrial centers of the Center-South may imply less rather than more competition in a frontier market. Analysis of directed colonization on the Amazon frontier therefore requires understanding how local market systems work.

Determination and Choice in Surplus Appropriation

Social processes, the forces to which they are subject, and the impact of public policies are not perfectly deterministic. A local market establishes relative prices, but farmers respond to these prices individually, by altering the quantity and combination of products offered. In Brazil's case of extreme spatial mobility of the labor force, farmers find ways to escape from an unfavorable market system and to seek other markets that are more beneficial to them.

Such adjustments, however, take time. Information about existing alternatives is limited, moving is expensive, and resources for a new undertaking are few and easily exhausted in each migratory step. In the short run, a farmer's margin of choice in a particular market system is effectively small. After arriving on a frontier, the farmer is in fact immobilized for a few years and subject to a system of surplus appropriation over which he exercises little or no control. In this sense, the market system determines the distribution of agricultural income. It is also in this sense that settlement policies that increase competition in frontier markets could benefit colonization.

This analysis therefore implies that colonization policy must seek to reduce the degree of concentration and interlinking within rural markets by promoting competitive and diversified commercial and institutional infrastructure in frontier areas. Specifically, it must promote markets that do not depress local product prices too far, and that do not excessively increase the price of land for colonists. As will be seen in the following chapters, market disequilibria contribute to indebtedness, speculation, exodus, devastation, and other counterproductive distortions of Amazon colonization.

Undeniably, all colonists do not take advantage of market opportunities in a given location in identical ways. They differ in objectives and ambitions, capacity and competence. They also differ as to the stage each one has attained in the family life cycle; their initial resources, knowledge, and prior experience; the fertility, size, and location of their plots; and in many other ways. The one thing that can be stated about the frontier with certainty is that it displays enormous variety in all its aspects.

The next step in evaluating Amazon colonization, therefore, is to incorporate the issue of individual variation in farming behavior into this chapter's somewhat deterministic analysis of market systems and income appropriation. Chapter 14 will present a model in which variations in farmers' individual reactions to local relative prices explain income, investment, accumulation, indebtedness, labor supply, deforestation, and other aspects of their behavior. Various elements typical of the frontier will be incorporated into the analysis, such as the length of time on a plot, conditions of access to land, and initial resources.

Notes

1. The classic works in this area are Sylos-Labini (1980) and Steindl (1976). See the bibliography in Guimarães (1982).

2. The fundamental works are Löesch (1967) and Cristaller (1966); in Brazil, see IBGE (1979c).

3. In this case, see Musumeci (1987) and the literature cited therein.

4. Chapter 15 will analyze data from a field survey of frontier merchants.

5. Chapters 6–10 analyzed data from a field survey of frontier institutions.

6. See the empirical sense given to the terms "local" and "external" economies in chapter 15.

7. Chapter 12 presented a discussion of the operation of usury-mercantile capital in Brazilian agriculture.

8. See, for example, Ozorio de Almeida (1977a).

9. Chapters 15 and 16 will show that the highest rates of farmer indebtedness occurred where commercial margins were greatest: in the private colonization projects of Mato Grosso.

10. The interlinking of rural markets, whether or not connected to sharecropping, is a common and well-studied phenomenon around the world. See, for example, Thorner and Thorner (1962), Bardhan (1984), Bhalla (1976), Newberry and Stiglitz (1979), Braverman and Srinivasan (1981), Bharadwaij (1974), Ransom and Sutch (1977), and Wharton (1962).

11. Chapters 16 and 18 will show that the highest rate of farmer indebtedness occurred where land prices were highest: in the private colonization projects of Mato Grosso.

12. This appears to be the case of official colonization in Pará, where more highways provided greater access to the market, as will be seen in chapters 15 and 16. Greater commercial competition apparently reduced margins charged by merchants and gave "official" colonists financial respite to invest and accumulate, especially when compared to "private" colonists in Mato Grosso.

13. This is apparently the case of private colonization in Mato Grosso, where

poorer roads and oligopsonistic business practices of southern colonizing firms reduced competition, as will be seen in chapters 15 and 16. High commercial margins, especially in the markets for land and agricultural products, squeezed colonists' initial financial resources and repressed investment and accumulation.

14. COLONISTS' MARKET RESPONSE

This chapter links hypotheses discussed in chapters 12 and 13, about the interactions between farmers and frontier markets, to the empirical evidence to be presented in part 4 of this book. It proposes that in the initial conditions of a frontier (i.e., in the absence of a wage labor market and with an abundant supply of land), farm family labor is a positive function of debt. This labor supply response, known as "debt peonage" in other contexts, provides the basis for indirect management of farm labor by merchants, via the "crop lien" mechanism of usury-mercantile capital.[1] It also shows that debt labor leads to labor-intensive but land-extensive farming and to "excessive" deforestation. Finally, accumulation by colonists is shown to depend on escaping from indebtedness, as well as on other conditions: initial resources brought to the frontier, technology, and favorable market prices.

The next two sections defend the use of microeconomic modeling of labor supply in the case of Amazon colonization and discuss some limitations of this particular effort. The fourth section ("A Microeconomic Model") presents the model and its implications for equilibrium and disequilibrium. The fifth section ("Hypothesis Testing") refers to supporting empirical evidence that will be presented in part 4, and the last section draws some general implications for colonization policy.

The Optimizing Migrant

In moving to the frontier, colonists had to deal with enormous costs—relocation, clearing, planting, isolation, poor health, and other hardships—all in order to attain the goal of a "better life."[2]

Evidently, such migrants were not imprisoned by inflexible traditions and behavior typical of their places of origin. The act of venturing onto the frontier was, in itself, a profound economic and social transformation, requiring courage to break with old customs and adopt innovative methods. They were choosing. The limits and restrictions on their choices were narrow, and the breach left open to them by an elitist and unequal society was small. As seen in part 1, the "closing of the frontier" from "within" and "without" was a reality. Yet those who went to the Amazon refused to become proletarianized, that is, to swell the ranks of the urban underemployed or to become rural migrant laborers.

In migrating and implanting themselves on the frontier, colonists became explicitly aware of their roles. Upon being interviewed, they showed their capacity to calculate income and expenditures and even knew very well how to mask the most relevant information—such as their indebtedness—from the interviewer's curious eyes. They remembered everything they brought with them to the frontier, even if they had come many years before. The decision to migrate had been a deliberate one, even if compelled by expulsion or penury, as was often the case. They knew how much they used of productive inputs and how much these had cost, as well as how much they earned from their own work.

Therefore, the analytical option adopted here is to interpret colonists' behavior in terms of "microeconomic rationality." This may not correspond exactly to what they declared, but it is consistent with observation of their behavior. Such a methodological decision, however, does not necessarily imply acceptance of all other consequences of the theory on which it is based. Individual producers may act to maximize their own income at the same time that they may be dealing with imperfect markets that are not in equilibrium. Allowing for equilibrium at one level—that of individuals' optimizing behavior—does not necessarily imply the acceptance of equilibrium for all other levels. The broad geographic relocations of both farmers and their whole economic environments, shown in parts 1 and 2 of this book, empirically justify a break with the "macro-micro" theoretical link. The interaction between optimizing farmers and markets in disequilibrium can and does occur in Brazilian agriculture in general, and on the Amazon frontier in particular. This chapter, then, deals with producers who seek to maximize their incomes without necessarily attaining this objective, because they are inserted into imperfect and interlinked markets, such as those discussed in the previous two chapters.

Regardless of disequilibria and imperfections in many rural markets, there is ample international literature attesting to the price sensitivity of agricultural producers. That is, a reasonable coexistence between optimizing farmers and concentrated markets is already well documented in the study of agricultural economics.[3] This chapter, therefore, analyzes individual farmers' choices within an economy that is admittedly segmented, heterogeneous, and "lumpy." Income is supposedly generated and appropriated within "pockets" of interconnected markets, such pockets being distributed unevenly through space and among sectors. This perspective is adequate for an economy like the Brazilian one, which is still in spatial formation, expanding over a vast territory as yet unincorporated into the market.

This presentation simplifies farmers' microeconomic behavior. It does not go into the merit of whether small farmers do or do not have a "peasant" logic, supposedly distinct from a "capitalist" one or from "microeconomic" rationality. Nor does it defend why colonists should be maximizing total income rather than some other variable. It does not question, as many do, whether they maximize anything at all, or if they are in some sense tied to conventional behavior rather than to economic calculation.[4] The motivation to migrate to a very distant place rather than to become proletarianized at home is taken to be evidence enough of a deliberate search for autonomy in production decisions. Thus, the model presented here is not a psychological or anthropological interpretation of small farmer motives. It presupposes a "deliberate peasant option," which is definitely distinct from an "unconscious" or "traditional peasant heritage."

The previous chapter proposed that the degree to which particular colonists remain at "subsistence" (i.e., in a nonmonetized economy) and the degree to which they enter the market economy depend upon how they interact with the market system they find on the frontier. The real income level they attain, whether they run a surplus or operate close to biological subsistence, is expected to depend upon relations of exchange, that is, upon the relative prices they encounter.[5]

The main findings are that: (1) family labor supply responds positively to indebtedness and (2) capital accumulation, whether or not it is an initial motive, is greater for those with more initial resources, better technology, and more favorable market systems. By implication, in the absence of a wage labor market during the initial stages of a frontier, merchants can monitor family labor indirectly through usury-mercantile operations. This result is particularly important because it links the hypotheses in chapter 12 to the empirical evidence in part 4 of the book.

Modeling Limitations

The microeconomic model in the next section combines some of the key variables that may influence colonists' behavior. It describes capital accumulation over time, subject to market restrictions and initial resources. As in any model, it represents a simplification of reality and emphasizes only a few characteristics of an agricultural frontier: (1) the discontinuity of beginning frontier agriculture, (2) total time since arrival on the plot, (3) costs of access to land and of settling on virgin soils, (4) costs of physical and social infrastructure, (5) chronic indebtedness, and (6) the fact that the realization of general economic objectives—settling, producing, and accumulating—requires more than one agricultural production period. Several of the model's limitations should be emphasized at the outset.

The complex issue of the impact of institutional, commercial, and physical infrastructure upon colonists' income is reduced to a single variable: "other current costs." This is sufficient, at this stage, for showing the impact of input markets, commercial services, or public services upon colonists' production behavior. The result, in this case, will be inadequate input markets: (1) farmers have to "internalize" the corresponding cost, and (2) this will compress current income and reduce accumulation.

Another simplification is the treatment given to land tenure. In spite of notorious and intricate varieties of sharecropping, renting, and purchase, the impact of tenure upon accumulation will figure in the model as a single item among expenditures: "land costs (aA)." This variable is taken as sufficient to focus on the *initial* cost of land, whatever its contractual arrangement, and on how this initial cost may hinder future performance by: (1) reducing colonists' initial resources for settlement, or (2) engendering current payments, such as rent, shares, or installments, all of which compress current operations, investment, and accumulation.

Various authors have studied the impact of interlinked markets upon small farmers, as occurs in the case of "usury-mercantile" operations that link product and credit markets.[6] Such "earmarked operations" are of fundamental importance for understanding the economic dynamic of the frontier, as was proposed in chapters 12 and 13. Nevertheless, such interlinked operations will not be made explicit here. Transactions are presumed to occur not as dependent reactions, but as simultaneous responses to relative prices. The objective here is to take into account, in the simplest possible fashion, the final impact of these transactions on farmer indebtedness. One can then focus on the role of debt in: (1) deforestation, (2) family labor supply, and (3) accumulation.

Other important issues were omitted. One such omission was the evolution of family labor over the life cycle. This is the basis for a large literature on survival strategies by small farmers, as was discussed in chapter 12. Nevertheless, the topic had to be left out so that emphasis could be placed on production, technology, accumulation, and market transactions. In fact, the findings in chapter 20 will suggest that the frontier experience is so strong as to overwhelm the usual effect of the family life cycle, which occurs in established agriculture. Econometric results in that chapter will even suggest inverse relationships between income and "age of household," and between income and family labor. Both findings contradict several of the expectations held before that field survey was analyzed.

Migrating to a frontier, it seems, imposes abrupt discontinuities on the evolution of a family unit. It is a "catastrophe" that breaks the smooth flow of family reproduction, regardless of its stage prior to arrival on the frontier. It does so as part of a family's general investment in itself. The study of this subject, however, would require more formal sophistication and more space than is available here. It is a theme that simply did not "fit" into the chapter.[7]

The model also omits questions of risk. On a frontier, uncertainty is very great. Information and experience are lacking, and the state intervenes massively with investment, subsidies, advance purchases, pricing and credit policies, and a host of other measures. Income variations, then, are extremely wide, and decisions to produce and to invest must take into account the risks involved. Producers do not maximize an assured income but rather an expected income that is based on a probability distribution. They are not subjected to stable prices and conditions but rather to high risks of loss that they can neither predict nor control.

Risk aversion may, in fact, help explain important aspects of colonists' behavior, to be observed in part 4. The most successful farmers diversified into commerce, while the least successful relied on chronic indebtedness to usury-mercantile capital (chap. 16). Both types of behavior could be interpreted as risk-averse management strategies, analogous to those of farmers around the world. Furthermore, the incredibly high accumulation rates observed among merchants (chap. 15) may also be viewed as a response to high risk on the frontier. The greater the probability of loss, the higher average returns must be in order to attract entrants to a market. On the other hand, merchants receiving high earnings invested in agriculture, with its much lower average return. This apparently irrational behavior may be explained, in part, as "portfolio diversification"—a rational reaction to a high-risk situation. Because of space limitations, however, it was not possible to incorporate issues of risk and imperfect information into the analysis.[8]

Another important omission of the model concerns the utility of working more or less, or of farming versus out-hiring. Previous debts reduce current income; incoming loans increase it. So the relation between debt and labor supply may have subjective "income effects" that are not taken into account here. Nor were possible subjective "substitution effects" taken into consideration. The impact of substitution effects on labor supply, however, has long been expected to be relatively weak at low income levels,[9] whereas the income effect should reinforce the labor supply response hypothesized in this chapter. Nonetheless, the analysis disregards utility and is carried out in terms of production decisions alone.

As usual in this type of model, the colonist is assumed to be passive. Being small in relation to the local economy, such producers should behave as "price takers." But the occupation of the frontier is an active historical event, in which the farmer frequently arrives even before the market. In the case of directed colonization, government or private colonizing firms conduct the process and directly influence market structures. In the case of spontaneous colonization, the local economy is formed without any planning, and market structures change with the number and relative power of incoming members. Since market structure and relative prices are implanted simultaneously with agricultural production, they should not be considered independent of it, as is done here.

These seven omissions—infrastructure, interlinked markets, tenancy, life cycle, risk, utility, and simultaneity—are not the model's only simplifications. Many others were made in order to keep the focus on frontier issues, as will be seen in the next section.

A Microeconomic Model

Indebtedness, Deforestation, and Labor Supply

Items 1–7 refer to current indebtedness and labor supply. Items 8–12 refer to accumulation and diversification.[10]

[1] Land Costs (aA)

In the case of land purchases, payment may be made in full (a_t=0 for t>0) or in installments (a_t>0 for t=0,1,...,n). In the case of renting or sharecropping, a_t>0 for t=0,1, ...,n. In the case of occupation, invasion, or squatting, a_t=0 for t=0,1,...,n. Payment refers to the value of land when it was purchased, independently of later investments (A in hectares; a in U.S. $/hectare).

In general, fixed costs are not part of microeconomic analysis since they "disappear" in the process of maximization. In this case, however, the price and original conditions of access to land may significantly alter colonists' behavior over time. Therefore, land costs are included in the model.

[2] Labor Costs (wL)

The cost of wage labor is its market price; the cost of family labor is its consumption of goods and services—some produced on the farm and others acquired in the market (L in hours worked each year; w in U.S. $/hour).

[3] Other Current Costs (cC)

All other goods and services obtained through market transactions: credit, transportation, warehousing, brokering, repairs, maintenance, agricultural equipment and other inputs, buildings, family consumption goods, other products and services; or those obtained through exchange or institutional or private transfers: financial assistance, technical assistance, health services, education, protection from violence, land registration, construction and maintenance of roads and bridges, and so forth. (C in units; c in U.S. $/unit).

[4] Budget Constraint (E)

Total annual expenditures (E) for labor, other current costs, and land are covered by own funds (pQ) and indebtedness (D). Given the seasonality of agricultural production, expenditures are made during the entire year, but receipts will occur only at the end of the production period. To finance production costs, then, producers must have on hand, at the beginning of each year, enough resources to last until the end of the harvest. If these resources are insufficient (or in excess), indebtedness (or investment) will occur (E in U.S. $).

$E_t = wL_t + cC_t + aA_t$, where t refers to the current agricultural year.

[5] Production (Q)

Agricultural production during one agricultural year is a continuous, twice differentiable function of land, labor, and other inputs.

$Q = Q\,(L,C,A)$; $Q_i>0$; $Q_{ii}<0$; $Q_{ij}>0$
for $i,j = L,C,A$.

For now, all income is assumed to derive from agriculture, whose product is sold (all or in part) at a price p. Nonmarketed output is valued at the same market price, so total income is pQ. Nonagricultural income will be considered in [12] below (Q in kilograms, p in U.S. $/kg.).

[6] Debt Constraint (D)

Incoming receipts from current loans (D_t) supplement current income (pQ_t). Obligations on previous debts ($D_t (i + 1)$, where i is the interest rate) add to current expenditures (E). Net income is defined as gross income (pQ_t) minus current expenditures (E_t) minus net indebtedness ($D = D_t - D_{t-1} (i+1)$):

[6a] $Y = pQ_t - E_t - D = 0$

Assuming there is no investment or dissaving and that net indebtedness is always null (these assumptions will be relaxed in [7c] and [9], below), then:

[6b] $D = D_t - D_{t-1} (i + 1) = 0$ where:
$D_t \geq 0$; $D_{t-1} (i + 1) \geq 0$ and [6c] $Y = 0$.

That is, current income (pQ_t) just covers current expenses (E_t) (Y, D, D_t, and D_{t-1} in U.S. \$, i in %).

[7] Maximization

The farmer's objective is to maximize net income, which is the same as maximizing current gross income (pQ_t) subject to expenditure and debt constraints (E_t + D) during each agricultural year. First order conditions for a maximum are that:

[7a] $pQ_i - p_i - dD/di = 0$

where p_i = w, c, a; and Q_i is the respective marginal product of a factor i; and

[7b] $dD/di = 0$ because of [6b].

In equilibrium, [7a] and [7b] are exactly satisfied. This means that [7a] collapses to the usual condition ($Q_i = p_i/p$), whereby each factor of production (L, C, A) is used up to the point where its marginal productivity is equal to its opportunity cost, that is, its real market price (w/p, c/p, a/p). Each year's current expenditure equals agricultural income, and the level of production varies only with relative prices. Farmers always participate in the market economy solely as purchasers of inputs and sellers of products. In this case, [7] defines a system of four equations with four endogenous variables (L, C, A, Q) and four exogenous ones (w, c, a, p). If second order conditions for a maximum are satisfied, these equations jointly determine demand for labor, inputs, and land (i.e., deforestation in a frontier economy), and supply of agricultural product:

L = L(w,c,a,p)—Labor Demand
C = C(w,c,a,p)—Demand for Inputs
A = A(w,c,a,p)—Demand for Land (deforestation)
Q = Q(w,c,a,p)—Supply of Products.

The system may be estimated by simultaneous least squares using survey data that include the endogenous and exogenous variables specified above, and encompassing a representative agricultural year.

The full econometric estimates for the hypotheses corresponding to equations [7], however, were not done in this book. Only the land demand and product supply equations in [7] were directly submitted to statistical testing in chapter 19, where land productivity (dQ/dA) turned out to be statistically sensitive to relative prices of land and agricultural product (a/p). (See table 56 in chap. 19.)

Given the restrictive assumptions [6b] of no dissaving and no investment, the first order conditions for equilibrium in [7] equate relative prices to relative productivity. When the system is in disequilibrium, [6b] is released. Kuhn-Tucker conditions compose the respective inequalities and make it possible to seek out "slack variables" that tend to move the system back toward equilibrium, even if such a state is never actually established. In this model, indebtedness (D_t, D_{t-1}) and investment (I) are the slack variables that balance the net income constraint. The implications of indebtedness will be discussed first; those of investment will be considered later.

Let [7b] now be an inequality [$D > 0 = D_t > D_{t-1}\ (i + 1)$]. Then own funds are insufficient to cover current expenses (E_t) plus debt repayment [$D_{t-1}\ (i + 1)$], so current debt and net debt must both be positive: $D = D_t - D_{t-1}\ (i + 1) > 0$. This means that [7a] now holds entirely.

Rearranging [7a] then yields:

[7c] $di/dD = 1/(pQ_i - p_i) > 0 \Rightarrow Q_i > p_i/p$.

This means that the response to indebtedness is positive, in terms of labor supply (dL/dD), land area (dA/dD), and other inputs (dC/dD), as long as marginal productivities are greater than respective real costs. In a new frontier: (1) there may yet be no land, labor, or input markets ($p_i = 0$), and (2) only the product market may be operative ($p>0$). The indebtedness response will then be positive as long as marginal productivities are positive ($Q_i > 0$). The initial phases of a frontier, then, should be of labor intensive family farming. This result is demonstrated as follows, in graph 1.

The horizontal axis indicates the quantity of total family labor supply, in hours per year, or in "effective workers" per year (see chap. 17, table 41). The vertical axis indicates the quantity of output. The slope of the ray from the origin indicates the real market wage rate (w/p). Farmers clear as much land (A_1) and work as much (L_1) as necessary to equate marginal productivity (Q_L) to the real wage rate (w/p), producing Q_1 along a production function with initially increasing and then decreasing marginal productivities.

The initial section of the production curve displays increasing marginal productivity of labor, justified by the condition of land abundance. The supply of land, however, comes only from deforestation, as fallow plots are never reused.[11] So [7c] is also an equation for small farmers' "demand for deforestation."

During the initial phase of a frontier, then, farmers work the land up to the point where the marginal product of labor is zero, which is shown in graph 1 by the horizontal tangent to the production curve A_1 at L_2, where $Q_L = 0$. In this sense, then, early frontiers are labor intensive.

The higher the market wage rate (w), and the lower are product prices (p), the more out-hiring and the less family farming there will be. The lower the market wage rate, and the higher are product prices, the more family farming and the less out-hiring. At the limit, when real wages rise above $(w/p)_1$, where $Q_L = Q/L$ (see graph 1), there is no family farming.

In the case of previous indebtedness ($D_{t-1} > 0$), requirements for repayment in kind demand that more than Q_1 be produced. Additional labor (L_2) on A_1, however, would reduce marginal productivity to zero, which contradicts condition [7c] whenever $w/p > 0$. More land is therefore deforested, adding A_2 to previous productive land and expanding production along a new production curve, Q_2. In order to appropriate a given level of income (pQ_1), then, farm families must work more and clear more land than before becoming indebted. The higher the volume of prior debt (D_{t-1}) or the higher the interest rate (i), the greater the impact of previous debt on deforestation and labor supply.

In case the farmer cannot reach Q_2, current indebtedness ($D_t > 0$) will act as an income supplement, as shown in graph 2. This reduces the reservation wage from $(w/p)_1$ to $(w/p)_3$ and increases labor intensity on each plot of land. That is, family farming persists even at marginal productivities below the real market wage rate.

Equation [7c] is of particular interest, as it refers to the labor supply response to indebtedness. This relationship is fundamental to the operation of usury-mercantile capital. Although this relationship was not tested statistically, it was supported indirectly by field data. Chapters 16 and 19 will show that those who were most deeply caught in consumer indebtedness (table 38) were those who farmed their plots

Graph 1. Debt Repayment, Deforestation, and Labor Supply

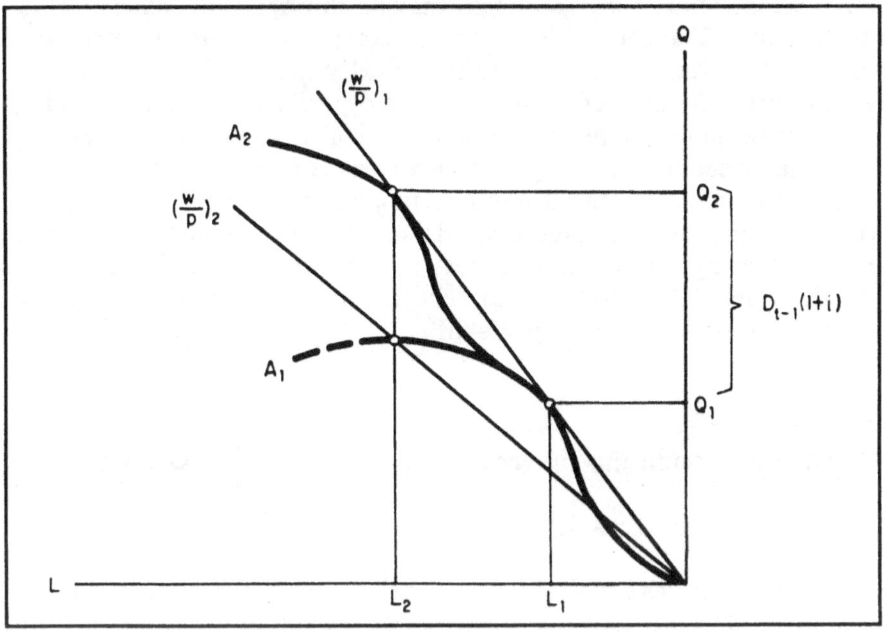

Graph 2. Current Indebtedness and Labor Supply

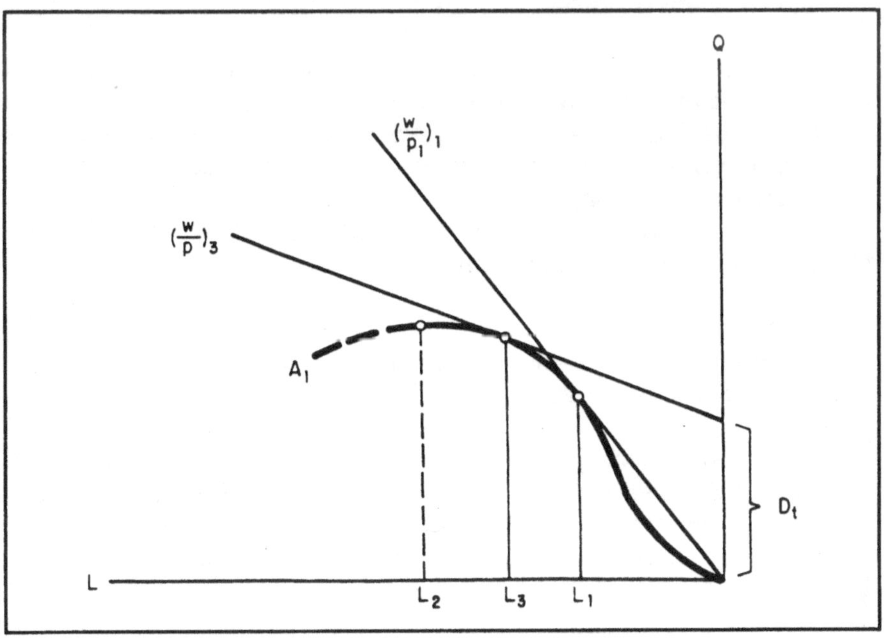

most land extensively (table 59), clearing and abandoning their plots in succession. Thus, "debt-peonage" may be an important cause of itinerant farming. The general issue of itinerancy, whose broad causes were reviewed in chapter 12, is found empirically to be highly significant in explaining colonists' performance—see especially chapters 20 and 21. The family labor supply response to debt also yielded significant and interesting econometric results when tested on another data set.[12]

In sum, under the stated assumptions, recurrent indebtedness ($D_{t-1} > 0$; $D_t > 0$) increases deforestation, labor supply, and labor intensity in family farming. Although the model, for simplicity of exposition, lumps previous debt (D_{t-1}) and current debt (D_t) together into D in [6], graphs 1 and 2 show that their impacts differ.

Accumulation

Some of the conditions for accumulation can now be examined.

[8] Initial Resources (R)

Initial resources consist of money, other financial assets, equipment, and other durable goods, plus stocks of consumer goods, inputs, and agricultural products originally brought to the plot (R in U.S. $).

[9] Investment (I)

Investment consists of clearing the forest, removing tree stumps, preparing the land, establishing pasture and permanent crops, building, acquiring durable goods and equipment, expanding stocks and herds, increasing physical or financial assets, and reducing debts (I in U.S. $).

Investment (or dissaving) occurs when own funds (pQ_t) more (less) than cover current expenses (E_t) and/or current indebtedness (D_t) more (less) than covers debt repayment [D_{t-1} (i + 1)]:

$$I \begin{cases} > 0 - \text{investment} \\ = PQ_t - E_t - D = 0 - \text{no investment or dissaving} \\ < 0 - \text{dissaving or increased indebtedness.} \end{cases}$$

Since most of frontier investment is limited to deforestation,[13] the demand for land (deforestation) in equation [7c] could also be considered an equation representing the demand for investment. This would transform investment into an endogenous variable, a function of market prices (P_i) and technology (Q_i).

[10] Settlement

In the year of settlement (t=0), expenditures (E_o) are met by initial resources (R) and may or may not cover the cost of initial investment ($I_o \geq R$) required for setting up a farm. So indebtedness may or may not occur from the beginning ($D_o \geq 0$). Access to land may occur through squatting (a=0) or some form of payment (a > 0). To facilitate the presentation, it will be assumed that all initial resources were spent in the first year of settlement. Therefore, no financial assets will be available for financing agricultural activities in later years:

$$D_o = R - (wL_o + cC_o + aA_o + I_o).$$

[11] Wealth (K)[14]

Wealth includes stocks of land, buildings, durable goods, herds, products, inputs, and financial assets at the end of a given agricultural year. The net worth recorded at the end of any year is the net worth from the previous year plus the value resulting from investment made during the current year (K in U.S. $).[15]

[11a] $K_t = K_{t-1} + I_t$

[11b] $R\,(r + 1)^n + \sum_{t=0}^{n} I_t\,(r + 1)^{n-t}$

where n is time elapsed since arrival, and r is the rate of return.

The rate "r" combines technical and financial components. For instance, deforestation increases the market value of land on two counts. First, it prepares land for production, the price of deforested areas being typically at least twice that of forested areas. Second, there is a capital gain component resulting from the general appreciation of real estate in frontier regions. This book does not differentiate between these two components, though later work shows each of them to be of substantial importancc.[16]

A farmer's wealth at any given moment depends on initial assets, time, and the annual volume of investment. Investment, in its turn, depends on prices (p_i) and technology (Q_i), as in [7c], and on there being current surpluses, as in [9]. Thus, market prices influence investment and accumulation on two counts: directly, via the indebtedness response; indirectly, by expanding or compressing the available surplus.

The level of accumulated wealth is therefore not considered an objective to be maximized in itself. It results from annual income maximization subject to budget and indebtedness constraints. The more favorable the market system, and the smaller the yearly indebtedness, the greater should be the rate of accumulation over time.

[12] Diversification

The case in which farmers invest all of their surplus in their own agricultural production is an exceptional one. It requires total coincidence between relative prices in the market and relative productivities. Given factor indivisibility, lack of knowledge about alternative technologies, limitations of initial resources, restrictive conditions of access to land, and other constraints, farmers rarely allocate resources in agricultural production so as to equalize marginal productivity to respective opportunity costs, as implied by system [7]. For this reason, they will frequently operate not only as farmers, but also as producers of nonagricultural goods and services demanded by local markets.

A farm family's income will diversify as farmers invest their surplus: becoming processors, opening a store, employing outside workers on their land, investing in durable goods or in stocks of inputs and products, making financial applications, or making contributions or transfers to others. If instead of surpluses farmers have deficits, then they compensate for their low incomes by borrowing, receiving transfers (whether private or official), hiring out family labor, renting part of the land to others, selling durables, or reducing stocks and other assets. In both cases—whether they have surpluses or deficits—farmers may eventually cease agricultural activity on their own plots altogether, becoming "100 percent" merchants or wage laborers, depending on existing relative prices and their responses.

A farm family's total income, then, has two components, one agricultural and the other nonagricultural. Maximization of total (agricultural and nonagricultural) income (W) proceeds as indicated in [7] above. Due to space limitations this extension is not presented here.

Hypothesis Testing and Policy Implications

A frontier includes a wide range of behaviors. The same set of relative prices are compatible with innumerable different individual outcomes, depending on other local conditions (e.g., type of colonization, soil fertility, technical assistance and health services); conditions from the place of origin (e.g., prior experience, previous migration, initial resources, region of origin); and a large number of variables that represent the influence of individual variations upon colonists' behavior (e.g., age, family size and composition, education, schooling, health). A large set of variables is needed to explain individual variation in responding to similar relative prices.

Specifying all such influences on colonists' performance in a stochastic model will not be carried out in this chapter. In general, farmer responses to prices and other economic and social stimuli are tested throughout part 4 against data from a field survey conducted in Amazon colonization projects in 1981–1982. Chapter 20, in particular, performs econometric estimations that statistically separate the influence of the local economic environment on the frontier from the influences of origin and of individual characteristics. The following list summarizes these findings:

(1) Labor Market

Productivity is found to be high enough for income per family worker to be well above the existing local minimum wage (chap. 17). This leads to relatively little labor market participation (both in-hiring and out-hiring). Wage income accounts for a mere 2 percent of total current income (chap. 16, table 38). This is consistent with implication [7a] that high agricultural productivity should lead to little out-hiring.[17]

(2) Input Market

Given several empirical difficulties, to be discussed in chapter 18 in the section on "Input Costs," implications regarding inputs could not be tested directly. The provision of technical and health services, however, was found to significantly improve current income and investment (chap. 20, tables 60–61).

(3) Land Market

Expensive land (as in private colonization) resulted in high productivity and land-intensive technologies. Cheap land (as in official colonization) resulted in low productivity land-extensive techniques, and itinerancy within colonization projects themselves. Hence, as predicted in [7c], the relative price of land was statistically significant in determining colonists' technology and degree of permanence (chap. 19, table 56).

(4) Product Market

The most unfavorable product market was in private colonization; the most favorable occurred in official colonization (chap.18). Colonists receiving the best prices (chap.18) were those with highest incomes (chap.16, tables 36 and 37).

(5) Financial Market

All colonists were heavily indebted, given that income from loans received was systematically higher than the value of current agricultural and nonagricultural income (chap.16, table 39). Farmers did not borrow because interest rates were low. Rather, colonizing firms charged such high prices for land (in the case of private colonization) and merchants charged such high prices for essential consumer goods (in the case of official colonization), that farmers' incomes were "squeezed" and they were led to incur debt, as current income became insufficient to cover current expenditures. Tied transactions, which linked credit to other markets (as discussed in chaps.12 and 13), were more important in determining colonists' performance than the operation of the formal financial market itself. In public colonization, consumer borrowing was associated with "excessive" deforestation (chap.19, table 55) as in graph 1. In private colonization, land-related borrowing was associated with "excessive" labor intensity (chap. 20, table 60), as in graph 2. As predicted in [11], the largest investors (chap.16, table 38) and those with the highest rates of accumulation (chap.17, table 41) were those with the highest rates of return.[18]

(6) Nonagricultural Activities

In general, there was low participation in nonagricultural activities (chap.16, table 37), but these activities were highly correlated with the highest incomes (chap. 20, table 60).[19]

The set of findings (1) to (6) refers to colonists' market responses in regions to which they migrated, that is, in colonization projects. To the degree that colonists are sensitive to local conditions and relative prices, government policy will have a greater margin for influencing their performance. The evidence presented in the next part of the book, and summarized in this section, shows that there was substantial farmer price responsiveness. The implications of this responsiveness for future colonization policies are discussed in the following concluding section.

Markets, Accumulation, and Colonization Policy

This chapter proposed that current income, labor supply, and deforestation are a function of relative prices and indebtedness. These conditions plus individual and origin characteristics, then, determine colonists' investment and prospects for accumulation, both within and outside agriculture.

The main policy implication of the model is that colonization should entail more than measures aimed merely at physical, institutional, and legal settlement (e.g., land, roads, titles). It must also include measures aimed at forming a market structure consistent with agricultural production and income appropriation by colonists. If this is not done, disequilibria in relative prices may provoke perverse and unexpected effects, such as diversion of labor, proletarianization, abandonment of plots, speculation, and other equally pernicious behavior already well-known on the frontier. These reactions, which represent "microeconomically rational" behavior under local market disequilibria, can lead to the failure of colonization as a whole.

The problem with Amazon colonization during the 1970s, however, was that basic trade-offs were disregarded. As shown in the following chapters, official colonization provided both cheap land and favorable commercial infrastructure, making it possible for many colonists to rapidly accumulate assets. In private colonization, though, land was expensive and commercial infrastructure was less favorable to farmers, thereby hindering accumulation.

Unfavorable results from the 1970s, however, do not imply the necessary failure of colonization in the future, if implemented in other ways. Colonists' market sensitivity, hypothesized in this chapter and empirically tested in part 4, means that proper colonization policies with attention to relative prices may permit much better performance for Amazon colonization in the future.

Before turning to colonists' performance, however, it is necessary to conclude the analysis of market influences on the frontier by presenting empirical evidence on merchants' behavior in colonization projects, as will be done in the next chapter.

Notes

1. See chapter 12 for a discussion on the "crop-lien" mechanism of usury-mercantile capital in the initial phases of a frontier.

2. According to Ferreira (1984) and M. Morais (1988), the principal motivation for colonists to migrate to the frontier is "to improve their standard of living (*melhorar de vida*).

3. See, for example, Paiva (1979), Delfim Neto (1965), and Pastore (1973) on the Brazilian case; for other countries, Behrman (1968), Falcon (1964), Jorgenson and Lau (1969), Massel (1967), Nakajima (1969), and others cited in Yotopoulos and Nugent (1976).

4. See references in notes 15 and 16 of chapter 12, and the discussion in this

regard in chapters 17–19.

5. This is not an argument of "unequal exchange." Instead, it recognizes that small farmers' subsistence is not a choice, but rather a result of their insertion into the market. See, in this regard, Janvry and Deere (1978).

6. See, for example, Newberry (1976, 1979a, 1979b), Braverman (1981), Braverman and Srinivasan (1981), and Braverman and Stiglitz (1981).

7. In the first proposal for this study (see Ozorio de Almeida, *Migrações internas. . .*, vol. 1), the theoretical model included not only production decisions but also the reproduction of the agricultural family unit. The empirical field data were subsequently collected for testing hypotheses generated by that model. However, they were never processed, and the corresponding theme was left out of the current text. For this reason, it was necessary to remove from the analysis issues of fertility, family exodus, hiring in and out, health, nutrition, education, and other aspects of "economic-demographic" management of family labor, whose study was originally planned. As the data are available, others may, one hopes, become interested in analyzing them, recreating the more broadly conceived original project.

8. Among the classic texts in this literature, see Telser (1958), Stein (1961), Ederington (1979), and, for Brazil, Melo (1983).

9. "If the additional worker phenomenon is viewed as an alternative to dissaving, asset decumulation or increasing debt in the attempts of families to maintain consumption in the face of declining income, such behavior is most likely to appear in families at low levels of wealth" (Mincer 1962, p. 75). See also Mincer and Cain (1969). For the case of rural labor supply, see references in note 3, above.

10. The symbols used in this theoretical model are the same as those used in chapter 13, though they are not used in presenting the empirical results in part 4.

11. See chapter 19 for empirical support for this statement.

12. Ozorio de Almeida (1977a).

13. See chapter 20 for empirical support for this statement.

14. Total "wealth" in this model is equivalent to "assets" in chapters 15, 17, 20, and 21.

15. This equation is tested in table 62 of chapter 21, which supports the hypothesis that initial resources are extremely important to colonists' accumulation on the frontier.

16. Ozorio de Almeida et al. (1990).

17. As will be seen in part 4, low productivity (chap.19) was associated with a high rate of out-hiring of wage labor (chap.16, table 37). See "other migrants in official colonization" in table 37.

18. Relatively high rates of accumulation (chap.17, table 42 and chap. 21, graph 5: see "Southerners in official colonization") were associated with greater investment (chap.16, table 38, and chap. 21, graph 4: see "Southerners in official colonization").

19. Finally, "southerners in official colonization" employed their greater agricultural surplus in nonagricultural activities more than others, thereby diversifying their activities (chap. 16).

15. FRONTIER MERCHANTS

According to the analysis developed in chapters 13 and 14, colonists' performance on the frontier depends largely upon their economic environment. This chapter completes the analysis of part 3 on how economic environments evolved on the frontier, along with colonization.

Colonists perceive their economic environment as a system of markets. Relative prices stimulate more or less production or speculation, accumulation or indebtedness, proletarianization or self-employment, monetization or subsistence, and so on. These prices are established by transactions between colonists and institutions, already discussed in part 2 of this book, and merchants, to be studied in this chapter.

Frontier merchants are the agents of Brazilian industry's expanding market. Although industry is spatially concentrated in the South-Southeast, its influence has expanded to the most remote points of the nation through the marketing of manufactured goods and inputs. This influence is changing over time, depending on the evolution of transactions between agriculture and the rest of the economy. Since the role of merchants in the rapid urbanization of the frontier has been neglected in the literature, this analysis of frontier merchants sheds light not only on rural aspects of the frontier, but also on urban ones.[1]

The theory of the firm and its market behavior is useful for studying merchants. It shows that the actions of each unit of production depend upon the degree of concentration in the market as a whole. Firms behave competitively in fragmented markets with easy entry; they adopt oligopolistic practices—such as mark-up pricing agreements, price leadership, collusion, and so on—in concentrated markets with barriers to entry.[2] It is thus possible to extract conclusions about an entire sector from observations on the behavior of only a few of its establishments. In particular, the margin practiced by each agent, then, is indicative of the degree of concentration in that agent's respective market: high margins (percentage of prices over costs) for some firms are indicative of a relatively concentrated market, while low margins imply a relatively competitive market. One cannot, with partial data, measure the total volume of commercial profit in a region, but one can deduce that certain markets are more profitable than others; that certain merchants take their profits from the local economy, while others take theirs from outside; that some markets are more concentrated than others, and so on.

This chapter is not theoretical, as are the other chapters in part 3. Its goal is to present findings based on a survey of merchants on the Amazon frontier of Pará and Mato Grosso. The project that generated the data, the theoretical issues that motivated the research, the empirical methods utilized, and the general findings are all presented in appendixes 1–3 of *Colonização dirigida na Amazônia*.[3] The present chapter is limited to describing field survey data on merchants and to analyzing their most immediate implications for colonization in the Amazon.

Since the sample was very small (only one-tenth as many merchants as colonists were interviewed in the field), these results should be considered merely exploratory. They remain interesting, nevertheless, due to the support they lend to hypotheses presented in chapters 12 and 13.

The next section classifies merchants according to how they mediate relations between frontier farmers and the rest of the economy. The third section measures profitability by different kinds of merchants. The fourth section measures rates of accumulation and reveals a strategy of agricultural diversification among merchants. The final section makes some comments on merchants as intermediaries between industry and agriculture during frontier expansion.

Types of Merchants

According to the model of market systems presented in chapter 13, many establishments operate local-external intermediation simultaneously in various markets—product, land, credit, and labor markets—and appropriate agricultural income in several combinations—commercial margins, rents, interest, and so on. It was not possible, then, to classify establishments strictly by the type of market they participate in, that is, by the kind of income they appropriate. This mobility between different markets is interesting in itself. The social identity of merchants seems to be determined less by the products they intermediate than by relations of clientelism and patronage that they establish with their clients and suppliers.[4] These relations often reproduce organizations typical of their regions of origin, though some variants reflect specific frontier conditions. This section classifies the surveyed merchants into five basic types, covering the principal combinations of local-external intermediation.

Frontier merchants establish a network of relationships with local farmers and outside clients and suppliers. Depending on their function in the marketing chain: they bring money into the area and take products away; or they bring merchandise and take money away; or they circulate money and merchandise only locally; or, finally, they combine different forms of intermediation in the same business.

Type A: Local Suppliers and External Clients

This type includes purchasers of agricultural and extracted products, sawmill operators and processors who resell externally.

The agricultural product market predominates among this type of merchant. It comprises truckers from outside—who appear only at harvest time to negotiate and haul away products—and small, medium, and large local establishments. The "classic" contingent of "usury-mercantile" capital is also part of this group, as described above.[5] At a given moment, however, there are various ways of operating as a merchant of Type A—that is, with local suppliers and outside clients. In addition to the usury-mercantile contingent already mentioned, there are also "simple" purchasers and processors who receive merchandise and pay money locally, and then redeliver merchandise and receive money from outside.

Type B: Outside Suppliers and Local Clients

These include bars, pool houses (*sinucas*), warehouses, pharmacies, grocery stores, clothing and shoe stores, odds and ends stores (*armarinhos*), agricultural equipment and input stores, stores for mechanical components and parts, and banks.

This type of merchant deals largely with manufactured goods and formal credit. Colonists' families who live in extreme isolation pay not only for products, but also for the relief from the loneliness of agricultural frontier living. Suppliers of consumer goods are often their principal social contact with the outside world. Input sellers are the principal means of technological improvement for farmers. Representatives from southern factories[6] regularly visit commercial establishments, no matter how small or remote, settling bills, updating stocks, and introducing novelties. Much more than formal rural extension agents, they constitute the main innovating influence upon small farmer technology.[7]

The supplier of consumer goods often advances merchandise between harvests, and awaits payment until after the harvest. When paid in kind, these merchants enter into the agricultural product market and become "usury-mercantile" operators similar to those described in Type A. The boundaries between these two types are tenuous, and classification into one or the other category depends on whether suppliers are predominantly local (Type A) or from the outside (Type B). When neither predominates, the merchant is classified as Type E (i.e., "mixed"), as defined below.

Purchases of manufactured inputs are often linked to credit transactions and may be tied to purchasing only specific products in extremely concentrated markets. As with classic "usury-mercantile" capital, the price charged for the good, or the rate of interest in the accompanying credit transaction, may become almost irrelevant to the farmers' purchasing decision. The main issue is absolute availability. Although the agents involved are "formal," their transactions become "informal" due to frontier conditions for market interlinking.

Type C: Local Suppliers and Local Clients

Included here are doctors, dentists, hotels, taverns, brothels, small local stores (*biroscas*), repair shops, others providing services, and processors who resell locally.

This type of merchant provides local services, although frequently using parts and components from outside. This group depends totally upon the local economy and tends to grow along with its level of economic activity and urbanization. When farmer-clients pay on account or in kind, the merchant enters the agricultural product market and may also become a "usury-mercantile" operator as in Types A and B. For lack of their own external clients, they often resell agricultural products to other local merchants.

Type D: External Suppliers and External Clients

This category is for roadside establishments.

This type includes enterprises that serve travelers at bus and truck stops. Although they depend on the external economy, many begin to provide services and to transact with local farmers, entering the markets for agricultural and industrial products. It is not uncommon for them to also adopt usury-mercantile practices typical of frontier commerce.

In areas near prospecting or large-scale projects (hydroelectric, mining, agro-industrial, and others), Type C can become Type D merchants. That is, the presence of a "foreign," more monetized clientele transforms a local operator into an external one.

For example, in Alta Floresta, in Mato Grosso, a large commercial infrastructure was implanted prematurely in relation to the growth of local agriculture. While farmers lacked income to activate the local mercantile capacity, commerce was sustained by gold prospecting. Because prospecting competes with agriculture for local labor, the colonizing firm expelled prospectors at gunpoint. Clearly, however, the prospectors had been useful in providing early demand for local urban infrastructure, which subsequently become beneficial to colonists. Prospectors have remained important for commerce in Alta Floresta ever since.[8]

Type E: Mixed Suppliers and Clients

This group includes combinations of all the above.

This type occurs more frequently in the initial phases of a frontier, when merchants deal with a little bit of everything. Some continue to operate in this way even after the frontier's consolidation.

This classification, according to local or external clients and suppliers, is summarized in chart 8. It permits an analysis of frontier merchants according to their insertion in the chains of intermediation that stretch from distant industrial centers all the way to the Amazon frontier. Although more than one hundred merchants were interviewed, inexperience led to inconsistencies, omissions, and the loss of many questionnaires, especially for Types D and E. For example, truck drivers were very difficult to contact, especially those who appear only at harvest time, and are clearly underrepresented. Those who were surveyed appeared more often in official than in private colonization projects, which reflects Pará's better road network, as already noted in chapter 7.

If all merchants were to operate in "pure" form, they would appropriate local agricultural income through their respective defining market transactions: Type A merchants (local-external) through commercial margins over the agricultural products they buy; Type B (external-local) through commercial margins over the industrial products they sell; Types C and E (local-local, and mixed) through commercial margins over local purchases and sales. Type D merchants (external-external) do not appropriate local agricultural income. To the extent that any of them enter into usury-mercantile transactions, they would also appropriate the corresponding interest.

Chart 8. Merchant Types

Type	*Suppliers*	*Clients*
A	Local	External
B	External	Local
C	Local	Local
D	External	External
E	Mixed	Mixed

In addition to the five types listed above, A through E, merchants were classified by origin: "southerners" (i.e., coming from Rio Grande do Sul, Santa Catarina, Paraná, and São Paulo) and "others." This distinction is due to expectations that southern merchants should differ from others in bringing to the frontier more knowledge and resources from their prior residence—the richest part of the country—than other merchants from poorer regions. Superior initial resources might then give southerners an advantage over others, in terms of their economic performance on the frontier. Part 4 of this book will test this hypothesis with reference to colonists. In the meeting of the classical "two Brazils" in the Amazon, the expectation was that those coming from the richer Brazil would fare better.

Finally, the last criterion by which merchants were classified refers to the type of colonization where they operate: official or private. Given the sample's composition, for reasons discussed in appendix 1 of *Colonização dirigida na Amazônia*, private colonization was surveyed only in Mato Grosso and official colonization only in Pará. It is interesting that private colonization is not only dominated by southern farmers, as will be seen in part 4, but that apparently these farmers also bring with them their merchants from the South.[9]

Private colonizers effectively planned the commercial sector of their projects. In official colonization, however, despite the best initial intentions and the *agrovilas*, the commercial sector was basically spontaneous.[10] The fact that the sample contained only southern merchants in Mato Grosso's private colonization is therefore significant.[11] The merchants who migrated to the western frontier probably arrived already inserted into chains of commercial intermediation, with clients and or suppliers from the South. That is, they pertained to the "central" sphere of the Brazilian economy, representing it and expanding it into the frontier.[12] This supposition is supported by data on profits presented below.

Profitability and Business Volume

Table 29 shows that the average current rate of profit,[13] or commercial "margin," was much higher in Mato Grosso than in Pará. Perhaps, as was seen in chapter 11, this is because the Mato Grosso merchants were within the sphere of influence of São Paulo, while those in Pará were within the influence of Belém—a much weaker center. The very small sample, however, makes statistical tests of these differences unfeasible, and the observed divergence is merely indicative of possibly more general differences.

Table 29 also shows that those who sell to the local population (Type B) were, on average, more profitable in Pará, while in Mato Grosso the most profitable were the purchasers of local produce (Type A). The completely local commerce of Pará had the lowest profit rates of all, while in Mato Grosso, the local economy sustained a much more profitable commerce. This is partly due to higher average incomes among Mato Grosso colonists and to their more highly monetized economy than that of Pará.[14] However, since farmers in Pará were also older and more diversified in their activities than those of Mato Grosso, their participation in nonagricultural activities was also greater.[15] Thus, they entered into competition in the commercial sphere, which must have reduced margins at the local level. Roadside commerce (Type D) had one case of extremely high profitability along the Transamazon Highway, but this type was not recorded at all in Mato Grosso.

Average Annual Receipts and Expenditures by Types of Merchants

Table 30 shows the average volume of operation for different types of merchants. In Pará, buyers (Type A) tended to have the lowest volume, while sellers (Type B) had the highest, with the exception of roadside merchants (Type D). In Mato Grosso the ranking is reversed. The most profitable types in table 29 also had the highest volume in each location. The significance of this difference between merchants will become clear below.

Comparing merchants and farmers is possible by contrasting the receipts and expenditure of table 30 with those of table 38 in the next chapter. On average, merchants operated with almost four times the amount of receipts ($42,000 vs. $11,000) and almost three times more in expenditures ($28,000 vs. $9,800) than colonists. That is, not only was the relationship between receipts and expenditures more favorable to commerce, but merchants' average turnover was three to four times greater than that of farmers.

Origin-destination comparisons between merchants and farmers are even more interesting. In official colonization, receipts and expenditures for southern merchants were only 50 percent greater than for southern farmers, a difference that is not statistically significant at the 10 percent level. Among the nonsoutherners, still within official colonization, merchants' receipts exceeded those of farmers by 11.7 times and expenditures by 6.5, both significant at the 10 percent level. In private colonization, however, the difference between merchants and farmers among southerners was 8.6 times for receipts and 5.4 times for expenditures, also statistically significant at the 10 percent level. That is, agricultural and nonagricultural business were not very different for southerners in official colonization. Nevertheless, the receipts of farmers and merchants were significantly different for the other groups, at least in a statistical sense. This result is important for interpreting the behavior of these groups, as will be discussed below.

Local and External Balances by Merchant Types

Table 31 disaggregates the data from the last two columns ("Total") of table 30 to make explicit the relation of each kind of merchant to the local and external economies. As described in chart 8, Type A merchants have expenditures in transactions with local agents and receive income from external agents, while those of Type B have the opposite situation: their receipts are local and their expenditures are external. For Type C, receipts and expenditures are with local agents; for Type D, both are with external agents; and in Type E, the agents are mixed, as would be expected from the classification criteria.

The average "balance" or "profit" volume for each type of merchant with respect to the *local* economy is in column 3 of table 31; the average balance for each type with the *external* economy is in column 6. The "total" line for each state refers to that part of average current profit volume that comes from local transactions and that part that comes from external transactions. Column 7 indicates current average profit volume for each merchant type and the overall average balance or profit volume.[16]

In Pará's overall average, merchant profits were realized on the frontier itself, especially through selling to colonists (Type B). Out of a total average profit of $76,026 (in col. 7), a share of 70 percent, or $53,895 (col. 3), came from the local economy and only 30 percent, $22,131 (col. 6), from outside.

In Mato Grosso, the opposite was observed. The local economy was practically balanced, and merchants' profits were realized externally, especially through the sale of agricultural products to the outside

Table 29. Number of Merchants by Type and Annual Current Average Profit Rates

Origin/ Destination	*Type*	*Southerners* Number (1)	Profitability (%) (2)	*Others* Number (3)	Profitability (%) (4)	*All* Number (5)	Profitability (%) (6)
	A	2	39.2	3	38.5	4	38.9
Public	B	2	30.5	7	76.6	10	72.3
colonization	C	1	28.2	2	7.4	3	5.3
in Pará	D	1	28.6	1	190.5	2	162.9
	E	—	—	2	47.2	2	14.7
TOTAL		6	30.8	15	52.0	21	50.9
	A	3	100.5				
Private	B	12	57.6				
colonization	C	5	80.4				
in Mato Grosso	D	—	—				
	E	—	—				
TOTAL		20	74.8				
	A	5	99.3			7	98.1
	B	14	56.1			22	63.3
Total	C	6	70.8			9	51.3
	D	1	28.6			1	66.1
	E	—	—			2	47.2
TOTAL		26	71.6			41	60.6

Source: Field survey.
Note: Types of merchants are described in chart 8.
Current Profit Rate = ([Receipts – Expenditures]/Receipts) x 100.

Table 30. Average Annual Receipts and Expenditures by Type of Merchant (U.S. $)

Origin/ Destination	*Type*	*Southerners* Receipts (1)	Expenditures (2)	*Others* Receipts (3)	Expenditures (4)	*All* Receipts (5)	Expenditures (6)
	A	10,233	7,346	5,691	4,108	7,398	5,329
Public	B	24,708	18,934	108,743	61,583	87,729	50,926
colonization	C	20,673	16,120	13,533	14,609	15,913	15,106
in Pará	D	43,911	34,144	483,538	166,342	263,580	100,248
	E	—	—	21,159	14,371	21,624	14,371
TOTAL		23,611	18,107	65,825	33,161	56,441	29,819
	A	348,681	173,854				
Private	B	105,235	66,787				
colonization	C	25,846	14,320				
in Mato Grosso	D	—	—				
	E	—	—				
TOTAL		121,904	69,726				
	A	213,801.8	107,250			153,658	78,148
	B	93,931	59,950			97,279	59,576
Total	C	24,983	17,624			19,659	12,995
	D	43,911	34,144			263,580	100,248
	E	—	—			21,159	14,371
TOTAL		98,944	58,286			42,318	28,743

Source: Field survey.
Note: Types of merchants are described in chart 8.

Table 31. Current Annual Balance, Local and External, by Type of Merchant (U.S. $)

Destination	Type	Local Economy Receipts (1)	Local Economy Expenditures (2)	Local Economy Balance (3)	External Economy Receipts (4)	External Economy Expenditures (5)	External Economy Balance (6)	Total Balance (7)
	A	—	5,329	-5,329	7,398	—	7,398	2,069
Public	B	87,729	—	87,729	—	50,926	-50,926	36,803
colonization	C	15,913	15,106	807	—	—	—	807
in Pará	D	—	—	—	263,580	100,248	163,332	163,332
	E[a]	10,812	7,191	3,621	10,812	7,191	3,621	7,242
TOTAL		64,490	10,595	53,895	74,878	52,747	22,131	76,026
	A	—	173,854	-173,854	348,681	—	348,681 1	174,827
Private	B	105,235	—	105,235	—	66,787	-66,787	38,448
colonization	C	25,846	14,320	11,526	—	—	—	11,526
in Mato	D	—	—	—	—	—	—	—
Grosso	E	—	—	—	—	—	—	—
TOTAL		50,843	167,273	-116,430	248,681	66,787	281,894	165,464
	A	—	78,148	-78,148	153,658	—	153,658	75,510
	B	97,279	—	97,279	—	59,576	-59,576	37,703
Total	C	19,659	12,995	6,663	—	—	—	6,663
	D	—	—	—	263,578	100,248	162,504	162,504
	E[a]	10,812	7,191	3,621	10,812	7,191	3,621	7,242
TOTAL		63,218	38,251	24,966	164,501	66,270	98,231	123,197

Source: Field survey.
Note: Types of merchant are described in chart 8.
[a]Values divided equally between local and external economies.

economy. Average total profit was more than double that of Pará: $165,464 (col. 7).

Sellers (Type B) and local commerce (Type C) had similar average volumes in both states. Besides the exceptional case of roadside commerce along the Transamazon Highway (Type D), the biggest difference between the two states was the agricultural product market (Type A). In this sector, Pará merchants had low average profit volume, $2,069 (table 31), and also low average profit rates, 38.9 percent (table 29); the merchants of Mato Grosso (according to the same tables) had much higher average profit volume, $174,827, and also much higher profit rates, 100.5 percent. These findings imply that official colonization had a more competitive marketing structure for agricultural products than the private colonization, where the market must have been more concentrated.

As seen in chapter 7, the road network in Pará grew much more rapidly than in Mato Grosso. Traditional northern and northeastern commerce in Pará was thus subjected to increasing competition against more recent southerners and Goianian merchants and truckers. Successful farmers of Pará diversified and initiated small businesses, increasing competition at the local level. Commerce in Mato Grosso, however, was "reserved" for the South.

Consequently, farmers in Pará benefited from more competition in the commercial sphere and obtained higher prices than in Mato Grosso, as will be seen in chapter 18. Local merchants' margins were squeezed "from below" by the relatively high prices received by farmers. As most of these merchants were still connected to the traditional agricultural product markets of the North-Northeast, less dynamic than that of the South, they had less opportunity to pass agricultural costs onward through the chain of intermediaries. Thus, their margins were also squeezed "from above." Much of the final appropriated surplus extracted by the product market in Pará did not, therefore, remain with local merchants. Some part remained with farmers; another part went to the commercial warehouses in Altamira, Marabá, and Imperatriz, from which products entered regional and national markets.

Private colonization, however, tended to be in locations distant from main highway arteries, reached by roads that were constructed and patrolled by the private colonizing firms themselves. Sometimes these firms had complete control over the traffic that entered and left their projects.[17] Private colonizers also frequently participated directly and on a large scale in the agricultural product markets. Oligopsonies or even monopsonies emerged "naturally" in these projects. The few additional buyers who did obtain entry into these markets enjoyed wider margins than would have been possible with greater competition.[18]

These margins expanded "downward" by depressing local agricultural product prices and "upward" by raising prices for southern manufactured goods. The final appropriation of surplus extracted from the product market in Mato Grosso, therefore, remained largely in the hands of local merchants themselves. Average profit in the agricultural product market (Type A) was 84(!) times higher in Mato Grosso than in Pará ($174,827 compared to $2,069), as seen above, in table 31. Once agricultural products were transported southward, the remaining surplus was appropriated beyond the frontier, when merchandise was resold elsewhere in the economy.

In sum, local level extraction of agricultural surplus through commercial profits existed in both Pará and Mato Grosso: by the purchase of agricultural goods produced locally and by the sale of manufactured goods produced externally. But in Mato Grosso average commercial profits were larger by far. The two types of colonization, official and private, differed in terms of agricultural product markets, which were much more concentrated in Mato Grosso than in Pará.

Chapter 18 will test these hypotheses. It will be seen that agricultural product prices in Mato Grosso were systematically below those of Pará. Such market concentration must have seriously reduced the profitability of farmers in private colonization, since they became steadily poorer over the years, as will be seen in chapter 21. Even the poorer colonists in official projects did better, benefiting perhaps from greater competition in the commercial sphere. By the end of the decade, many had surpassed settlers in private colonization, who had been much better off on arrival.

But the story of colonists belongs in another part of the book. The following tables describe accumulation by frontier merchants and their diversification into agricultural production.

Accumulation and Diversification

Table 32 shows that, on average, merchants had been in the area for only three years, with very little variation between southerners and others, in both Mato Grosso and Pará.

As was seen in table 29, current profitability was much higher in Pará, almost double that in Mato Grosso. Table 32 shows, however, that the difference between Pará and Mato Grosso was reversed over the years. After arrival on the frontier, the rate of total accumulation in commerce (table 32) in Pará was greater than that of Mato Grosso.[19]

This result suggests several possible interpretations. On the one hand, it is possible that business during the survey year in Pará was not as good as in Mato Grosso for merely circumstantial reasons. On the other hand, merchants in Pará may have begun on a small scale and grown over time,

Table 32. Time on Plot and Accumulation Rates by Type of Merchant

Origin/ Destination	Type	*Southerners* Time (months) (1)	*Southerners* Accumulation Rate (%) (2)	*Others* Time (months) (3)	*Others* Accumulatio Rate (%) (4)	*All* Time (months) (5)	*All* Accumulatio Rate (%) (6)
Public colonization in Pará	A	22.0	6.9	42.0	10.3	32.0	10.1
	B	30.7	22.9	27.8	20.7	28.6	21.0
	C	36.0	4.1	10.0	19.6	23.0	15.0
	D	8.0	47.7	36.0	27.8	21.0	29.5
	E	72.0	6.4	—	—	72.0	6.4
TOTAL		34.6	22.6	30.6	19.3	32.1	19.7
Private colonization in Mato Grosso	A	35.3	14.0				
	B	28.0	15.6				
	C	43.5	10.0				
	D	19.5	8.2				
	E	—	—				
TOTAL		31.7	13.0				
Total	A	30.0	13.9			28.3	13.2
	B	28.7	16.0			28.3	17.7
	C	41.0	10.3			33.3	11.3
	D	15.7	30.4			19.2	28.2
	E	72.0	6.4			72.0	6.4
TOTAL		32.4	13.4			31.9	14.5

Source: Field survey.
Note: Types of merchants are described in chart 8.
Accumulation rate is the ratio of current assets to original assets raised to the 1/t power where: $[(\text{Assets}_t/\text{Assets}_o)^{1/t}] \times 100$ (t=time in months), all minus 100.

while in Mato Grosso merchants may have begun as large scale as they were to be and therefore grew little. It is strange that in spite of being more competitive, the market in Pará should appear more propitious for commercial accumulation than that of Mato Grosso. These issues will be reconsidered further on.

In Pará the oldest commerce was "mixed" (Type E), while in Mato Grosso it was "local" (Type C). Thus, undifferentiated commerce tends to be the first to arrive. This is exactly in accordance with the literature reviewed in chapter 12. Such merchants tend to practice the usury-mercantile relations ("crop lien") typical of the frontier's initial phase. Consumer goods credit between harvests is tied to future purchases of agricultural products at harvest time. With the exodus of small farmers, typical of the frontier's second phase, merchants become more specialized in their dealings with farmers and transactions become more highly monetized. The durability of these older merchants, then, may signify either that they change over time or that a sizable enough contingent of their small farmer clients hang on. Such "survivors" would justify the local persistence of informal credit services for borrowed consumption provided by "local" and "mixed" merchants.

In all, the highest rate of accumulation among merchants occurred among the "external" (Type D) in Pará, typically roadside operations. Others rates were fairly similar, being generally higher among "sellers" (Type B) than "buyers" (Type A).

The absolute average monthly rate of accumulation was extremely high. Considering that monthly inflation in 1981 was 3 percent to 6.5 percent, one can estimate by subtracting from the figures in table 32 that the real rate of accumulation in frontier commerce was between 8 percent and 10 percent per month during the period. This level is high compared with that of frontier farmers, whose rates are estimated in chapter 17 to be only 1.1 percent per month during the same period. Frontier commerce, therefore, was thriving more than agriculture.

Participation in Agricultural Activities

Table 33 divides current assets (working capital) by fixed assets for merchants' agricultural and nonagricultural activities. It shows that commerce used much higher proportions of working capital to fixed capital than agriculture. Starting a business, then, required substantial liquidity, which must have constituted an important barrier to entry into this sector by farmers. This barrier may have been largest (the volume of required working capital greatest) in the sectors selling manufactured products (Type B) and in those in "external" commerce (Type D), which perhaps accounts for their respective higher margins relative to other sectors.

Table 33. Current Assets/Fixed Assets in Agricultural and Nonagricultural Activities by Type of Merchant (%)

Destination	*Type*	*Agricultural*	*Nonagricultural*	*Total*
	A	—	10.0	9.0
Public	B	0.4	167.0	116.0
colonization	C	—	71.3	34.0
in Pará	D	—	263.0	224.9
	E	1.8	—	1.8
TOTAL		0.6	103.1	80.5
	A	2.0	60.3	43.7
Private	B	0.0	101.5	42.8
colonization	C	1.2	32.1	28.3
in Mato Grosso	D	—	—	—
	E	—	—	—
TOTAL		0.7	71.0	42.2
	A	1.8	46.0	35.3
	B	0.1	125.9	62.0
Total	C	0.4	39.4	30.0
	D	—	231.0	101.1
	E	1.9	—	1.8
TOTAL		0.7	81.7	52.8

Source: Field survey.
Note: Types of merchants are described in chart 8.

Table 34 calculates the percentage of agricultural income, investment, and assets in total income, total investment, and total assets of merchants.[20] In spite of the extremely irregular information, there is an interesting participation by merchants in agriculture. Although agricultural income and assets are small percentages of their respective totals, fully one-quarter of merchants' investments went to agriculture (25.3 percent), generally for purchasing land. This proportion was almost twice as high in Mato Grosso (29.4 percent) as in Pará (15.2 percent). Although agricultural earnings were a relatively low percentage (7.2 percent in Pará and 0 percent in Mato Grosso) of merchants' total income, agriculture was apparently absorbing a significant portion of commercial surpluses.

This finding would suggest that agricultural profitability was higher than commercial, since one does not generally disdain a more lucrative sector to invest in a less lucrative one. Nevertheless, accumulation was much lower in agriculture than in commerce, as will be seen when comparing these findings with those of chapter 17. Agricultural investment by merchants, therefore, is difficult to interpret and deserves greater attention, as will be done in the next section.[21]

The Evolution of Frontier Commerce: Some Reflections

The high rates of accumulation observed above do not merely reflect the profitability of commerce itself, but also result from various other factors that operate simultaneously. On the one hand, merchants generally have their fixed assets in urban areas, and their properties appreciate much more rapidly than rural ones given the accelerated rate of frontier urbanization noted in chapter 2. On the other hand, the accumulation rates reported here do not include merchants who fail or close, nor small marginal businesses neglected by the survey. The real average commercial accumulation rate, then, may be lower than that observed.

To the extent that there is appropriation of agricultural surplus by commerce, this would swell the commercial accumulation rate and reduce the agricultural accumulation rate. Such would occur through oligopsonized transactions, which transfer income from farmers to merchants. Merchants would then integrate vertically, by investing in agriculture, in order to appropriate agricultural surplus directly. They would be able to avoid the unfavorable prices that face other farmers, for, being merchants, they dictate their own prices. As will be seen in the next chapter, many of the more successful farmers tried to do the same by entering commerce. They probably did so in order to raise their own prices as well and to expand their own total profitability.

Many merchants came to the frontier initially intending to buy land, especially in Pará, but did not succeed in doing so on arrival. They

Table 34. Participation in Agricultural Activities by Type of Merchant (%)

Destination	*Type*	*Income*	*Investment*	*Assets*
Public colonization in Pará	A	—	10.0	—
	B	6.2	21.8	2.0
	C	12.1	39.0	4.6
	D	6.7	—	2.0
	E	—	—	16.6
TOTAL		7.2	15.2	10.8
Private colonization in Mato Grosso	A	—	21.0	8.1
	B	—	40.6	41.0
	C	—	5.6	—
	D	—	—	—
	E	—	—	—
TOTAL		—	2.9	23.2
Total	A	—	18.8	0.4
	B	5.9	34.9	15.5
	C	2.6	16.1	1.3
	D	6.1	—	0.2
	E	—	—	16.6
TOTAL		3.0	25.3	7.5

Source: Field survey.
Notes: Types of merchants are described in chart 8.
Participation is measured as the share of agricultural activities divided by the total, multiplied by 100.

became merchants only as an intermediate stage, planning to transfer some day into agriculture. As discussed in chapter 12, landed property on the frontier consolidates after awhile. This movement accompanies the demise of family farming and of usury-mercantile capital. Some merchants then become direct agricultural producers. They hire wage labor on their own farms rather than manage agricultural labor indirectly through indebtedness. This may explain why local commerce (Type C) in Pará, the oldest merchant type, also had the highest rates of participation in agricultural activities: 12.1 percent of income, and 39 percent of investment.

On the other hand, as previously mentioned, many farmers, and especially the southerners of Pará, invested their agricultural profits in business, diversifying their activities along with their increasing income. They were interviewed as merchants, but they began as farmers. That is, a reciprocal movement between merchants and farmers existed, principally in Pará where barriers to entry for both sectors were apparently smaller than in Mato Grosso. The price of land, the key barrier to entry in agriculture, was much lower in official colonization, and roads, the key route to markets, were better in Pará. Thus, one would expect Pará merchants to be greater investors in agriculture than Mato Grosso merchants.

It is odd, then, that the principal agricultural investors in this sample were not the merchants from Pará, but rather those from Mato Grosso! Perhaps the far greater volume of business and profits in Mato Grosso weakened the barrier posed by more expensive land. Perhaps the chain of intermediation with respect to the South was more rigid in Mato Grosso, barring expansion of operations within merchants' own commercial sector. Large-scale southern industrial suppliers and clients may not easily alter the quotas reserved for their frontier representatives. This may frustrate their growth as merchants.Thus, they may turn to land purchasing as a store of value, as a speculative investment, or even as a means to expand productive activities. The available data cannot resolve this question, and these doubts must remain unresolved for the meantime.

The Outpost of Capitalism

Private colonization in Mato Grosso brought from the South not only farmers, but also an entire commercial structure. Close ties with clients in "central" markets, added to enormous difficulty of access to colonization areas, created barriers to entry in commerce and formed concentrated agricultural product markets. The result was extremely high average profit margins in frontier commerce, compared to agriculture, especially in Mato Grosso.

In the official colonization of Pará, local agricultural product merchants suffered from strong competition by outside truckers as well as from successful farmers who diversified their activities toward commerce. All had relatively easy access to local suppliers of raw materials and, also, found it relatively easy to resell agricultural product outside the frontier, given the expanded road network. The market for manufactured goods from the South, however, was much more difficult to enter. Therefore, the highest commercial margins in Pará were observed among the merchants most protected by barriers to entry: those who sold southern industrialized products to the local economy.

Throughout the frontier, the oldest type of merchant was in local commerce. This type is the most likely to practice the classic extraction of surplus through the sale of consumer goods between harvests in exchange for future agricultural product. But its margin was the lowest of all and it tended to be supplanted over time by other types of commerce linked to the industrial economy outside. The resale of industrialized products was important in all frontier locations and had much higher margins than local commerce. The highest margins of all, however, were obtained in Mato Grosso through monopsonization of the agricultural product markets. In Pará, this method of appropriating agricultural surplus remained weak, as already mentioned, due to the greater competition made possible by easy access to roadways and more competitive markets.

From arrival until the time of interview, frontier merchants had high rates of accumulation. The key barrier to entry in commerce appears to have been the large amount of working capital necessary, especially in trading with manufactures. The principal barrier to entry in agriculture was the cost of land. Many merchants invested their high profits in land, especially those of Mato Grosso. Thus, being a merchant on the western Amazon frontier seems to have been an excellent business.

Finally, note that agricultural profits may have been higher than those to be reported in the next chapter. If not, why would merchants have wanted to invest in agriculture? Perhaps there was a way for farming to be profitable. If one arrived with sufficient working capital to finance current operations and with sufficient assets to satisfy banking collateral requirements, one could escape the vicious circle of usurious indebtedeness. In this sense, it is interesting to stress that a large part of the bank loans taken on by merchants were for agriculture, not commerce.[22]

Frontier urban activity is not only commercial. A large part is linked to the state, as was seen in part 2. This preliminary study of frontier merchants contributes to improving our understanding of rapid urbanization in the Amazon. Although this issue has generated various distinct interpretations, the data presented here show that the market function of frontier cities is very important. Cities concentrate and export local agricultural surpluses to the rest of the economy. Frontier towns in the Amazon house market systems that act as a type of siphon, appropriating income and linking frontier agriculture to the industrial capitalism of the South. The next chapter will analyze the effects of these market systems on frontier colonists.

Notes

1. Chapter 2 points to the importance of the "urban frontier."

2. See Guimarães (1979, 1980, 1982, 1983a, 1983b), Bain (1951, 1969), Hall and Hitch (1983), Modigliani (1958), Sylos-Labini (1980), and Scherer (1970).

3. The data for this part of the field survey are described in detail in A. Santos (1985), in *Migrações internas*, vols. 3 and 4 and appendix. Antonio José Alves Júnior developed the typology and the tables used in this section. The selection of survey locations is in appendix 2 of *Colonização dirigida na Amazônia*.

4. Musumeci (1988), chapter 6, analyzes the social relationships between merchants, clients, and suppliers. She shows how merchant resources originated in personal relations and how flows of merchandise, credit, and money were established between merchants, local farmers, and the rest of the economy.

5. See Musumeci (1988) and chapter 12, above.

6. Gomensoro (1985) shows that industrial production of agricultural inputs is strongly concentrated in São Paulo and Rio Grande do Sul.

7. See Musumeci (1988).

8. See A. Santos (1985) and C. Santos (1988).

9. It is well known that private colonizing firms brought entire communities from the South, as from Paraná to Mato Grosso. For example, in the private project of Alta Floresta, the local bus company brought up all of the immigrants by bus from a single origin, a small town in Paraná, to the colonization project. Upon arrival, vehicles did not return but, instead, became the transportation system for the same community in its new locale.

10. Colonizing firms and cooperatives were not part of the "merchant" survey, since they were included in other surveys of "institutions," discussed in chapters 8 and 9. See B. Ferreira (1984) on nonagricultural sector planning in private colonization, and A. Santos (1985) on the high proportion of merchants in official colonization who were in commerce "by chance" and not "by intention."

11. The tables in this chapter, therefore, are blank in the areas corresponding to "Others" in "Private Colonization in Mato Grosso" as there were no observations in *this* category.

12. The word "central" refers not to the official (IBGE's) "Center" region of Brazil, but rather to the hierarchical function of Brazilian industrial "centers," located in the South and Southeast regions. It is a term derived from "central place" theory, in the same sense employed in chapter 11.

13. The "current profit rate" is measured as income minus expenditures,

divided by expenditures. This refers to the current percentage return to working capital during one given production period. It can also be used as a proxy for the firm's "mark-up" or "margin" of prices over costs. The "rate of accumulation," analyzed in the section "Accumulation and Diversification," refers to the rate of increase of fixed assets over one or more production periods. See note 20 below.

14. See chapter 16.

15. Ibid.

16. The terms "balance" and "profits" are used interchangeably to indicate the simple difference between annual receipts and expenditures.

17. A good example is Alta Floresta, where access depended on crossing the Teles Pires River by ferry. Since the ferry was owned by the colonizing company, this firm had total control over access to the project. See B. Ferreira (1984).

18. This is a prediction of oligopoly theory. The greater the barriers to entry, the greater the price charged over unit cost. In this case, the barriers are distance and the difficulty of access, while the market is that of commercial intermediation. See sources already cited in note 2, above.

19. In this book, the "rate of accumulation" is the percentage increase during a unit of time (in table 32 the time unit is one month) in the real value of merchants' fixed and financial, agricultural and nonagricultural, assets (i.e., of all merchants' wealth). Given the fluidity with which funds go to and from productive and family uses, it is impracticable to measure only productive commercial assets independently of consumer assets.

20. The definitions of these three variables—income, investment, and assets—are in *Colonização dirigida na Amazônia*, appendix 1.

21. See also the discussion in this regard in A. Santos (1985).

22. Ibid.

Sharecropper family: Northeasterners in Alta Floresta, Mato Grosso

Successful colonist: family, home, and fields in Boa Esperança (Good Hope), Mato Grosso

PART 4: THE COLONISTS

This part of the book presents the principal empirical results from a field survey of directed colonization projects in the Amazon, conducted in 1981–1982. General issues and the literature on colonization in the Amazon were discussed previously, in part 1, "The Dimensions of the Frontier"; part 2, "The Frontier and the State"; and part 3, "The Frontier and the Market." This part focuses upon the field data and their implications in light of the issues raised in previous chapters.

Chapter 16 describes the structure of colonists' economic transactions. Chapter 17 presents data on colonists' levels of real income and accumulation. It further estimates the costs of job creation and provides a rough calculation of the costs and benefits of Amazon colonization. Chapter 18 analyzes prices in colonization projects and identifies market segmentation in the frontier economy. Chapter 19 examines the technological and environmental consequences of small farming at prevailing relative prices. Through econometric analysis, chapter 20 shows the importance of the frontier's economic environment for determining colonists' incomes, investments, and accumulation. Finally, chapter 21 shows how the influence of colonists' places of origin weakens over time, and argues that the influence of the local-level economic policy increases correspondingly.

It is worth recalling that the methods of collecting and organizing data, as well as the data themselves, are entirely original. No other field survey on the Amazonian frontier has described the microeconomy of the small producer with such rigor or presented transaction accounts with such detail, as has been done in this study. Consequently, this part of the book is not comparable to other research, and no further bibliographical references will be made.

The tables that follow are based on field data collected in the directed colonization projects of the Amazon during the years 1981 and 1982. In all, 700 farmer interviews were conducted, yielding a final sample size of 498. All values are reported in U.S. dollars converted at the average exchange rate of 1981 (Cr. $96.65/U.S. $). All tables consist of simple averages per household, calculated for four subgroups of migrants: southerners or other migrants in private or public projects. The distinction between types of project seeks to test the hypothesis that private settlement was more efficient than public settlement in terms of colonists' performance. The distinction between places of origin is necessary because of the general expectation that southerners have had an edge over "other migrants" when the "two Brazils" meet in the Amazon. Unfortunately, there were so few "nonsouthern" colonists in private colonization that it became impossible to analyze this subgroup statistically, so it was excluded from the tables.

Although the sample variance is rather large, comparisons between simple means reveal much about the different situations encountered. Appendixes 1 through 3 of *A colonizacão dirigida na Amazônia*, from which this book is extracted, describe the field research. They explain sampling procedures and the choice of suvey locations in terms of how representative they are of different circumstances in Amazon colonization. They also describe the sample, the questionnaires, and variable definitions. These appendixes include statistical analysis of the data, each variable's average and standard deviation, statistical tests of differences between means, simple correlations between all of the variables, and graphs of distributions. For lack of space, however, it was impossible to reproduce all this statistical information here. Map 19 indicates survey locations and table 35 summarizes basic sample information. The volumes with complete descriptions are available for consultation at the libraries of FEA/UFRJ and IPEA in Rio de Janeiro.

Since all of the data collected in private colonization come from the state of Mato Grosso, findings for this group may be presented equally in terms of state (Mato Grosso) or type of colonization (private). Similarly, all official colonization data come from the state of Pará, so this state will be synonymous with public colonization. By implication, official colonization in Pará is considered representative of conditions of official colonization in the Amazon in general, and private colonization in Mato Grosso is considered representative of private colonization in the Amazon in general. The period referred to by the field survey—the agricultural year from 1 July 1980 to 30 June 1981—crowns the Decade of (directed) Colonization. It is, therefore, appropriate for an evaluation of the results of this program for the 1970s as a whole.

Map 19. Location of Surveyed Colonization Projects

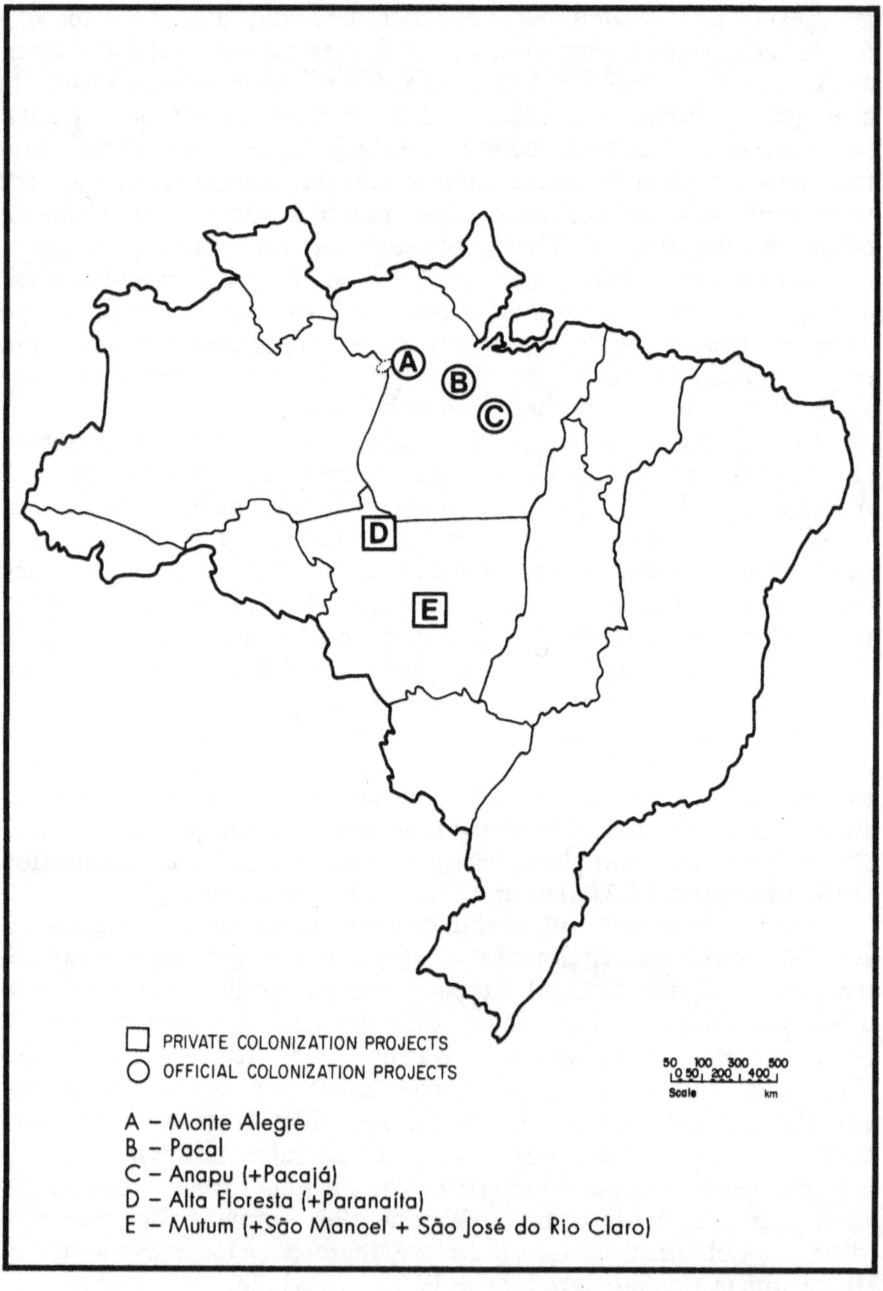

Table 35. Sample Distribution

Location	Rural Population[a]		Question-naires	Persons per Questionnaire[b]	Surveyed Population	Difference between Population and Sample	
	Nº (1)	% (2)	Nº (3)	Nº (4)	Nº (5)=(3) x (4)	% (6)	% (7)=(6)–(2)
Pará							
Pacal	9,756	19	120	7	840	24	+5
Anapu	5,680	11	74	7	518	15	+4
Pacajá	2,929	6	23	7	161	5	-1
Monte Alegre	13,136	25	53	6	371	11	-14
TOTAL - 1	31,501	61	270	7	1,890	—	-6
Mato Grosso							
Alta Floresta	10,910	21	119	7	833	24	+3
Paranaíta	3,908	7	46	7	322	9	+2
São J. Rio Claro	3,221	6	38	4	152	3	-3
Mutum	2,427	4	22	12	264	8	+4
São Manoel	332	1	3	10	30	1	0
TOTAL - 2	20,618	39	228	7	1,601	45	+6
TOTAL	52,119	100	498	7	3,491	100	0

(5/1) = Surveyed Population/Rural Population = 3,491/52,119 = 7%.
Source: Field survey.
[a]Resident population in official census sectors corresponding to each surveyed location.
[b]Average household size in each location.

16. THE APPROPRIATION OF INCOME IN DIRECTED COLONIZATION

This chapter analyzes the economic performance of colonists using "balance sheets" of their market transactions. For example, a negative balance on transactions linked to agriculture (sale of products and purchase of inputs) with a positive balance on nonagricultural transactions (businesses, outhiring, etc.) would imply that agriculture is being subsidized by other activities. This is not uncommon for the initial years of settlement. Alternatively, a positive balance in agriculture, with a negative financial account, would imply that agricultural income was being used to pay loans. This may occur due to investment or to chronic consumer borrowing. Thus, income and expenditure flows in each type of transaction reveal farmers' positions with respect to the surrounding market system. These positions are fundamental elements in evaluating the performance of directed colonization during the 1970s.

Chapter 13 discussed the general issues and literature that frame the presentation of data in this chapter. That framework is adapted here to the actual diversity of concrete situations on the frontier. Each table presents data on income, expenditures, and balances—grouped by specific types of transactions—summarizing the interaction between colonists and the surrounding economy.

The "Family Farming Account" (table 36) includes only market transactions. It refers to sales of agricultural products and extractive outputs, as well as to purchases of inputs and consumer goods. The "Nonagricultural Account" (table 37) involves exchange in other markets—labor, land, business, credit. It also includes official or private transfers whether or not related to productive activities. The "Financial Account" (table 38) refers to loans received and extended, and to debt payments made or received. These three balance sheets—agricultural, nonagricultural, and financial—comprise the farmer's "Monetary Account" (table 39). The "Monetary and Nonmonetary Account" (table 40) adds the subsistence economy to the market economy, thereby measuring the real total standard of living for the farm family. This way of organizing information, derived from the analysis in chapter 13, links income levels to systems of surplus appropriation through market transactions.

Each balance sheet is expressed in average values for each migratory group. The percentages reported refer to shares of a value in each particular group's total *income.* That is, each type of income and expenditure is expressed as a share of total *income* in each account. This presentation reveals the relative position of each immigrant group vis-à-vis the rest of the economy.

Given the large amount of information to be analyzed, this chapter begins the evaluation of directed colonization by considering only a few issues. For reasons discussed in previous chapters, the tables refer to large groups of migrants distinguished by origin—southern or other—and by destination—official or private colonization. No further disaggregation is done here, whether by location in the Amazon, time on the plot, or any other. Following chapters will present successively more detailed analyses, which reveal the many interrelationships existing among the diverse factors that influence colonists' performance. This chapter concentrates, then, upon the relationship between colonists and the market, and on the forms by which their current income is appropriated.

The main findings in this chapter concern the vicious circle of indebtedness that compromises colonists' abilities to appropriate income. Especially in private colonization, colonists became heavily indebted to pay for their land. In official colonization, by contrast, the pattern differed according to migrants' place of origin: southerners became indebted in order to invest, while other migrants became indebted in order to consume. Nonagricultural opportunities and nonmonetary income were both smaller than expected in colonization projects.

Family Farming Account

In table 36, each cell shows the "agricultural family's current balance," indicating to what degree agriculture covered current family and production expenditures. Sales refer only to agricultural products, and purchases refer only to agricultural inputs, including wage payments and family consumption. Only monetized transactions are included, that is,

Table 36. Family Farming Account
(a) Southerners

Destination	Receipts U.S. $	Receipts %	Expenditures U.S. $	Expenditures %	Balance U.S. $	Balance %
Pará: Public colonization						
Agriculture	7,102.0	100	3,551.0	50	3,351.0	50
Family	—	—	1,954.4	28	-1,954.0	-28
TOTAL	7,102.0	100	5,505.4	78	1,596.4	22
Mato Grosso: Private colonization						
Agriculture	5,148.4	100	3,812.8	74	1,335.8	26
Family	—	—	2,048.7	40	-2,048.7	-40
TOTAL	5,148.4	100	5,861.3	114	712.9	-14
Total						
Agriculture	5,671.0	100	3,753.8	66	1,917.2	44
Family	—	—	2,029.0	36	-2,029.0	-36
TOTAL	5,671.0	100	5,782.8	102	-111.8	-8

Table 36. Family Farming Account
(b) Others

	Receipts		*Expenditures*		*Balance*	
Destination	*U.S. $*	*%*	*U.S. $*	*%*	*U.S. $*	*%*
Pará: Public colonization						
Agriculture	2,088	100	1,024.7	51	1,063.3	49
Family	—	—	1,345.0	65	-1,345.0	-65
TOTAL	2,088	100	2,369.7	116	-281.7	-16
Mato Grosso: Private colonization						
Agriculture	—	—	—	—	—	—
Family	—	—	—	—	—	—
TOTAL	—	—	—	—	—	—
Total						
Agriculture	—	—	—	—	—	—
Family	—	—	—	—	—	—
TOTAL	—	—	—	—	—	—

Table 36. Family Farming Account
(c) All

Destination	Receipts U.S. $	Receipts %	Expenditures U.S. $	Expenditures %	Balance U.S. $	Balance %
Pará: Public colonization						
Agriculture	3,612	100	1,794.1	50	1,817.9	50
Family	—	—	1,530.2	35	-1,530.2	-35
TOTAL	3,612	100	3,324.3	85	287.7	15
Mato Grosso: Private colonization						
Agriculture	—	—	—	—	—	—
Family	—	—	—	—	—	—
TOTAL	—	—	—	—	—	—
Total						
Agriculture	4,316	100	2,718.0	64	1,597.6	36
Family	—	—	1,870.7	43	-1,870.7	-43
TOTAL	4,316	100	4,588.8	106	-273.1	-6

Source: Field survey.
Note: Blank sections reflect the fact that there were only southern migrants in the private colonization projects of Mato Grosso.

those effected in exchange for money.

The table shows that southerners in Pará had the highest current agricultural income ($7,102) and expenditures ($5,505). Other migrants in Pará had the lowest current agricultural income and expenditures ($2,088 and $2,369, respectively). Meanwhile, the colonists of Mato Grosso (all of whom were southerners, as mentioned earlier) were between these two extremes (with current income and expenditures of $5,148 and $5,861, respectively).

The ways in which these groups were inserted into the market economy differed greatly and interestingly. First, the levels of family expenditures were closer among all groups than were income levels. Second, production expenditures used up a larger share of agricultural income in Mato Grosso (74 percent) than in Pará (50 percent for southerners and 51 percent for other migrants). Third, family expenditures consumed a greater share of total income among other migrants (65 percent) than among southerners generally (28 percent in Pará and 40 percent in Mato Grosso).

It is also evident from this table that the "agricultural economy" was relatively more monetized in Mato Grosso than in Pará—and was perhaps more advanced technologically, as well. Within Pará, other migrants were poorer than southerners since their agricultural income could not cover necessary family expenditures. The family farm economy, then, tended to generate deficits for different reasons in different places: in Mato Grosso, because of high agricultural expenditures; among the other migrants in Pará, because of insufficient family income. The only ones who produced more net agricultural income than they consumed within the family were the southerners of Pará.

Nonagricultural Income

The transactions shown in table 37 indicate that nonagricultural income was higher in Mato Grosso ($1,371) than in Pará. This was largely due to higher rental receipts since sharecropping was much more common in Mato Grosso than in Pará. Thus, migrants in Mato Grosso "imported" systems of organization of production typical of the old coffee economy of Paraná. Among the southerners of Pará, the principal nonagricultural source of income came from business ($353), as was observed in a different study.[1] Among other migrants, out-hiring was the principal nonagricultural income source ($614).[2] The highest nonagricultural expenditure in Mato Grosso was interest payments; in Pará, it was the institutional transfer payments, especially taxes and tariffs. This aspect of Pará may reflect greater fiscal enforcement on farmers in official colonization projects. Southerners showed deficits in

Table 37. Nonagricultural Account
(a) Southerners

Destination	Receipts U.S. $	Receipts %	Expenditures U.S. $	Expenditures %	Balance U.S. $	Balance %
Pará: Public colonization						
Rents	103.4	12.0	354.9	41.2	-251.6	-29.2
Interest	3.1	0.3	436.7	50.7	-433.6	-50.4
Transfer	139.7	16.2	1,082.4	123.7	-942.7	-109.5
Wages	259.7	30.2	—	—	259.7	30.2
Business	353.9	41.2	343.5	39.9	10.4	1.3
TOTAL	860.9	100.0	2,222.4	140.0	-1,361.5	-158.1
Mato Grosso: Private colonization						
Rents	483.1	35.2	452.1	32.3	31.0	2.2
Interest	23.8	1.8	800.8	58.3	-777.0	-55.8
Transfer	234.9	17.0	213.1	15.5	21.8	1.6
Wages	397.3	29.0	—	—	397.3	29
Business	231.8	17.0	114.8	8.4	117.0	8.6
TOTAL	1,371.0	100.0	1,580.0	114.5	-209.0	-14.4
Total						
Rents	386.0	31.0	10.3	0.8	375.7	30.2
Interest	18.7	1.5	706.7	57.0	-688.0	-55.5
Transfer	212.1	17.0	304.3	24.5	-92.2	-7.5
Wages	361.0	29.0	—	—	361.0	29.0
Business	266.0	21.5	177.0	14.3	89.0	7.8
TOTAL	1,244.7	100.0	1,198.3	96.3	45.5	4.0

Table 37. Nonagricultural Account
(b) Others

Destination	Receipts U.S. $	Receipts %	Expenditures U.S. $	Expenditures %	Balance U.S. $	Balance %
Pará: Public colonization						
Rents	165.6	26	73.4	11.9	92.2	15.0
Interest	62.0	9	145.9	23.7	-83.9	-13.6
Transfer	70.3	10	221.4	36.0	-151.1	-26.0
Wages	253.4	37	—	—	253.4	37.0
Business	122.0	18	70.3	11.4	-51.7	6.6
TOTAL	614.6	100	510.0	83	104.5	17.0
Mato Grosso: Private colonization						
Rents	—	—	—	—	—	—
Interest	—	—	—	—	—	—
Transfer	—	—	—	—	—	—
Wages	—	—	—	—	—	—
Business	—	—	—	—	—	—
TOTAL						
Total	—	—	—	—	—	—
Rents	—	—	—	—	—	—
Interest	—	—	—	—	—	—
Transfer	—	—	—	—	—	—
Wages	—	—	—	—	—	—
Business	—	—	—	—	—	—
TOTAL						

Table 37. Nonagricultural Account
(c) All

Destination	*Receipts* U.S. $	%	*Expenditures* U.S. $	%	*Balance* U.S. $	%
Pará: Public colonization						
Rents	147.0	21.1	158.3	22.6	-11.3	-1.6
Interest	10.0	0.0	233.9	33.3	-223.9	-33.2
Transfer	92.0	13.2	484.2	69.0	-392.2	-55.9
Wages	256.7	36.8	—	—	256.7	36.6
Business	192.4	27.6	153.1	21.8	39.3	5.6
TOTAL	698.1	100.0	1,021.2	146.0	-331.4	-47.0
Mato Grosso: Private colonization						
Rents	—	—	—	—	—	—
Interest	—	—	—	—	—	—
Transfer	—	—	—	—	—	—
Wages	—	—	—	—	—	—
Business	—	—	—	—	—	—
TOTAL						
Total						
Rents	296.0	29.3	292.8	29.1	3.2	0.3
Interest	21.8	2.2	1,217.8	120.8	-1,206.5	-119.7
Transfer	157.2	15.6	360.0	35.7	-202.8	-20.1
Wages	322.8	32.1	—	—	322.8	32.1
Business	210.0	21.9	135.6	13.5	74.4	7.4
TOTAL	1,007.8	100.0	2,006.2	199.1	-998.4	-99.1

Source: Field survey.

their nonagricultural current exchanges—both those in Mato Grosso and those in Pará—which means that either the agricultural or financial accounts were funding these exchanges. Other migrants showed surpluses, although at a low level of operation, which means that either the agricultural or the financial accounts were being funded by these market transactions.

Income shares indicate that colonization in Mato Grosso was relatively more monetized and made greater use of sharecropping finance and credit. Pará, instead, had more formal institutional presence, with its attendant fiscal burden. Those who most frequently resorted to the labor market to complement their income were other migrants in Pará—precisely those with the lowest incomes, both agricultural and nonagricultural.

The low total value of nonagricultural income among colonists is surprising.[3] Thus, agriculture was still, by far, the major source of income in directed colonization. Yet, some colonists did establish businesses, indicating that they had generated enough working capital or that they had a high level of initiative. Until the time of the interview, however, the fruits of such talents were still predominantly being realized in agriculture and not outside of it.

These findings contrast with those obtained in the previous chapter concerning the agricultural activities of merchants. Among farmers with businesses, the largest income sources are agricultural; among merchants with farms, the largest incomes come from business. This reflects an empirical definition: interviewees were classified as farmers if their largest source of income at the time was agricultural, and as merchants if their main income came from business. These relative proportions suggest high mobility between the two categories: some farmers, especially in Pará, began small businesses and expanded them, integrating "forward"; some merchants, especially in Mato Grosso, invested their large profits in agriculture, integrating "backward." The mobility between sectors may have been more, and the segmentation of economic opportunities may have been less, therefore, than the evidence in chapter 18 will suggest.

Contrary to expectations, transfers were not an important part of farmers' income. The balance for taxes and tariffs, which included the imputed value of social and technical assistance, was actually negative in Pará; that is, settlers received less than they contributed! The southerners in Pará paid a great deal for the assistance they received. However, as will be seen below,[4] they also apparently benefited more from this assistance in terms of the agricultural income that it generated. This may mean that the impact of technical assistance upon agricultural performance and income is greater, in terms of future output, than the current value directly transferred.

Financial Account

"Disinvestments" are reductions in assets (e.g., sales of durable goods) and increases in liabilities (e.g., incoming funds through taking in loans)—both of which increase current disposable income during a given year. "Investments" include increases in assets (e.g., purchases of durable goods) and reductions in liabilities (e.g., paying back debts)—both of which reduce current disposable income during the year. Physical investments and disinvestments refer to durable goods, buildings, land (including improvements and clearing), and animals (including fattening, births, and deaths). Financial investments and disinvestments refer to transactions involving financial assets.

Table 38 shows that southerners, on average, were similar in Pará and Mato Grosso in terms of total financial receipts ($7,371 and $7,643, respectively), and also in terms of indebtedness ($6,219 in Pará and $6,548 in Mato Grosso). Debts represented 84 percent and 86 percent of total financial income, respectively. Meanwhile, debt payments in Mato Grosso ($3,470 or 44 percent of total financial income) were almost double those in Pará ($1,800 or 24 percent of total financial income). These expenditures consisted mainly of payments for land purchases, which were much more expensive in private than public colonization, as seen earlier. For this reason, physical investment was lower in private colonization (26 percent) than in official projects (33 percent). Other migrants were the ones who invested the most as a share of financial income (43 percent) in spite of much lower absolute values of investment. Southerners in official colonization registered more physical investment in their plots than any other group.[5]

All three groups showed positive financial balances, indicating that they were using the financial account to cover deficits in current expenditures. This suggests that information on debt repayments may have been omitted, as will be discussed further on.

The Monetary Balance

As can be seen in table 39, the monetary accounts did not exactly balance, probably due to problems in data collection and to rounding errors. On average, some 12 percent of farmers' total monetary income remained unaccounted for. The greatest error is found among the southerners in Pará (28 percent), while among the other two groups the errorsare 11 and 9 percent. Since the largest positive balances are in financial accounts, interviewees probably underreported their debt repayments. In fact, this was the principal problem in conducting interviews, in spite of efforts to resolve it through (or perhaps precisely because of) exhaustive and repeated requests. The colonists were suspicious of how such information would be used. Their positive monetary balance, therefore, could be attributable in large part to undeclared debt payments. This, in turn, suggests that a large part of credit was still of an "informal" nature at the time (i.e., practiced within a "usury-mercantile" circuit), as described in part 3 of this book, especially in chapter 12.

Of the three migrant groups identified, those with the greatest monetary income were southerners in official colonization ($15,333), closely followed by southerners in private colonization ($14,162) and, finally, at a much lower level, by other migrants in official colonization ($5,648).

Agricultural income was 39 percent of total receipts: highest among southerners in Pará (46 percent), lowest in Mato Grosso (36 percent). Nonagricultural income was small, never surpassing 10 percent of the total. The largest source of income, in all cases, came from financial transactions, around 52 percent, especially in Pará. Yet public project colonists had not brought enough assets with them to sell in such volume. Only heavy borrowing can account for such a high level of financial receipts in the financial account. In Mato Grosso, however, the high proportion of financial income may indicate "dissaving" of initial resources brought from the South, as is consistent with other indicators to be discussed below.

Family farming expenditures were slightly larger than financial expenditures, with nonagricultural expenditures being lowest. Among southerners in Pará, financial expenditures absorbed only 28 percent of income, but among the other migrants in Pará, and southerners in Mato Grosso, financial expenditures absorbed 39 percent. If the aforementioned omitted debt payments are added to these financial expenditures (i.e., if they are all attributed to undeclared debts, as discussed above), then financial payments become the principal expenditure for colonists in this sample.

Recalling the three previous tables, concerning the family-farming, nonagricultural, and financial accounts, the following conclusions can be drawn:

1. Southerners in Mato Grosso were borrowing to cover their previously contracted debts, generally incurred when purchasing land. They had deficits in both their agricultural and nonagricultural balances, and production was not yet sufficient to cover their financial obligations. Consequently, they had to decapitalize, or to borrow further, in order to meet these obligations.

2. Southerners in Pará were borrowing to invest. In spite of relatively high institutional payments, their family-farming balances were in

Table 38. Financial Account
(a) Southerners

Destination	*Receipts*		*Expenditures*		*Balance*	
	U.S. $	*%*	*U.S. $*	*%*	*U.S. $*	*%*
Pará: Public colonization						
Physical	1,151.6	16	2,458.3	33	-1,306.8	-17.7
Financial	6,219.3	84	1,800.3	24	4,419.0	60.0
TOTAL	7,371.0	100	4,258.7	57	3,112.2	42.0
Mato Grosso: Private colonization						
Physical	1,094.7	14	2,013.4	26	-918.6	-12.0
Financial	6,548.3	86	3,470.2	44	3,078.1	42.0
TOTAL	7,643.0	100	5,483.7	72	2,159.3	28.0
Total						
Physical	1,119.5	15	2,147.0	29	-1,027.5	-13.7
Financial	6,405.6	85	3,018.1	40	3,387.5	45.0
TOTAL	7,525.0	100	5,165.0	69	2,360.0	31.0

Table 38. Financial Account
(b) Others

	Receipts		*Expenditures*		*Balance*	
Destination	*U.S. $*	*%*	*U.S. $*	*%*	*U.S. $*	*%*
Pará: Public colonization						
Physical	659.1	32	931.1	43	-272	-11
Financial	1,813.0	68	923.0	32	850	36
TOTAL	2,472.1	100	1,854.1	75	618	25
Mato Grosso: Private colonization						
Physical	—	—	—	—	—	—
Financial	—	—	—	—	—	—
TOTAL	—	—	—	—	—	—
Total						
Physical	—	—	—	—	—	—
Financial						
TOTAL	—	—	—	—	—	—

Table 38. Financial Account
(c) All

Destination	*Receipts* *U.S. $*	*%*	*Expenditures* *U.S. $*	*%*	*Balance* *U.S. $*	*%*
Pará: Public colonization						
Physical	111.8	3	1,632.7	48	-1,520.9	-44.7
Financial	3,291.2	97	1,189.9	35	2,101.3	61.8
TOTAL	3,403.0	100	2,822.6	83	580.4	17.0
Mato Grosso: Private colonization						
Physical	—	—	—	—	—	—
Financial	—	—	—	—	—	—
TOTAL						
Total						
Physical	1,010.9	17	1,807.6	31	-796.7	-13.8
Financial	4,782.2	83	2,233.8	39	2,548.4	44.0
TOTAL	5,793.0	100	4,041.3	70	1,751.7	30.0

Source: Field survey.

surplus. They invested more in agriculture than any other group.

3. Other migrants in Pará were borrowing to consume. Their family-farming balance was insufficient to cover consumption expenditures, and their nonagricultural activities, especially part-time wage labor, were also unable to provide for family consumption.

4. Nonagricultural income was small for all groups: the surrounding economy was new and simple; urban centers were distant from one another; the labor market was incipient; opportunities to complement income from nonagricultural sources were restricted. Southerners in Pará were the most successful at opening small businesses and prospering, but even so, the proceeds were small as a share of total income. Agriculture remained the principal opportunity for accumulation in directed colonization.

Monetary and Subsistence Account

In estimating the monetary and nonmonetary balance, values were imputed to all goods produced, used, or exchanged in kind by farmers. Values were also imputed to production goods (both agricultural and nonagricultural), family consumption goods (collecting firewood, animal feed, construction, clearing, etc.). Many of these goods had no local market—such as firewood—or the local market was only marginally developed—as in the case of corn. So values had to be determined for these goods by taking the amount of time spent on the associated tasks and valuing this time at the equivalent daily wage rate. Since the labor market was also marginal in these regions at that time, there tends to be overestimation of the value of the nonmonetary economy. Some occasionally absurd results arose. For example, in the case of cattle feed, the estimated value of feed corn turned out to be higher than that for the cattle that consumed it. This occurred because corn was not usually marketed, while the market for cattle was more generalized. These and other accounting problems arose because accounting concepts, which assume fully established markets, were applied to areas where such markets are still incomplete. In spite of such problems, the findings are quite interesting, as can be seen in table 40.

Southerners in official colonization projects obtained the highest total real (monetary and nonmonetary) yearly income ($17,449). They were closely followed by southerners in private colonization ($16,912). Other migrants in official colonization received incomes well below the other two groups, around $7,650 per year.

On average, nonmonetary "expenditures" corresponded to almost one-fourth of total income (23 percent). Among colonists in Mato Grosso, this share was much smaller (10 percent), while it was significantly higher for the other migrants in Pará (32 percent). These expen-

Table 39. Monetary Account
(a) Southerners

Destination	*Receipts* U.S. $	*Receipts* %	*Expenditures* U.S. $	*Expenditures* %	*Balance* U.S. $	*Balance* %
Pará: Public colonization						
Current account:						
Family farming	7,102.0	46	5,505.4	36	1,596.4	10
Nonagricultural	860.9	6	2,222.4	8	-1,361.5	-2
Financial account	7,371.0	48	4,258.7	28	3,112.2	20
TOTAL	15,333.9	100	11,985.5	72	3,348.4	28
Mato Grosso: Private colonization						
Current account:						
Family farming	5,148.4	36	5,861.3	41	712.9	-5
Nonagricultural	1,371.0	10	1,580.0	11	-209.0	-1
Financial account	7,643.0	54	5,484.7	39	2,158.3	15
TOTAL	14,162.4	100	12,926.0	91	1,236.4	9
Total						
Current account:						
Family farming	5,671.0	39	5,782.8	40	-111.8	-1
Nonagricultural	1,244.7	9	1,095.7	11	149.0	-2
Financial account	7,525.0	52	5,164.0	36	2,361	16
TOTAL	14,440.8	100	12,042.5	87	2,398.2	13

Table 39. Monetary Account
(b) Others

	Receipts		*Expenditures*		*Balance*	
Destination	*U.S. $*	*%*	*U.S. $*	*%*	*U.S. $*	*%*
Pará: Public colonization						
Current account:						
Family farming	2,088.0	37	2,372.4	42	-284.4	-3
Nonagricultural	614.6	11	510.0	10	104.5	1
Financial account	2,945.7	52	2,195.6	39	750.1	13
TOTAL	5,648.2	100	5,079.1	91	570.0	11
Mato Grosso: Private colonization						
Current account:	—	—	—	—	—	—
Family farming	—	—	—	—	—	—
Nonagricultural	—	—	—	—	—	—
Financial account	—	—	—	—	—	—
TOTAL	—	—	—	—	—	—
Total						
Current account:						
Family farming	—	—	—	—	—	—
Nonagricultural	—	—	—	—	—	—
Financial account	—	—	—	—	—	—
TOTAL	—	—	—	—	—	—

Table 39. Monetary Account
(c) All

Destination	Receipts U.S. $	%	Expenditures U.S. $	%	Balance U.S. $	%
Pará: Public colonization						
Current account:						
Family farming	3,612.0	47	3,324.3	43	287.7	4
Nonagricultural	701.5	9	1,021.2	13	-319.8	-4
Financial account	3,403.0	44	2,874.2	37	528.8	7
TOTAL	7,716.5	100	7,219.9	93	983.0	7
Mato Grosso: Private colonization						
Current account:	—	—	—	—	—	—
Family farming	—	—	—	—	—	—
Nonagricultural	—	—	—	—	—	—
Financial account	—	—	—	—	—	—
TOTAL	—	—	—	—	—	—
Total						
Current account:						
Family farming	4,315.6	39	4,588.8	41	-273.1	-2
Nonagricultural	1,007.8	9	1,178.4	11	-170.7	-2
Financial account	5,793.0	52	4,041.2	36	1,751.7	16
TOTAL	11,116.3	100	9,808.6	88	1,306.8	12

Source: Field survey.

ditures include all production of inputs, construction for productive purposes, and forest clearing realized by the farmers themselves. Nonmonetary "income"—so-called own-consumption (food, firewood, etc.)—was smaller than nonmonetary expenditures in Pará (12 percent for southerners and 26 percent for other migrants). This was not so in Mato Grosso, where nonmonetary income comprised 16 percent of total income. This shows that agricultural production in Pará was still less dependent on purchased inputs than in Mato Grosso—which was more highly monetized, by contrast. On the other hand, it indicates that southerners in Pará, with surpluses in the family-farming account, resorted little to own-consumption as a response to monetary income constraints. Meanwhile, other migrants in Pará and colonists in Mato Grosso ran deficits in their family-farming accounts and complemented their monetary income with more own-consumption. This practice, in the case of private colonization, helps explain the greater intensity of family labor utilization already observed elsewhere.[6]

The most surprising finding in table 40 is the low nonmonetary share of total income: between 12 percent and 26 percent. Colonists practiced subsistence, or "peasant," agriculture in the sense of *self-employment* of family labor. But this did not imply subsistence agriculture in the sense of own-consumption! The presence of product markets was very important among small frontier farmers, in spite of their being located literally on the edge of untouched forests. These colonists, therefore, should be considered "monetized peasants."

Real Income: Monetary and Nonmonetary

Tables 36–40 describe accounting relationships between the frontier economy and the external economy in directed colonization in the Amazon at the end of the 1970s. According to the analysis presented in chapter 13, the tables display the structure of transactions that linked colonists to the wider economy, which can be summarized as follows.

Total annual income per family was, on average, between $17,449 and $7,650. Agricultural income generated a substantial surplus relative to production expenditures, but it was not enough to cover family expenditures. This was true for southerners in Mato Grosso as well as for other migrants in Pará (table 36). The nonagricultural economy was of little help in correcting these deficits since it constituted only a small share of total income (table 37). Borrowing was the key source for the funds necessary to cover family-farming expenditures, especially for other migrants in Pará (table 38), as it accounted for more than half of all of farmers' receipts (table 39). For southerners in Mato Grosso, land payments consumed so much of their income that little was left over for current expenditures or investment (table 38). For others in Pará,

Table 40. Monetary and Subsistence Account
(a) Southerners

Destination	*Receipts* *U.S. $*	*%*	*Expenditures* *U.S. $*	*%*	*Balance* *U.S. $*	*%*
Pará: Public colonization						
Monetary	15,332.7	88	11,986.6	69	3,346.0	19
Nonmonetary	2,117.0	12	2,913.6	17	-796.7	-5
TOTAL	17,449.6	100	14,900.0	86	2,549.4	14
Mato Grosso: Private colonization						
Monetary	14,161.4	84	12,926.0	77	1,235.3	7
Nonmonetary	2,751.1	16	3,792.0	10	-1,040.9	-6
TOTAL	16,912.6	100	16,718.0	99	194.5	1
Total						
Monetary	14,440.8	85	12,560.8	74	1,880.0	11
Nonmonetary	2,515.2	15	3,516.8	21	-1,001.5	-6
TOTAL	16,955.0	100	16,077.6	95	877.3	5

Table 40. Monetary and Subsistence Account
(b) Others

Destination	*Receipts* U.S. $	%	*Expenditures* U.S. $	%	*Balance* U.S. $	%
Pará: Public colonization						
Monetary	5,648.2	74	5,079.1	67	569	7
Nonmonetary	2,003.1	26	2,424.2	32	-442	-6
TOTAL	7,650.2	100	7,505.4	99	147	1
Mato Grosso: Private colonization						
Monetary	—	—	—	—	—	—
Nonmonetary	—	—	—	—	—	—
TOTAL	—	—	—	—	—	—
Total						
Monetary	—	—	—	—	—	—
Nonmonetary	—	—	—	—	—	—
TOTAL	—	—	—	—	—	—

Table 40. Monetary and Subsistence Account
(c) All

Destination	*Receipts*		*Expenditures*		*Balance*	
	U.S. $	*%*	*U.S. $*	*%*	*U.S. $*	*%*
Pará: Public colonization						
Monetary	7,717.5	79	7,168.1	73	549.4	6
Nonmonetary	2,037.2	21	2,573.2	27	-536.0	-6
TOTAL	9,754.8	100	9,741.3	100	13.4	—
Mato Grosso: Private colonization						
Monetary	—	—	—	—	—	—
Nonmonetary	—	—	—	—	—	—
TOTAL	—	—	—	—	—	—
Total						
Monetary	11,116.3	82	9,808.6	72	1,307.9	10
Nonmonetary	2,364.2	18	3,130.9	23	-766.7	-6
TOTAL	13,481.6	100	12,940.5	95	541.1	4

Source: Field survey and table 39.

consumption borrowing was so high relative to income that they had to resort most heavily to the nonmonetary economy (table 40).

Therefore, two types of vicious circles can be gleaned from farmers' transactions: (1) the high cost of private land led southerners in Mato Grosso to display an unexpected pattern of receipts and expenditures, and provoked chronic borrowing; (2) other migrants in Pará, by contrast, displayed a pattern of receipts and expenditures that is typical of exchange within a system of usury-mercantile capital; this pattern involved a large "subsistence" component (i.e., own-consumption) and chronic consumer borrowing. In both cases—land debt or consumption debt—a large part of the income generated by colonists was appropriated by other agents: in Pará by merchants; in Mato Grosso, by colonizing firms. These "captive" interlocked transactions reduced the amount of income appropriated by farmers and restricted their ability to save, invest, and accumulate.

The classic system of usury-mercantile capital was not generally present in Mato Grosso's colonization. Settlers there interacted with banks and firms affiliated with the capitalism of the Center-South, as seen in chapters 11 and 15. They were therefore more highly monetized and "formal." Nevertheless, they were still submitted to "captive" transactions, but of a different sort. Merchants in private colonization had relatively strong economic power and operated in concentrated markets. Their high margins, previously noted in chapter 15, especially in the agricultural product markets, were "costly" to farmers in terms of reducing the agricultural income they appropriated.[7]

In Pará, on the other hand, two types of farmers were found operating side by side. As suggested in chapter 12, they may have represented distinct phases of an advancing frontier. One of these groups was composed of family "subsistence" farmers who were indebted to support their consumption. These would be typical of the frontier's first phase, that of clearing the land and initial settlement. Many of these were later to join the subsequent rural exodus. The other group was composed of farmers who invested and accumulated. These would be typical of the frontier's second phase, that of land concentration and rural exodus. Many will probably remain in the area after landed property becomes consolidated. This cross-section sample, then, captured in one moment of time both kinds of farmers, representing vestiges and foreshadowings of the distinct phases of an advancing frontier.

Borrowing and Investment

In sum, southerners in Mato Grosso were relatively more monetized in agricultural production and spent relatively more on inputs per unit of output. They had lower absolute income levels, however, than southerners in Pará in spite of higher receipts from rents and nonagricultural activities, and were unable to balance their current transactions. Since they paid high prices for land, they became indebted and overloaded with high interest payments. They sought to mitigate this vicious circle in their monetary transactions through recourse to own-consumption in agriculture.

In Pará, southerners obtained the highest incomes. They ran surpluses in their family-farming accounts in spite of paying relatively high taxes. They borrowed to invest, in agriculture as well as in businesses, and resorted much less to own-consumption. Para's southerners were also more successful than other migrants in taking advantage of existing market opportunities and of official transfers. This may have been due to their previous experience in developed regions of the country, where cooperatives, extension work, and other support mechanisms are commonplace.

Other migrants in Pará were the poorest group. They did not earn enough even to cover their family-farming expenditures. Consequently, they resorted to wage labor, consumer borrowing, and own-consumption to cover their current deficits.

There is some evidence of the operation of usury-mercantile capital among the colonists interviewed in this period. These interlinked transactions are revealed via a strong positive current account for agriculture and a large negative balance in the nonmonetary financial account. Such a structure of transactions suggests that agricultural production was being used to repay debts in kind. On average, nonmonetary transactions were a small share of total financial accounts, serving merely as a complement to current income (own-consumption) and to investment (clearing and construction), and contributing almost nothing for transactions in kind. But for the poorest group, other migrants in Pará, these transactions were a large share (one-third) of total expenditures.

This evidence of heavy borrowing for consumption by other migrants in Pará suggests that the usury-mercantile relationship may have been undergoing a process of monetization. Consumption credits advanced during the year, and payments in kind at harvest time may have been intermediated by money. With the strong presence of the market throughout the frontier, it may well be that the relationship between merchants and farmers, although interlinked and dependent as in the classic usury-mercantile case, was already monetized.

Contrary to expectations, the most impressive "captive" transactions observed did not occur among the other migrants in Pará, nor were they linked to the marketing of agricultural produce as in the "classic" usury-mercantile relationship. Rather, they occurred among southerners in Mato Grosso as a result of the high value of land payments. Over half of the income these colonists generated was committed to interest and principal repayments owed on their plots. In this case, debts were not incurred because of family consumption, but rather because of land. Product market concentration (see chap. 15) and low prevailing agricultural product prices (see chap. 18) made it difficult for these colonists in Mato Grosso to escape their initial debt. They remained, therefore, in a vicious circle of debt and low income until the end of the decade.

The next chapter continues the analysis of colonists' performance in directed colonization. It will examine to what extent colonization covered its opportunity costs in the wider economy and will make a rough calculation of the benefits and cost ratio of directed colonization during the 1970s.

Notes

1. See appendixes 3 and 4 of *A colonização dirigida na Amazônia.* This finding is consistent with predictions of the model presented in chapter 14.

2. This finding was predicted by the model presented in chapter 14.

3. This apparently contradicts the finding in chapter 20 that nonagricultural activity has a strongly positive influence on current income. The discrepancy will be discussed at that point.

4. In chapter 20, technical assistance is shown to be highly and positively correlated with current income, even though this chapter showed that its value represents a small share of the value of current income. This point will be further discussed in that chapter.

5. *A colonizaçào dirigida na Amazônia,* appendix 4.

6. Ibid.

7. Chapter 18 will show that agricultural product prices imposed by merchants in the private colonization of Mato Grosso were significantly lower than those of official colonization in Pará.

17. COSTS AND BENEFITS

According to chapters 13 and 14, the appropriation of income by colonists and their rates of accumulation depend upon relative prices in the markets in which they transact. Chapters 15 and 16 showed that income appropriation by colonists was hampered by market concentration on the frontier, a topic that will be further examined in chapter 18. This chapter argues that in spite of unfavorable markets, directed colonization was a successful rural income distribution policy.

It will be seen that the cost per job created in Amazon colonization was indeed high: $36,869. Yet incomes and accumulation rates in directed colonization more than covered settlers' opportunity costs in both labor and capital markets. Even the poorest groups had average real income levels that amounted to more than twice the minimum wage per worker. Considering the entire period, from start-up to 1981, farmers obtained average capital accumulation rates comparable to interest rates in the financial market. By the end of the 1970s, directed colonization was reaching its break-even point.

Data and concepts on income variables come from the same sources as in the previous chapter. References pertaining to capital accumulation are in the corresponding section.

Real Level of Living

Returning to chapter 16 and separating out own-consumption from other nonmonetary items in table 40, the average value for own-consumption turns out to be surprisingly close to that of monetary outlays with family consumption in table 36. This similarity exists within each group and between migrant groups: southerners and others. Both figures, "own consumption" and "monetary outlays for consumption," are shown in table 42 under these respective headings. Their similar values suggest that different types of farmers target for similar real levels of living and similar compositions in consumption between purchased and own-consumed goods. This implies that income above the target real consumption level would tend to be used for investment.[1] When income falls short of target consumption, the difference is covered by indebtedness, given that nonagricultural income sources are still few on a frontier.[2]

As was seen in chapter 16, economic behavior differed greatly among migrant groups. For example: public settlement's southerners were the greatest investors, and private settlement's southerners were the most indebted. Such large differences in productive behavior among groups contrasts with their homogeneity in family consumption levels. On average, total family real consumption per year was greater in Mato Grosso ($4,060) than in Pará ($3,156). Within Pará, it was greater among southerners ($3,656) than among the others ($2,943). These differences, however, are much smaller than the total income differentials already observed in chapter 16.

In order to estimate an average imputed wage rate, total real consumption per family has to be divided by the number of effective workers per household. Although there is strong seasonality in agriculture, the intensity of labor (hours per day) varies less over the agricultural year than the type of work that is done. Deforestation, stump removal, burning, soil preparation, planting, weeding and other crop treatment, harvesting, warehousing, extractivism, repairing, construction, transportation, animal care, and so on all demand long hours all year round. Since adults frequently worked longer hours than a typical urban workday, an "effective worker" was estimated by the total annual working hours observed divided by an urban equivalent: 8 hour workday x 25 working days per month x 12 months per year = 2,400 working hours per year. This calculation corrects the downward bias that would have been introduced if the number of workers per family were to be estimated on the basis of the number of active adults. It also corrects the overestimate that would arise from attributing full worker status to part-time workers, such as children, teenagers, and the elderly.

Dividing total real family consumption by the number of "effective" workers per family, according to table 41, yields total consumption per worker, the next line of table 42. One can see that frontier farming "paid" family labor roughly according to the urban labor market:[3] more among southerners (1.1 minimum wages per effective worker, based on the 1981 harvest time minimum wage) and less among the others in Pará (0.87

Table 41. Effective Workers per Family

Destination	Origin Southern	Other	Total
Pará	3.11	3.19	3.16
Mato Grosso	3.44	—	—
TOTAL	3.35	—	3.29

Source: Field survey.
Note: 1 "effective worker" = 8 hs/day x 25 days/month x 12 months/year = 2,400 hours/year.

minimum wages per effective worker). The average family level for the sample as a whole is around one minimum wage per effective worker.

Comparing table 42's "level of living" and table 40's "total income," one is struck by the fact that a farmer's average turnover was twelve times the family's own remuneration level. It should thus be remembered that the figures in table 42 refer not to production but to consumption. They approximate the idea of a real "level of living" per family, or worker. This is the appropriate variable for comparison with urban wage rates from the point of view of the farmer's decision to migrate to either an agricultural frontier or an urban center.

If the frontier's nonmonetary economy were to have been overestimated[4] and if its share of total income were lower than accounted for, the estimated real level of living in table 42 would also be too high. This, however, was not the case. Nonmonetary income was, on average, a small percentage of total monetary income: only 20 percent. As a matter of fact, it is possible that the real level of living is underestimated, rather than overestimated. This is because some of the omitted loans noted in the previous chapter, also about 20 percent of total monetary income, were probably used for family consumption. Since it is unclear which bias was greater, underestimation due to consumer loans, or overestimation due to nonmonetary income, one will have to consider them as roughly equal. Thus, real average consumption per effective family worker at the end of the 1970s is estimated at one minimum wage. At decade's end, then, migration to the frontier made about as much economic sense to settlers as entry into the urban labor market.

Capital Accumulation Rates

Frontier farming seems to have been a "good deal" in terms of capital market alternatives, as can be seen in table 43.

Capital accumulation rates[5] were measured comparing the value of initial assets[6] upon arrival to that of assets in 1980–1981, discounted by time on the plot, according to the standard formula in table 43. As the value of all initial assets was updated to 1981, the calculated rates are in real terms. One can see in table 43 that asset values accumulated at a real rate of 1.6 percent per month and 20 percent per year! Rates were highest for Pará's southerners (25 percent per year), intermediary for Mato Grosso's southerners (21 percent annually), and lowest for others in Pará (13 percent per year).

The evolution of these rates over time was very different among migrant groups, as one would perhaps expect. In Pará, both southerners and others had low real accumulation rates (7.8 percent and 3.6 percent per year, respectively) during the start-up phase (0–3 years), but compensated in subsequent years with much higher rates (28.2 and 27.6 percent). In Mato Grosso, settlers had incredibly high real rates in the initial phase (49.5 percent annually) that later fell to much lower levels (11.3 and 14.1 percent per year).

Being a settler, therefore, was, financially, a good arrangement in the public colonization of Pará and seemingly improved with time. After initial start-up difficulties, settlers obtained, on average, a 28-percent annual accumulation rate, yielding double the initial investment every 2.4 years! In Mato Grosso, being a settler began as a real bonanza, with investment doubling in less then two years! During succeeding phases, these high rates fell to 13 percent, which doubles one's capital every 5.7 years. Even in Mato Grosso, however, settlement seems not to have been bad business.

The most widespread alternative for small savers in Brazil are savings accounts that pay real interest rates of 0.5 percent monthly (6 percent annually). If these rates are taken to be the opportunity cost for low income investors, then settlement covered its financial opportunity cost by a wide margin. Many other interest rates could conceivably be used for comparison, but none is as generally accessible as are federal savings accounts.

As mentioned before, the sample includes different kinds of settlers. In Pará, many recent migrants were northeastern itinerant farmers who cleared plots and left them soon afterward in a transient economic path devoid of capital accumulation. These eternal pioneers reduced the average accumulation rate observed among all those who had arrived one to three years previous to the survey. Settlers who had remained three to six or more years on their plots were mostly survivors relative to the rural exodus. They made up a successful group that was effectively accumulating capital.

Table 42. Real Level of Living (in U.S. $)

Destination	*Southern*	*Origin* *Other*	*Total*
Pará (public settlement)			
Monetary outlays	1,964	1,345	1,530
Own-consumption	1,679	1,598	1,622
Total per family	3,656	2,943	3,152
Total per worker[a]	1,175	922	997
Minimum wages per worker[b]	1.11	0.87	0.94
Mato Grosso (private settlement)			
Monetary outlays	2,048		
Own-consumption	2,011		
Total family	4,060		
Total per worker[a]	4,180		
Minimum wages per worker[b]	1.11		
General Total			
Monetary outlays	2,029		1,870
Own-consumption	1,906		1,801
Total family	3,935		3,672
Total per worker[a]	1,174		1,116
Minimum wages per worker[b]	1.11		1.05

Source: Tables 36 and 41.

[a]1 effective worker = 8 hs/day x 25 days/month x 12 months/year = 2,400 hours/year.

[b]Monthly minimum wage on 5/1/81: Cr$8,464.80 x 12 months = Cr$101,577.60 = U.S. $1,057.66 per year.

In Mato Grosso, recent arrivals included ex–small farmers from the South whose holdings had appreciated greatly during the upturn of the economic cycle of the early 1970s. After selling their former plots, they brought the corresponding resources with them to the frontier. The apparently high accumulation rate among these migrants therefore does not correspond to capital accumulation on the frontier. Rather, as new capitalized migrants joined those already there, an influx of capital was transferred from one region to another. Older settlers who had been on the frontier from three to six years or more no longer lived off the southern economy. Since they depended solely on the frontier, their average accumulation rate was much lower than that of recent arrivals.

It should be noted that an increase in the value of settlers' assets, measured here as capital accumulation, may not come from productive investments. A part of it may reflect speculative increases in asset values, especially land. Part of the measured accumulation rate may therefore be due to "capital gains" and not "capital accumulation." This issue cannot be analyzed with the available data. The main point in this section is that, for whatever reason, directed colonization in the Amazon greatly increased the value of settlers' assets, especially in the case of older colonists in official settlement.[7]

Cost per Job Created

According to table 41, there were, on average, 3.3 effective workers per rural family in the sample. Since average family size was 7,[8] one can estimate approximately 2.1 family members per effective worker in Amazon colonization.

Urban families frequently have lower labor force participation than rural families, due to more access to education, retirement benefits, transfers, other income, and possibly to other activities, such as religion, entertainment, and so on. Urban families also tend to be smaller than rural ones, but as the labor force participation rate is also lower, the resulting average number of effective workers per family may be similar. The estimate of 2.1 family members per effective worker will thus be extended to the population as a whole.

Multiplying this number (2.1) by $5,578, the per capita cost of directed colonization estimated in chapter 10, yields an estimate of public investment per job created in directed colonization of $11,713. This value represents only the social/institutional part of investment in job creation; it excludes individual investments in creating an agricultural or commercial establishment on the frontier. The same field survey used in this part of the book estimates that resources brought by farmers and merchants who migrated to colonization projects were similar in each

Table 43. Capital Accumulation Rates (%)

Destination	*Time in Years*	*Southern*		*Origin Other*		*Total*	
		Monthly	*Annual*	*Monthly*	*Annual*	*Monthly*	*Annual*
Pará:	1–3	0.6	7.8	0.3	3.6	0.4	4.5
Public settlement	4–6	2.1	28.8	2.4	28.7	2.2	28.7
	6 +	2.1	28.1	2.0	27.6	2.0	27.7
TOTAL		1.9	25.0	1.3	13.0	1.5	19.4
Mato Grosso:	1–3	4.1	49.5	—	—	—	—
Private settlement	4–6	0.9	11.3	—	—	—	—
	6 +	1.1	14.1	—	—	—	—
TOTAL		1.8	21.5	—	—	—	—
Total	1–3	3.8	48.8	—	—	3.8	43.7
	4–6	1.4	18.1	—	—	1.6	20.2
	6 +	1.7	20.6	—	—	1.9	25.3
TOTAL		1.8	23.4	—	—	1.6	20.3

Source: Field survey.
Note Rate of return = ([(total assets/initial resources) 1/time on plot] x 100) - 100.

region, though widely different across regions. Poorer migrants in Pará (public colonization) brought an average of $5,000 per family. Richer migrants in Mato Grosso (private colonization) brought an average of $28,000 per family. The weighted average of the two regions is $7,115.

These initial resource values may seem high for a supposedly "dispossessed" population, especially values from Mato Grosso. In fact, many settlers, particularly those from the Northeast who went to Pará, arrived without a penny and relied on wage labor for one or more years until they had saved enough to set themselves up minimally on their own plots. They then cleared a small area at a time and expanded slowly. Others, especially those from the South who went to Mato Grosso, arrived with capital from the sale of their previous properties, and cleared most of their plots immediately. Start-up costs in agriculture, however, must have been relatively high. As can be seen by comparing tables 40 and 42, even among small farmers average turnover was twelve times greater than average family consumption.

Dividing the overall average private cost per family ($7,115) by the average number of effective workers per family (3.3) from table 41 yields an average private cost of $2,156 per worker. Adding this cost to the average social cost already estimated ($11,713) yields a total cost, social and private, per job created in Amazon directed colonization during the 1970s of $13,900.

This figure should be compared to an alternative one. If one were to divide the cost per family in directed settlement projects, seen in chapter 8 ($4,000), by the average number of effective workers per family (3.3) calculated here, the result would be an average "direct" cost per worker of approximately $1,212 within directed settlement projects. This is quite close to the settlement figures calculated by FAO and IPEA, shown in table 44, which include only direct settlement costs. By taking into account not only such "direct" costs (chap. 8) but also "indirect" costs such as those of homogenizing (chap. 7) and complementing (chap. 9), the estimated cost per job created was here multiplied more than ten times.

The "complete" estimate ($13,900) is conceptually more adequate, for the period under study, than the "partial" estimate cited in the above paragraph ($1,212). During the 1970s, there was no possibility for Amazon colonization that did not necessarily involve the indirect costs of implanting legal, physical, and social infrastructure in the region at $13.9 thousand per worker. At that time, however, the same number of people could have been settled at less than one-tenth of the cost by an agrarian reform in already established regions, which would have demanded only settlement (at $1.2 thousand per worker). These figures reflect the real political choice that was actually made during the 1970s, to settle the Amazon when it was still mostly intact. A further discus-

Table 44. Costs per Job Created: Other Sources

Activity	*Source*	*Cost (in U.S. $1,000)*
Agriculture and ranching	SUDAM	70
	SUDENE/IPEA	25
Amazon settlement	IPEA	2
	FAO/IBRD	1.9
Industry	SUDAM	32
	SUFRAMA	18
	SUDENE/IPEA	24
Services	SUDAM	55

Source: Mahar (1978), p. 128, table IV.6 (my conversions).

sion of colonization versus agrarian reform follows in chapter 22. Every qualification made in chapter 10 concerning deficiencies in these same data, or in the calculations and concepts, applies again here.

It may not be strictly correct to compare such broad-based costs as those estimated here with other job-creation costs more narrowly defined elsewhere. Those presented in table 43, for instance, include only direct outlays in each estimate. Note that this book's estimate of the cost of Amazon colonization, at $13,869 per worker, is quite cheap compared to the cost of job creation in urban activities (industry or services) or even in large-scale agriculture or ranching (see table 44). Thus, not only did colonization make economic sense for the individual migrant, as seen in the sections "Real Level of Living" and "Capital Accumulation Rates" above, it also made "planning" sense, in terms of job-creation costs in the economy as a whole.

Tentative Cost-Benefit Ratios

The total cost per job created by colonization during the 1970s was estimated in the previous section as approximately $13,900. This figure can now be multiplied by the estimated average number of effective workers per family (3.3), yielding a cost of $45,900 per settled family. During the agricultural year of 1980–1981, total annual income per family according to table 40, was $13,500.

In spite of great variations within the sample, average income did not vary significantly between new and older settlers. There was even a slight tendency for income to decline over time, as will be seen in chapter 21, graph 4. Thus, one year's income may be a reasonable approximation to average income in other years. Average time on the plot was five years: less for southerners in Mato Grosso and Pará (3 years) and more for others in Pará (8 years). Multiplication of weighted average time (5 years) by weighted average annual income ($13,500) yields an estimated weighted average income generated by settlers since their arrival on their plots of $67,500. This would be an extremely rough estimate of the benefit of colonization per settled family. Dividing this figure on benefit per family ($67,500) by the estimated cost per family ($45,900) yields a tentative benefit-cost ratio of 1.47.

As all others in this chapter, this figure must be regarded with extreme caution. Since the economic performance of southerners in public projects was generally better than for either of the other groups, the benefit-cost ratio may also have been higher for them than for other migrants in the same projects, or for southerners in private settlement. The calculation made here, therefore, is a gross overall approximation of the "true" cost-benefit ratios, and is offered only for the sake of providing a broad order of magnitude on the issue.

Given the huge variations among different groups of settlers, the average for the total sample is not very relevant in itself. The use of confidence intervals instead of averages would have been preferable. Different discount rates should have been applied to cost and income flows to increase comparability of the resulting ratio to alternatives in the rest of the economy. None of these adjustments was made, however, due to the dearth of information on which they would be based and the precariousness of the data used. The tentative conclusion that can be made in this section, however, is that, possibly, colonization had already more than paid for its cost by the end of the 1970s.

The "Reasonable" Performance of Colonization

Income appropriated by frontier settlers remunerated agricultural capital and labor at levels compatible with their alternatives in financial and labor markets. In terms of measured costs and benefits, colonization seemingly contributed to society more than it took during the 1970s. This conclusion is based exclusively on the conventional and imprecise economic measurements, without taking into account so-called positive or negative externalities.

On the positive side, given political resistance to land reform in established areas, colonization gave some of the landless population the opportunity to become autonomous small farmers. Many affirmed that they preferred to earn less on their own land than more working for someone else.[9] Given observed real income data, what they earned turned out to be more, and they were certainly on land of their own. In return for this option, they apparently produced more than they had cost society as a whole. Measurement of the value of land ownership itself was not attempted.

On the negative side, alternative uses for the natural resources involved in colonization were also not taken into account. Several such alternatives can be envisaged. To begin with the least probable, the land would perhaps have been more productive in large-scale agriculture and ranching than in colonization. Second, given colonization, agricultural technology could have been less devastating to the ecology than the type actually used. This issue was mentioned in chapter 4 and will be addressed again in chapter 19. Third, forest extractivism, such as rubber tapping, would perhaps have been less destructive and more profitable than either farming or ranching. Last but not least, the forest could have been preserved whole due to its value as a natural resource in its own right, independent of any economic product it might provide. The measurement of the value of any of these alternatives to colonization is not attempted here. This book's objectives are merely to measure colonization's direct economic costs and benefits. Within all stated limitations, this chapter proposes that colonization's benefits during the 1970s more than covered its cost.

The next chapter will examine relative prices in Amazon colonization projects. These prices monitored agricultural income appropriation, whether by settlers or other agents with whom settlers transacted. They are therefore crucial to an evaluation of the economic performance of directed settlement in the Amazon.

Notes

1. According to verbal communication by Geraldo Müller (IPPUR/UFRJ, 1987; see also G. Müller 1987), settlers only begin to invest as of ten minimum wages. The data given here, however, indicate that the capacity to invest begins at much lower income levels, practically as soon as subsistence is covered.

2. See table 37.

3. About half the urban labor force in Brazil earns one institutionally set "minimum wage" or less. For this reason, the minimum wage can be considered a reasonable upper bound opportunity cost for self-employment in frontier agriculture.

4. See text for table 40.

5. "Capital accumulation" is taken to mean an increase in the real value of all physical and financial assets, whether due to appreciation (above general inflationary levels) or to quantitative additions to stocks of production and consumption durables, buildings, and so on. Small farmers easily transfer

resources from consumption to production in agriculture, commerce, and so on. Therefore, comparisons over time refer to family property as a whole. Appendix 1 of *A colonização dirigida na Amazônia* defines the exact empirical meaning of assets among Amazon colonists interviewed in field research. A rate of "capital accumulation" had to be calculated, instead of the more usual "rate of return," because information was not available on income produced by farmers during each year since arrival. To the extent that not all income is reinvested in the farm, the rate of capital accumulation will be smaller than the rate of return. On the other hand, to the extent that speculation appreciates assets beyond their real productivity, it will be greater than the rate of return.

6. "Initial assets" brought by settlers to the Amazon are defined and measured in appendix 1 of *A colonização dirigida na Amazônia.*

7. Subsequent work by the author on Amazon colonization during the 1980s differentiates productive investment from capital gains. It shows that appreciation in land values, especially in Pará, was the main motive for colonists' rising total asset values in the recent decade, though not necessarily in Mato Grosso.

8. See table 36. "Family" members include the nuclear group (father, mother, offspring), the extended family, and nonblood relatives, or *agregados,* who partake of household consumption and production

9. B. Ferreira (1984).

18. MARKET SEGMENTATION

The value a farmer appropriates from a given level of agricultural production depends upon relative prices in market transactions with inputs and outputs. The higher are product prices and the lower are input prices, the larger the share of total value that a farmer appropriates and the larger his resultant income. Relative prices, in turn, depend upon how local merchants operate and are linked to markets in the rest of the economy. Price setting in one frontier location will be different from that in another, depending on how commercial chains connect local merchants to distinct parts of the external market. Chains that carry products to concentrated markets may entail mark-up pricing, barriers to entry, and other mechanisms typical of oligopolistic price setting. Those that carry merchandise to competitive markets may set prices more competitively.[1] Different price-setting behaviors in one location may provoke large variations in prices between merchants in the same market. When different prices are charged for equivalent products, "market segmentation" can be said to occur.

In conformity with the analysis in chapter 12, colonists' behavior should vary with the phase of frontier advance in which they find themselves. In the early phases, many become imprisoned in a vicious circle of indebtedness, as seen in chapter 16. Chronic debt may come through consumption transactions with usury-mercantile capital, through land transactions due to "excessively high" prices for land, or through other means. It causes a large contingent of colonists to give up and leave, swelling the rural exodus from the frontier, as seen in chapter 2. Some, however, create cooperatives or organize as a local community, so as to bargain for better prices than they would obtain by competing among themselves. These and other farmer reactions will increase or diminish the price-setting power of local merchants and affect the degree of market segmentation on the frontier.

Different segments of a given market appropriate different shares of total value. Colonists' income, therefore, and colonization's performance in general, will depend on the degree of rural market segmentation. For empirical purposes, a market will be considered "homogeneous" if similar products have prices that are not statistically different from each other, and "segmented" if there is a statistically significant difference between prices charged by different agents.

This chapter will test hypotheses concerning local market segmentation, which requires disaggregation within locations. Data come from the same locations analyzed in the three previous chapters, which are now made explicit: three public colonization projects in Pará—Pacal, Anapu/Pacajá (along the Transamazon Highway), and Monte Alegre (further north)—and three private colonization projects in Mato Grosso—Alta Floresta/Paranaíta, Mutum, and São José do Rio Claro.[2] This chapter also differs from the previous ones in that it is not merely descriptive, but aims to test empirical hypotheses statistically.

Average prices paid or received by each colonist were weighted by the quantities transacted in each purchase or sale with respect to each product and input. Simple tests on differences of means were used to investigate the hypothesis of market segmentation in each location: between migrants, between locations, and also between types of colonization. When the differences in the means were statistically significant at the 10 percent level, the result was presented with a small letter-exponent to the corresponding mean. Two or more means with the same letter-exponent signify that they are statistically different at the 10 percent level of significance.

All relevant pairs and all local combinations were tested: (1) southerners versus "others" in each location in official colonization projects; (2) official colonization versus private colonization among southerners; and (3) official colonization versus private colonization in general. The absence of an exponent above an average indicates that it is not statistically different from any other average at the 10 percent significance level. Joint chi-square tests were not done within and between groups, since the objective here is not merely to determine any differentiation whatever on the frontier, but to identify how each subgroup is differentiated from the others already chosen for comparison.

The findings suggest that the land market is strongly segmented, and that the agricultural product market is also segmented, with more concentration in private colonization than in the official. The manufactured product market, however, appears to be homogeneous across frontier areas that are very distant from one another and have a minimum of communication between them. This supports earlier evidence from chapters 11 and 15, with respect to the domination by southern industrial capital over the market for manufactured goods on the frontier.

Agricultural Product Prices

This section compares average prices obtained by colonists when selling each of the principal agricultural products: rice, beans, corn, coffee, cocoa, sugarcane, and pepper. Only the first three annual crops were cultivated in all locations; the others, being perennial, were still being implanted in some places and were totally absent wherever an institutionalized marketing system was lacking. Annual crops, then, make up a general undifferentiated system of production and commercialization on the frontier, while perennial crops integrate into a structure of production and commercial distribution specific to each product. Thus, sugarcane was planted where sugar mills existed; cocoa was cultivated where CEPLAC was active; pepper was planted where pepper purchasers operated, and so on. Soy was only beginning to expand as a major crop during the survey period, and therefore is not analyzed in this chapter.

Rice is a universal crop that is produced both for commercial and subsistence purposes throughout the country. It was part of the commercial structure in all research locations, as may be seen in table 45. For this reason it was chosen as a "base" product for the purposes of comparison and statistical testing. It is strange to note that, at the time, though rice was the predominant cash crop for the southerners of Mato Grosso, it was of less importance to the southerners of Pará. Immigrants' origins (all southerners, in this case), then, had less to do with the crop that they planted than expected. The marketing chain that linked each location to its specific dominant "central" market was apparently more important than farmers' origin. Returning to table 45, then, Anapu/Pacajá in Pará and Mutum in Mato Grosso were dominated by the rice market, which accounted for 86 percent and 99 percent, respectively, of the total value of marketed agricultural products.[3] Marketing in other locations was more varied.

Rice, Beans, and Corn

Tables 46, 47, and 48 suggest that Pacal was a relatively homogeneous market—that is, without differentiation between the prices paid to southerners and others for rice, corn, and beans. Probably the proximity

Table 45. The Share of Rice in the Value of Principal Commercial Crops (%)

Destination	*Origin*		
	Southerners	*Others*	*All*
Public colonization in Pará:			
Pacal	7.14	10.85	9.06
Anapu/Pacajá	72.34	87.43	86.19
Monte Alegre	2.92	12.28	6.43
SUBTOTAL	7.93	22.85	16.08
Private colonization in Mato Grosso:			
Alta Floresta/Paranaíta	58.60	—	—
Mutum	99.36	—	—
São J. do Rio Claro	20.31	—	—
SUBTOTAL	65.60	—	—
TOTAL	34.39	—	29.84

Source: Field survey.
Note: (Value of rice sales)/(Value of rice + bean + corn + coffee + cocoa + cane + pepper sales) x100.

of Altamira directed the greater part of production toward that market, eliminating small monopsonists in local enclaves. In other official colonization projects, however, segmentation was clearly manifested. Southerners obtained higher prices than others in Anapu, Pacajá, and Monte Alegre.[4] In private colonization, price variation was not systematic between locations. In the market for rice, the region's principal cash crop, Mato Grosso prices were significantly lower than those in Pará. For the other crops of marginal importance, the prices in Mato Grosso were higher.

In the specific case of rice, table 46 shows that southerners within official colonization obtained higher prices than other settlers. They also obtained higher prices than southerners in private colonization. At the local level, in Anapu/Pacajá and in Monte Alegre, which have very different and isolated markets, there were significant price differences

Table 46. Average Rice Prices (U.S. $/Kg.)

Destination	*Origin*		
	Southerners	*Others*	*All*
Public colonization in Pará:			
Pacal	0.13	0.14	0.14
Anapu/Pacajá	0.14[a]	0.13[a]	0.13[c]
Monte Alegre	0.23[b]	0.12[b]	0.14[c]
SUBTOTAL	0.14[d]	0.13	0.13[f]
Private colonization in Mato Grosso:			
Alta Floresta/Paranaíta	0.13	—	—
Mutum	0.14	—	—
São J. do Rio Claro	0.11	—	—
SUBTOTAL	0.13[d,f]	—	—
TOTAL	0.16	—	0.13

Source: Field survey.
Note: Repeated letter exponents indicate differences in the means that are statistically significant at the 10 percent level.

between southerners and others. But this difference was not significant in the case of Pacal. As suggested above, perhaps the influence of the nearby market of Altamira blurred the difference between southerners and others in this location. On average, official colonization had higher prices than private.

In the case of beans, table 47 shows that within official colonization projects, southerners again got better prices than others in Monte Alegre and in Anapu/Pacajá, although in the latter case the difference is not statistically significant. Anapu/Pacajá and Monte Alegre are different from one another and in relation to Pacal, which, perhaps because of its proximity to Altamira, shows little internal price differentiation. Private colonization had higher bean prices than the official, which were highest in Alta Floresta.

For corn, table 48 shows that southerners also had higher prices than others in the official colonization projects of Anapu/Pacajá, as well as in Monte Alegre, although the difference is statistically significant only at

Table 47. Average Bean Prices (U.S. $/Kg.)

Destination	*Origin*		
	Southerners	*Others*	*All*
Public colonization in Pará:			
Pacal	0.88	0.95	0.92[c]
Anapu/Pacajá	1.27	0.93	0.97[c]
Monte Alegre	0.96[b]	0.64[b]	0.65[c]
SUBTOTAL	0.89	0.84	0.88[d]
Private colonization in Mato Grosso:			
Alta Floresta/Paranaíta	1.00[f]	—	—
Mutum	—	—	—
São J. do Rio Claro	0.78[f]	—	—
SUBTOTAL	0.98[d]	—	—
TOTAL	0.93	—	0.90

Source: Field survey.
Note: Repeated letter exponents indicate differences in the means that are statistically significant at the 10 percent level.

the level of Pará as a whole. Anapu and Monte Alegre are different from one another, but not with respect to Pacal. Southerners in private colonization received different prices in different locations: as a whole, they obtained higher prices than those in official colonization.

In sum, the three crops present distinct patterns with respect to the prices reported by colonists in each location. The next section looks at prices reported by merchants in these same locations.

Prices of Merchants

Tables 46, 47, and 48 show prices received by farmers. Among rice merchants, declared prices in each location were generally a little higher than those reported above, although they preserved the differentiation already noted. Many merchants are also processors, who buy rice in the hull from colonists and resell processed rice, often back to the colonists themselves. Comparing the prices in tables 46 and 49, one sees that the

Table 48. Average Corn Prices (U.S. $/Kg.)

Destination	Origin		
	Southerners	*Others*	*All*
Public colonization in Pará:			
Pacal	0.08	0.09	0.09
Anapu/Pacajá	0.10	0.09	0.09[c]
Monte Alegre	0.10	0.10	0.10[c]
SUBTOTAL	0.09[a]	0.09[a]	0.09[b]
Private Colonization in Mato Grosso:			
Alta Floresta/Paranaíta	0.10[d]	—	—
Mutum	0.13[d]	—	—
São J. do Rio Claro	0.09[d]	—	—
SUBTOTAL	0.10[a,b]	—	—
TOTAL	0.10	—	0.10

Source: Field survey.
Note: Repeated letter exponents indicate differences in the means that are statistically significant at the 10 percent level.

higher the merchants' margins, the lower the prices for colonists, as would be expected. Given that processing technology was similar across locations, unit processing costs must also have been very similar. The observed difference in margins, therefore, may be largely related to different degrees of market concentration across locations. The low prices paid to rice farmers in Mato Grosso, then, may have been generated in part by the more concentrated market structures in that state, relative to Pará.

In table 49, processing margins are very large, ranging from 245 percent to 355 percent. It is worth recalling that even though they appear high, these calculations underestimate the value actually appropriated by processors, since they do not incorporate the value of the hull that they keep and resell as cattle feed. Such large margins must indicate a high level of monopsonistic power exercised by frontier merchants, conferred upon them by the distance to central markets.[5]

Table 49. Average Rice Prices According to Merchants

Destination	*Type of Rice* *With Hull (U.S. $/Kg.) (1)*	*Processed (U.S. $/Kg.) (2)*	*Margin (%) (3)*
Public colonization in Pará:			
Pacal	—	0.72	—
Anapu/Pacajá	0.15	0.41	267
Monte Alegre	0.17	0.42	245
SUBTOTAL	0.16	0.42	255
Private colonization in Mato Grosso:			
Alta Floresta/Paranaíta	0.10	0.32	355
Mutum	—	—	—
São J. do Rio Claro	0.15	0.48	311
SUBTOTAL	0.11	0.39	339
TOTAL	0.13	0.40	308

Source: Field survey.
Note: Column 3 = [(2) – (1) / (1)] x 100.

In this case, freight charges are not part of merchants' costs, at least not directly, since prices were charged and paid at business headquarters. Nevertheless, all of the goods exported or imported on the frontier indirectly incorporated substantial transportation costs relative to goods transacted in main consumer centers, since freights impose a discount on sale prices and add to purchase prices. Distance and transport costs therefore cause adverse terms of trade for the frontier, relative to the rest of the economy. Transport costs constitute barriers to entry into local markets, and thereby inflate margins beyond the effect of market concentration in each location. The wide margins observed here indicate that potential competitors for frontier merchants were very distant and would have had to pay high transport costs to enter these markets. Local margins thus capture merchants' high degree of relative monopsony: not only among themselves in each frontier location, but also on the frontier as a whole relative to markets elsewhere.

Principal Perennial Crops

Table 50 shows that the price of coffee in Pará is three times higher than that in Mato Grosso, with great variation among locations. Mato Grosso's disadvantage in coffee prices in comparison to Pará could reflect differences in quality as much as higher commercial markups, as was already verified in the case of rice. Relative distances to the central markets cannot sufficiently explain such great price differences. Although Mato Grosso is less accessible than Pará, as was seen in chapter 7, it is not much more remote.[6] Certainly, distance alone is not enough to explain a price difference of 300 percent relative to Pará.

Pepper is a cash crop only in Pará, comprising a homogeneous market along the Transamazon Highway, but a segmented one in Monte Alegre, where prices obtained by southerners were significantly higher than those received by others. Average farmers' prices were consistent with merchants' prices in the same localities (see tables 49 and 50). The number of observations, however, is insufficient for statistical testing.

In general, perennial crops had more fragmented markets and greater variance than the annuals, being also less widely cultivated. Some were still getting started and had markets that were also incipient, as was the case of cocoa. Pepper was not a cash crop in Mato Grosso projects, perhaps for lack of a specialized marketing structure. Coffee, a southern specialty from Paraná, is shipped from Mato Grosso and Pará to strongly differentiated external markets.

Perennial crops are a way for farmers to consolidate their holdings and accumulate wealth. Nevertheless, market uncertainties increase the riskiness of this path of agricultural accumulation through diversification. In the absence of an adequate policy to support perennial crops, their spread on the frontier seems to have been retarded according to this survey. Many successful colonists, then, diversified into nonagricultural activities, as was seen in chapter 16, rather than into perennials, as will be seen in the next chapter.

Input Costs

Average costs incurred by colonists with respect to current expenditures (e.g., freight and sacking), equipment (tractors, power saws, and sprayers), hired labor, credit, and land were compared. Only in the case of land were systematic and statistically significant price differences found. The credit, input, and labor markets were not found to be segmented, either within or between locations. This may be due in great measure to evasion and deliberate omission of information by colonists, especially

Table 50. Average Price of Principal Perennial Crops (U.S. $/kg..)

Destination	*Crop*	*Origin* *Southerners*	*Others*	*All*
Public colonization in Pará:				
Pacal	Coffee	2.40	1.02	1.16
	Pepper	0.61	0.62	0.61[c]
Anapu/Pacajá	Coffee	0.90	—	0.90
	Pepper	—	0.63	0.63[c]
Monte Alegre	Coffee	—	—	—
	Pepper	0.69[a]	0.56[a]	0.64[c]
SUBTOTAL	Coffee	1.58	1.02	1.13
	Pepper	0.62	0.60	0.62[b]
Private colonization in Mato Grosso:				
Alta Floresta/Paranaíta	Coffee	0.38	—	—
	Pepper	—	—	—
Mutum	Coffee	—	—	—
	Pepper	—	—	—
São J. do Rio Claro	Coffee	0.39	—	—
	Pepper	—	—	—
SUBTOTAL	Coffee	0.38[b]	—	0.73
	Pepper	—	—	0.62
TOTAL	Coffee	1.03	—	0.59
	Pepper	0.62	—	0.62

Source: Field survey.
Note: Repeated letter exponents indicate differences in the means that are statistically significant at the 10 percent level.

about the credit market and, above all, with respect to "informal" or "usurious" transactions. There were also multiple imprecisions in data collection, for which reason the respective costs are not presented here. Neither was it possible to study the prices of family consumption goods, given the great diversity involved and difficulties in comparing distinct consumer baskets.

Chapters 15 and 17 showed very different rates of accumulation between merchants and farmers, merchants' rates being much higher. Their respective creditors were also very different: merchants borrow mostly from banks; farmers borrow heavily from merchants. As previously discussed in chapter 12, then, rates of interest for both should also be very different: (1) if farmers' creditors were to follow the logic of "usury-mercantile capital," they would seek to maximize volume received in agricultural produce, not interest rates. It is even possible, then, for the interest rates charged by merchants to farmers to be lower than the rates paid by merchants to banks; and (2) if farmers' creditors were to follow the logic of "directly productive capital," then they would seek to maximize their specific income (i.e., interest itself). In this case, it is very possible that the interest rate paid by farmers would be higher than that paid by merchants.

Both of these possibilities, interesting and important though they are, could not be investigated with the current data base that collected inconsistent information from farmers and insufficient information from merchants. Such data were much more tricky to collect than was initially foreseen during the survey preparatory phase, and their absence is unfortunately harmful to the analysis.

The price of land, however, was adequately collected and it revealed systematic differences of great interest, given the crucial importance of land on a frontier. Land price differences were found to be consistent with the implications of the model developed in chapters 13 and 14, as will be seen next.

The Price of Land

The average price of land in each location was calculated separately for forested areas, cleared areas, and those planted with pasture, temporary crops, perennial crops, and *capoeiras* (abandoned fields). Variations among individual lots reflect appraisals by local extension services and by colonists themselves about the probable purchase price, given variations in fertility, accessibility, and so on. The final result is the average price per hectare for land in each location, presented in table 51.[7]

At first glance, land prices on the Amazon frontier in general seem absurdly cheap. Comparing tables 51 with 46–48, one sees that the price of 1 hectare of land (19 cents) was, on average, little more than the price of 1 kilogram of rice (13 cents), less than one-quarter of the price of 1 kilogram of beans (88 cents), and not quite double the price of 1 kilogram of corn (10 cents). Absolute prices are meaningless, however, given the uniformly low absolute level of real income derived from frontier farming, seen in the previous chapter. Only relative comparisons, therefore, should be made.

Lots in private colonization cost almost four times those belonging to southerners in official colonization, and eight times those belonging to

Table 51. Total Price of Land (U.S. $/ha.)

Destination	*Origin*		
	Southerners	*Others*	*All*
Public colonization in Pará:			
Pacal	0.13	0.12	0.13[a]
Anapu/Pacajá	0.02	0.02	0.02[a]
Monte Alegre	0.12	0.04	0.07[a]
SUBTOTAL	0.12[b,c]	0.06[c]	0.08[c]
Private colonization in Mato Grosso:			
Alta Floresta/Paranaíta	0.46[d]	—	—
Mutum	0.22[d]	—	—
São J. do Rio Claro	0.20[d]	—	—
SUBTOTAL	0.29[b,e]	—	—
TOTAL	0.19	—	0.19

Source: Field survey.
Note: Repeated letter exponents indicate differences between means that are statistically significant at the 10 percent level.

"others" in official projects. A hectare in Alta Floresta was valued twenty times higher than one in Anapu/Pacajá. These differences were much greater than the differentials in the total value of assets (which included the value of land) among the same groups of colonists: southerners in private colonization owned assets 57 percent more valuable than southerners in official projects, and three times more so than "others."[8]

Such a large gap in land prices cannot be justified in terms of the supposed advantages of private colonization versus official projects. Chapter 8 showed that total investment per lot in private colonization was less than half that of the official. Neither is the difference in land prices justified by supposed marketing advantages of private colonization. The preceding tables in this chapter indicate exactly the opposite: prices for farmers in Mato Grosso were worse than in Pará. Finally, land price differences cannot be imputed to land quality or productivity differences, because these also run in the opposite direction (see chap.

19). None of these justifications, therefore, explain the observed differences in land prices between private and official projects. These indicate strong market segmentation in the real estate market between the two types of colonization at the end of the 1970s. Furthermore, as discussed in chapter 8, the initial price differential was even larger. Prices charged by private colonizing firms were one hundred times larger than those charged by INCRA. The field data, therefore, reveal subsequent market adjustment, with more rapid appreciation in the price of land in official colonization projects than in private ones. This point will be taken up again below.

The real estate market was also differentiated among locations within each state, but this differentiation was much smaller than between states. In Pará, the most valuable land (found in Pacal) was much cheaper than the cheapest land in Mato Grosso (in São José do Rio Claro). This is surprising. The soil of Pacal is very fertile and comparable only to that in some areas of Rondônia, being greatly superior to any of the soils in areas researched in Mato Grosso. The price of land on the frontier, therefore, does not depend so much upon quality as upon the type of colonizer who brings it to market, whether private firm or official agency.

Within official colonization, southerners' land was more valuable than that of others, although this difference was statistically significant only at the level of the total sample, not at the local level. This is strange, since in each project the quality of soil occupied by southerners was notoriously better than that of the others, especially in the case of Pacal. Southerners frequently purchased their land selectively in official colonization projects, usually from older colonists who were leaving. Other migrants generally received their land directly from INCRA, often after a time squatting on project outskirts, and had less opportunity to choose. In addition to selecting better land, southerners may have acquired lots that had been improved, that were better located, and that were more productive than the lots of other migrants. Certainly, southerners' invested more in their lots, so that the land had appreciated more since acquisition. This was seen in chapters 16 and 17, where rates of accumulation were compared.

In sum, within official colonization, differences in land prices between southern settlers and others are consistent with differences in assets, productivity, and product prices. Between official and private colonization, however, differences in land prices are much greater than and run counter to observed differences in total assets, productivity, or agricultural prices. Thus, land price differences reflect the large initial gap in the price of land charged by INCRA and private colonizers. Relatively high prices for land and relatively low prices for agricultural products are a poor combination for private colonization. They are consistent with patterns already observed in earlier chapters: greater disinvestment and indebtedness for southeners in Mato Grosso relative to those in Pará. This issue will be taken up again later.

Relative Prices and Income Appropriation

Price differences were greater for land than for agricultural products. In private colonization, land was valued three times more than in official colonization. Given that private colonization firms generally obtained land through public auction, the average purchasing cost was far lower than that which they charged to their settlers. The gap between purchase and sale prices, once the cost of implanting a project is discounted, represents the private colonization firms' profit.

Providing cheap land to small farmers in official colonization projects is part of a social policy of rural income distribution on the frontier. The appropriation of cheap land by colonization firms for later resale at a high profit to settlers should not have been a part of the same social policy. The price of land in private colonization became so high (in a relative, not absolute, sense) that small farming became untenable.

Southern settlers were able to sell their products at higher prices, on average, than other migrants in official colonization, in spite of apparently similar input costs. Between official colonization in Pará and private colonization in Mato Grosso, there was significant differentiation in product markets, especially for rice. Relative prices in official colonization, therefore, were more favorable to income appropriation by settlers, on two counts: more competitive product markets and lower land prices.

Reconsidering the results of chapters 15 and 17, the rates of accumulation obtained by merchants were much higher than those of settlers, and this differential was much greater in private colonization projects than in official ones. Those differentials are consistent with the price differences seen in this chapter. Although accumulation in agriculture was considerable, a large part of the surplus produced by farmers was apparently absorbed by merchants through the relative prices that they commanded in rural markets.

The more concentrated were rural markets, the greater the margins enjoyed by merchants, the lower prices they paid to farmers the higher the rate of accumulation for merchants, and the lower that rate for farmers. These appear to have been the tendencies for private colonization in Mato Grosso during the 1970s. The more competitive were rural markets, the smaller were merchants' margins, the higher the prices paid to farmers, the lower the rate of accumulation obtained by merchants, and the higher that of farmers. These appear to have been the tendencies in official colonization in Pará during the period.

Frontier Stages and the Segmentation of Economic Opportunities

A Digression

Returning to the paradox presented in chapters 15, 16 and 17, commerce was more lucrative on the frontier than agriculture. Even so: (1) merchants invested much in agriculture, and (2) colonists invested little in commerce. This behavior would be difficult to understand, given that rates of accumulation in commerce were four to five times greater than those in agriculture. Such contradictions are suggestive of distinct functions for commerce and agriculture in the different phases of frontier advancement. It is worth summarizing these functions here, in terms of the propositions advanced in chapter 12.

Merchants may view land mostly as a store of value. In acquiring it, they expect it to appreciate over time, with the general intensification of settlement. Perhaps it is also a way of increasing the scale of their business operations. Established marketing chains may limit merchant activity to a specific link in the chain of intermediation and to a particular scale, preventing their expansion within commerce. By going into agriculture, merchants overcome such barriers, expanding their general level of operation.

Additionally, agricultural production may be a logical step for certain kinds of merchants, that is, for those who begin as "indirect employers" of agricultural labor in the initial phases of a frontier through usury-mercantile transactions. After this initial period ends, many small farmers emigrate, landed property consolidates, wage labor appears, and agricultural and merchant operations change from "usury-mercantile" to "directly productive." Some merchants then become direct agricultural producers.

Schematically, merchants can thus be classified as "capitalist operators" from the start, in the sense that their opportunity costs since arrival on the frontier would always be the accumulation of capital. They would rate themselves as "successful" when their rate of accumulation is at least as high as the prevailing interest rate in the financial market. Chapter 15 showed that the average rate of accumulation obtained by frontier merchants was exceptionally high, particularly when compared with their farmer clients, as examined in chapter 17.

For many farmers, however, agriculture may never have been a "capitalist activity." In other words, their aim may never have been to appreciate invested capital. Instead, they may have always exercised a "peasant option" in relation to the labor market. These farmers may be principally seeking autonomy in work decisions and an escape from the alternative of wage labor, whether urban or rural. Although monetary income was a high proportion of total income, as was seen in chapter 16, colonists may have preferred simply "to produce their own wage" on the frontier, rather than work for others elsewhere. In this case, they would identify not with small capitalists, which they are to some degree, but mainly with the labor force, to which they also belong.

Formally, the opportunity cost of this kind of farmer, then, would not be the remuneration of capital, but of labor—that is, not the interest rate, but the wage level. They would rate themselves as "successful" when earning as much as or more than they could aspire to in the best alternative employment. Table 41 made this comparison with reference to the urban minimum wage. Its implication is that a small farmer would be satisfied in obtaining earnings above this wage, even though his rate of return would be lower than that of local merchants.

The opportunity set for farmers and merchants may thus be different during different stages of a frontier's advance. Initially unable to hire labor in agriculture, merchants would derive profit only from commerce. The subsequent closure of the frontier, with private appropriation and concentration of land ownership and the formation of a local labor market, allows former merchants to hire wage laborers and, in this way, to operate directly in agriculture.

Small farmers would remain on a frontier as long as it was capable of paying their families a salary equivalent to or above that obtained in the labor market. They would move from frontier to frontier, being successively expelled by closure, as long as income earned in each location was to remain above the wage labor alternative. Farmers who continue as such during and after consolidation and exodus would eventually have to become "capitalists." With the demise of market interlinking, trading partners would become "pure" and survival would then require a change in economic objectives. Merely covering the wage level would prove insufficient, and earning a competitive return on capital would become necessary. Some would evolve toward this objective after arrival, once the vicious circle of dependency on "usury-mercantile" capital is successfully overcome; others would arrive at the frontier with this objective already in mind and with the means to attain it. The process of economic incorporation of the frontier would end, then, when markets become fully established and operate as in the rest of the economy.

In sum, many small farmers may come to the frontier as a reaction against wage employment and may make economic decisions with reference to their opportunity costs in the labor market. Many merchants may come to the frontier as part of the expanding northward movement of southern capitalism and may make economic decisions with reference to their opportunity costs in the capital market. The frontier economy is therefore segmented, because migrant behavior is dictated by different opportunity costs: wages versus interest rates. This segmentation is similar to that observed in the urban economy, where many self-employed workers also "produce their own wage," in what is usually called the "informal labor market."[9]

The above statement, that a colonist's opportunity cost is the wage rate while a merchant's is the interest rate, is not meant to be absolute or deterministic. Small farmers on the frontier want to and do on occasion obtain competitive rates of return, while merchants frequently fall below these rates. Some colonists diversify, progress, and become merchants: they were not interviewed in the "farmer" category but in that of "merchants," in spite of having started out in agriculture. Many merchants failed and left the frontier; their profitability was certainly much lower than that obtained among the interviewed survivors. Mobility does exist between segments. All that is affirmed here, then, is that the frontier economy offers distinct "opportunity sets" for different agents. In spite of all the interactions between them, farmers and merchants apparently tend to move in distinct economic circuits (i.e., in segmented markets).

There is an ample literature on labor market segmentation to which justice cannot be done in the space available here. A great deal of evidence and an enormous diversity of perspectives exist with respect to the informal sector in Brazil, Latin America, the rest of the Third World, and even in advanced countries, to which reference was made in the beginning of this chapter. There are also many theoretical discussions involved, such as whether different rates of accumulation, as observed on the frontier, imply the absence of a single interest rate in the economy, or whether such would be consistent with competitive equilibrium, and so on. These theoretical discussions, in turn, recall older controversies concerning the nature of capital and many other issues too far afield from the topic of Amazon colonization, so they will be left aside.

Returning, then, to frontier prices, one must now examine the issue of how colonists react to the economic environment they encounter on the frontier. Farmers respond to prices in conformity with their objectives and constraints. The next chapter examines these reactions with respect to agricultural production and technology. The following chapter analyzes a broader set of farmer reactions to frontier economic environments.

Notes

1. Chapter 15 refers to the literature on the theory of the firm's behavior in different market structures.

2. *Migrações internas*, vols. 1–6 and appendix 3 of *A colonização dirigida na Amazônia* contain a description of these locations, the criteria for choosing them, and an explanation of how representative they are of directed colonization situations in the Amazon.

3. Later, during the 1980s, Mutum specialized in soy and practically abandoned rice. During the survey period reported here, however, this had not yet occurred.

4. This result supports predictions of the model in chapter 14, according to which higher product prices stimulate more investment and higher profits. As seen previously, southerners in official colonization invested the most (table 38) and had the highest rates of return (table 42).

5. See chapter 15 for a discussion on the relation between commercial margins and the degree of concentration among merchants.

6. Chapter 7 shows that Pará's accessibility by road was much greater than that of Mato Grosso by the end of the 1970s.

7. The market value reported in interviews with farmers, merchants, and institutions in each location is presented here. This does not always correspond to prices observed in actual transactions. In many cases, the land had not been purchased, but had been squatted on for several years and was later obtained from INCRA at an institutionally set cost. Presumably, the values expressed here are close to what the cost of purchasing the land would have been at the interview date.

8. See appendix 3 of *A colonização dirigida na Amazônia*.

9. See the works cited in note 16 of chapter 12, and the recent review of the informal market literature in Ozorio de Almeida and Rebello de Castro (1989). The relation between small firms in urban and rural areas has been studied recently, not only in underdeveloped nations, but also in developed countries, as in Paci (1982) and Bagnasco (1988).

19. AGRICULTURAL STRATEGIES

This chapter examines how frontier farming responds to the relative prices analyzed in the previous chapter, and tests some of the hypotheses of chapter 14. Price responses lead to two different technological strategies: one intensive and the other extensive. Given market restrictions and prevailing relative prices, different types of frontiers offer distinct stimuli to agricultural technology. Low land prices and high input prices stimulate land-extensive low level technology. High land prices relative to industrial inputs stimulate land-intensive technology. The relative prices of agricultural products stimulate different crop combinations.

A relevant price, however, is not necessarily that which is directly observed. To obtain bank credit for specific purposes, farmers may be compelled by a bank to purchase equipment that they had not planned to buy. The equipment price, then, has little to do with the decision to purchase. The sale of agricultural produce to a particular merchant may also be obliged by the debts incurred between harvests to maintain family consumption; product price, again, may have little to do with the decision to sell. In addition to these, there are many other market distortions in agriculture in general, and in frontier agriculture in particular. Nonetheless, overall, one can expect that some correspondence must exist between the economic environment—such as relative prices—and settlers' production decisions.

The immense issue of agricultural technology in the Amazon cannot be reduced simply to a response to relative prices. It is clear that when producers arrive in a particular location, they bring with them knowledge and agricultural practices learned in their regions of origin. Whether land is cheap or expensive, it cannot instantaneously make agricultural techniques more or less intensive. There must be a period of adjustment to market conditions before settlers respond to new comparative advantages. The issue of how much time settlers take to respond to local economic conditions will be addressed in chapter 21. This chapter is limited to observations on colonists' "average" responses at a given moment in time. Such averages will mask differences between recent settlers, who still practice an agriculture like that of their previous region of residence, and older settlers, who have learned to take advantage of local opportunities on the frontier.

The findings indicate that by the end of the 1970s agriculture in the deforested lands of Mato Grosso colonization was more intensive than in Pará: both in terms of production per hectare of cultivated land and in terms of the proportion of cultivated to fallow land. This higher intensity of land use is consistent with relatively higher land costs in Mato Grosso. In Pará, southerners and others had low productivity, which is consistent with the relatively cheap lands in that state. In official colonization, however, an important differentiation arose with respect to agricultural technology. Taking advantage of surpluses ensuing from cheap land, southerners invested more than others, covering a relatively high proportion of total cultivated area with perennial crops. Other migrants, who had lower income, less investment, and a smaller percentage of total deforested area under cultivation, also had less acreage in perennial crops, although their position improved over time. Low cost land distribution, therefore, effectively facilitated accumulation, especially among the southerners of Pará. But inexpensive land also encouraged underuse of deforested land, thereby promoting "excessive" destruction of natural resources in Amazon colonization in general.

The data used in this chapter come from the field survey presented in previous chapters. To test the hypothesis of a relation between technology (this chapter) and relative prices (chap. 18), tables remain disaggregated by field locations.

The Intensive Strategy

The intensive strategy, or so-called modern technology, raises productivity per hectare through industrial inputs (e.g., machinery, chemical pesticides, and chemical fertilizers). Although this technology may be highly questionable in the Amazon,[1] it does increase land productivity, at least in the short run. This is in itself beneficial, as greater land productivity reduces the amount of deforestation for any given level of output. The diffusion of the intensive strategy could thus diminish the deforestation provoked by colonization.

However, the ecological problems of farming in the Amazon clearly go beyond the problem of deforestation alone. Pollution and environmental disequilibria provoked by industrial inputs are also important issues. Alternative technologies more appropriate to the Amazon, such as intercropping, rotation, use of perennial crops, and others previously mentioned, can also raise output per hectare, without harm to the ecology. Given a certain degree of deforestation, sustainable agroforestry reduces the destruction of a region's natural resources. These alternatives will be examined in the subsequent section, after a look at annual crops and their productivity.

Annual Crops

Average Rice Yields

Table 52 shows that average rice yields were much higher for southerners in Monte Alegre than for settlers anywhere else in the sample. This is consistent with the higher prices obtained by these settlers, as seen earlier in table 46. Many of these "southerners" of Monte Alegre were actually seed producers of Japanese descent, who operated through a very successful cooperative. Aside from them, southerners in Pará were not statistically different from others in terms of productivity, in spite of the significant price differentiation in this state, seen earlier.

Within each state, there were other intriguing local productivity differences. Surprisingly, the directions of these differences were generally opposite to price differences (chap. 18), as can be seen by comparing tables 46 and 52. On average, rice productivity in Mato Grosso was 25 percent higher than that of Pará, in spite of prices being 10 percent lower. Productivity in Alta Floresta was 24 percent above that of Mutum, in spite of prices being 13 percent lower. At the local level, therefore, prices do not seem to have been a stimulus to productivity. The principal productivity differences were observed at the state level, between Pará and Mato Grosso.

Average Bean Yields

Table 53 shows that average bean yields in Mato Grosso were also higher than in Pará, and Alta Floresta's settlers had higher yields than those in other locations in Mato Grosso. In this case, productivity differences matched price differences. Within Pará at the local level, however, productivity differences were once again inverse to price differentials, as can be seen by comparing tables 47 and 53. Productivity in Pacal was greater than in Anapu, although prices in Pacal were lower. Both of these gaps were statistically different at the 10 percent level. Once again, price did not appear to stimulate productivity at the local level.

Table 52. Average Rice Yields (Kg./ha.)

Destination	Origin: Southerners	Origin: Others	All
Public colonization in Pará:			
Pacal	984.00	1,194.22	1,096.62[c]
Anapu/Pacajá	887.79	1,101.43	1,068.79[c]
Monte Alegre	2,160.00	834.07	1,010.86
SUBTOTAL	1,043.47[b]	1,088.97	1,077.38[a]
Private colonization in Mato Grosso:			
Alta Floresta/Paranaíta	1,540.65[d]	—	—
Mutum	1,244.52[d]	—	—
São J. do Rio Claro	807.58[d]	—	—
SUBTOTAL	1,352.02[a,b]	—	—
TOTAL	1,232.29	—	1,166.39

Source: Field survey.
Note: Repeated letter exponents indicate differences in the means that are statistically significant at the 10 percent level.

Average Corn Yields

In the case of corn, table 54 shows yet again that Mato Grosso had higher yields than Pará, and that within Mato Grosso the highest yields were those of Alta Floresta. These differences do not always follow the price differentials, which is also true in comparing southerners versus others in each of Pará's locations. In this case, then, the productivity-price relationships are not systematic at the local level.

Relative Prices and Productivity

The above comparisons show that average yields in Mato Grosso were always higher than in Pará. Within Mato Grosso, the yields in Alta Floresta were the highest; within Pará, Pacal, with its fertile lands, always had higher yields than Anapu. Nevertheless, contrary to expectations, output per hectare did not follow previously observed product price differences.

Until now, we have been working only with absolute prices. The model developed in chapter 14, however, compares productivity to

Table 53. Average Bean Yields (Kg./ha.)

Destination	*Origin* *Southerners*	*Others*	*All*
Public colonization in Pará:			
Pacal	256	309	286
Anapu/Pacajá	302	229	253
Monte Alegre	120	204	297
SUBTOTAL	260	284	277[d]
Private colonization in Mato Grosso:			
Alta Floresta/Paranaíta	339[f]	—	—
Mutum	180	—	—
São J. do Rio Claro	195[f]	—	—
SUBTOTAL	335[d]	—	—
TOTAL	293	—	288

Source: Field survey.
Note: Repeated letter exponents indicate differences in the means that are statistically significant at the 10 percent level.

relative prices. This will be done next, by comparing rice productivity in each location to the relative prices of rice-to-land. Rice is chosen here because it was the most important commercial crop in these locations during the period, as was seen in table 45. The results of these calculations are shown in table 55.

In Pará, where land prices were low, the relative price for rice was above unity. In Mato Grosso, where the price of land was high, the relative price for rice was lower than unity. Comparing these relative prices to yields, it becomes apparent that yields were low where land prices were low (in Pará) and high where the land price was high (in Mato Grosso, especially in Alta Floresta). The correlation coefficients between these two variables—productivity and relative prices—are negative. In all cases, these correlations are statistically significant at the 10 percent level or better, as shown in table 56.[2]

Chapter 18 showed that variations in agricultural output prices were small compared to large differences in land prices between Pará and Mato Grosso. The much larger land price variations seem to exert a far

Table 54. Average Corn Yields (Kg./ha.)

Destination	Origin Southerners	Others	All
Public colonization in Pará:			
Pacal	855	863	859
Anapu/Pacajá	1,533	615	704
Monte Alegre	925	943	941
SUBTOTAL	914	814	844
Private colonization in Mato Grosso:			
Alta Floresta/Paranaíta	1,527	—	—
Mutum	1,230	—	—
São J. do Rio Claro	1,092	—	—
SUBTOTAL	1,255	—	—
TOTAL	1,148	—	1,005

Source: Field survey.
Note: Repeated letters exponents indicate differences in the means that are statistically significant at the 10 percent level.

stronger influence over productivity than the smaller product-price variations. That is, low-yield cultivation seems not to be conducted on expensive land. The only exception to this rule is apparently the case of the highly productive southerners of Monte Alegre, whose cheap land bore extremely high productivity and high prices. But this seems to have been due to an efficient local cooperative. This special case shows that "pulling" product price upward raises productivity even on poor land!

Average Yields for Principal Perennial Crops

In the Amazon, the principal perennial crops are coffee, cocoa, pepper, and rubber. In Pacal, sugarcane is also planted, due to especially fertile land and the existence of a sugar mill and alcohol distillery. Because they are recent, however, many of these crops were not yet in full production at the time of interview, which made comparison between locations impossible. Average yields for the two principal perennials (coffee and pepper) are shown in table 57.

Table 55. Relative Prices and Rice Yields (kg./ha.)

Destination	*Origin*					
	Southerners Relative		*Others Relative*		*All Relative*	
	Prices	*Yields*	*Prices*	*Yields*	*Prices*	*Yields*
Public colonization in Pará:						
Pacal	1.01	984	1.17	1,194	1.10	1,096
Anapu/Pacajá	6.77	887	6.05	1,101	6.09	1,069
Monte Alegre	1.92	2,160	2.83	834	2.46	1,011
SUBTOTAL	1.14	1,043	2.12	1,089	1.63	1,077
Private colonization in Mato Grosso:						
Alta Floresta /Paranaíta	0.28	1,541	—	—	—	—
Mutum	0.64	1,245	—	—	—	—
São J. do Rio Claro	0.58	808	—	—	—	—
SUBTOTAL	0.46	1,352	—	—	—	—
TOTAL	0.86	1,232	—	—	1.15	1,166

Source: Tables 46, 51, and 52.
Note: Price of rice divided by the price of land. Yields are measured in kilograms per hectare.

Table 56. Simple Correlations between Productivity and Relative Prices

Destination	*Origin*		
	Southerners	*Others*	*All*
Pará:			
Public colonization	-0.18	-0.06	-0.06
Mato Grosso:			
Private colonization	-0.32	—	—
TOTAL	-0.27	—	-0.15

Source: See text.

As with rice, corn, and beans, the productivity of coffee was also much higher in Mato Grosso than in Pará, and, within Mato Grosso, the highest productivity was found in Alta Floresta. These differences are to be expected given the different land prices already noted above. As for pepper, it is not a typical crop in Mato Grosso. Pará's higher productivity for this crop, concentrated in Monte Alegre, was due to the local cooperative, as noted above.

Average Yields According to Other Sources

Yield differences between locations on the frontier are interesting, but the absolute level of observed productivity is even more relevant. Comparing tables 52, 53, 54, and 57 with table 58, one sees that productivity on the frontier was generally very low by any criterion. In the case of perennials, low yields were probably, at least in part, a function of their immaturity within regions of recent occupation. Coffee and pepper take time to produce, and their productivity increases over the years. This explanation, however, does not suffice for the annual crops whose average productivities in Pará were also lower than state averages: 21 percent lower for rice and 10 percent lower for corn. This is clear evidence of low technology for settlers in Pará during the period.

It is surprising to see in table 58 that rural extension agents and banks demand higher productivity than state, or even national, averages. Their services required yields much higher than those actually obtained by farmers in colonization projects. This gap aggravated settlers' loan repayment difficulties and reduced the role of bank credit in leveraging a process of accumulation. As a result, farmers turned to local money

Table 57. Average Yields for Principal Perennial Crops (kg./ha.)

Destination	*Crop*	*Origin* *Southerners*	*Others*	*All*
Public colonization in Pará:				
Pacal	Coffee	289	162	200
	Pepper	693	736	713
Anapu/Pacajá	Coffee	800	300	415
	Pepper	—	300	300
Monte Alegre	Coffee	—	—	—
	Pepper	1,129	330	789
SUBTOTAL	Coffee	417	145	236
	Pepper	780	650	719
Private colonization in Mato Grosso:				
Alta Floresta/Paranaíta	Coffee	696	—	—
	Pepper	—	—	—
Mutum	Coffee	—	—	—
	Pepper	—	—	—
São J. do Rio Claro	Coffee	485	—	—
	Pepper	—	—	—
SUBTOTAL	Coffee	599	—	—
	Pepper	—	—	—
TOTAL	Coffee	550	—	396
	Pepper	780	—	731

Source: Field survey.

lenders and became trapped in the vicious circle of chronic indebtedness discussed in previous chapters.

Relatively low productivity in Pará and relatively high productivity in Mato Grosso were consistent with land prices in each state. Product prices, which were higher in Pará, appear to have had little effect on encouraging productivity; land prices appear to have been more impor-

Table 58. Average Yields According to Other Sources (kg./ha.)

Location	*Crop*	*Agricultural (1) Census*	*EMATER (2) Assisted*	*EMATER (2) Nonassisted*	*Banks (3)*
Pará	Rice	1,266	1,800	900	1,900
	Corn	944	2,100	1,000	1,980
	Coffee	904	—	—	—
	Pepper	3,054	—	—	—
	Rice	1,310	1,800	900	1,900
Mato Grosso	Corn	1,705	2,100	1,000	1,980
	Coffee	1,336	—	—	—
	Pepper	1,098	—	—	—
	Rice	1,565	—	—	—
Brazil	Corn	1,779	—	—	—
	Coffee	872	—	—	—
	Pepper	2,715	—	—	—

Sources: (1) *Anuário estatístico do Brasil, 1981*; (2) field survey; (3) field survey.

tant. Since the price of land was much higher in Mato Grosso, physical productivity was also greater in this state than in Pará.

The next section examines another aspect of settlers' low productivity, which is the generalized practice of land extensive agriculture.

The Extensive Strategy

The extensive strategy applies as much to small as to large farmers. In the case of family-based agriculture, settlers clear 3 to 4 hectares in order to plant annual crops for two or three years, taking advantage of the fertility of recently cleared land. Thereafter, they abandon the land, forming a *capoeira*, and deforestation moves on. When small farmers own their lots, they may or may not create pasture from the lands they no longer cultivate. When they do plant pasture, they typically raise very few cattle on it. Surrounding large landowners may rent these pastures for their own cattle—at extremely low levels of productivity.[3] When small farmers are squatters or tenants, they usually plant pasture expressly for landowners. Thus, they incorporate into their behavior the expectation of future expulsion from current plots and subsequent occupation by ranchers.[4] This is the classic sequence of the moving frontier, described in chapters 2 and 12. Its consequences are land extensive agriculture and ranching and low level technology for both large and small producers.

The mobility of "extensive" small farmers reflects the low cost of land on the frontier, whether occupied by squatters, renters, sharecroppers, or even small owners. After clearing the forest, small farmers rarely remain for long in their lots. Soon they sell them to someone else, abandon them, or are expelled from them. Whatever the case, such land is surely not seen as a "fixed" factor to be preserved and recovered for permanent reuse. Rather, it is viewed as a variable factor, an input, that one uses up and throws away or leaves behind, resuming the same process farther on. The implications of land extensive technology for the devastation of the Amazon are obvious. The deforested area is a large and growing multiple of the area in use.

As already discussed in chapters 4 and 5, a "modern" form of extensive cultivation exists that may be less destructive than the current pattern of moving frontier. Land rotation and crop rotation, for instance, are cheap with respect to purchased inputs and, by reusing deforested lands, reduce the destruction of natural resources per unit of output. By plowing the soil less, polluting the rivers less, and provoking less environmental disturbance, a "modern extensive strategy" could turn out to be even more appropriate to the Amazon's natural resources than the intensive techniques discussed above.[5] The next section examines the evidence from colonization projects regarding the use of land in agriculture.

Agricultural Land Use

Table 59 shows the use of land observed in directed colonization. Each lot was classified into areas inappropriate for agriculture—due to topology, flooding, rockiness, inadequate soil structure, or other reasons—and those appropriate for agriculture. Land considered inappropriate for agriculture comprised only 1.6 percent of the total. In Pará, southerners had the lowest share of unusable land (0.2 percent), reflecting the importance of the fertile lands of Pacal. The others had higher proportions of unusable lands, reflecting the large share of this migrant group on the poor soils of Monte Alegre.

Usable lands were classified into areas still covered by virgin forest and areas in use. The forest covered approximately 50 percent of the lots in Pará, the legal limit for official colonization. This shows that many of the settlers had already cleared beyond these limits, since there was a large recent contingent who had merely begun to clear their lots. In Mato Grosso, the proportion of forested land was higher, 61.4 percent, reflecting the fact that colonization projects in this state were much more recent.

Land in use was further divided according to type of utilization, whether for crops or other uses. Since soy was still incipient in this period, the major annual crops were basically rice, beans, and corn. Small quantities of other crops were destined principally for family consumption. Perennial crops were largely coffee and pepper, with some sugarcane and cocoa, and small areas planted with guaraná and rubber.

After two or three years of using an area of recently cleared land for annual crops, a farmer usually exercises one of various options: (1) to continue to grow these crops, but intensify the use of chemical inputs to combat pests and decreasing soil fertility, which implies growing monetary expenditures per unit of output; (2) to plant perennial crops, which require years of constant expenditure until these begin to yield; (3) to plant pasture; or (4) to leave the area fallow or in *capoeira*. Other alternatives, such as crop or land rotation, which maintain soil fertility and save on chemical input expenditures, are, as yet, little used in frontier agriculture. Another technique that is also rarely used is crop and cattle rotation. In colonization projects, herds are typically small and pastures are rented or retained as a store of value, rather than for productive ends in themselves.[6] Other than cultivation, therefore, table 59 distinguishes between land in pasture and *capoeira*.

Aside from showing the general structure of land use for each group

Table 59. Land Use

Destination			*Origin*					
		Southerners			*Others*			*All*
	Area (ha.)	*As Share of Land (%) All*	*Used*	*Area (ha.)*	*As Share of Land (%) All*	*Used*	*Area (ha.)*	*As Share of Land (%) All*	*Used*

Destination	*Southerners Area (ha.)*	*Southerners As Share of Land (%) All*	*Southerners Used*	*Others Area (ha.)*	*Others As Share of Land (%) All*	*Others Used*	*All Area (ha.)*	*All As Share of Land (%) All*	*All Used*
Public colonization in Para:									
Forest	4,899	52.0	—	10,415	53.8	—	8,739	53.2	—
Temporary	870	9.2	19.3	1,721	8.9	20.8	1,463	9.0	20.3
Perennials	1,021	10.8	22.6	844	4.4	10.2	898	6.5	14.6
Pasture	1,539	16.3	34.1	3,715	19.2	44.9	3,054	18.2	41.1
Capoeira	1,087	11.5	24.1	1,989	10.3	24.1	1,808	10.7	24.1
Unsuitable	10	0.1	—	681	3.5	—	477	2.4	—
TOTAL	9,426	100.0	100.0	19,365	100.0	100.0	16,346	100.0	100.0
Private colonization in Mato Grosso:									
Forest	17,977	61.4	—	—	—	—	—	—	—
Temporary	5,908	20.2	54.3	—	—	—	—	—	—
Perennials	1,486	5.1	13.7	—	—	—	—	—	—
Pasture	2,056	7.0	18.9	—	—	—	—	—	—
Capoeira	1,425	4.9	13.1	—	—	—	—	—	—
Unsuitable	442	1.5	100.0	—	—	—	—	—	—
TOTAL	29,294	100.0	—	—	—	—	—	—	—

Destination					*Origin*				
		Southerners			*Others*			*All*	
	Area (ha.)	*As Share of Land (%) All*	*Used*	*Area (ha.)*	*As Share of Land (%) All*	*Used*	*Area (ha.)*	*As Share of Land (%) All*	*Used*
All Colonization:									
Forest	14,484	59.1	—	—	—	—	12,938	56.6	
Temporary	4,562	17.5	44.0	—	—	—	3,483	13.9	33.2
Perennials	1,362	6.5	16.3	—	—	—	1,165	5.7	14.2
Pasture	1,918	9.3	23.4	—	—	—	2,600	13.1	31.4
Capoeira	1,335	6.5	16.3	—	—	—	1,634	8.3	19.8
Unsuitable	327	1.2	—	—	—	—	461	1.7	—
TOTAL	23,988	100.0	100.0	—	—	—	22,231	100.0	100.0

Source: Field survey.
Note: "Used Land" refers to deforested lands that are suitable for agriculture.

of colonists, the table also notes the percentages of usable *deforested* land that is covered by annual crops, perennial crops, pastures, and *capoeiras*. These additional percentages reveal the technical intensity of land use by eliminating the interference of deforestation itself (i.e., duration of occupation), since recent settlers have more forested land than others, and some settlers have more unusable lands than others. This provokes an interference that should be controlled for.

In Pará, little of the cleared and usable land was under annual crops, while in Mato Grosso these crops accounted for 54 percent of the cultivated land. This higher proportion reflects the greater degree of mercantilization of settlers in Mato Grosso, as already shown in table 45, especially in the case of rice in Mutum. On the other hand, the area in perennials was small in Mato Grosso (14 percent) compared to Pará. These two percentages suggest that Mato Grosso southern settlers aimed at technical intensification of annual crops, which is consistent with the high productivity, specialization, and monetization already noted. This strategy is quite different from that of southerners in Pará, who had the highest proportion of perennials (23 percent), more than double that of the other two groups (10 percent).

Since none of the groups had much cattle, pasture can be considered to be basically fallow land. Adding pastured areas to land in *capoeira* shows that in Pará, fallow land occupied 58 percent of the land in use by southerners and 70 percent of the area in use by others. In other words, southerners cultivated 40 percent of usable deforested area while others cultivated only 30 percent. Meanwhile, in Mato Grosso, agriculture occupied 70 percent of usable cleared lands, a proportion that was more than double that of the others in Pará.

In each case, land-extensive agricultural technology on the frontier reflects itinerant experience prior to arrival, as settlers continue to clear the forest and subsequently to abandon (or semiabandon) the land. But relative prices considered in the previous chapter may also have had their role. The high price of land in private colonization may have increased land intensity in Mato Grosso, and the cheap lands of public colonization may have decreased land intensity in Pará. Since prior itinerancy was greater in Mato Grosso than in Pará,[7] extensive cultivation should also have been greater, not smaller. Within Pará, southerners used lands that were slightly more expensive and obtained slightly better product prices by practicing an agriculture that was a little more intensive than that of the other migrants. But the differences were small, compared to the difference between states. These findings are consistent with the very great differences in the price of land and productivity between states. Apparently, then, land prices influenced not only productivity, but also the intensity of land use.

Relative Prices, Technology, Itinerancy, and Deforestation

Agricultural technology on the frontier appears to have been a function partly of the price of land. When land prices were very low, colonists repeated their prior pattern of itinerancy on their own plots. After using them up, or after reaching the legally imposed clearing limit, they apparently lacked the technical or financial capacity to remain on the same soil. The land distributed to public project settlers, and cleared by them, thus fell into the hands of others. When land was expensive, however, it was used much more intensively. In this case, high land costs consumed settlers' financial resources and pushed them to high-profit annual crops. Since they could not wait for the fruition of long-term investments, as is necessary for perennial crops, private project settlers concentrated upon the annuals.

Expensive land, then, is consistent with an intensive strategy and is conducive to reuse, thereby keeping settlers longer on their land. On the other hand, its high financial costs repress investment and capital accumulation. This can lead the settler to give up on the frontier and to resort to return migration, as indeed did occur significantly in private colonization.[8]

Cheap lands are consistent with an extensive strategy and allow for investment and accumulation of capital at the individual level; but its social cost is high in terms of excessive deforestation and underuse of deforested land.

Clearly, the principal actors devastating the Amazon are not the small farmers who cut the forest little by little as they plant their crops. Large-scale agricultural-ranching concerns that use powerful equipment, defoliants, and other chemical inputs certainly cause much more rapid and extensive damage to the environment. Similarly, other large-scale projects, such as hydroelectric dams and mining, may have a much greater destructive impact than colonization. The results presented in this chapter do not imply that one should take land from small farmers, much less reserve it for the large. But these findings do serve as warning about the vicious circle of primitive extensive technology and its implications with respect to any policy of land distribution.

Land distribution, whether in colonization or in agrarian reform, aims to break a previously temporary relationship to the soil, conferring permanent title to the producer. Transitory settlement of land is a Brazilian social fact, not only among the dispossessed, but also among landowners, as will be seen in the next chapter. The tendency seen in this chapter of recent landowners to retain their extensive techniques and to fall back on their prior itinerancy, therefore, is relevant as much for colonization as it would be for agrarian reform.

A life experience of accumulation gained in going from place to place, rather than establishing oneself on a single plot, must surely have an influence upon producers' technologies. The legal fact, then, of conferring title to settlers may not be sufficient to reform the social fact of their previous itinerancy. One must also create a new technological fact: reform producers' agricultural practices and transform their technology from extensive to intensive. Or, better, change them from "primitive extensive" practices to "modern extensive" ones.[9]

In this regard, rural extension, for instance, should be adapted to the technological demands of the humid tropics. Mixed agricultural-forestry management, intercropping, rotation, and other techniques are appropriate to the heterogeneous ecology of the Amazon. Grains generally rely on a "modern" intensive technology, based on large tracts of homogeneous crops that are foreign to Amazonian natural conditions and take a toll on the environment. New emphasis should be placed on trees and root crops, more kindred to the local ecology. Genetic improvements, grafting, intercontinental interchange of species, "escape" mechanisms for dealing with plant maladies, and several biotechnological advances are promising in the direction of ecologically balanced agroforestry in the Amazon. Additional measures would be to introduce new high-unit-value crops and to build processing facilities in local urban centers for traditional crops, both of which would help compensate for high transport costs out of the region. All of these measures raise the local value productivity of the cleared land and would contribute to reducing itinerancy and diminishing "excessive" deforestation per farmer. Aside from such economic and technological initiatives, several legal procedures would also reduce deforestation. One obvious measure is to enforce the prohibition on clearing more than 50 percent of the plots. Another is to unite forest reserves into "bunches" inside each settlement project and to give title to plots only half the size distributed until now.

These results, and their implications, suggest that the general objective of any continuing colonization in the Amazon must change. Colonization must aim to create a legal and economic environment consistent with a new technology and a new social fact: that of retaining farmers on their land. Otherwise, unfavorable relative prices and excessive indebtedness will continue to reduce the appropriation of income by colonists, and will keep expelling them from their plots, even after they become landowners. Their relation with the distributed lands will continue to be as transitory and extensive as they were on the lands they farmed before.

The interaction of colonists with the economic-institutional environment in the Amazon does not begin on the frontier itself, but prior to it.

As was mentioned in chapter 8, private colonizing firms recruited their settlers in the South, where rural capitalism was advancing via mechanization, improved commercialization, new crops such as soybeans, rising local land prices, and the concentration of land ownership. Official colonization, on the other hand, attracted mostly northeastern and other migrants. It sought to reverse the political blockade against agrarian reform in the Northeast, by giving "land for landless people, and people for unpeopled lands."[10] That is: the institutional environments and the colonists of the frontier came jointly. They did not confront one another for the first time in the Amazon, and they did not each result from an independent process.

Thus, it may be that the correlations found in this chapter were not causal connections, but a mere series of coincidences, such as the following. More technically sophisticated colonists from the South were channeled to Mato Grosso by private colonizing firms, while less technified colonists, especially northeasterners, were brought to Pará by INCRA. Land was expensive under private colonization and cheap in official colonization because these two types of colonizers had different objectives. Colonizing firms charged more for land because they wanted profits and knew that the productivity of their chosen colonists would be high. INCRA charged less because it did not aim at profits, but merely to put poor farmers on the land, and expected their productivity to be low. Southerners in Pará were less productive than those of Mato Grosso, not because of cheaper land but because they came from less productive subregions of the South than those that fed private colonization. If all these are merely coincidences, then relative prices would not be the cause of technological behavior. Rather, they and productivities would be joint occurrences, having been created within the same social process that generated the frontier.[11]

The available data cannot statistically distinguish these two possibilities: whether there is a causal or merely a coincidental relationship between relative prices and productivity. Sample bias, excluded variables, and simultaneous determination may have a lot to do with the correlations observed. One can state only that the data are compatible with both hypotheses.

No social processes are perfectly deterministic, no matter how all-encompassing they may appear. Individual variations occur, generating unpredictable outcomes. Amazonian colonization cannot be understood merely as a technological response to relative prices. Individual outcomes may occur within the evolution of wider forces, but they respond to a wide range of other impacts beyond the market determinants discussed up to this point. The next chapter introduces statistical analyses of a large number of influences upon settlers' performance.

Notes

1. See Bibliography and discussion in chapters 4 and 5.

2. This is a statistical test of the hypotheses of the model developed in chapter 14.

3. M. Ribeiro (1986) shows that cattle productivity on the frontier is low and, in addition, represses technological change in cattle raising in the Center-South. His work is interesting, as it indicates that usury-mercantile capital appears on the frontier, even among firms that operate with directly productive capital in the rest of the economy. The same meat and dairy multinationals who contract suppliers through usual market transactions in the Center-South resort to usury-mercantile lending practices to ensure their raw materials on the frontier.

4. "Work a year, work a year, in the other plant grass. The tithe is grass . . . Work two years on some land and: That's it! . . . If 'he' wanted it for cattle, then I had to move on, because of the cattle" (translation from itinerant farmer quotation in Garcia Júnior 1975, pp. 11–12).

5. See note 1, above.

6. This is not the case for farmers near the immense floodplains of the Amazon. These areas are inundated six months each year, but during the dry period they sustain cattle that could not survive in colonists' small dry pastures. Ownership of Amazon floodplains is undefined, since the navy has rights to the banks of all navigable rivers. As long as it continues to be a land for common use, recalling the old English "commons" from the era before "enclosure," it will continue to be useful for cattle raising by small farmers. The Amazon thus has environmental conditions and space enough for cattle to come to constitute an important element of appropriate small-scale technology.

The conflict between large and small farmers in the Amazon over the floodplains is similar to that between large and small fishermen over lagoons and lakes that are also immune to appropriation. It is also similar to the case of mining, where conflicts between prospectors and large mining companies are already notorious. See C. Santos (1988).

7. See appendixes to *A colonização dirigida na Amazônia*, and B. Ferreira (1984).

8. J. Santos (1985b).

9. "Modern extensive" technology is rotational agro-forestry. It is the technology that is least harmful to the Amazonian ecosystem and contrasts with "primitive extensive" technology, which deforests a great deal of land and forms much *capoeira*. It also contrasts with "intensive" technologies, whose mechanical and chemical inputs are directly damaging to nature. See the discussion in this regard in chapter 5.

10. A phrase attributed to Brazilian President Emílio Garrastazu Medicí and recorded in a mural near the headquarters of INCRA's main colonization project along the Transamazonian Highway in Brasil Novo.

11. I am indebted to José Graziano da Silva for this critique.

20. DIFFERENTIATION ON THE FRONTIER

This chapter expands upon the analysis of the performance of colonization developed in the previous chapters of part 4. It compares the influence of the destination economic-institutional environment with other influences that colonists bring from regions of origin or those that are individually specific. To the extent that local (destination) influences predominate in determining colonists' performance, there is a role for local-level policy tools—such as marketing, titling, technical assistance, and so on—in improving colonization outcomes.

The destination economic-institutional environment is made up of different types of infrastructure: physical, legal, social, commercial, services, and production activities. It determines farmers' opportunities, such as forms of access to land, operation of diverse markets, and others. Though colonists react differently to their environments and to the relative prices within them, there are some common elements in their reactions. These could be monitored by policy to increase the effectiveness of colonization programs

Colonists' *origins* determine the resources they bring, not only their economic assets, but also their culture and knowledge of agricultural techniques from previous experiences elsewhere. These experiences include (1) tenancy—ownership, squatting, or renting land; (2) community—living and working closely with others or avoiding collective decisions; (3) institutional interactions—favorable or negative experience with public and private institutions; and (4) numerous other events in the past that alter current behavior on the frontier. To the extent that origin influences prevail in determining colonization outcomes, farmers will be relatively insensitive to local-level policies aimed at improving colonization outcomes, farmers will be relatively insensitive to local-level policies aimed at improving colonization outcomes.

Individual variations in behavior across similar origins and destinations come from personal characteristics. Age, family size, family labor availability, time on the plot, area already cleared, level of formal education, intelligence, courage, health, aspirations, ambitions, and numerous other factors vary among individuals and alter their agricultural performance. To the extent that individual variations prevail in determining colonization outcomes, then farmers will be relatively insensitive to local-level policies aimed at improving colonization outcomes.

This chapter presents a statistical analysis of these broad groups—destination, origin, individual—of variations among colonists. It seeks to identify broad tendencies and to interpret which are the dominant influences over the behavior of farmers in directed colonization. The process of differentiation on the frontier, however, is complex and multidimensional. It cannot be understood with reference to any limited set of indicators, not even by the large number of factors taken into account here.

Although this chapter employs regression techniques, it does not develop its own theoretical model. The theoretical analysis of the influence of the local (destination) economic-institutional environment on the performance of colonists was presented in chapters 12–14, and the empirical evidence in this regard was presented in chapters 15–19. Now, the importance of the frontier environment as a whole will be tested vis-à-vis other influences upon colonists. More specifically, this chapter will test the extent to which colonists' performance—variations in income, investment, and assets—can be attributed to the destination frontier environment and how much corresponds to other influences: *origin* and *individual* characteristics.

According to the analysis developed in chapter 14, colonists' current income is a function of their reactions to current relative prices in their principal transactions, given resource constraints: land area, family labor, and so on. Colonists' accumulation is a function not only of these elements but also of the initial resources that they brought to the frontier with them, and of time since arrival. This would imply that income should be a function of the local economic environment, while accumulation would be a function of local and origin influences. These hypotheses will be tested in the following sections.

All the information comes from the same field survey, already utilized in chapters 15–19, taken among small agricultural producers in official colonization projects in Pará and private projects in Mato Grosso.[1] The analysis undertaken does not include calculating expansion factors to enhance the generalizability of results. Estimated coefficients are valid for this particular sample, not for the Amazon as a whole. To the degree that the adopted criteria, the sampling process, and observational precision have generated a representative sample, then the results indicate the relative influences of the analyzed variables on the Amazon frontier as a whole. Time and resource limitations for field research and analysis, described elsewhere,[2] prevented drawing more from the data than the findings that follow.

The next section presents an econometric model for interpreting variations among colonists, through regressions and analysis of covariance. The following five sections estimate what part of the variation between colonists could be attributed to the migrants' destination economic-institutional environment and which are explained by diverse conditions of "origin" and "individual characteristics." The last two sections present conclusions and discuss their implications.

A Multivariate Regression Model

Three variables are chosen to represent colonists' performance: income, investment, and assets. *Income* refers to the sum of all receipts during the agricultural year 1980–1981, on current as well as financial accounts, for all members of the unit of production.[3] *Investment* refers to the sum of all productive expenditures effected in that year and that are not aimed toward generating income during the same year.[4] *Assets* were all durable production and consumption goods, both physical and financial, possessed at the end of the agricultural year in 1981.[5] They represent total wealth, "net worth," or "patrimony" of the colonists. An "increase in wealth" is similar, but not exactly equal, to the concept of "capital accumulation," used in chapters 15, 17, and 21. All these terms will be used synonymously in this chapter. All three variables include agricultural and nonagricultural monetary and nonmonetary receipts and expenditures.

Each of these three variables was analyzed as an independent variable in multiple regressions with respect to the same group of "independent" variables: seventeen in all. The values of coefficients and the statistical significance of their estimates were different in the three regressions, as would be expected. These are all presented in tables 60–62. Subsequent regressions omitting variables with low statistical significance are not reported because, as already noted, the objective of this work is not to measure absolute impacts, but merely to test hypotheses regarding the existence, direction, relative magnitude, and significance of effects.

When variables come from survey data, there is an inherent tendency for collinearity, this being a typical problem of cross-section analyses. The presence of collinearity among variables in the same regression, however, does not bias coefficients: it merely underestimates their standard errors.[6] In spite of low levels of statistical significance, variables may still be relevant, though their separate effects are not distinguishable in one particular sample. The nature of the relationships between them, however, is indicated by the regression results. In this specific case, simple correlations between variables tend to be low, which is suggestive of low collinearity among them.[7]

The omission of relevant variables in a regression is more problematic for the purpose of this study than the inclusion of collinear variables. Omitted variables introduce biases into the estimated coefficients for included variables.[8] In a situation of multicausality, as studied here, one can never be certain of having included all of the relevant variables. Therefore, the possibility of bias caused by omitted variables is always present. This is a risk that every exploratory study must run.

Other sources of estimation bias are measurement errors in the variables themselves and model misspecification. Some relationships require multiple equation specifications and, within each equation, some variables may have a linear relationship with the dependent variable, while others do not. No attempt is made here to rigorously specify functional relationships. To the degree that linearity is a "misspecification," there will be biases in the estimated coefficients.[9] This problem also cannot be avoided, given the preliminary nature of the analysis. Findings are presented in three tables, each with a different dependent variable: income (table 59), investment (table 60), and assets (table 61).

Variables of *origin* do not refer to migrants' place of birth, but rather to their agricultural experience prior to arrival on the frontier: their last place of residence ("southerner" or not), number of previous migratory stages ("experience of prior itinerancy"), having been a landowner sometime in another location ("prior ownership"), and the value of monetary and material resources that they had when they began to clear their current plot ("initial resources").[10]

Destination variables refer to the economic-institutional environment that the migrants found on the frontier, including: type of colonization project ("private" or "public"), total value of technical assistance ("agricultural transfers"), health and other social services ("nonagricultural transfers") and tenancy ("sharecropper," "occupant," or "colonist").[11]

Individual variables refer to personal or family unit characteristics:

duration of marriage of the head of household; the number of annual hours worked by family members in agricultural activities on the current plot ("agricultural hours"); the number of hours worked annually in other activities ("nonagricultural hours"); total cultivated area ("cultivated area"); and the time elapsed since beginning economic activity on the current plot, measured in months ("time on plot"). In the regressions referring to income, the colonists' total wealth ("assets") are also included; and in the regression for investment, both "assets" and "income" are included.[12]

The following chart shows how independent variables (X) are grouped into origin variables (A), local variables (B), and individual variables (C). In each table, Regression A includes only the first stage regression with the four origin variables. Regression B includes the origin variables and the six destination variables, comprising the first and second stages of estimation. Regression C includes three stages of estimation, with origin variables, destination variables, and the seven individual variables, for a total of seventeen independent variables. Chart 9 presents the general scheme of estimation.

Hypothesis testing was done for each variable using the t-statistic individually, and for each group of variables (origin, destination, and individual) using an F-test collectively. When a coefficient indirectly reached a 1 percent significance level according to the t-test, it was given a small exponent "a"; with 5 percent significance it was given a "b"; if it reached 10 percent significance, it was given a "c." The same coefficients were applied for the significance levels attained by the F-statistic, with reference to groups of coefficients, as indicated below each regression at the bottom of each table.

These F-statistics show the contribution of each group of variables to reducing the sum of square residuals, as well as the degree of statistical

Chart 9. Framework for Econometric Estimation

Regression A:	$Y_i = a_0 + a_1 x_{a1} + \ldots + a_n x_{an}$.	(1st stage)
Regression B:	$Y_i = b_0 + b_1 x_{a1} + \ldots + b_n x_{an} +$	(1st stage)
	$+ b_{n+1} x_{b1} + \ldots + b_{n+m} x_{b(n+m)}$	(2nd stage)
Regression C:	$Y_i = c_0 + c_1 x_{a1} + \ldots + c_n x_{an} +$	(1st stage)
	$+ c_{n+1} xb_1 + \ldots + c_{n+m} x_{b(n+m)} +$	(2nd stage)
	$+ c_{n+m+1} x_{c1} + \ldots + c_{n+m+p} x_{c(n+m+p)}$	(3rd stage)

where i=3, n=4, m=6, and p=7; and a, b, c are the coefficients of regressions A, B, and C, respectively.

Table 60. Regressions and Analysis of Covariance for Annual Current Income

(Coefficients with standard errors in parentheses)

Independent Variables	*Regression A*		*Regression B*		*Regression C*	
A. Origin Variables						
Southerners	319.51	(268.95)	382.68	(270.69)	357.97	(193.32)[b]
Exp. of itinerancy	268.89	(97.72)	17.33	(79.12)	-0.69	(60.11)
Exp. of ownership	16.96	(294.83)	446.37	(239.81)[b]	46.56	(176.83)
Initial resources	0.21	(0.03)[a]	0.19	(0.03)[a]	0.01	(0.02)
B. Destination Variables						
Private coloniz.			-597.06	(286.94)[b]	-236.75	(225.82)
Agric. Transfers			52.63	(2.94)[a]	26.07	(2.37)[a]
Nonagric. transfers			0.27	(2.73)	1.96	(1.91)
Sharecroppers			771.15	(336.05)[b]	-270.09	(240.34)
Occupants			567.49	(365.51)	-2.47	(263.14)
Definitive title			594.39	(233.65)[a]	94.39	(172.34)

Independent Variables	*Regression A*		*Regression B*		*Regression C*	
C. Individual Variables						
Age					0.48	(6.81)
Agric. hours					-0.04	(0.03)
Nonagric. hours					0.08	(0.03)[a]
Cultivated area					17.75	(1.58)[a]
Time on lot					2.96	(2.40)
Assets					0.09	(0.02)[a]
Current income					—	—
General Statistics						
Constant	223.51	(264.94)	8.74	(244.10)	-253.02	(241.53)
R-square	0.13		0.50		0.78	
F	16.57		44.53		92.04	
Degrees of freedom	5,443.00		11,443.00		17,391.00	
Analysis of covariance	Reg.0*-RegA		Reg.A-Reg.B		Reg.B-Reg.C	
Difference in squared residuals (1×10^6)	533.00		1,306.00		993.00	
Degrees of freedom	7,443.00		16,443.00		28,391.00	
F	10.87[a]		19.90[a]		17.05[a]	

Note: Levels of significance: a = 1% level; b = 5% level; c = 10% level.
*Not presented in this table.

Table 61. Regressions and Analysis of Covariance for Investment

(Coefficients with standard errors in parantheses)

Independent Variables	*Regression A*		*Regression B*		*Regression C*	
A. Origin Variables						
Southerners	32.83	(144.82)	44.71	(184.82)	-78.55	(164.11)
Exp. of itinerancy	161.04	(52.62)[a]	142.15	(54.02)[a]	53.77	(50.81)
Exp. of ownership	-9.00	(158.75)	-25.87	(163.74)	-87.78	(149.50)
Initial resources	0.13	(0.02)[a]	0.12	(0.02)[a]	0.01	(0.02)
B. Destination Variables						
Private Coloniz.			11.10	(195.91)	-15.86	(191.15)
Agric. transfers			10.29	(2.01)[a]	-8.93	(2.28)[a]
Nonagric. transfers			6.32	(1.87)[a]	-4.98	(1.62)[a]
Sharecroppers			-252.12	(227.99)	-495.98	(203.49)[a]
Occupants			-72.66	(249.56)	-225.52	(222.45)
Definitive title			-47.14	(159.53)	282.88	(145.74)[b]

Independent Variables	Regression A		Regression B		Regression C	
C. Individual Variables						
Age					-3.46	(5.76)
Agric. hours					0.01	(0.02)
Nonagric. hours					-0.01	(0.02)
Cultivated area					-7.71	(1.53)[a]
Time on lot					-3.07	(2.04)
Assets					0.39	(0.04)[a]
Current income					0.39	(0.04)[a]
General Statistics						
Constant	-0.18	(145.23)	122.32	(166.67)	443.93	(204.45)[b]
R-square	-0.15		0.22		0.48	
F	19.84		12.35[a]		22.26	
Degrees of freedom	5,443.00		11,443.00		18,391.00	
Analysis of covariance	Reg.0*-Reg.A		Reg.A-Reg.B		Reg.B-Reg.C	
Difference in						
squared residuals (1×10^6)	177.00		71.00		277.00	
Degrees of freedom	7,443.00		16,443.00		29,391.00	
F	12.40[a]		2.30		6.60[a]	

Note: Levels of significance: a = 1% level; b = 5% level.
*Not presented in this table.

Table 62. Regressions and Analysis of Covariance for Assets

(Coefficients with standard errors in parentheses)

Independent Variables	*Regression A*		*Regression B*		*Regression C*	
A. Origin Variables						
Southerners	1,165.79	(619.14)[b]	-4.27	(723.76)	-108.17	(537.15)
Exp. of itinerancy	1,236.91	(224.96)[a]	824.84	(211.54)[a]	1,125.87	(157.51)[a]
Exp. of ownership	-78.91	(678.71)	554.74	(641.19)	-549.64	(490.63)
Initial resources	1.02	(0.08)[a]	0.97	(0.07)[a]	0.66	(0.05)[a]
B. Destination Variables						
Private coloniz.			366.36	(767.19)	1,625.69	(622.34)[a]
Agric. transfers			82.81	(7.86)[a]	16.69	(6.53)[a]
Nonagric. transfers			7.18	(7.32)	12.84	(5.28)[a]
Sharecroppers			2,896.29	(900.63)[a]	590.53	(667.20)
Occupants			1,321.68	(977.27)	-404.68	(730.93)
Definitive title			1,864.16	(624.71)[a]	813.49	(477.20)[b]

Independent Variables	Regression A		Regression B		Regression C	
C. Individual Variables						
Age					-1.97	(18.94)
Agric. hours					-0.15	(0.07)[b]
Nonagric. hours					-0.03	(0.08)
Cultivated area					-63.80	(3.10)[a]
Time on lot					9.14	(6.67)[c]
Assets					—	—
Current income					—	—
General Statistics						
Constant	-1,124.58	(621.41)[b]	-2,086.15	(662.66)[a]	-2,323.47	(661.28)[a]
R-square	-0.39		0.52		0.77	
F	70.74[a]		49.24[a]		94.90[a]	
Degrees of freedom	5,443.00		11,443.00		16,391.00	
Analysis of covariance	Reg.0*-Reg.A		Reg.A-Reg.B		Reg.B-Reg.C	
Difference in squared residuals (in trillions)	11.0		4.0		7.0	
Degrees of freedom	7,443.0		16,443.0		27,391.0	
F	41.9		7.8		14.6	

Note: Levels of significance: a = 1% level; b = 5% level; c = 10% level.
*Not presented in this table.

significance of this contribution. In the "A" regressions, where only one stage of estimation was undertaken, this measures the contribution of variables of origin. In the "B" regressions, with two stages of estimation, this statistic measures the contribution of destination variables (second stage), given the inclusion of origin variables (first stage). In the "C" regressions, with three stages of estimation, this statistic measures the contribution of individual variables (third stage) given the inclusion of variables of origin (first stage), and destination (second stage). A group of variables may be significant according to the F-test even though some of its coefficients do not individually pass their t-tests.

The main purpose is to test the influence of the local economic-institutional environment (destination variables) versus the influence of the other two groups—origin and individual. If the destination group of variables turns out to be more significant than the other two groups, then locally implemented policy probably has an important role in influencing colonization performance. If, on the other hand, this group turns out less significant than one or both of the others, then settlement outcomes probably depend more on predetermined (origin and/or individual) characteristics than on policy. This implies fewer "degrees of freedom" in orienting future Amazon colonization in desired directions.

The most important finding to look for in the sections that follow then, is that resulting from the second stage of estimation. Its reduction in the residual sum of squares will be compared to the reduction effected by the other two stages. In the case where this contribution is greater, the environment is probably the stronger influence upon performance in a strictly statistical sense. By implication, then, performance of colonization could be affected by policy tools, such as marketing, titling, technical assistance, and so on. In the opposite case, the influences of origin and individual variation probably drive a process of "natural selection" not very sensitive to colonization or economic policies.

Statistical results are presented in the following sections. Contrary to previous chapters, monetary values are in Brazilian currency (1981 cruzeiros) and coefficients have no correspondence to orders of magnitude in U.S. dollars.

Current Income

In the analysis of colonists' current income, the regression on the entire set of independent variables reaches an R^2 of 0.78, significant at the 1 percent level (see table 60). Each of the three blocks of variables is significant at the 1 percent level. According to the analysis of covariance at the bottom of table 60, the largest contribution to the reduction of unexplained variation (residual sum of squares) comes from Regression

B (destination variables: 1.3 trillion),[13] followed by Regression C (individual variables: 993 billion). Regression A (origin variables) contributes least by this measure (533 billion). In other words, within the limits of this analysis, the economic-institutional environment has the greatest explanatory power for variation in colonists' current income.

Origin Variables

As a group, origin variables not only contribute the least, but their coefficients are also quite sensitive to the inclusion of the other two blocks of variables. It is worth considering the variables separately.

"Being a southerner" only has a strongly positive influence (it shows the greatest and most significant coefficient in the regression) once the variables of group C ("individuals") are included in the regression.

Prior experience variables—itinerancy and previous ownership—have unstable coefficients when other groups are included. Itinerancy is not significant and changes sign; prior ownership has a strong positive influence in Regression B, but loses its value and significance with the inclusion of group C (individuals), probably because of correlation with current assets. Initial resources are significant and positive, but only in the absence of individual variables. Again, they are probably affected by the inclusion of current assets.

In sum, the origin variables included in the regression seem to suffer from collinearity with those that reflect individual attributes and contribute relatively little to the explanation of current income.

Destination Variables

Destination variables contribute most to the reduction of residual error for current income. It is interesting to note that the sign for being in private colonization is negative, despite the positive sign for being a southerner among the origin variables. Since the colonists in private colonization were almost entirely southerners, the positive impact of being from the South becomes apparent only in official colonization. This result confirms the previous findings in chapters 16–19.

Means and simple correlations[14] also show that southerners received more technical assistance than others, another positive and significant factor. They were also more likely to have definitive title to the land, another positive influence. Contrary to expectations, therefore, the influence of private colonization upon current income is not positive. Instead it becomes negative once one controls for the independent effects of southern origin, receiving technical assistance, and having title to land.

Initially in this study, private colonization was expected to be a successful solution for land distribution on the frontier, resolving many problems in official projects. However, the data on "excessively" high land prices seen in chapters 8 and 18, plus the high indebtedness of private project settlers seen in chapter 16, reversed this expectation. The result of this regression, therefore, reinforces the conclusion that private colonization is not an effective solution for rural income distribution. This point is of great importance and will be referred to again further on.

To be a sharecropper or squatter has a negative influence on income, once individual variables are controlled for (in phase C of estimation), but this result does not attain statistical significance. Simple correlations among these variables, however, are also negative, as shown by the detailed data presented in appendix 3 of *A colonização dirigida na Amazônia*.

In sum, destination variables are those that contribute most to explaining current income, especially variables for technical assistance and title holding. That is, going to an official project without becoming a landowner and without receiving institutional assistance does not significantly raise farmers' incomes. This reinforces results from previous chapters, to the effect that the local economic-institutional environment is an important element for explaining colonists' income. By implication, there is room for influencing the performance of frontier farmers through specific colonization policies.

Individual Variables

Individual variables contribute less to the reduction of squared residuals than destination (environment) variables, but more than origin variables. Introducing these individual variables strongly affects the signs and values of the other previously included variables, always in the expected direction. In this way they act as "control" variables that allow for better identification of the influences of origin and destination.

Duration of marriage has a positive sign, as expected, but it is not statistically significant. Unexpectedly, total hours of family labor dedicated to agriculture are neither positive nor significant. Income thus seems to be relatively unaffected by the family life cycle, since it is not significantly higher among "mature" families (i.e., those with a greater supply of family labor). Even more surprising, it is not the hours of agricultural work, but rather the hours of nonagricultural work—whether in business, employment on other lots, or work of another kind—that most influences family income. These findings apparently contradict those of chapter 16, whereby nonagricultural income was a small percentage of total income on average. Probably only a few high-income families had a high percentage of nonagricultural activity, not enough to affect the average figures. Simple correlations among the same variables, however, are positive, as shown in appendix 3 of *A colonização dirigida na Amazônia*.

The negative and weak statistical relationship between family work and income suggests the interference of excluded variables. One is years of schooling, though there is little evidence of its impact on Third World farm income. Another is technology. Low technology would mean that lower income (and productivity) requires more family labor per given level of output. On the other hand, the positive relationship between nonagricultural work and current income reinforces previous findings. The most successful colonists among "other migrants" in official colonization were those strongly linked to the labor market. Among southerners also in official colonization, the most successful were those who accumulated many plots and/or entered into business. Both cases were little representative of the classic family producer (or "peasant") situation, in which it was expected that agricultural work would have a positive influence on income. This point will be taken up again later.

Finally, among the individual variables, cultivated area obviously shows a positive and significant influence; time on the plot is also positive but it is not significant. These variables "classify" farmers into old and recent, large and small. In this way, they act as "control" variables, the better to reveal the impact of other included variables.

In sum, in analyzing current income, individual variables contribute more to a reduction of residuals than do origin variables and less than destination (environment) variables. Cultivated area was the main single positive influence among all variables.

Local Economic-Institutional Environment and Current Income

Combining all of the information on current income, the principal positive influences were southern origin, not being in private colonization, receiving technical assistance, cultivated area, and nonfarm work. This set of variables portrays southerners' strategies in official colonization. They cultivated larger areas, sought more technical assistance, diversified their activities, often in the direction of commerce, and thereby attained the highest current incomes. The local economic-institutional environment of official colonization, therefore, was apparently the most propitious to increasing colonists' incomes. This finding has important policy implications. Success within colonization would not, thus, be merely a result of "natural selection," a reward for the "better" colonists. Rather, successful colonization would be inducible by appropriate settlement policies, at the local level.

Current income, however, is a flow that is drained each year. Prospects for future income depend on investment, which will be examined next.

Investment: Individual Discontinuity

The regression on colonists' investment has an R^2 of 0.48, much lower than that of current income, discussed above, and also lower than the regression for assets, to be seen below. The group of variables considered together, though, is statistically significant at the 1 percent level (see table 61).

The three groups of variables—origin, destination, and individual—are all significant at the 1 percent level. According to the analysis of covariance at the bottom of table 61, the greatest contribution to the reduction in squared residuals comes from the individual variables (277 billion), followed by the origin variables (177 billion). The destination variables contribute the least (71 billion). In other words, the local economic-institutional environment explains little of the variation in investment, which responds above all to influences of a personal nature.

Origin Variables

Origin variables have some influence upon investment, above all those that indicate prior itinerancy and initial resources. But both of these lose significance with the subsequent introduction of individual variables. This is probably due to collinearity with assets, as was also seen in the analysis of current income. Being a southerner and former landowner did not have significant effects and even presented some negative signs, contrary to expectations. It also appears that itinerancy may enrich and teach colonists how to invest during their wanderings before arriving at the frontier. This is an important result, to be reconsidered later. In all, however, origin variables did not have a strong influence over investment.

Destination Variables

In the case of investment, destination (local environment) variables are those that contribute least to the reduction of squared residuals as a group, in direct contrast to the effect on current income. Being in private colonization does not have a statistically significant effect, which even becomes negative after the inclusion of individual variables. Receiving technical or social assistance has a positive sign only in the absence of the individual variables; with these included, the signs also become negative and significant at the 1 percent level. That is, those who receive assistance invest the least! Being a sharecropper or squatter reduces investment, and being a landowner significantly increases investment, as would be expected.

The local economic environment on the frontier exercises a weak influence over investment. Its only impact was through the holding of land title. Since investment occurs above all in the first years on the plot (see below), colonists have few alternatives upon arrival: basically, they have to clear forest off the land and prepare the soil for planting. Local differences were not sufficient to provoke variations in these basic start-up activities.

Individual Variables

Individual variables contribute the most to the reduction of squared residuals in the investment regression. They also strongly alter the sign and significance of other included variables. Older units, those that have been longer on their plots and have more cultivated area, all invest less than younger units (negative sign on age), more recent arrivals (negative sign on time on plot), and smaller farms (negative sign on cultivated area). This shows that the principal forms of investment being captured in the sample are those incurred during the initial stages on the plot, when families are young, recently arrived, and have not yet cleared much land. There is little investment among older units once this initial effort of starting up has been accomplished. As would be expected from a microeconomic analysis of production, assets and current income have positive signs and are significant.

In sum, individual variables, above all those related to life cycle and start-up, are those that most contribute to explaining investment. In all, however, these regressions have the lowest R^2, compared to those in the other two tables.

Implantation and Rupture

Investment was found to be the dependent variable that is most sensitive and difficult to explain. It is not determined by past experience, nor by local conditions. It reflects an intention to raise one's standard of living, the knowledge of how to do it, a disposition to overcome routine, and confidence that the desired objective is worth the risk. All of these elements demand a much more sophisticated model than is presented here. These findings offer a preliminary description rather than a theoretical interpretation of investment behavior.

The principal positive influences on investment are land title and time on the plot. Investments typical of older, consolidated units—such as expansion of perennial crops, construction, additions to equipment, and so on—were small, and their variation counted for relatively little. They were "washed out" by the large initial effort required to deforest the land and begin farming. In fact, many older farmers had invested little over time and had reduced their initial endowment—as was the case in private colonization. Others diversified into nonfarm activities—as was the case for southerners in official colonization. The regression, therefore, points to divergent paths among different types of colonists. These different trajectories are clearly seen in appendix 3 of *A colonização dirigida na Amazônia*.

The negative sign on age, even though not statistically significant, is interesting. Once again, the situation of the frontier reverses expectations. Normally, there should be a positive relation between investment and maturity of the family unit: the more adult children present, the greater the surplus labor available for investment. Perhaps a large number of farmers were already highly monetized and dispensed with the "working capital" supplied by family labor.[15] Perhaps, as suggested before, the jolt of migrating great distances, clearing the forest, and starting a farm in the Amazon frontier is an overwhelming disruption of the softer, smoother, and more prolonged impact of the family life cycle upon investment. Behavior in discontinuity must surely differ from that under conditions of permanence in the same place.

The influence of local economic-institutional environments upon investment is relatively small. Its contribution to the reduction in the unexplained residuals is the smallest of all and corresponds to merely a fourth of the contribution of individual variables. On the frontier, therefore, investment was an individual undertaking.

Assets: Itinerant Accumulation

The regression for colonists' assets obtains an R^2 of 0.77, significant at the 1 percent level for the entire set of variables (see table 62). According to the analysis of covariance at the bottom of the table, the three blocks of variables are highly significant, each at the 1 percent level. The greatest contribution to reducing residual error, in this case, comes from origin variables (11 trillion), followed by individual variables (7 trillion). Destination conditions contribute least to explaining assets (4 trillion). In other words, the local economic-institutional environment explains little of the variation in the value of assets. This variation is attributable principally to the influence of colonists' origins.

Origin Variables

The most significant origin influences are prior itinerancy and initial resources.[16] After including the other two groups of variables, southern origin ceases to be significant and turns negative, as also occurs with previous land ownership. Strangely enough, the simple correlation between initial resources with itinerancy is larger than with previous land ownership, as can be seen in appendix 3 of *A colonização dirigida na Amazônia.* Surprisingly, then, itinerancy itself could be a means toward accumulation. This point will be further discussed below.

Destination Variables

Being situated in private colonization projects, receiving agricultural and nonagricultural transfers, and having title to the land are all positive and significant factors. That is, wealthier colonists brought more with them in the first place, were in private colonization, owned their land, and received more technical and social assistance.[17]

Individual Variables

Among these variables, the only positive influence is time on the plot. It is strange that all the other variables have negative signs, such as work dedicated to agriculture (significant at the 5 percent level), and cultivated area (significant at the 1 percent level). Thus, the value of assets was not the result of local agricultural activity, but was related to previous experience and accumulation.

This regression comprises a partial test of the fundamental equation of chapter 14 (equation 12). That model relates initial resources, time, area, hours, and price variables (omitted from these regressions) with total accumulated assets. The statistical significance of initial resources and time on the plot, thus, support the model's predictions. Frontier agriculture cannot be analyzed as that of established regions. Past conditions and the stage of operation on the plot are of crucial importance in understanding accumulation by colonists.

Summarizing the results of the three blocks of variables, the principal positive influences upon assets are itinerancy, initial resources, transfers, title holding, situation in private colonization projects, and time on the plot. The implications of these results will be discussed here and in the following chapter.

Itinerant Accumulation

These regressions on assets describe a complex process diverging paths of accumulation. Separate paths are more clearly revealed in an examination of averages and simple correlations,[18] which, due to space limitations, cannot be presented here. The two main stories are identified as follows.

(1) In private colonization, southerners had more assets (positive sign) because they brought them from outside. Thus, current capital did not represent greater accumulation on the frontier itself. Over time, their capital actually depreciated. They lost what they had from selling their previous properties (negative sign for southerners and previous property ownership). To compensate for these losses, southerners in private colonization intensified family labor. Perhaps they came from the South with more work-oriented habits than the northeasterners and others, as common prejudice holds. Overworking the family, however, did not reverse their dissaving (negative sign on hours of agricultural and nonfarm work and for cultivated area).

(2) In official colonization, southerners and other migrants accumulated through recourse to institutional, technical, and social assistance (positive sign on agricultural and nonagricultural transfers). However, since "others" were earlier arrivals than southerners (positive sign on time on the plot), they had time to grow. By the end of the decade, they had already accumulated greater wealth, even, than that of southerners in private projects.[19]

Of the three groups of explanatory variables tested, the local economic-institutional environment contributed least to the reduction of unexplained variation in assets (only one-third of the reduction in squared residuals furnished by origin variables). Those who accumulated on the frontier, then, were those who had already accumulated elsewhere before.

Conclusions and Unexpected Results

This chapter analyzes colonists' performance on the frontier with regard to three alternative measures: current income, investment, and accumulated assets. Each measure has different implications and is influenced in distinct ways by conditions of origin, destination, and colonists' individual characteristics. To summarize:

(1) The principal influence on variation of current income was the local economic-institutional environment in the region of destination. Of particular importance were technical assistance and holding title to land, both of which acted directly upon agricultural operations in the observed period. Income levels were higher among landowners, who received the most institutional assistance, especially in official colonization. Otherwise, colonists tend to fall into the vicious circle of indebtedness, which favored income appropriation by other agents, such as merchants and colonizing agencies. Basic colonization policies,

therefore, such as titleholding and various services, directly increased colonists' income.

(2) The principal influence on variation in investment was individual variables, especially those linked to the early stages upon the land. Moving to the frontier broke the continuous evolution of the family life cycle in established agriculture and interfered with usual investment decisions. The most difficult task on the frontier was the start-up cost of clearing the land and establishing oneself. This is the investment variation captured by the survey data. It was so overwhelming as to dwarf the impact of local variations in different local economic-institutional environments. These destination variables influenced investment only indirectly, via current income.

(3) Origin variables were the principal influence on variation in assets, especially prior itinerancy and initial resources brought from outside to the new plot. In this case, accumulation was more rapid for southerners and slower for other migrants, and it required agricultural and nonagricultural assistance. Local conditions affected accumulation only indirectly, through their impact on current income and investment decisions made over the years. In sum: colonists in private colonization were wealthier, not because they accumulated on the frontier itself, but rather because they had brought more assets with them. Colonists in the official projects, however, had assets that were amassed on the frontier itself.

(4) Unexpectedly, being in private colonization did not in itself exercise a positive influence on income, investment, or accumulated assets, once the independent influences of holding title, receiving technical assistance, bringing resources from regions of origin, and time on the plot were controlled for. Farmers in private colonization, then, showed high average levels of income, accumulated capital, investment, and title holding; however, they were disinvesting, falling into debt, and living on what they had originally brought with them. Farmers in official colonization who had access to technical and social assistance and titleholding performed well; with time, they attained levels of income and assets similar to those of private colonization. No independent influence appeared in these tests to indicate that private colonization was more efficient than official colonization in terms of income, investment, or asset accumulation by the colonists.

(5) Another surprise was discovering that the maturity of the family unit (in terms of duration of marriage and available labor hours for agricultural work) did not exercise a significant influence upon income, investment, or asset accumulation. "Mature" families (i.e., those with many members of working age) were expected to invest more and achieve higher rates of accumulation than young families. Neverthe-

less, neither age nor the number of hours dedicated to agriculture had the expected influence. In the dynamic process of migration, the family life cycle apparently does not influence performance on the frontier. Duration of marriage was, apparently, "truncated from below." Colonists tended to arrive with families already formed, venturing to the frontier only with a family age profile favorable to family labor farming. Thus, variations in age of marriage and agricultural work hours on the frontier itself were small and had little explanatory power over performance. This is not to say that the life cycle had had no influence prior to arrival, only that such influence was not observable on the frontier.

(6) Apparently, itinerancy was not a vicious circle that reproduced low income on the frontier. To the contrary, and unexpectedly, itinerancy appears to have been conducive to accumulation. Many colonists brought resources to the frontier precisely because they had taken advantage of the opportunities found in passing from one place to another before. Also, unexpectedly, having been a landowner before coming to the frontier was not in itself a positive or significant influence. What mattered for colonization performance were the resources brought in, whether or not they came from previous agricultural properties.

This result implies an unexpected relationship between colonists and the land. Each property is apparently a transitory stage in a life strategy for which accumulation is practiced *with* itinerancy. These small farmers successively purchased, appreciated, and sold lands. Their accumulation occurred within the same family, but not on the same land.

A nomadic style implies that simple ownership of land may not have much impact on farmers' technology. Practices of soil conservation and investments with long maturation may be unattractive to those who do not plan to remain long. The same could be true of low degrees of community participation on the frontier. The variable means presented in appendix 3 of *A colonização dirigida na Amazônia* indicate extreme isolation: less than one institutional contact per month. Living on the fringes of society may lead one to discredit deeper involvement with, or greater social responsibility for, an institutional environment that one plans someday to leave. These issues will be recalled in the next chapter.

(7) Another result worth emphasizing is the importance of out-hiring and technical and social assistance to current income, investment, and assets. Work off the plot may, apparently, raise family income significantly, as do technical and social assistance. Health care is an especially important determinant of the capacity to invest and accumulate. This result, however, contradicts that obtained in chapter 16, where nonfarm income was shown to be a small proportion of total income, averaging around only 10 percent. Among all members of each group, nonfarm

activities may well have been a small portion of total income in general, but a large share of income among the most successful. The averages shown in chapter 16, then, may have masked the success of some colonists in their differentiation, analyzed in this chapter.

This conclusion implies, in turn, that planning for colonization projects in the future cannot neglect the nonagricultural component. It is fundamental to establish communities close to one another and to provide incentives for the emergence of local-level urban activities that create alternative employment for members of agricultural families. At the same time, basic services, and especially health services, must be provided to the population. Without them, agricultural profitability and growth will be undermined.

This chapter expanded the analysis of colonists' reactions to the economic and institutional environments of the frontier. With respect to colonists themselves, it emphasized the diversity of experiences and own resources. With respect to local frontier environments, it revealed differences in the supply of social and economic infrastructure. The environment was seen to be fundamental in the determination of colonists' current income. Systems of captive transactions, as are typical of private colonization and also of sharecropping, were shown to be clearly harmful to the appropriation of income. Official colonization offered opportunities to titled colonists which gave them advantages in appropriating the income they generated. The next chapter concludes this econometric analysis, focusing on how colonists' reactions changed over time.

Notes

1. A description of the sample, definitions of all the variables, explanations of statistical methods, and consolidated tables with all means, standard errors, and simple correlations are summarized in appendixes 1–3 of *A colonização dirigida na Amazônia.*
2. *Migrações internas,* especially vols. 2 and 4, Ozorio de Almeida (1985a), and *A colonização dirigida na Amazônia.*
3. Equivalent to table 40 "Total Receipts," "Monetary and Nonmonetary Balance," and to "TC," item 10 of figure A.1.1.4 of appendix 3 of *A colonização dirigida na Amazônia.*
4. Equivalent to S1 of figure A.1.2.3 of appendix 3, of *A colonização dirigida na Amazônia.*
5. Equivalent to FF of figure A.1.3.3 of appendix 3, *A colonização dirigida na Amazônia.*
6. Johnson (1963), chapter 8.
7. See appendix 3 of *A colonização dirigida na Amazônia.*
8. Johnson (1963), chapter 6.
9. Ibid., chapter 9.

10. Origin variables in terms of appendix 3 of *A colonização dirigida na Amazônia*: southerners (XM), prior itinerancy (EXI), prior ownership (SP2), initial resources (TT1).

11. Destination variables in terms of appendix 3 of *A colonização dirigida na Amazônia*: private colonization (XM1), agricultural transfers (I2), nonagricultural transfers (I3), sharecroppers (T2A), occupants (T2B), titled (T2D).

12. Individual variables in terms of appendix 3 of *A colonização dirigida na Amazônia*: age (T2), agricultural hours (H2), nonagricultural hours (H3), cultivated area (AD), time on lot (Y1), assets (AT), current income (RAT).

13. Units refer to Brazilian current *cruzeiros* and have no importance in the discussion of empirical results.

14. See appendix 3 of *A colonização dirigida na Amazônia.*

15. See the discussion in chapter 12.

16. This result is predicted by the model developed in chapter 14, equation (12), according to which accumulation would be a function of initial resources, time, and other variables.

17. See appendix 3 of *A colonização dirigida na Amazônia.*

18. Ibid.

19. Ibid.

21. ITINERANCY AND ADAPTATION TO THE AMAZON

This chapter uses graphs to summarize the econometric results of chapter 20, showing differentiation among colonists on the Amazon frontier. It shows that income and investment did not rise over time in Amazon colonization. The impact of local economic institutions upon colonists' accumulation, however, was positive and grew over time, as the influence of their regions of origin began to weaken. The final section of this chapter summarizes the principal conclusions of part 4 of the book. The terminology used here is the same as that of the previous chapters: "assets," "wealth," and "capital" are used equivalently and the measured increase in their value is called a process of "accumulation."

Differentiation on the Frontier: Summary of Findings

The combined survey information on colonists seen until now reveals a general process with many variations, which can be grouped into four broad and distinct trends.

Some southerners in Pará who had prior experience with agriculture took advantage of the institutional benefits and cheap land of official colonization. They accumulated in agriculture and diversified into nonagricultural activities.

Some southerners in Mato Grosso who had sold their land in the South and bought relatively expensive land in private colonization worked their families a great deal in agriculture. Subsequently, they became indebted and disinvested, or reduced accumulation. Many of them eventually planted pasture, more for speculative than for productive purposes.

Other migrants in Pará, with less money and less experience than southerners, entered official colonization, usually after years as squatters. Although many eventually quit and sold their land "rights," often to southerners, others remained and laid claim to property titles. In time they learned to use official assistance, obtain credit, invest, and accumulate. After enough years, many even surpassed the performance levels of farmers in private colonization.

Finally, those who entered private colonization without money to buy land became sharecroppers in perennial crops, such as coffee. Limited by rigid labor contracts, these workers lasted only briefly, five years at most, on their plots. Their future options were to become local landless laborers or to emigrate again to other frontiers.

The graphs below summarize these distinct trends for the first three types of colonists (i.e., excluding sharecroppers). Income, investment, and assets refer to the same variables analyzed in chapter 20. Each graph was calculated by multiplying the average values of the independent variables from appendix 3 of *A colonização dirigida na Amazônia* by their respective coefficients, shown in tables 60, 61, and 62. This effectively turned each multiple regression into a simple linear function, with an intercept and only one dependent variable: time on the plot. It is a schematic simplification that illustrates general tendencies for each of the three groups.

Graph 3 suggests that the only group that increased its average income after arriving on the Amazon frontier was "other" migrants in official colonization. Older southerners in both states had lower income than the more recent arrivals, which is shown by the negative slope. This is surprising. An important factor depressing colonists' incomes must have been adverse relative prices in concentrated input and product markets, as was discussed in part 3 and chapter 18. Also, colonists' inadequate agricultural techniques are certainly responsible, in part, for stagnant or declining income over time. In the absence of adequate rural extension, as was discussed in chapters 4, 5, and 19, farmers did not evolve from annual to perennial crops, as is needed to preserve soil fertility and to increase agricultural productivity.

In spite of the high rates of accumulation observed in chapter 17, then, southerners' incomes did not improve with time. Only other migrants improved their incomes after arrival, although with modest gains. Given the large variation in the sample, however, one cannot be certain if the positive slope in graph 3 is statistically significant. Whatever the benefit of colonization to colonists' incomes, it was primarily due to migration itself and to the gap between average incomes on the frontier and in origin regions, as seen in chapter 17.

Graph 4 shows that investment declined over time. This is consistent with previous observations that colonists' principal investment involved initial clearing of the forest and establishing themselves on their plots. Relatively low investment in later years is worrisome and helps explain the stagnant or even declining incomes seen in graph 3.

Graph 5 shows that southerners in official colonization accumulated the most assets on the Amazon frontier. That is: their asset profile has the highest positive slope. Other migrants in Pará and southerners in Mato Grosso have slightly increasing and parallel accumulation trends, starting from very different levels.

In sum, at the end of the 1970s, private colonization still subsisted on resources brought from the South. Over time, income and investment declined, leaving little accumulation in the Amazon itself. By contrast, colonists in official colonization were accumulating capital, even if investment was higher in the initial phases and declined over time. Overall, southerners in official projects were the most successful Amazonian colonists.

The Importance of the Passage of Time Before and After the Frontier

Previous chapters showed that, contrary to expectations, itinerancy was not a movement merely among the poor. For many, it was a process of generating valuable knowledge, both agricultural and nonagricultural, empowering colonists to enrich themselves by diversifying their frontier activities. However, there is a transition between origin influences, which are stronger in the beginning and weaken with time, and destination influences, which are weak at first and become stronger later on. During the first years, colonists' performance was strongly influenced by prior experience and resources accumulated prior to arrival. As time passed, the impact of prior experience weakened, as local factors became dominant.

This transition was tested by repeating the three groups of regressions in chapter 20 and distinguishing all variables according to time since arrival: one to three years; three to six years; and six or more years. To do this, each variable was multiplied by intercept and slope dummy variables (0,1) for each period. The number of independent variables was tripled, then, in comparison with tables 60, 61, and 62 and the number of coefficients became enormous. These regressions are not reported here because of space limitations and also because many time-specific variables were not statistically significant, while others behaved in nonsystematic ways.

The principal result of this new test, however, was a positive and significant (5 percent level) relationship between itinerancy and accumulation. According to these results, little experience of prior itinerancy

Graph 3. Total Annual Income

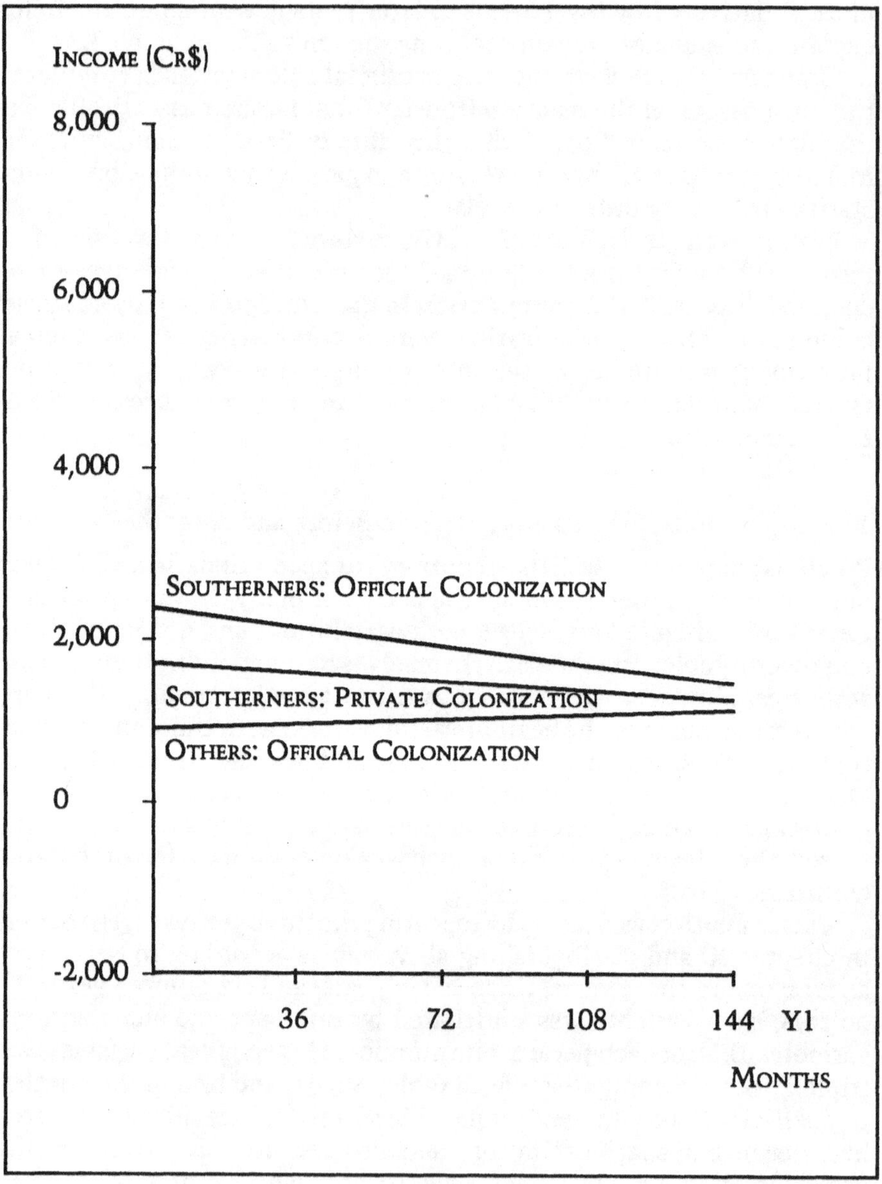

Graph 4. Investment

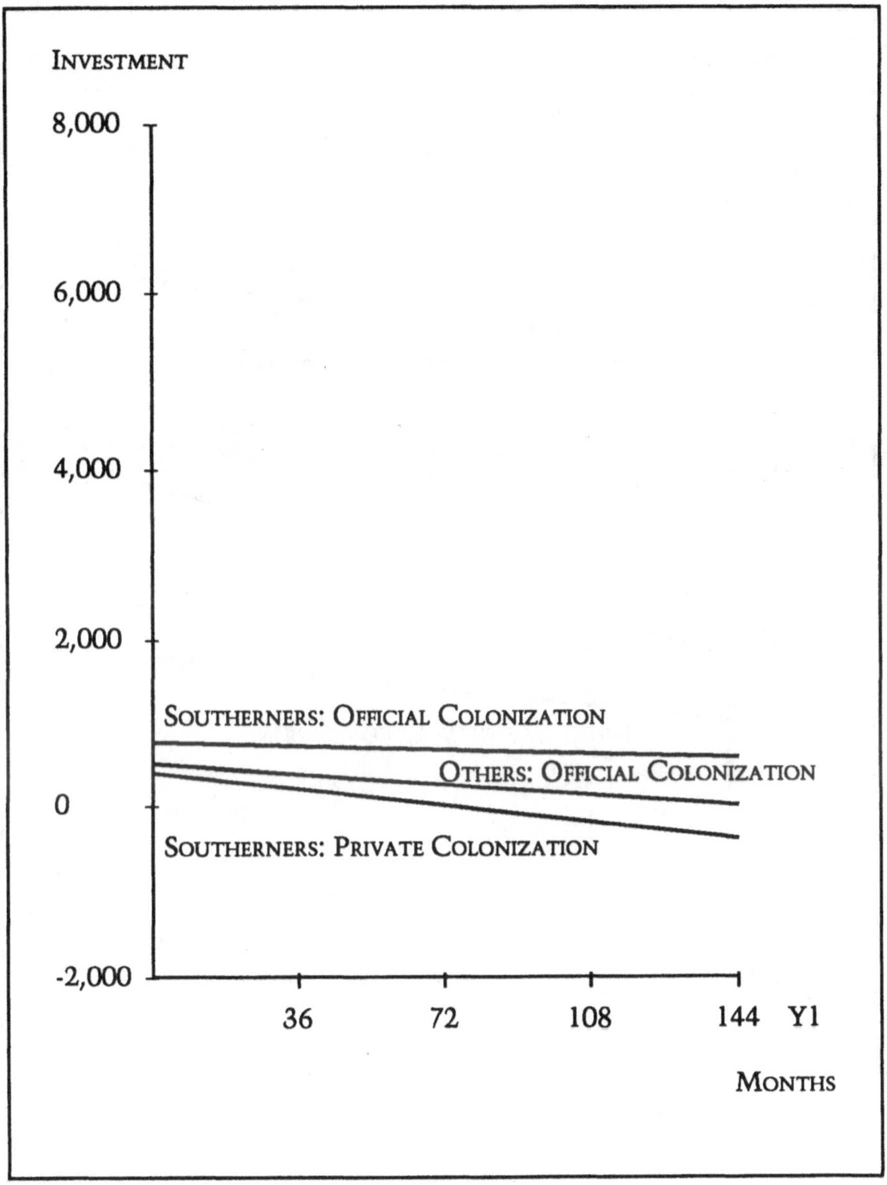

Graph 5. Total Assets

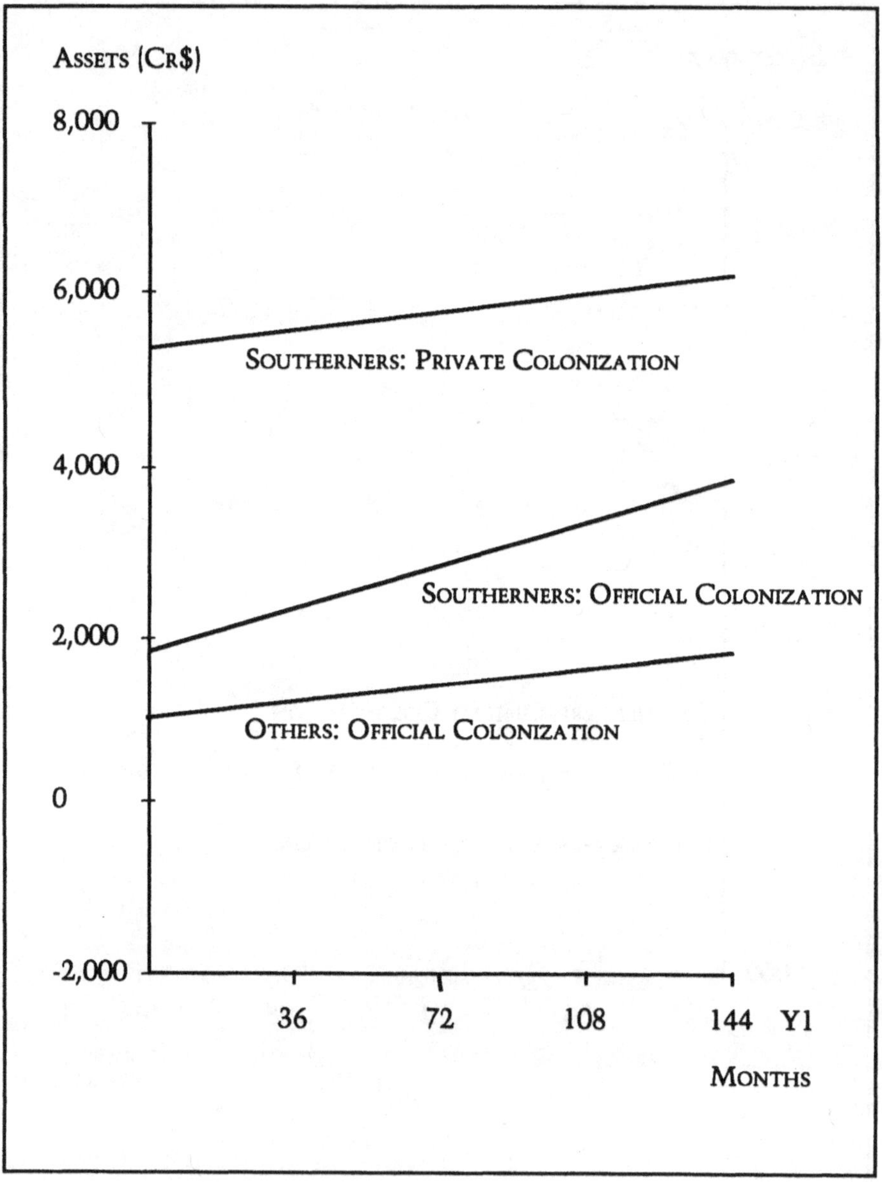

Graph 6. Itinerant Accumulation

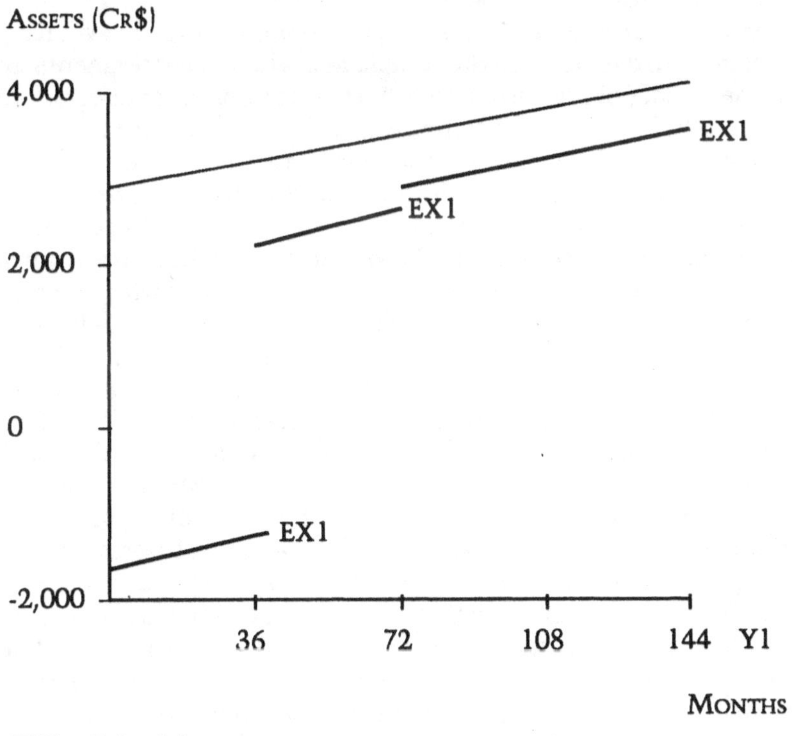

EX1—Prior Itinerancy

implies less accumulation on the frontier, while more prior itinerancy implies greater accumulation on one's own plot of land. Excluding itinerancy from the regression for assets would, therefore, shift the estimated function downward.

This shift, however, varies with time. In the first years, the impact of prior itinerancy is greater. Excluding this variable, then, causes a large downward shift in the function. In the following years, the impact of prior itinerancy is smaller. Excluding the variable from the regression causes successively smaller downward shifts in the function. Three such exclusion tests are illustrated by the three line segments in graph 6. The axes and definitions are the same as for graph 5, and the data come from the coefficients reported in table 62 and from the means in appendix 3 of *A colonização dirigida na Amazônia.*

The three groups of colonists shown in the previous graphs were aggregated in one average line in graph 6, representing the average path of asset growth over time in the sample as a whole. Line segments, then, show the impact of prior itinerancy over time upon all colonists. This is clearly much larger at the beginning and diminishes with time.

The absence of any prior itinerancy experience means that this variable is equal to zero, which is the same as excluding it from the final regression of table 62 for the first three years. The level of accumulated assets in the initial period would be very low, then, in comparison with the prior estimated average. This is apparent in comparing the general line with the segment in the lower left corner of graph 6, for 0–36 months. In other words, recent colonists who were very itinerant before arrival accumulated more; those who had been less itinerant accumulated less. As discussed in chapters 2 and 12, the pioneers who clear the land on the frontier's first phase belong to this contingent of "recent" colonists. The majority of them soon left again, enlarging the subsequent rural exodus.

After these first three years, prior itinerancy loses much of its impact. Its absence is equivalent to excluding this variable altogether from the final regression of table 62 for those on the frontier from three to six years. The level of accumulated assets in this intermediate period would be lower than the overall average estimated in chapter 20. This is apparent by comparing the general line with the intermediate segment (from 32 to 72 months) in graph 6. Yet this segment is also much closer to the general average than that of the prior period. In other words, among "intermediate" colonists, those who were itinerant before arriving accumulated more than those who were not itinerant. But the difference was smaller than among recent colonists. The influence of prior itinerancy, therefore, diminished with time. In this transitional phase, many of the interviewed colonists probably reemigrated, joining the rural exodus on the frontier's second phase; only some established themselves longer in the area.

For "old" colonists (i.e., those with more than six years on their plot), prior itinerancy was already very distant. The sedentary practices of the past years already counted for more than the experience prior to arrival. The impact of itinerancy on frontier accumulation was smaller than in the preceding phases, even if it was still positive and significant. The lack of any prior itinerancy is the same as excluding the variable from the last regression of table 62 for all those with more than six years on the plot. The level of accumulated assets in these advanced years would be lower than the average, as seen by comparing the respective segment with the general line in graph 6, from 72 to 144 months. The difference relative to the general average, however, is much smaller than for the preceding two phases. In other words, among "old" colonists, those who were itinerant before arriving still accumulated more than those who were not itinerant. But the difference relative to the mean is very small. These are the "survivors" who did not reemigrate during the rural exodus of the frontier's second consolidating phase. By maintaining stable links with the land, they learned to take advantage of their new environment.

Graph 6 therefore summarizes the transmission of influences from origin to destination upon farmers' performance on the frontier. As the origin loses its influence, experience on the frontier in managing local economic and institutional environments certainly gains force. Such are the dominant influences upon current income, as seen in the previous chapter. This interaction over time, between colonists and their "baggage" on the one hand, and environment and its "opportunities" on the other, is the key to colonization performance.

As seen in the previous chapter, access to institutional assistance was fundamental, among local impacts. Some arrived knowing better how to make use of supportive institutions; others learned how to do so over time. This is true even though such services were seriously deficient for everyone: roads were in ruins, schools and health services were lacking, credit was insufficient, and social isolation was drastic. Improving local institutional environments would certainly have a strong positive impact on colonists' performance.

Accumulation Trends: Before and After the Frontier

It is important to remember that the itinerancy analyzed in this chapter is a different kind from that initially expected—small sequential shifts by nonlandowners. However, a different itinerancy was found here, unforeseen by most studies on small farming in Brazil. Many small producers buy and sell rural real estate all over the country, progressively accumulating capital in the process of moving from place to place. This strategy of prior accumulation is associated with the capital growth that migrants achieve later on the frontier. Contradicting the expectations of chapter 12, then, itinerancy is not necessarily a low-income trajectory. On Brazil's shifting frontier, there are some small "itinerant landowners" who are relatively successful and little studied in the specific literature.

Origin, destination, and individual factors condition migrants' performance on the frontier, but do not determine it. As measured in the previous chapter, these factors statistically account for three-quarters of the variation in income and assets, and for half the variation in investment, as seen by the R^2 of tables 60–62. Given the same local institutional-economic environments (there called "destination" variables) and many of the same personal conditions (there called "origin" and "individual" variables), colonists still differ among themselves. Prior experiences, initial resources, time on the plot, family labor, and so on, are important, but they are not everything.

To analyze the remaining variation is beyond the scope of this book. Migrants' behavior cannot be explained by any finite set of characteristics. All that could be attempted here was to describe some of their economic characteristics, and to organize, measure, and compare the most probable influences upon colonists' performance.

In sum, the findings presented in part 4 of the book about small farming in the Amazon after ten years of directed colonization are surprising in many ways. Colonists' standard of living appeared reasonable in comparison with urban wages. The subsistence economy was small, since nonmonetary income was a small portion of total income. Yet indebtedness was high. Relative prices were more favorable to the farmers of Pará than to those of Mato Grosso, and official colonization appears to have been more successful than private colonization in terms of colonists' performance. Investment depended on the stage of implantation on the plot, apparently little influenced by the family life cycle. Itinerancy continued on settled plots, even when colonists were already landowners. Itinerancy also appeared to be a potential strategy of accumulation through owning properties successively, not merely a vicious circle of indigent mobility. Finally, past experiences weakened and local influences became increasingly effective over time. This implies that appropriate settlement policies can act positively upon colonists and that colonization can be successful if conducted correctly.

This chapter concludes the empirical part of the book. It suggests that farmers have a slow response to local stimuli. This finding is of fundamental importance for the effectiveness of any land distribution policy, whether in colonization or agrarian reform—the topic of the next chapter.

22. COLONIZATION AND AGRARIAN REFORM: THE CURRENT DEBATE

This chapter draws current policy implications from the findings in this book and brings the discussion up to the present. The objective is to bring the book's conclusions to bear on a general discussion of trade-offs between the two main types of land distribution schemes in Brazil today: colonization—a historical reality—and agrarian reform—a political hypothesis. No additional information is brought forward and no comparisons are made with actual experiences of agrarian reform in other countries, such as Mexico, Taiwan, Korea; no mention is made of the literature on agrarian reform. Since colonization and agrarian reform both aim at settling similar contingents of small farmers, issues in common, such as those involving technology and scale of agricultural production, are also left out of the discussion. Finally, complementary or alternative distributive measures, whether fiscal, educational, health-related, or other, are not analyzed, as they do not alter the comparison between the two main types of land distribution: colonization and agrarian reform. A brief mention is made of how land distribution evolved during the 1980s, drawing out the continuity of processes that began during the 1970s.

The next section summarizes the most important findings of the book as a whole. The following three sections compare colonization and agrarian reform from differing points of view in their effectiveness as land redistribution policies. The fifth section summarizes the results of my more recent research into the colonization of the Amazon during the 1980s and points to the predictive value of the 1970s. The concluding section restates the general argument of the book as a whole. Topics do not follow the order of previous chapters, and the presentation necessarily repeats what has come before. No sources or bibliography are cited, as the material covered has been referred to in earlier parts of the text.

The conclusions of this chapter are important for considering any land redistribution measures to be implemented in the future. The main lesson is that without substantial investment in technology and in economic, social, and physical infrastructure, and without an initial period of protection "against the market," the success rate of any settlement scheme will be much lower than desired. This lesson is certainly as true for agrarian reform as for colonization. Any land distribution is expensive and requires a long-term sustained commitment for improvement of rural income distribution to be a general and firm result.

Summary of Findings

Evaluation of directed colonization in the Amazon during the 1970s requires consideration of many interlinked aspects. One of them is that the agricultural frontier in Brazil has been a short-lived moving phenomenon. Vast areas of the national territory are swept by a migratory wave that swells at first in a given area, but soon afterward passes it by. During the 1970s, the frontier areas of the previous decades were already experiencing rural exodus, land property reconcentration, and urbanization. During the 1980s, a good part of the 1970s frontier studied here was already on the same path. Since at least the 1960s, the advance of the Brazilian frontier has involved a greater increase in urban population than in rural population, that is, the frontier is more an urban phenomenon than a rural one.

Only 3 percent of the Amazon is known to be suitable for small farming at present technological levels. This area had been completely appropriated by the end of the 1970s. In this sense, then, the "enclosure" of the Amazon frontier had already occurred by the end of the Decade of Colonization. Had there been serious and intensive rural extension work at the time, much more land could have been opened up to small farmers on soils less suitable for them, but still available. The need for such a large-scale technical and institutional effort was not foreseen; therefore it was not made. Land occupation from then on generated growing social conflicts for remaining fertile soils, as is confirmed by increasing press coverage on the upward spiral of violence in the Amazon during the 1980s.

Rough calculations, based on admittedly imprecise information, yield several surprising results about Amazon colonization during the 1970s. Real living standards were higher than alternatives in the urban labor market and capital accumulation rates were higher than prevailing interest rates. This would imply that colonization was covering its private opportunity cost during the period. Public and private investment in physical and social infrastructure in the region cost around $45,900 per settled family and $13.9 thousand per job created during the 1970s. Those values are actually quite low when compared to alternative values found elsewhere in the economy. On average, annual income generated by settlers was $13,500. Estimates indicate that, since arrival on the frontier, accumulated benefits were greater than costs. In other words, colonization returned to society more than it took during the decade.

In many ways, however, the price paid by society as a whole for shifting millions of people to the Amazon was high. Natural access to the region is through rivers that flow northward from the frontier. Demographic, economic, and administrative centers, however, are in the opposite direction: to the south of the frontier. Thus, the Brazilian state took responsibility for building an expensive road and communications network that inverted access to the Amazon, linking it to the more developed parts of the country.

At the same time that the state expanded its scope of action in the Amazon, a varied and complex commercial and institutional infrastructure was established, bringing the migrant economy under the influence of southern industrial capitalism. During the initial phases of frontier settlement, agricultural production and income appropriation were based on usury-mercantile capital, whereby small family farmers and merchants interacted through the crop lien mechanism. In subsequent phases, many small farmers departed, markets consolidated, directly productive capital came to predominate in agriculture and commerce, wage labor increased, and frontier areas became progressively integrated into the general economy.

As these sequential phases of occupation evolved in each area, they led to very different market systems at distinct points of the frontier. These different markets were observed principally in relation to land prices and agricultural product prices. In public colonization, land was cheap, markets were fairly competitive, and product prices were higher than in private projects. This enabled settlers to invest in permanent crops, raise productivity over time, diversify into commerce and other businesses, and accumulate—faster for southerners and slower for other migrants. In private colonization, land was expensive, markets were highly concentrated, and agricultural product prices were low. This combination provoked indebtedness, inhibited investment, and curtailed accumulation, even though productivity was relatively high.

In Mato Grosso's private settlement projects, colonists became deeply indebted by purchasing expensive land. The main cost of private colonization was purchasing the land. In this case, it was mostly the settler who paid for it. In Pará's public settlement projects, many settlers took advantage of cheap land, exhausted its fertility and deforested successively, passing on from plot to plot. They remained itinerant in spite of ownership, sometimes within the same settlement project. The main cost of public colonization was unproductive devastation. In this case, it was mostly "nature" who paid for it.

These "itinerant landowners," found in public-directed settlement projects, turned out to be the most successful colonists in the 1970s. They had settled in many different places before, buying, leasing, and selling the land successively as they moved on with the agricultural frontier. Less experienced migrants generally had fewer initial resources and took longer to get established. With time, however, many poorer migrants learned to take advantage of local level technical and social assistance, as well as of the commercial and physical infrastructure available in public projects.

Success, however, took time. In the beginning, it depended mostly on migrants' previous know-how; later, it depended more on migrants' ability to take advantage of local economic opportunities. In sum:

1. Cheap land distribution was a successful social policy for its direct beneficiaries. The benefit to the settler of migrating to the Amazon frontier was a substantial gain in earnings and capital accumulation, relative to alternatives elsewhere in the economy. The benefit of Amazon colonization to the whole economy was that total directly incurred costs were less than the private value of settlers' earnings.

2. Settlers' low technology brought about great environmental destruction in the Amazon. A policy of appropriate technology generation and diffusion is urgently needed to avoid "excessive" deforestation and devastation in Amazon colonization. Only then will small farmers adopt technical alternatives that are at once less harmful to the environment and consistent with relative prices on the frontier.

3. Land distribution requires compatible prices and markets. Small farmers were sensitive to the economic environment to which they migrated, in spite of habits and practices brought from home regions. This sensitivity increased with time, which implies that the effectiveness of settlement policies should also increase over time. Thus, the problems with colonization in the past may have been due mainly to insufficient attention to market factors. This implies that future colonization policies could become more successful than previous ones, if market issues—relative prices, credit, and so on—are dealt with adequately.

4. Merchants, not settlers, were those who most benefited from colonization projects in the Amazon. The clearing of large areas of virgin forest and the destruction of vast stretches of the Amazon environment served southern industry and commerce more than it did farmers. This

is a significant and serious leakage in what should have been an income redistribution policy.

5. The costs and imbalances of Amazon colonization could have been much attenuated if Brazilian land distribution issues had been seen as a whole from the beginning. Any future land-based distributive program must henceforth be on guard not to repeat past mistakes. The precedent from which to learn is that of Amazon colonization: the only large-scale Brazilian land distribution experience to date.

6. The experience of directed colonization during the 1970s shows that any land redistribution policy must resist a general tendency toward rural exodus. Settlers must be protected from market forces that accelerate their expulsion, and this protection must last long enough to ensure a process of accumulation. However, the policy instruments available to colonization are typically slow to take effect. This is due in part to the slow demise of settlers' ingrained itinerancy. Many failed projects—abandonment or resale of plots, reconcentration of landed property, urbanization, and unemployment—were due to the insufficiency and discontinuity of necessary measures. There were also some successful projects. The interviewed settlers of the late 1970s were survivors who had benefited from colonization. They are not representative, however, of the whole set of migrants who entered directed settlement projects in the decade's early years.

Colonization and Agrarian Reform: Some Economic Issues

Ultimately, colonization and agrarian reform aim to redistribute income in rural areas. Both compete with other redistributive measures, such as fiscal policy, education, health, and so on. Since an ample discussion of all aspects of rural income redistribution is beyond the scope of this book, this section and the following two will focus only on colonization and agrarian reform, and on some of the trade-offs between them. Although based on the analysis of Amazon colonization during the 1970s, these are the key contemporary questions for considering land distribution today.

Land distribution provides individuals with an important asset: land itself. The objective of the distribution is to give a dispossessed rural workforce the means by which to generate incomes above their current labor market alternatives. When such an objective is achieved, a land distribution policy can be considered successful.

The distributed asset—land—is not a form of remuneration, but a factor of production. It allows the worker to appropriate from the production process a larger share of total income than if he had only his own labor to contribute. A laborer with nothing else to work with is paid only for his labor, while a laborer who works with his own land is remunerated for both factors of production: land and labor.

The distributed asset—land—is a good that, in any capitalist economy, has a market of its own. In a society where private property in general tends to concentrate, so does distributed land. As it appreciates in value, its price rapidly surpasses a small farmer's expectations of future income, and small plots soon begin to be sold to larger holders. The general dynamics of concentration in a capitalist economy apply to any asset, and there is no reason why land should be excluded from it.

A landed rural worker who earns joint returns to land and labor, raises his future income expectations as his current productivity and income increase. Therefore, his asking price should also increase, as should the time he stays on the land before selling out. If and when he does sell, the more he will charge, the greater will be the variety of productive options he will then have in the general economy. He can then either buy land elsewhere, go into an urban business, invest in training or education, or find himself some other economic activity. Whatever his choice, it is made possible by the originally distributed asset, which elevated the farmer's, or ex-farmer's, position on the income distribution ladder. Thus, land distribution may be considered a successful income distribution policy even when those benefited by it do not forever keep the land they receive, or even remain forever rural.

"Success," however, takes time. Many years are needed for agriculture to flourish. Clearing forests, planting permanent crops, building, and so on, all take many years. The formation of a market system favorable to farmers' income appropriation takes even more time. Without suitable commercial and institutional infrastructure, accumulation in agriculture is jeopardized. The poorer the worker originally, the less prior experience he has and the less assistance he receives, the longer it will take him to raise his income level in agriculture. If local markets are too concentrated, then unfavorable prices will prevent the farmer from ever accumulating.

The success of a land distribution policy, therefore, depends on some elements related to farmers themselves and on other elements independent of them. At the farmers' level, agriculture must be made sufficiently productive to elevate future income expectations substantially, thereby increasing farmers' bargaining power in the land market. At the local level, surrounding rural markets must permit enough farmer appropriation of agricultural income for accumulation to occur. Finally, since reaping the benefits from the distributed land takes time, the institutional environment must operate in a way that is deliberately favorable to retaining small farmers on the land.

Economic Conditions for Land Distribution

Transforming the economic and social position of a large number of people is not done overnight. Countervailing forces must be contained for as long as necessary for both farmers and their markets to become established. This implies innovation regarding *legislation*, *territoriality*, and *duration* of the measures to be taken. Each of these issues will now be briefly discussed.

Legislation must be such as to specify the exceptionality of land vis-à-vis other forms of private property. Land must be legally redefined as an asset that can be distributed for social ends without affecting the distribution of other forms of private property. The issue, then, is not to justify distribution based on poor use of land by previous owners, as is done today in Brazil, but to base distribution solely upon the expected benefit for future owners. It is a form of attaining a legitimate social objective, improving rural income distribution that results in the reallocation of a specific asset: land. The selection of future landowners should be done in the most effective way possible, so as to maximize benefits relative to costs. Thus, distribution should be intended neither as punishment for the neglect of some nor as reward for the militancy of others.

Distribution should also not be expected to serve as a step toward eliminating property rights in the economy in general. As in any capitalist system, the forces that generate concentration usually will continue to do so during the distributive process. By recognizing this general tendency, it becomes possible to exert specific controls during the operation of a given distributive measure, in order to increase its effectiveness. The necessary legal instruments, therefore, cannot be the classical ones of agrarian reform that aim at a permanent and wide-ranging modification in the landed property structure. Rather, limited measures that target distribution within specific project areas for restricted periods of time may turn out to be much more effective.

As for the *duration* of distributive policies, they should also last long enough for small farmers to substantially elevate their income levels and the value of their properties. The better the soil, the more experienced the settlers, the more resources and technical assistance they get, and the more favorable the market system, the faster will results come. There is no definite deadline for success, however. By what can be gleaned from the experience of directed colonization, it takes at least a decade for settlers to consolidate their holdings. Distribution policies that operate against concentrative forces must interfere in land transactions for a period of several years. Only when benefited farmers "come of age" can an area be considered "emancipated," according to the terminology of settlement projects.

Territoriality depends on what kinds of outlays are to be incurred. Geographical concentration in medium-size settlement projects has scale economies in physical and social infrastructure. Dispersion implies resorting to already existing local infrastructure and reduces direct outlays. Yet it demands adequate coordination that is expensive in itself. Without it, settlers will end up as deprived of institutional support as the Amazon frontier people of the 1970s.

In the specific case of frontier settlement (i.e., colonization), much higher direct costs are sure to be incurred than in the case of settlement in established areas. The provision of formerly nonexistent physical and social infrastructure was discovered in this book to be many times more expensive than settlement itself. An additional social cost of frontier settlement is the fact that it provokes destruction of previously untouched natural resources.

The only cost saved by frontier settlement vis-à-vis agrarian reform is that of legal contestation by, and financial compensation to, ex-proprietors. On a frontier, this problem is relatively small, as land values are lower and landownership is less consolidated than elsewhere. Once incorporated into federal holding, land can be distributed directly by the state. Even though during the 1970s federal distribution was extremely concentrative, it need not continue to be so. In other areas, where landed property is consolidated, the contestation problem is much greater. Courts, of course, treat land as a form of private property just as any other. As long as this definition lasts, any changes in the current property structure will remain legally indefensible. Thus, modification in current legislation is more essential to land reform than to colonization.

The argument thus returns to legal issues. Since the Brazilian Constitution of 1988, the elaboration of a new legal base for land distribution is increasingly urgent. Punitive legislation against unproductive landlords is ineffective and insufficient, as it does not ensure subsequent protection against reconcentration. What is now needed is legislation that will identify specific tracts of land as a type of asset different from those in the rest of the economy for purposes of distribution.

Within a given area, land should be considered as an "earmarked" factor of production for the benefit of a targeted landless labor force. Such an approach to distribution would not affect the property structure of other factors, whether in agriculture or in other sectors, nor would it threaten the institution of private property per se. Without such an explicit *legal* "exceptionality clause," along with well-defined *duration* and *territoriality*, the whole economic power structure feels endangered by land distribution and reacts politically against agrarian reform, perpetuating the present impasse.

Economic Contradictions in Land Distribution

During the last few years, there has been increasing social unrest in rural areas of Brazil. Increasing numbers of landless workers are organizing to demand land and violent reaction has escalated. There can be no doubt that land distribution is urgently needed. The number affected and the economic benefits to be derived are substantial.

However, different types of costs involved in directed colonization and agrarian reform must be carefully weighed and openly discussed by the general public. Without broad political backing, the state may yield to interest groups that oppose distribution, as happened midway through the 1970s, and as also occurred in the drafting of the 1988 Constitution. In such circumstances, even when initiated, land distribution will be halted by incomplete measures. Income distribution in rural society, then, will not be altered.

Incomplete measures are in fact counterproductive. The provision of legal, physical, and social infrastructure increases land values, attracts nontarget groups, and speeds up property reconcentration, as has been happening in many parts of the Amazon since the 1970s. Distributionist legislation such as the "Estatuto da Terra" of the 1960s, which does not specify territoriality, threatens all landowners indiscriminately. This stimulates "conservative modernization" and expels workers from the countryside, who then increase the ranks of the landless. This is what has been happening in the South of the country since the 1960s. Incomplete distributive measures thus tend to subvert their own intention.

It is disappointing to realize that land distribution generally leads to subsequent reconcentration. The fact that distributed land does reconcentrate afterward, however, need not be interpreted as a policy failure, as long as the target population makes good use of the distributive period. No land reform in a highly mobile, constantly shifting population such as Brazil's can be definitive. It may have to be taken up over and over again in later periods and in new locations. Ignoring the temporality/territoriality of land distribution means passing legislation inconsistent with the constant flow of the labor force in a dynamic capitalist system.

Who benefits from land distribution depends on how rapidly reconcentration occurs. The experience of Amazon colonization shows that merchants and outside capitalist farmers moved into frontier agriculture soon after the pioneer frontier phase was over. They, and not the original colonists, reaped the main benefits from the social, physical, and market infrastructure implanted by colonization projects. Without adequate "buffer" legislation, agrarian reform would probably go the same way. Political resistance to land distribution may, therefore, be less than feared if nontarget groups expect to be its ultimate beneficiaries.

Who pays for land distribution—ex-landowners, settlers, society, or nature—will also be crucial in determining how strong political resistance to such measures will be, and how effective such resistance will be in the end. In an agrarian reform, the lands that are distributed were previously someone's property. Public compensation for expropriation transfers this cost, partially or totally, to society as a whole, depending on the percentage it covers of the land's real value. Expropriation without complete compensation imposes part of the private cost on ex-landowners. Private payments by settlers transfer part of the burden back to the private sector. The costs of arranging the necessary institutional coordination, legislation, and physical, economic, and social infrastructure are paid by the public sector. According to the experience of the 1970s, such costs are considerable when compared to the cost of land. Finally, if land distribution uses virgin forests, its cost is paid for not by any specific contemporary local social group, but by all those who consider the natural environment part of their own heritage, or that of humanity as a whole.

In addition to the issue of direct cost and who will pay for it, other social costs of land distribution vary according to which combination of component measures in a land distribution "package" is actually enforced. Charging little for the land is an invitation to technological backwardness and land devastation. It leads farmers to waste and abandon the land they receive and to practice low-productivity itinerant agriculture in spite of becoming landowners. Charging too much for the land provokes indebtedness and a search for immediate profits, repressing investment. Both cases—cheap or expensive land—reduce accumulation. Setting adequate relative prices for land and other goods crucial to the small farmer economy should be part of any land distribution program. The prices for land, agricultural products, industrial goods, and credit must be consistent with income appropriation by small farmers. Without consistent relative prices, accumulation on distributed lands will be less than would have been possible otherwise.

Rural market equilibrium in itself is not enough to ensure small farmer accumulation, however. Technological development and diffusion of new agricultural techniques adequate for family farming are crucial to raising productivity. This implies a broad institutional-scientific effort to generate technologies adapted to the specific conditions of the Brazilian environment, both in the humid tropics of the Amazon and in other regions of the country.

Undertaking the costs of land distribution—whether agrarian reform or colonization—without providing small farmers with conditions for accumulation is questionable. Doing so in the Amazon is even worse. Virgin forests once destroyed never return the same. Indian cultures, once jeopardized, never recover. Devastation can never again be fully repaired. Paying such high natural and social costs without at least raising settlers' incomes merely spreads poverty around, adding insult to injury. Thus, Amazon colonization during the 1970s teaches us that land distribution must be taken as a broad set of policies in precarious equilibrium. Otherwise, it does more harm than good.

Land Distribution during the 1980s

The long-term results of land distribution during the 1970s are only now beginning to be evaluated. Whether small farming is in any sense "sustainable" in the humid tropics is something that can be ascertained only after many years of observation. The effects of alternative agricultural technologies on the Amazon environment take time to become manifest. The adequacy of economic and social policies for promoting stable communities of small farmers in what were once frontiers must withstand the test of time. So we do not know today any more about Amazon colonization than what has been included in this book.

My own current research on Amazon colonization shows that many of the trends that started during the 1970s intensified subsequently, during the 1980s. The demand for Amazon land continued to grow until the mid-1980s, then tapered off, as the general economic crisis removed conditions for migration. Land values in the South fell off, and speculative sales of *minifundia* in the southern states no longer financed long-distance migratory flows as massive as those of the 1970s. Although land values in the established regions of the country did not appreciate as quickly as they had before, they nonetheless skyrocketed in the Amazon. Road penetration and growth of towns attracted new business and laid down conditions for a new set of capitalist farmers to buy up original family farms, even inside colonization projects. Many of those who sold their land reaped large capital gains. Many of those who still remained on their plots had become, by the end of the 1980s, speculators rather than farmers. This was especially true of the state of Pará. Relatively cheap land, plus greater road accessibility, led to various forms of "speculative accumulation," such as are predicted in this book.

Agricultural technology continued to be inadequate for the Amazonian environment in all colonization projects. Even when appropriate technologies were attempted, economic policies were unfavorable to them. Such was the case of perennials (e.g., coffee and cocoa) and tree crops (e.g., rubber), all of which take many years to yield, during which time they impose heavy costs on farmers for the correct treatment of growing shrubs. Because of the general credit crunch, however, official long-term credit was insufficient. This drove small farmers into usurious "informal" debt with local informal lenders. Many went bankrupt, sold out, and swelled the rural exodus from directed colonization projects. Evidently, "sustainable" agriculture requires a more favorable economy than Brazil had to offer during the protracted crisis of the 1980s. The need for adequate economic infrastructure for colonization to be successful is another of the predictions of this book.

Some colonists did turn out to be highly successful, in the economic sense, during the 1980s. They accumulated wealth at high rates through their farming, not through speculation. They also constituted stable and prosperous rural communities. Ironically, however, the most economically successful colonists were precisely those who adopted what are considered to be the most inadequate technologies for the humid tropics. Whenever they had enough resources—own capital and/or short-term bank credit—they adopted the southern "technological package" of intensive chemical and mechanical inputs and, mostly, went into soybean production. Nowadays, however, the economic basis for these "successes" has ended. Price subsidies to soy production in distant regions have become unbearable in Brazil's current crisis. Thus, "successful" colonization was the least "sustainable" of all, both in the economic sense and in the ecological sense. This was especially true of the case of private colonization in the state of Mato Grosso. Relatively expensive land to begin with led to "excess technological intensification," as is also predicted in this book.

Aside from continuing the colonization projects undertaken during the 1970s, INCRA started some new ones during the 1980s, mostly to resolve increasingly violent land disputes. Meanwhile, a new movement of land distribution emerged during the mid-1980s. With the ending of a military dictatorship of twenty years' duration and the popular election of state governors, political demand for land led to local programs of agrarian reform, the largest being in the state of Pará. Settlement there was done on lands disappropriated from the old extractive oligarchy. An evaluation of the results of these land distribution schemes is just beginning and cannot be included here. The main point to note is that, after the 1970s, land distribution, even in the Amazon, was no longer possible without disappropriation of private lands, yet another of the predictions in this book.

As this book goes to press in early 1992, revisiting the same communities studied in 1981 shows massive urban growth, extreme diversification of activities, and a wide variety of experiences. Many of those who sold off their land started small businesses in local towns. Others complain heavily about the government, but stick to the land they have.

There is no pattern of return migration discernible. Unemployment and underemployment in the rest of the economy mean that Amazon settlement is apparently still the better alternative for those who went there. New movements into the forest seem to come mostly from the towns that were set up during the 1970s. Thus, Amazon land distribution does seem to have had an income-distributive effect after all, even though the property of land itself reconcentrated subsequently. This trend, finally, was also predicted in this book.

In sum, pressures for agrarian reform and colonization are stronger than ever in Brazil. They did not end with the 1970s, but continued into the 1980s and will grow during the 1990s. Until the 1991 Brazilian censuses are published, and until my own follow-up fieldwork, currently under way, is analyzed, not much more can be said now about the evolution of Amazon colonization during the 1980s. The region is too vast for generalizations, the number and types of actors are constantly increasing, and the interests involved have become much more complex than they were during the 1970s. Not only are Brazilian public and private agents interested in the Amazon, there is now an enormous number of foreign firms, foreign nongovernmental organizations, foreign journalists, and foreign academic researchers in the area. The penetration of markets and institutions into the Amazon is no longer a merely Brazilian East-to-West or South-to-North phenomenon, as portrayed here. The Amazon is becoming internationalized at a rate beyond what was foreseen in this book.

The main issues, however, are the same now as then. By mapping them out, literally and figuratively, this book provides the basic analytical and factual framework from which new information can subsequently be interpreted. That interpretation, however, must await the next book.

Conclusion

This book aimed to present Amazon colonization during the 1970s, the "Decade of Colonization," in broad perspective. It brought together information on the physical, demographic, institutional, and economic dimensions of directed settlement in the basin, and it set out some of the costs and benefits involved. The social and political issues are complex. Many of them continued into the 1980s and persist in the 1990s. A better understanding of them, inside and outside Brazil, will, I hope, contribute to effective collaboration among all parties interested in the Amazon today.

The expansion of the Amazon frontier altered degrees of freedom for political maneuvering in Brazil. The agrarian reform that was not undertaken twenty years ago can no longer be carried through in the terms formerly intended. Yet, it is still possible to provide some benefit to the dispossessed in the countryside by distributing land. Any land distribution, however, whether in the Amazon or in lands closer by, requires common sense. One should not charge too much for the land, pay too little for agricultural products, permit technologies that are too unproductive, starve the farmer of needed physical, economic, and social infrastructure, or attract large landowners and drive off the small.

Land distribution policies should admit neither devastation for the benefit of property concentration nor conservation to the detriment of distribution. In searching for the right combination, we can make use of the experience accumulated in directed colonization during the 1970s. An ample land redistribution program, in the Amazon and outside it, can still help many people and considerably improve rural income distribution in Brazil. All this can be achieved in a much less predatory way than has been done to date. We need only to want to do so.

23. POSTSCRIPT: THE MANY DIMENSIONS OF THE AMAZON FRONTIER

The Amazon is larger than any assertion that can be made about it. It has always attracted adventurers and dreamers, whose imagination it has captured the world over. Its name comes from an ancient Greek myth, and it continues to give rise to fantastic and grotesque heroes in modern film and literature such as Aguirre and Galvez. The destruction and burning of the forest is provoking growing protest in industrialized nations. Whether living in temperate zones or in the tropics, more and more people and organizations feel that they have rights to defend and that they are part, in some sense, of what happens in the Amazon.

The relation between the Amazon and Brazilian society, however, is quite different. Real heroes such as Chico Mendes, champion of rubber tappers, die, slain by the region's violence and greed. Big Brazilian cities scorn the countryside, in a way that is symmetric to the relation between these cities and the developed world. In London, for example, Rio de Janeiro is considered as a place where "there are snakes in the middle of the street." Yet, in Rio, the same idea holds in relation to Altamira, in Pará. Each metropolis is ignorant and contemptuous of its provinces.

Inversely, provinces know and value their metropoli. Since the 1970s, as the Amazon becomes progressively incorporated into Brazilian society, everything that happens in Rio de Janeiro, São Paulo, or in the international sphere now gets to the frontier. Television news coverage and *carioca* soap operas are ubiquitous in towns and villages. Metropolitan fashions, jargon, and values are known in the Amazon, although their adoption in local urban centers is filtered by indigenous customs. The former "two Brazils" are now integrated into only one. Language, consumption habits, industrial production, information, and aspirations are increasingly similar all over the country. But interregional cultural exchange is asymmetric. This blocks the perception of the frontier by those who live in the southern cities of Brazil

Finding in one community *gaúchos* with their *chimarrãos*, Japanese with their *gueixa* house, and *maranhenses* with their adobe homes, in the midst of the forest's fallen tree trunks, is to witness vast cultural differences being integrated by the frontier. As one penetrates the immense continent, whether slowly navigating wide and tortuous rivers, traveling on dusty roads through endless wilderness, or flying over silent forest carpet that extends from horizon to horizon, one cannot help but be fascinated by such great spaces. Going to the frontier means freedom from the "savage" competition of the segmented and concentrated economy in the rest of the country. A frontier gives vent to pressures for individual assertion and search for better opportunities in what is thought to be free land.

The quest for free land is the classic dream of all frontier people. Even though often unfulfilled, it guides their actions. That this is so can only be understood by being there. The frontier spirit cannot be identified or defined, but it certainly can be felt in the air.

There is a magical dimension in the task of changing one's destiny. It makes the small great and the weak strong. A southerner who arrived without a penny and cleared "virgin" forest with "his own hands" now has large stretches covered by plantations. A gunman who fled from justice in the Northeast and became an *invasor* on a river bank now runs a busy inn of his own. A prostitute who first set up a roadside bar and then became a usurer in the rice market now accumulates various plots in a colonization project where only one is formally allowed. All have become very different from what they were before coming to the frontier. With land ownership, they acquired new social and economic ties, took on new roles, and matured as social actors.

Those who could not make it are no longer there to be seen. They returned to their regions of origin, remained in local overcrowded towns, or left in search of yet another frontier. Those who are failing are becoming poor and defeated, as are so many others, both urban and rural, throughout Brazil. They become part of an unemployed and marginalized urban population, where they are perhaps no worse off than in cities elsewhere. The difference lies in the shattered hopes they once had, which brought them to the Amazon in the first place. So the myth is still there, even among the failures.

Convincing such a society that natural resources are scarce and that the Amazon should be preserved is difficult indeed. The myth of plentiful free land is persistent. Not frontier adventurers, city technocrats, or even the rest of public opinion has ever placed great value on environmental conservation until foreign pressure increased in the past few years. There are still few national interest groups who are effectively involved in propagating the new values being imported from industrialized societies. It will take many years of patient debate to convince the actors involved, as well as to reach a reasonable portion of Brazilian public opinion, of conservationist points of view. Only then will effective conservation legislation be passed and enforced.

There is, therefore, an economic and cultural logic behind Amazon devastation. Landless workers, wage laborers, settlers, merchants, large farmers, ranching or mining groups, hydroelectric planners, and other government agents all participate in it. Last, but not least, there is southern industrial capitalism, whose markets are being expanded by the Amazon's occupation. Substituting the logic of devastation with a logic of conservation will depend, in part, on each side's recognizing the legitimacy of the other's positions and on the capacity of the Brazilian state to negotiate compromises that will be consistent with such divergent interests. An urgent task for the future is the creation of an appropriate forum for this domestic debate. The fact that the international questioning of Amazon occupation has picked up before the national discussion has progressed, in a sense, puts the "cart before the horse."

It is, of course, impossible to grasp a reality as loaded with emotion as is the Amazon issue while wielding only the poor instruments of economics. People are more than their exact measurement in a given moment in time; they are a potential for action in themselves and in others. A social process is more than a local phenomenon; it is also the many repercussions it provokes across space and time. The Amazon frontier entails a possibility of national redefinition and growth much greater than any "opportunity cost" an economist can quantify.

To perceive complexity, however, does not mean that one can transmit it. I hope that the tables of this text, the statistical hypothesis testing, and the tedious measurements that support each finding do not provoke an impact contrary to that which was intended. The objective was not to exhaust the reader but to impart some awareness of the many dimensions of Amazon colonization.

GLOSSARY

Terms

Agregados. Household members who are not blood relatives.

Babaçu. A nut from which oil and fiber are extracted.

Biroscas. Small stores spread throughout the countryside that sell almost everything that local inhabitants buy.

Bodegueiros. Small rural traveling merchants, having a role similar to *biroscas*.

Caboclo. Local inhabitant of the Amazon, though not belonging to any Indian tribe.

Capixabas. People from the state of Espírito Santo.

Capoeira. Land left idle after being cleared and exhausted from cultivation.

Cariocas. People from the city of Rio de Janeiro.

Cerrado. Area with savannalike vegetation covering approximately one-third of Brazil and located roughly in the Center-West region.

Chimarrão. A hot drink made of the mate herb, drunk in the South of Brazil.

Estatuto da Terra. National legislation passed in 1965 instituting land reform.

Gaúchos. People from the state of Rio Grande do Sul.

Gleba. A large tract of land.

Grileiros. "Land grabbers," large-scale operators, who usually falsify property registries.

Guaraná. A powder made from bark and used medicinally as well as in soft drinks and refreshments.

Invasor. Forceful squatter.
Maranhenses. People from the state of Maranhão.
Mineiros. People from the state of Minas Gerais.
Seringueiros. Rubber tappers.
Sinuca. Pool hall.

Acronyms

BASA. Banco da Amazônia (Bank of the Amazon).
BINAGRI. Biblioteca Nacional de Agricultura (National Agricultural Library).
CEDEPLAR. Centro de Desenvolvimento e Planejamento Regional do Centro de Ciências Econômicas (UFMG) (Regional Development and Planning Center of the Economic Science Center of the Federal University of Minas Gerais).
CEPLAC. Comissão Executiva do Plano de Lavoura Cacaueira (Executive Commission for the Cocoa Development Plan).
CNPAF. Conselho Nacional de Pesquisa Agro-florestal (National Council for Agro-Forestry Research).
CNT. Conselho Nacional de Turismo (National Tourist Council).
DNER. Departamento Nacional de Estradas de Rodagem (National Highway Department).
EMATER. Empresa de Assistência Técnica e Extensão Rural (Technical Assistance and Rural Extension Enterprise).
EMBRAPA. Empresa Brasileira de Pesquisas Agrícolas (Brazilian Agricultural Research Enterprise).
EMBRATER. Empresa Brasileira de Assistência Técnica e Extensão Rural (Brazilian Technical Assistance and Rural Extension Enterprise).
FAO. Food and Agriculture Organization of the United Nations.
FEA. Faculdade de Economia e Administração (UFRJ) (Economics and Administration College of the Federal University of Rio de Janeiro).
FIBGE. *See* IBGE.
FUNAI. Fundação Nacional do Índio (National Indian Foundation).
GEBAM. Grupo Executivo do Baixo Amazonas (Lower Amazon Executive Group).
GETAT. Grupo Executivo do Araguaia e Tocantins (Araguaia and Tocantins Executive Group).
IBDF. Instituto Brasileiro de Desenvolvimento Florestal (Brazilian Institute for Forestry Development).
IBGE. Instituto Brasileiro de Geografia e Estatística (Brazilian Geographical and Statistical Institute).

ICOTI. Instituto de Cooperação Técnica Intermunicipal (Intercounty Technical Cooperation Institute).

INCRA. Instituto Nacional de Colonização e Reforma Agrária (National Institute for Colonization and Agrarian Reform).

INPES. Instituto de Pesquisas (INPES/IPEA) (Research Institute linked to IPEA and SEPLAN).

IPEA. Instituto de Pesquisas Econômicas Aplicadas (SEPLAN) (Institute for Research in Economics and Administration subordinated to SEPLAN).

IPLAN. Instituto de Planejamento do Instituto de Planejamento Econômico e Social (SEPLAN) (Social and Economic Planning Institute subordinated to SEPLAN).

IPPUR. Instituto de Planejamento e Pesquisa Urbana e Regional (Institute for Urban and Regional Planning and Research of the Federal University of Rio de Janeiro [UFRJ]).

NAEA. Núcleo de Altos Estudos da Amazônia (Nucleus of High Level Studies on the Amazon belonging to the Federal University of Pará).

PROTERRA. Land purchase credit program.

RADAM or RADAMBRASIL. Radar para a Amazônia (Radar for the Amazon).

SEMA. Secretaria Especial do Meio Ambiente (Special Secretariat for the Environment).

SENAR. Serviço Nacional de Aperfeiçoamento Rural (agricultural training program).

SEPLAN. Secretaria de Planejamento (Secretary of Planning).

SESP. Serviço Especial da Saúde Pública (Special Public Health Service).

SUCAM. Superintendência de Campanhas de Saúde Pública (Superintendency of Public Health Campaigns).

SUDAM. Superintendência de Desenvolvimento da Amazônia (Superintendency for the Development of the Amazon).

SUDECO. Superintendência de Desenvolvimento da Região Centro-Oeste (Superintendency for the Development of the Center-West).

SUDENE. Superintendência de Desenvolvimento da Região Nordeste (Superintendency for the Development of the Northwest).

SUFRAMA. Superintendência da Zona Franca da Manaus (Superintendency of the Manaus Free Trade Zone).

UFRJ. Universidade Federal do Rio de Janeiro (Federal University of Rio de Janeiro).

USDA. United States Department of Agriculture.

BIBLIOGRAPHY

Ablas, Luiz Augusto Queiroz. Movimentos migratórios e relações de troca entre estados na dinâmica espacial do desenvolvimento brasileiro. Ensaios Econômicos. São Paulo: IPE, 1985, 47.

Ab' Saber, A. N. Zoneamento ecológico e econômico da Amazônia: questões de escala e método. In *Seminário sobre tecnologia para os assentamentos humanos no trópico úmido.* Manaus: CEPAL, April 1987.

Afonso, Frederico Monteiro. *A cacauicultura da Amazônia.* CEPLAC/MINAGRI. Itabima: CEPLAC, 1979.

Agarwala, A. N., and S. P. Singh. *The economics of underdevelopment.* London: Oxford University Press, 1958.

Agroanalysis. *Cerrado* (Ensaio Especial), 10(9):2–15, September 1986.

Albuquerque, Maria Beatriz de, and Maurício David (eds.). *El setor agrário em América Latina.* Stockholm: Instituto de Estudios Latino-Americanos, 1979, pp. 125–137.

Almeida, Alfredo Wagner B. de, and Neide Esterci. Trabalho e subordinação no sertão cearense. *Revista de Ciências Sociais,* 10(1/2):95–103, 1979.

Amaral, C. M. Aspectos da comercialização na agricultura de baixa renda—Vale do Ribeira, Estado de São Paulo. Master's thesis, Universidade de São Paulo, 1975.

Amin, Samir, and Kostas Vergopoulos. *A questão agrária e o capitalismo.* Rio de Janeiro: Paz e Terra, 1977 (Pensamento Crítico, 15).

Andrade, Manuel Correia de. *A terra e o homem no Nordeste.* São Paulo: Brasiliense, 1964.

Aragon, Luis E., and L. J. A. Mougeot (eds.). *Migrações internas na Amazônia: contribuições teóricas e metodológicas.* Belém: NAEA/UFPa, 1986.

Aransberg, C., and S. Kimball. Relações de crédito na Irlanda rural. *Antropologia do direito: estudo comparativo de categorias de dívida e contrato.* Rio de Janeiro: Zahar, 1973.

Araújo, Edson Avelino de. Fronteira agrícola e formação de centros comerciais urbanos em Goiás, 1930–1955. Master's thesis, Belo Horizonte, CEDEPLAR/UFMG, 1981.

Araújo, Uilson Melo. Resposta da oferta agrícola aos preços mínimos. Master's thesis, Rio de Janeiro, EPGE/IBRE, 1985.

Archetti. Peasant studies: an overview. In *International Research in Rural Studies Progress and Prospects*. New York: Wiley, 1978.

Arrow, K. J. Toward a theory of price adjustment. In *The Allocation of Economic Resources*. Palo Alto, Calif.: Stanford University Press, n.d.

Arruda, Hélio Palmas de. *Colonização oficial e particular*. Brasília: INCRA/MINAGRI, 1978.

Asselin, V. *Grilagem: corrupção e violência em terras do Carajás*. Petrópolis: Vozes/Comissão Pastoral da Terra, 1982.

Assunção, Luiz Márcio de Oliveira. O trabalho fora da propriedade: o caso das famílias dos pequenos proprietários rurais no município de Piracicaba (S.P.). Master's thesis, São Paulo, ESALQ/USP, 1984.

Bacha, Edmar Lisboa, and H. S. Klein (eds.). *A transição incompleta: Brasil desde 1945*. Rio de Janeiro: Paz e Terra, 1986. 2vols. (Coleção Estudos Brasileiros 93–94).

Baer, Werner, et al. *Dimensão do desenvolvimento brasileiro*. Rio de Janeiro: Campus, 1978, pp. 301–337.

Bagnasco, Arnaldo. *La construcione sociale del mercato*. Bologna: Il Mulino, 1988.

Baiard, Amilcar. *Subordinação do trabalho ao capital na lavoura cacaueira da Bahia*. São Paulo: Hucitec, 1984 (Estudos Rurais, 4).

Bain, Joe S. Relation of profit rate to industry concentration: American manufacturing, 1936–1940. *Quarterly Journal of Economics*, 65(3):293–324, August 1951.

———. *Barriers to new competition*. Cambridge, Mass.: Harvard University Press, 1956.

———. Price leaders, barometers and Kinks. *Journal of Business*, 30(3):193–203, July 1960.

———. *Industrial organization*. New York: Wiley, 1969.

Banaji, J. Summary of selected parts of Kautsky's the agrarian question. *Economy and Society*, 5(1), 1976.

Barbosa, Túlio. *Desempenho do setor agrícola; a questão fundiária no período 1979–84*. São Paulo: USP/IPE, 1985 (Trabalho para Discussão Interna, 6).

Bardhan, P. *Land, labour and rural poverty: essays in development economics*. New York: Columbia University Press, 1984.

Bardhan, P., and A. Rudera. Interlinking of land, labour and credit relations: an analysis of village survey data in east India. *Economic and Political Weekly*, 13, February 1978.

Barrel, W. F., and Peter Phills. *The applications of cost-benefit analysis to transport investment projects in Britain*. Amsterdam: Elsevier, 1971.

Bastos, Maria Inês, and Elbio Gonzales. O trabalho volante na agricultura brasileira. In *Reunião nacional de mão-de-obra volante na agricultura* 1. Botucatu: UNESP, 1975, pp. 11–33.

Baumfeld, Carlos Minc. *Mercado de trabalho e mobilidade da força de trabalho na agricultura brasileira; uma análise crítica na formulação de Gaudemar.*

Rio de Janeiro: FEA, 1983 (Texto Didático, 22).
———. *A reconquista da terra. Estatuto da terra, lutas no campo e reforma agrária.* Rio de Janeiro: Jorge Zahar Editor, 1985.
Becker, Bertha Koiffman. Uma hipótese sobre a origem do fenômeno urbano numa fronteira de recursos do Brasil. *Revista Brasileira de Geografia,* 40(1), January/March 1978.
———. Os deserdados da terra. *Ciência Hoje,* 3(17):24–34, March/April 1985a.
———. Fronteira e urbanização repensadas. *Revista Brasileira de Geografia,* 47(3/4): 357–371, July/December 1985b.
———. O papel das cidades na ocupação da Amazônia. In *Seminário sobre tecnologia para os assentamentos humanos no trópico úmido.* Manaus: CEPAL, April 1987.
Behrman, Jerry R. *Supply response in underdeveloped agriculture.* Amsterdam: North-Holland, 1968.
Bell, C., and P. Zuzman. Bargaining theoretic approach to cropsharing contracts. *American Economic Review,* 66(4):578–588, September 1976.
Belluzzo, Luiz Gonzaga, et al. *Comercialização e formação de preços.* Campinas: UNICAMP, 1970.
Benetti, Maria Domingues. Endividamento e crise no cooperativismo empresarial do RGS: análise do caso FECOTRIGO/CENTRALSUL—1975–83. *Ensaios FEE,* 6(2):23–55, 1986.
Bennema, J., K. J. Beek, and M. N. Camargo. *Um sistema de classificação da capacidade de uso da terra para levantamentos de reconhecimento de solos.* Brasília: Ministério da Agricultura, 1964.
Bentes, Rosalvo Machado. A Zona Franca e o processo migratório para Manaus. Master's thesis, Belém, UFPA/PLADES, 1983.
Berquó, Elza. A fecundidade rural-urbana dos estados brasileiros em 1970. *Revista Brasileira de Estatística,* 38(51):251–303, July/September 1977.
Berry, Brian R. Tamanho de cidades e desenvolvimento econômico: síntese conceitual e problema de política com especial referência ao Sul e SE asiático. In S. Faissol, *Urbanização e regionalização.* Rio de Janeiro: IBGE, 1978, pp. 45–46.
Bhaduri, A. Agricultural backwardness under semi-feudalism. *Economic Journal,* 83(329):120–137, March 1973.
———. On the formation of usurious interest rates in backward agriculture. *Cambridge Journal of Economics,* 5, March 1977.
Bhalla, S. New relations of production in Haryana agriculture. *Economic and Political Weekly,* 11, March 1976.
Bharadwaj, K. *Production conditions in Indian agriculture.* Cambridge: Cambridge University Press, 1974.
BINAGRI. *Estudos básicos para o planejamento agrícola.* Brasília: BINAGRI, 1979 (Série Aptidão Agrícola das Terras, 11–16, 18).
Binswanger, Hans P. *Brazilian policies that encourage deforestation in the Amazon.* Washington, D.C.: World Bank, April 1989 (Environmental Department Working Paper, 16).
Binswanger, Hans P., and M. Rosenzweig (eds.). *Contractual arrangements, employment and wages in rural labor markets in Asia.* New Haven: Yale University Press, 1981.

Boisier, Sérgio, et al. *Desenvolvimento regional e urbano; diferenciais de produtividade e salários industriais*. Rio de Janeiro: IPEA/INPES, 1973 (Relatórios de Pesquisa, 15).

Boserup, Esther. *The conditions of agricultural growth: the economics of agrarian change under population pressure*. Chicago: Aldine, 1965.

Bottomley, A. Monopolist rent determination in underdeveloped areas. *Kyklos*, 19:106–117, 1966.

Bradby, B. The destruction of the natural economy. *Economy and Society*, 4(2), 1975.

Brandt, Vinícius Caldeira. Desenvolvimento agrícola e excedente populacional na América Latina (Notas Teóricas). *Novos Estudos CEBRAP*, (14):101–118, October/December 1975.

———. Do colono ao bóia-fria: transformação na agricultura e constituição do mercado de trabalho na Alta Sorocabana de Assis. *Novos Estudos CEBRAP*, (19):37–92, January/March 1977.

———. População e força de trabalho no desenvolvimento da agricultura brasileira. São Paulo: CEBRAP, 1979, mimeo.

Braverman, Avishay. Sharecropping and interlinking of agrarian markets. In *Landlords, Tenants and Technological Innovations*. Washington, D.C.: World Bank, 1981 (World Bank Development Research Center Discussion Papers, 31).

Braverman, Avishay, and T. N. Srinivasan. Agrarian reforms in developing rural economies characterized by interlinked credit and tenancy markets. In H. P. Binswanger and M. Rosenzweig (eds.), *Contractual arrangements, employment and wages in rural labor markets in Asia*. New Haven: Yale University Press, 1981

Braverman, Avishay, and J. Stiglitz. *Sharecropping and the interlinking of agrarian markets*. Washington, D.C.: World Bank, 1981.

Brito, Maria do Socorro, and T. Solange. O papel da pequena produção na agricultura brasileira. *Revista Brasileira de Geografia*, 44(2):191–261, April/June 1982.

Bruit, Hector. Essência e aparência das relações de produção no campo. *Economia e Desenvolvimento*, 1(3), 1982.

Bunker, Stephen G. Barreiras burocráticas e institucionais à modernização: o caso da Amazônia. *Pesquisa e Planejamento Econômico*, 10(2):555–600, August 1980.

———. Os programas de crédito e a desintegração não-intencional das economias extrativas de exportação do médio Amazonas do Pará. *Pesquisa e Planejamento Econômico*, 12(1):231–260, April 1982.

Calvente, Atila Torres. Formações não capitalistas no movimento de ocupação da Amazônia: colonização agrícola em Rondônia, 1970–1980. Master's thesis, Brasília, Instituto de Ciências Humanas/Departamento de Economia/UnB, 1980.

Câmara Neto, Alcino Ferreira. O processo de modernização da agricultura. In A. L. Ozorio de Almeida et al., *Biotecnologia e agricultura: perspectivas para o caso brasileiro*. Petrópolis: Vozes, 1984, pp. 15–40.

Camargo, J. M. A. Transição para o capitalismo; uma análise teórica do aparecimento do trabalho assalariado. *Pesquisa e Planejamento Econômico*,

11(2):443–468, August 1981.

Camargo, José Franciso de. Êxodo rural no Brasil; formas, causas e conseqüências econômicas principais. Rio de Janeiro: Conquista, 1960.

Capdeville, Duarte. Hierarquia de localidades centrais em áreas subpovoadas: o caso de Rondônia. *Revista Brasileira de Geografia,* (39):135–146, April/June 1977.

Carabias, M. J. Experiencias productivas en el trópico húmedo mediano. In *Seminário sobre tecnologia para os assentamentos humanos no trópicos úmidos.* Manaus: CEPAL, April 1987.

Cardoso, Fernando Henrique, and Enzo Faletto. *Dependencia y desarrollo en América Latina.* Mexico City: Siglo XXI, 1978.

Cardoso, Fernando Henrique, and Geraldo Müller. *Amazônia: expansão do capitalismo.* São Paulo: Brasiliense, 1977.

Carneiro, Maria José. Vidas imigrantes. *Ciência Hoje,* 4(24):66–72, May/June 1986.

Carvalho, Afrânio de. *Reforma agrária.* Rio de Janeiro: Ed. O Cruzeiro, 1963.

Carvalho, David Ferreira. Formas de acumulação e dominação do capital na agricultura e campesinato na Amazônia. Master's thesis, Belém, NAEA/UFPa, 1984.

Carvalho, José A. Magno de. Estimativas indiretas e dados sobre migrações: uma avaliação conceitual e metodológica das informações censitárias recentes. *Revista Brasileira de Estudos de População,* 2(1):31–74, January/June 1985.

Carvalho, José A. Magno de, et al. *Migrações internas na Amazônia.* In J. M. M. Costa, *Amazônia: desenvolvimento e ocupação.* Rio de Janeiro: IPEA/PNPES, 1979.

Carvalho, Rejane Vasconcelos. O estado e os programas de apoio à pequena produção. *Revista de Ciências Sociais,* 10(1/2):131–143, 1979.

Castro, Ana Célia. Modernização e diferenciação social da produção familiar agrícola no Brasil: efeitos do crédito rural. *Encontro Nacional de Economia,* 9. Olinda, 8–11. December 1981. Brasília: ANPEC, pp. 501–519.

———(coord.). *Estado e agricultura: avaliação e perspectivas da política científica e tecnológica.* Rio de Janeiro: CPDA/UFRRJ, 1983.

Castro, Ana Célia, and J. M. F. J. Silveira. Inovações biológicas para a agricultura: da via híbrida à engenharia genética. In C. M. Castro and G. Martine (eds.), *Biotecnologia e sociedade: o caso brasileiro.* Campinas: UNICAMP/ALMED, 1985, pp. 92–119.

Castro, Claudio Moura. *High technology in intermediate countries: The case of Brazil.* Brasília: IPEA/IPLAN/CNRH, 1983.

Castro, Claudio Moura, and G. Martine (eds.). *Biotecnologia e sociedade: o caso brasileiro.* Campinas: UNICAMP/ALMED, 1985.

Castro, Paulo Rabello de. *Barões e bóias-frias: repensando a questão agrária no Brasil.* Rio de Janeiro: CEDES/APEC, 1982 (Coleção Grandes Temas, 1).

CDEP. *A questão agrária brasileira.* Recife: Comissão de Desenvolvimento Econômico de Pernambuco, 1962.

CEDEPLAR. Migrações internas na região Norte: estudo de campo da região de Marabá. Belo Horizonte: CEDEPLAR/UFMG, 1977 (3 vols.).

———. Migrações internas na região Norte: o caso do Acre. Belo Horizonte: SUDAM/UFMG/FUNDEP, 1979a.

———. Ocupação agrícola da Amazônia: primeiros estudos para fixação de diretrizes. Brasília: Ministério da Agricultura, 1979b.

CEPAL/PNUMA. Sistemas ambientales y estrategias para ampliar la frontera agropecuaria en América Latina. In *Seminário sobre tecnologia para os assentamentos humanos no trópico úmido*. Manaus: CEPAL, April 1987.

Chalout, Norma B. R. *Settlement along the Trans-Amazon highway: planning and reality*. Cambridge: Center of Latin American Studies, 1980.

Chaung, S. N. S. *The theory of share tenancy*. Chicago: University of Chicago Press, 1969a.

———. Transactions costs, risk aversion and the choice of contractual arrangement. *Journal of Law and Economics*, 12(2):23–42, April 1969b.

Chayanov, A. V. *The theory of the peasant economy*. Homewood, Ill.: Irwin, 1966.

Clark, Colin. *Population growth and land use*. New York: St. Martin's Press, 1968.

Cochrane, T. T., and P. A. Sánchez. Ecosystem research: land resources and their management in the Amazon region: a state of the knowledge report. In S. B. Hecht (ed.), *Amazonia: agriculture and land use research*. Columbia: University of Missouri Press, 1982.

Colinvaux, P. A. The past and future Amazon. *Scientific American*, May 1989, pp. 68–74.

Collins, Norman R., and Lee J. Preston. *Concentration and price-cost margins in manufacturing industries*. Berkeley: University of California Press, 1968.

———. Price-cost margins and industry structure. *Review of Economics and Statistics*, 51(3):271–286, August 1969.

Conselho Nacional de Transportes. *Plano de viação: evolução histórica 1808–1973*. Rio de Janeiro: Ministério dos Transportes, 1974.

Contador, Claudio Roberto (ed.). *Tecnologia e desenvolvimento agrícola*. Rio de Janeiro: INPES/IPEA, 1975a (Monografia, 17).

———. *Tecnologia e rentabilidade na agricultura brasileira*. Rio de Janeiro: IPEA/INPES, 1975b (Relatório de Pesquisa, 28).

Contador, Claudio Roberto, and L. R. Ferreira. *Estudo preliminar sobre fertilizantes*. Rio de Janeiro: IPEA, 1983.

Coradini, O. L., and A. Frederico. *Agricultura, cooperativas e multinacionais*. Rio de Janeiro: Zahar, 1982.

Costa, José Marcelino Monteiro. *Amazônia: desenvolvimento e ocupação*. Rio de Janeiro: IPEA/INPES, 1979 (Monografia, 29).

Costa, Manuel Augusto (ed.). *Migrações internas no Brasil*. Rio de Janeiro: IPEA/INPES, 1971 (Monografia, 5).

Costa, Sarah H. *Os padrões de formação familiar e suas relações com condições de saúde em regiões de fronteira*. Rio de Janeiro: ENSP, 1981, mimeo (Subprojeto 3 da Pesquisa: "Migrações internas").

Cristaller, W. *The central places of Southern Germany*. Englewood Cliffs, N.J.: Prentice-Hall, 1966.

Cunha, Aércio dos Santos. Rural poverty and agricultural modernization in Brazil. PhD diss., Vanderbilt University, 1978.

Cunha, Paulo Vieira da. A organização dos mercados de trabalho: três conceitos alternativos. *Revista de Administração de Empresas*, 19(1), January/March 1979.

Cunha, Teresinha Helena de Alencar. Terra da promissão—luta pela subsistência de um povoado na frente de expansão do sudoeste do Maranhão. Master's thesis, Rio de Janeiro, Museu Nacional/UFRJ, 1977.

CVRD. *Cerrado: Um projeto nacional de abastecimento e exportação de grãos*. N.p., n.d.

David, Maria Beatriz de Albuquerque. *O papel atual da fronteira agrícola*. Rio de Janeiro: INPES/IPEA (Texto para Discussão Interna, 63).

Delfim, Neto A., et al. *Agricultura e desenvolvimento econômico no Brasil*. São Paulo: Universidade de São Paulo, 1965.

Delgado, Oscar (coord.). *Reformas agrárias en la América Latina; procesos y perspectivas*. Mexico City: Fondo de Cultura Económica, 1965.

Dias, Guilherme Leite da Silva. Estrutura agrária e crescimento extensivo. Master's thesis, São Paulo, Faculdade de Economia e Administração, 1976.

———. (coord.). *Alternativas de desenvolvimento para grupos de baixa renda na agricultura brasileira*. São Paulo: EMBRAPA/PURDUE, 1977.

———. *Pobreza rural no Brasil; caracterização do problema e recomendações de política*. Brasília: Comissão de Financiamento da Produção, 1979.

———. *O papel da agricultura no processo de ajustamento*. Belo Horizonte: ANPEC, December 1988.

Dias, Guilherme Leite da Silva, and Manoel Cabral de Castro. Colonização dirigida no Brasil: considerações críticas sobre o sistema de implantação de projetos. São Paulo: FIPE/M.A., 1976, mimeo.

DIEESE. Estatuto da terra e a reforma agrária. *Boletim do DIEESE*, (4):5 April 1985a.

———. Reforma agrária: uma necessidade inadiável. *Boletim do DIEESE*, (5):3–5, August. 1985b.

DNER. *Mapa rodoviário*. Rio de Janeiro: Ministério dos Transportes, 1962, 1969, 1971, 1975, 1980 (Publicação por Estado).

———. *Anuário estatístico*. Rio de Janeiro: Diretoria de Planejamento, 1982.

Domar, E. The causes of slavery and serfdom: a hypothesis. *Journal of Economic History*, 30(1):18–32, March 1970.

Domínguez, C. Investigación y desarrollo tecnológico diferenciado para el aprovechamiento económico de distintos ambientes del trópico cálido húmedo colombiano. In *Seminário sobre tecnologia para assentamentos humanos no trópico úmido*. Manaus: CEPAL, April 1987.

Durand, E. L. H. Tecnología para la intensificación del uso de las áreas colonizadas de la selva alta del Peru. In *Seminário sobre tecnologia para assentamentos humanos no trópico úmido*. Manaus: CEPAL, April 1987.

Ederington, L. H. The hedging performance of the new futures markets. *Journal of Finance*, 34(1): 157–169, March 1979.

Eichner, A. S. A theory of the determination of the mark-up under oligopoly. *Economic Journal*, 83(332):1.184–200 (December), 1973.

EMBRATER. *Ação integrada de apoio aos pequenos produtores rurais em projetos de colonização e assentamento do INCRA e do PROTERRA/FUNTERRA*. Plano operacional anual. Brasília, 1985.

Emmanuel, A. *Unequal exchange*. London: New Left Books, 1973.

Erber, Fábio Stefano. Política científica e tecnológica no Brasil: uma revisão da literatura. In João Sayad (ed.), *Resenhas de economia brasileira*. São Paulo: Saraiva, 1979, pp. 117–197.

Esterci, Neide. Conflito no Araguaia: peões e posseiros contra a grande empresa. PhD diss., São Paulo, DCS/FFLCH/USP, 1985.

Falcon, Walter P. Farmer response to price in a subsistence economy: the case of West Pakistan. *American Economic Review*, 54:131–37, May 1964.

FAO. A framework for land evaluation. *Soils Bulletin* 32. Rome, 1975.

FASE. *Pesquisa sobre força de trabalho agrícola em regiões de fronteira*. Rio de Janeiro: FINEP/INAN/FASE , 1978/1979, 4 vols.

Ferreira, Brancolina. O estado e a reprodução da pequena produção: reflexões em torno de um caso de colonização compulsória. PhD diss., Universidade de Brasília, 1980.

———. *A terra e seu significado para o pequeno produtor na fronteira*. Brasília: IPEA/IPLAN, 1981, mimeo (Subprojeto 4 da pesquisa "Migrações Internas").

———. *A relação dos colonos com a terra*. Brasília: IPLAN/IPEA, 1984.

Ferreira, Ignes Costa Barbosa, and Maria P. de Oliveira. Ceres et Rio Verde: deux moments de l'expansion de la frontiere agricole dans Etat de Goiás. *Cahiers des Sciences Humaines*, 22(3/4):281–295, 1986.

Fialho, Ildeu Pereira M. Os aventureiros da terra e a aventura do capitalismo na fronteira amazônica oriental. Master's thesis, Rio de Janeiro, CPDA/UFRRJ, 1982.

FINEP. *Problemas de formação do campesinato*. Rio de Janeiro: convênio FINEP/IPEA/IBGE/UFRJ, 1977 (Projeto Emprego e Mudança Sócio-Econômica do Nordeste).

Fleury, Maria Tereza Lane. Cooperativas e produtores agrícolas em uma sociedade capitalista. Master's thesis, Universidade de São Paulo, Faculdade de Filosofia, 1980.

Fonseca, M. G. D. *Inovações mecânicas na agricultura: questão para debate*. Rio de Janeiro: CPDA/UFRRJ, 1983.

Forman, Shepard, and Joyce Riegelhaupt. Market place and marketing system. Toward a theory of peasant economic integration. *Comparative Studies in Society and History*, 12(2):188–212, April 1970.

Foweraker, Joe. *A luta pela terra; a economia política da fronteira pioneira no Brasil de 1930 aos dias atuais*. Rio de Janeiro: Zahar, 1981.

Frank, A. G. *Capitalism and undervelopment in Latin America: historical studies of Chile and Brazil*. New York: Monthly Review Press, 1969.

Freitas, M. N. A. Rizicultura na pequena produção paraense. Master's thesis, Belém, NAEA/UFPa, 1985.

Friedmann, H. World market, state and family farm: social basis of household production in the era of wage labour. *Comparative Studies in Society and History*, 20(4):545–586, 1978.

From, Gary, et al. *Perspectives on regional transportation planning*. Washington, D.C.: Lexington Books, 1973.

Furtado, Celso. *Formação econômica do Brasil*. 10th ed. São Paulo: Editor Nacional, 1970 (Ciências Sociais, 23).

Gall, N. *Letter from Rondônia: a report on the Brazilian frontier*. New York: International Fact-Finding Center, Carnegie Endowment for International

Peace, 1977.

Garcia, Ronaldo. *Seminário sobre a questão agrária no Brasil.* Brasília: CEPER/ Associação de Sociólogos, 1979.

Garcia Júnior, Afrânio Raul. *Terra de trabalho; trabalho familiar de pequenos produtores.* Rio de Janeiro: Museu Nacional/UFRJ, 1983.

Gastal, Edmundo. O processo de transformação tecnológica na agricultura. *Caderno de Difusão de Tecnologia,* 3(1):155–169, January/April 1986.

Guademar, Jean Paul. *Mobilidade do trabalho e acumulação de capital.* Lisbon: Estampa, 1976.

Geertz, C. *Agricultural involution.* Berkeley: University of California Press, 1963.

Ghose, A. K. Indebtedness, tenancy and the adoption of new technology in semi feudal agriculture. *World Development* 4, April 1976.

Gomensoro, Sônia Maria R. *Biotecnologia para produção de alimentos básicos de consumo popular.* Rio de Janeiro: FEA/UFRJ, 1984.

———. *Tecnologia para produção de alimentos básicos.* Rio de Janeiro: FEA/ UFRJ, 1985.

———. *Desenvolvimento de novos setores intensivos em tecnologia no Brasil: biotecnologia.* Rio de Janeiro: STI/IEI/FEA, 1986.

Goodland, R. J. A., and H. S. Irwin. *Amazon jungle: green hell to red desert?* Amsterdam: North-Holland, 1975.

Goodman, David. Expansão da fronteira e colonização rural: recente política do desenvolvimento no Centro-Oeste do Brasil. In Werner Baer et al., *Dimensão do desenvolvimento brasileiro.* Rio de Janeiro: Campus, 1978.

———. Algumas implicações da biotecnologia para a agricultura dos países em desenvolvimento. In C. M. Castro and G. Martine (eds.), *Biotecnologia e sociedade.* Campinas: UNICAMP/ALMED, 1985, pp. 66–91.

———. Economia e sociedade rurais a partir de 1945. In E. Bacha and H. S. Klein (eds.), *A transição incompleta.* Rio de Janeiro: Paz e Terra, 1986, pp. 113–176.

Goodman, David, and Michael Redclift. The bóias-frias: rural proletarianization and urban marginality in Brazil. *International Journal of Urban and Regional Research,* 1(2):348–364, 1977.

———. *From peasant to proletarian capitalist development and agrarian transitions.* Oxford: Basil-Blackwell, 1981.

Gouru, P. *The tropical forest world: its social and economic conditions and its future status.* London: Longmans, 1961.

Graham, Douglas H., and Sérgio Buarque de Hollanda Filho. *Migrações internas no Brasil: 1872–1970.* São Paulo: FIPE/USP/CNPQ, 1984 (Relatórios de Pesquisa, 16).

Graziano da Silva, José. (coord.). *Estrutura agrária e produção de subsistência na agricultura brasileira.* São Paulo: Hucitec, 1980a.

———. Estrutura fundiária e relações de produção no campo brasileiro. In *Segundo encontro nacional de estudos populacionias.* Aguas de São Pedro: 1980b.

———. *A modernização dolorosa; estrutura agrária, fronteira agrícola e trabalhadores rurais no Brasil.* Rio de Janeiro: Zahar, 1981.

———. *O progresso técnico e as especificidades da agricultura.* Campinas: UNICAMP, 1983.

———. *O que é a questão agrária?* São Paulo, Brasiliense, 1985.

———. *O progresso técnico na agricultura.* Campinas: UNICAMP, November 1988 (Texto Didático).

Graziano da Silva, José, et al. *Tecnologia e campesinato.* Campinas: DEPE/PROTAAL, 1982.

———. Tecnologia e campesinato: o caso brasileiro. *Revista de Economia Política,* 3(4):21–56, October/December 1983.

Griffin, K. *Land concentration and rural poverty.* London: Macmillan, 1976.

Guanziroli, Carlos. *Estimativa dos custos de expansão da fronteira agrícola.* Rio de Janeiro: DPUR/UFRJ/IPEA. 1985–1986, 7 vols.

Guia 4 Rodas. *Mapas rodoviários e mapas verticais.* São Paulo: Editora Abril, 1966, 1970, 1975, 1980.

Guimarães, Alberto Passos. *A crise agrária.* Rio de Janeiro: Paz e Terra, 1979.

Guimarães, Eduardo Augusto. Organização industrial: a necessidade de uma teoria. *Pesquisa e Planejamento Econômico,* 9(2): 517–530, August, 1979.

———. *Formação de preços no oligopólio.* Rio de Janeiro: FEA/UFRJ, 1980, mimeo.

———. *Acumulação e crescimento da firma: um estudo de organização industrial.* Rio de Janeiro: Zahar, 1982 (Biblioteca de Ciências Sociais—Economia).

———. *Barreiras à entrada.* Rio de Janeiro: FEA/UFRJ. 1983a (Texto Didático, 19).

———. *Economias de escala e barreiras à entrada: uma formalização.* Rio de Janeiro: IEI/UFRJ, 1983b (Texto para Discussão, 16).

Gusmão, R. P., and O. V. Mesquita. Estrutura espacial do desenvolvimento rural na região do cerrado. *Revista Brasileira de Geografia,* 43(3):419–448, July/September 1981.

Gutierrez, M. C. *Estimativa econométrica da relação entre a penetração das estradas e o avanço da fronteira agrícola brasileira.* Rio de Janeiro: FEA/UFRJ, 1983 (Trabalho de Iniciação Científica).

Haddad, Paulo Roberto (ed.). *Planejamento regional: métodos e aplicação no caso brasileiro.* Rio de Janeiro: IPEA/INPES, 1972, pp. 7–51 (Monografia, 8).

Hall, R. L., and C. J. Hitch. Price theory and business behaviour. *Oxford Economic Papers,* (2):12–45, May 1939.

Harris, Donald J. The circuit of capital and the "labor problems" in capitalist development. *Social and Economic Studies,* 37, nos. 1–2, March/June 1988, pp. 15–31.

Harrison, B. Rural growth centers: a strategy for the rural development of low income countries. A research proposal. N.p.:1967, mimeo.

Hébette, Jean (coord.). Natureza, tecnologia e sociedades: a experiência brasileira de povoamento do trópico úmido. In *Seminário sobre tecnologia para assentamentos humanos no trópico úmido,* Manaus: CEPAL, 27–30 April 1987.

Hébette, Jean, and Rosa E. Acevdeo Marin. *Colonização espontânea, política agrária e grupos sociais.* Belém: NAEA/Universidade Federal do Pará, 1977.

———. *Colonização para quem?* Belém: Universidade do Pará/NAEA, 1979 (Amazônia Pesquisa, 1).

———. *O estado e a reprodução social: Ariquemes—Rondônia.* Belém: NAEA/UFPa, 1982 (Série Seminário e Debates, 9).

Hecht, S. B. (ed.). *Amazonia: agriculture and land use research.* CIAT Séries 03E-82. Columbia: University of Missouri Press, 1982.

Hees, Dora Rodrigues, Maria Elizabeth de Paiva Correa de Sá, and Tereza Coni Aguiar. A evolução da agricultura na região Centro-Oeste na década de 1970. Rio de Janeiro: DEGEO/IBGE, 1984, mimeo.

Hemming, John, et al. *Change in the Amazon jungle: the frontier after a decade of colonization.* London: Manchester University Press, 1985, 2 vols.

Henriques, Maria Helena F. T. A dinâmica demográfica de uma área de fronteira: Rondônia. Relatório de pesquisa no. 1: conceitos básicos e descrição preliminar da área. Rio de Janeiro: IBGE/DESPO, 1980, mimeo.

———. A política de colonização dirigida no Brasil: um estudo de caso, Rondônia. *Revista Brasileira de Geografia,* 46(3/4):393–424, July/December, 1984.

———. A dinâmica demográfica de uma área de fronteira: Rondônia. *Revista Brasileira de Geografia,* 47(3/4):317–356, July/December 1985.

———. Os colonos de Rondônia: conquistas e frustrações. *Revista Brasileira de Geografia,* 48(1):3–42, January/March 1986.

Ianni, Octávio. *A classe operária vai ao campo.* 2nd ed. São Paulo: Brasiliense/CEBRAP, 1977 (Cadernos CEBRAP, 24).

———. *A luta pela terra: história social da terra e da luta pela terra numa área da Amazônia.* Petrópolis: Vozes, 1978.

———. *Colonização e contra reforma agrária na Amazônia.* Petrópolis: Vozes, 1979a.

———. *Ditadura e agricultura: o desenvolvimento do capitalismo na Amazônia, 1964–1978.* Rio de Janeiro: Civilização Brasileira, 1979b.

IBASE. Brasil: O campo em chamas. *Cadernos do Terceiro Mundo* (94):18–29, October 1986.

IBGE. *Amazônia brasileira.* Rio de Janeiro: Conselho Nacional de Geografia, 1944.

———. *Áreas de atração e evasão populacional no Brasil, no período 1960–1970.* Rio de Janeiro: SUEGE (Série Estudos e Pesquisas, 4).

———. *Censo agropecuário—1960.* Vol. 2. Rio de Janeiro: Departamento de Censos, 1964.

———. *Censo agrícola—1960.* Vol. 1. Rio de Janeiro: Departamento de Censos, 1970.

———. *Censo demográfico—1960.* Vol. 1. Rio de Janeiro: Departamento de Estatísticas de População, 1970.

———. *Divisão do Brasil em microrregiões homogêneas.* Rio de Janeiro: IBGE, 1971.

———. *Divisão do Brasil em regiões funcionais urbanas.* Rio de Janeiro: DEGEO, 1972a.

———. *Sinopse do censo demográfico—1970.* Vol. 1. Rio de Janeiro: IBGE, 1972b.

———. *Censo agropecuário—1970.* Vol. 2. Rio de Janeiro: Superintendência de Estatísticas Primárias. 1973a.

———. *Censo demográfico—1970.* Vol. 2. Rio de Janeiro: Departamento de Censos 1973b.

———. *Censo demográfico—1975.* Rio de Janeiro: Departamento de Censos. 1979a.

———. *Censo agropecuário—1975*. Rio de Janeiro: IBGE, 1979b.

———. (Orlando Valverde, coord.). *A organização do espaço na faixa da Transamazônia*. Rio de Janeiro: IBGE/INCRA, 1979c.

———. *Regiões de influência das cidades*. Rio de Janeiro: IBGE, 1980.

———. *Modernização da agricultura no sudoeste de Goiás*. Rio de Janeiro: IBGE, 1982.

———. *Censo agropecuário—1980*. Rio de Janeiro: IBGE, 1983.

———. *Sinopse preliminar do censo agropecuário—1985*. Vol. 1. Rio de Janeiro: IBGE, 1985.

ICOTI. *A rede funcional urbana do Amazonas*. Manaus, 1976.

Incao e Mello, M. C. D'. *O bóia-fria: acumulação e miséria*. Petrópolis: Vozes, 1975.

INCRA. Metologia para programação operacional dos projetos de assentamento de agricultores. Brasília, 1971, mimeo.

———. *Informe sinóptico sobre o projeto integrado de colonização*. Altamira. Brasília, 1973.

———. *Cadastro de imóveis*. Brasília, 1978.

———. *Programa de colonização oficial*. Brasília, 1981a.

———. *Resumo geral do desempenho do sistema fundiário*. Brasília, 1981b.

———. *Departamento de Recursos Fundiários*. Brasília, 1982b.

———. *Programa de assentamento do polígono de Altamira*. Brasília, 1982a.

———. *Programação operacional, projetos fundiários*. Brasília, 1982c.

———. *Relação das empresas de colonização particular e empresas de migração*. Brasília: Departamento de Projetos e Operações (DPC), 1982d.

———. *Anais do simpósio internacional de experiência fundiária*. Salvador, August 1984.

INPES/IPEA. *Aproveitamento atual e potencial dos cerrados*. Rio de Janeiro: 1973 (Série de Estudos para o Planejamento no. 2).

INTERIOR. *A vez do cerrado*, 3, no. 17, May/June 1977, pp. 46–51.

IPEA. *Desenvolvimento regional no Brasil*. Brasília: IPLAN/IPEA, 1976.

Irmão, José Ferreira. Agricultural policy and capitalist development in Northeast Brazil. Master's thesis, Recife, UFFE/PIMES, 1984.

Janvry, A. de. The political economy of rural development in Latin America: an interpretation. *American Journal of Agricultural Economics*, (57):490–499, 1975.

Janvry, A. de, and C. D. Deere. *A theoretical framework for the analysis of peasants*. Berkeley: University of California, 1978 (Texto para Discussão da Giannini Foundation).

Jatobá, Jorge, et al. Expansão capitalista: o papel do estado e o desenvolvimento regional recente. *Pesquisa e Planejamento Econômico*, 10(1):273–318, April 1980.

Johnson, J. *Econometric methods*. New York: McGraw-Hill, 1963.

Johnston, Bruce, and Peter Kilby. *Agricultura e transformação estrutural: estratégias econômicas de países em desenvolvimento*. Rio de Janeiro: Zahar, 1977.

Jorgenson, D. W., and L. S. Lau. An economic theory of agricultural behaviour. *Meeting of the Far Eastern Econometric Society*. Tokyo, 4 June 1969.

Juarez, J. Santos. Relações de produção na agricultura de pequena produção no território Federal do Amapá. In *Encontro Pipsa (Grupo I)*. Macapá: 16–18 October 1980, mimeo.

Kageyama, Angela, and José F. Graziano da Silva. Progresso técnico e subordinação do trabalho ao capital na agricultura. *Boletim ABRA*, 10(4/5):49–54, July/October 1979.

———. *Produtividade e progresso técnico na agricultura*. Campinas: DEPE/IFCH/UNICAMP, 1982 (Texto para Discussão, 12).

———. Os resultados da modernização agrícola dos anos 70. *Estudos Econômicos*, Universidade de São Paulo, 13(3):537–560, September/December 1983.

———. Política agrícola e produção familiar. *Anais do Congresso Brasileiro de Economia e Sociologia Rural*, 24. Vol. 1. Brasília: SOBER, 1986, pp. 199–222.

———. *A dinâmica da agricultura brasileira: do complexo rural aos complexos agroindustriais*. Campinas: UNICAMP, n.d.

Katzman, Martin Theodore. *Cities and frontiers in Brazil; regional dimensions of economic development*. Cambridge, Mass.: Harvard Universtiy Press, 1977.

Kautsky, Karl. *La cuestión agraria*. Paris: Ruedo Ibérico, 1974.

Kidd, G., et al. *Assessment of future environmental trends and problems: agricultural use of applied genetics and biotechnologies*. Washington, D.C.: OTA, 1981.

Kinzo, Mary Dayse. Colonização e as transformações na estrutura de classes; de posseiros a colonos. Master's thesis, Brasília, DCS/ICH/UnB, 1982.

Klinge, H. *Journal of Soil Science*, 16:95, 1965.

———. *Acta Amazônica*, 1971.

Laclau, E. Feudalism and capitalism in Latin America. *New Left Review*, (67), 1971.

Lacorte, M. H. C. Estrutura da rede rodoviária do Estado do Rio de Janeiro: uma contribuição metodológica. Master's thesis, Universidade Federal do Rio de Janeiro, Departamento de Geografia, 1976.

Landini, J. R., A. D. Souza, and M. A. Monteiro. As funções das relações não-capitalistas na agricultura brasileira. *Cadernos CERU*, (16), November 1981.

Lavinas, Lena, et al. *A urbanização na fronteira*. Vols. 1 and 2. Rio de Janeiro: IPPUR/UFRJ, 1987.

Lehmann, David (ed.). *Agrarian reform and agrarian reformism: studies of Peru, Chile and India*. London: Raber and Raber, 1974.

Lemos, M. B. Um estudo comparativo sobre a formação de organização da produção de arroz do Brasil (1950–1970). Master's thesis, Departamento de Economia/UNICAMP, 1977.

Lena, Philippe. Expansão da fronteira agrícola em Rondônia: evolução da estrutura agrária e o aproveitamento dos lotes. *Anais do Seminário da expansão na fronteira agropecuária e o meio ambiente na América Latina*. Brasília: UnB/CEPAL/PNUMA/ANPEC/CNPq, 1981.

———. Aspects de la frontiere Amazonienne. *Cahiers des Sciences Humaines*, 22(3/4):319–343, 1986.

Lenin, Vladimir I. *The development of capitalism in Russia* (*The collected works*, vol.3). Moscow: Progress Publishers, 1964.

Leontieff, Wassily, Anne P. Carter, and Peter A. Petsi. *The future of the world economy, a United Nations study*. New York: Oxford University Press, 1977.

Levy, Maria Bárbara. *História financeira do Brasil colonial.* Rio de Janeiro: IBMEC, 1979 (Coleção História Financeira do Brasil, 1).

Lewis, A. W. Economic development with unlimited supplies of labor. In A. N. Agarwala and S. P. Singh, *The economics of underdevelopment.* London: Oxford University Press, 1958.

Lima, P. R., T. B. Vergolino, and Y. Sampaio. *Emprego, renda e miséria no Nordeste rural.* Recife: PIMES/UFPe, 1978 (Série de Pesquisa).

Lima, R. A. M. *Direito agrário, reforma agrária e colonização.* Rio de Janeiro: F. Alves, 1975.

Lima Sobrinho, Barbosa. *Problemas econômicos e sociais da lavoura canavieira.* Rio de Janeiro: Zélio Valverde, 1945.

Lindoso, Felipe José. O campesinato e o mercado; circuitos comerciais e reprodução camponesa. Master's thesis, Rio de Janeiro, PPGAS/MN/UFRJ, 1983.

Lipietz, A. *O capital e seu espaço.* São Paulo: Nobel, 1988.

Loesch, August. *The economics of location.* New York: Wiley, 1967.

Lopes, Eliane Sérgio Azevedo. Colonização agrícola em Rondônia: a relação parceleiro-agregado como manifestação de resistência à expropriação. Master's thesis, Rio de Janeiro, CPDA/ICHS/UFRJ, 1983.

Lopes, Juarez R. Brandão. Desenvolvimento e migrações: uma abordagem histórico-estrutural. *Novos Estudos CEBRAP* (6):127–142, October/December 1973.

———. Do latifúndio à empresa: unidade e diversidade do capitalismo no campo. *Cadernos CEBRAP,* (26), 1976.

———. Capitalist development and agrarian structure in Brazil. *International Journal of Urban and Regional Research,* 1978.

———. Desarrollo capitalista y estrutura agrária en Brasil. In Maria Beatriz de Albuquerque and Maurício Dias David (eds.), *El sector agrário en América Latina.* Stockholm: Institute of Latin American Studies, 1979, pp. 125–137.

Loureiro, Maria Rita Garcia. *Parceria e capitalismo.* Rio de Janeiro: Zahar, 1977.

———. Terra, família e capital. São Paulo: FGV, 1980, mimeo.

———. Contribuição para a análise das transformações recentes na agricultura brasileira. *Revista de Administração de Empresas,* 21(1):83–86, January/March 1981.

———. Pequena empresa na agricultura—família e processo de trabalho. *Revista de Administração de Empresas,* 24(1):33–36, January/March 1984.

Lu, Martin. Os grandes projetos da Amazônia: integração nacional ou (sub) desenvolvimento regional? *XI Encontro Nacional de Economia.* Belém: ANPEC, December 1983.

Machlup, F. Theories of the firm: marginalist, behavioral, managerial. *American Economic Review,* 57(1):1–33, March 1967.

Magalhães, Luis M. S. Impasses e alternativas na Amazônia ocidental. *Ciência Hoje,* 6(31):25–29, May 1987.

Mahar, Dennis J. *Desenvolvimento econômico da Amazônia: uma análise das políticas governamentais.* Rio de Janeiro: IPEA/INPES, 1978 (Relatório de Pesquisa, 39).

Maluf, Renato Sérgio J. A expansão do capitalismo no campo: o arroz no Maranhão. Master's thesis, Caminas, UNICAMP, 1977.

Marcier, Maria Hortense Ferro Costa. Padrões alimentares de um grupo camponês numa situação de expropriação no Estado do Maranhão. Master's thesis, Rio de Janeiro, Museu Nacional/UFRJ, 1977.

Martine, George. *Migrações internas e alternativas de fixação produtiva; experiência recente de colonização no Brasil.* Brasília: CNRH/PNUD, 1978 (Relatório Técnico, 37).

———. Rondonia and the fate of small producers. Brasília.

———. A colonização de Rondônia: continuidades e perspectivas. Brasília: CNRH/PNUD, 1980, mimeo.

———. *A evolução recente da estrutura de produção agropecuária: algumas notas preliminares.* Brasília: CNRH/PNUD, 1987a.

———. Migração e absorção populacional no trópico úmido. *Seminário sobre tecnologia para assentamentos humanos no trópico úmido.* Manaus: CEPAL, 27–30 April 1987b.

Martine, George, and Lício Camargo. *Crescimento e distribuição da população brasileira: tendências recentes.* Brasília: CNRH/PNUD, 1983 (Texto para Discussão 5/82).

Martins, José de Souza. *Capitalismo e tradicionalismo: estudo sobre as contradições da sociedade agrária no Brasil.* São Paulo: Pioneira, 1975.

———. Terra e liberdade: luta dos posseiros na Amazônia Legal. *Boletim da ABRA,* 9(1), January/February 1979.

———. Lutando pela terra: índios e posseiros na Amazônia Legal. *Revista de Ciências Sociais,* 11(1/2):7–28, 1980.

———. *Os camponeses e a política no Brasil.* Petrópolis: Vozes, 1981.

———. *A militarização da questão agrária.* Petrópolis: Vozes, 1984.

Marx, K. *Capítulo inédito do Capital: resultado do processo de produção imediato.* Porto: Escorpião, 1975.

Massel, B. F. Farm management in peasant agriculture: an empirical study. *Food Research Institute Studies,* 7(2):205–215, 1967.

Mata, Milton da, et al. *Migrações internas no Brasil: aspectos econômicos e demográficos.* Rio de Janeiro: IPEA/INPES, 1973 (Relatório de Pesquisa, 19).

Meillassoux, C. From reproduction to production: a Marxist approach to economic anthropology. *Economy and Society,* 1(1), 1972.

Meirelles, S. M. P. A questão da saúde na Amazônia. *Seminário sobre tecnologia para assentamentos humanos no trópico úmido.* Manaus: CEPAL, 17–30 April 1987.

Melo, Fernando Homem de. A *composição da produção no processo de expansão da fronteira agrícola brasileira.* São Paulo: USP/IPE, 1983 (Trabalho para Discussão Interna, 17).

Mendonça de Barros, José Roberto, and D. H. Graham (eds.). *Estudos sobre a modernização da agricultura brasileira.* São Paulo: IPE/USP, 1977 (Série IPE; Monografia, 9).

Menezes, M. A. O atual estágio de conhecimento sobre os recursos naturais na Amazônia: pressuposto para definição de uma política de ocupação. II Encontro Nacional de Estudos Populacionais. Aguas de São Pedro: ABEP, October 1980.

Mincer, Jacob. Labor force participation of married women. *Aspects of labor economics.* Princeton, N.J.: National Bureau of Economic Research, 1962.

Mincer, Jacob, and Glen C. Cain. Urban poverty and labor force participation: comment. *American Economic Review*, March 1969, pp. 185–194.

Ministério da Agricultura. *Mapa esquemático dos solos das regiões Norte, Meio-Norte e Centro-Oeste do Brasil.* Rio de Janeiro: MA-CONTAP-USAID/ Brasil (Boletim Técnico, 17), 1975a.

———. *Oferta e demanda de recursos de terra no Brasil.* Brasília: SUPLAN, 1975b.

——— *Aptidão agrícola das terras.* Brasília: BINAGRI, 1979.

———. *Mapa de solos do Brasil na escala 1:5.000.000.* Rio de Janeiro: EMBRAPA/ SNLCS, 1981.

Ministério do Interior. *Plano de desenvolvimento integrado do Vale do Xingu e Tapajós.* Rio de Janeiro: MINTER/SUDAM/SONDOTÉCNICA, 1976, 4 vols. (Relatório Final).

Ministério das Minas e Energia. *Levantamento de recursos naturais.* Rio de Janeiro: Projeto RADAMBRASIL, 1974/1980.

Ministério da Reforma e do Desenvolvimento Agrário. *Proposta para a elaboração do I Plano Nacional de Reforma Agrária da Nova República—PNRA.* Brasília: MIRAD, 1985.

Miranda, Mariana. Government colonization projects and the expansion of the agricultural frontier: a case study in Altamira. Seminar on regional development alternatives in the third world. Belo Horizonte: Fundação João Pinheiro, 1982.

Miranda Neto, Manoel José de. *O dilema da Amazônia.* Petrópolis: Vozes, 1979.

———. *A expropriação dos alimentos: análise das relações entre a produção agrícola familiar e o capital comercial: um estudo de caso da Amazônia.* Rio de Janeiro: Achiamé, 1985.

———. *Dominação pela fome: economia política do abastecimento.* Rio de Janeiro: Forense Universitária, 1988.

Modigliani, F. New developments on the oligopoly front. *Journal of Political Economy,* 66(2):215–232, June 1958.

Monteiro, Paulo S. *Projeto de expansão da fronteira agrícola.* Rio de Janeiro: INTERBRÁS, 1990.

Morais, Fernando, et al. *Transamazônia.* São Paulo: Brasiliense, 1970.

Morais, Maria da Piedade. *A dimensão social da fronteira: a terra e o pequeno produtor.* Rio de Janeiro: FEA/UFRJ, 1988 (Monografia de Economia).

Moran, Emílio F. *Developing the Amazon. The social and economic consequences of government directed colonization along Brazil's Transamazon Highway.* Bloomington: Indiana University Press, 1981.

———. *The dilemma of Amazonian development.* Boulder, Colo.: Westview Press, 1983.

Moreira, Roberto José. A pequena produção e a composição orgânica do capital. *Revista de Economia Política,* São Paulo, 1(3):41–56, July/September 1981.

Mougeout, Luc J. A. *Alternative migration targets and Brazilian Amazonia's closing frontiers.* Swansea, Wales: University College of Swansea, 1984. (Centre for Development Studies, Monograph 18).

Moura, Hélio A. de. O balanço migratório do Nordeste no período 1950/1970. *Revista Econômica do Nordeste,* 10(1):47–86 (January/March) 1979.

——— (coord.). *Migrações internas—textos selecionados.* Fortaleza: CAEM 1980, pp. 251–265.

Moura, Maria da Conceição de Almeida. Da necessidade do assalariamento. *Boletim Informativo PIPSA*, (2):105–112, July 1979.

Mueller, Charles C. O estado e a expansão da fronteira agropecuária na Amazônia brasileira. *Estudos Econômicos*, São Paulo, USP, 13(3):657–679, 1983a.

———. Fronteira, frentes e a evolução recente da ocupação da força de trabalho rural no Centro-Oeste. *Pesquisa e Planejamento Econômico*, Rio de Janeiro: 13(2):619–660 (August), 1983b.

———. *Gênese de estratégia agrícola no Brasil: uma interpretação.* Brasília: Fundação Universidade de Brasília, 1983c (Texto para Discussão, 104).

Müller, Geraldo. Estado, estrutura agrária e população: ensaio sobre integração e incorporação regional. São Paulo: CEBRAP, 1980.

———. *O complexo agro-industrial brasileiro.* São Paulo: ESP/FGV/Núcleo de Pesquisa e Publicações, 1981 (Relatório de Pesquisa, 3).

———. *Agricultura e industrialização do campo no Brasil.* São Paulo: PUC, 1982 (Cadernos PUC de Economia, 12).

———. Nas asas das estatísticas rumo às fronteiras. São Paulo: CEBRAP, 1987.

Müller, Geraldo, and V. Cardoso. *Amazônia, desenvolvimento sócio-econômico e política de ocupação.* São Paulo: CEBRAP, 1975.

———. O agrário brasileiro e a medição do dinâmico e do atrasado. Lavinas, 1987.

Müller, Keith Gerald. Colonização pioneira no sul do Brasil: o caso de Toledo, Paraná. *Revista Brasileira de Geografia* 48(1):83–139, January/March 1986.

Musumeci, Leonarda. Notas sobre campesinato de fronteira e o mito da "terra liberta." Rio de Janeiro, 1980, mimeo.

———. *Pequena produção e modernização da agricultura: o caso dos hortigranjeiros do Estado do Rio de Janeiro.* Rio de Janeiro: IPEA/IMPES, 1987 (Série PNPE, 15).

———. *O mito da terra liberta; colonização "espontânea," campesinato e patronagem na Amazônia Ocidental.* São Paulo: ANPOCS/Vértice, 1988.

Nakajima, C. Subsistence and commercial farms: some theoretical models of subjective equilibrium. In C. R. Wharton (ed.), *Subsistence agriculture and economic development.* Chicago: Aldine, 1969.

Nakano, Yoshiaki. A destruição da renda da terra e da taxa de lucro na agricultura. *Revista de Economia Política*, São Paulo, 1(3):3–16, July/September, 1981.

Neira, E. Espacio y tecnología en el trópico húmedo. *Seminário sobre tecnologia para os assentamentos humanos no trópico úmido.* Manaus: CEPAL, 27–30 April 1987.

Nerlove, M. *The dynamics of supply: estimation of farmers' response to price.* Baltimore: Johns Hopkins University Press, 1958.

Newberry, D. M. G. *Risk sharing, sharecropping and uncertain labour markets.* Stanford, Calif.: IMSS, 1976 (Technical Report, 202).

———. *Risk, uncertainty and agricultural development.* New York: Agricultural Development Council, 1979a.

———. Sharecropping, risk-sharing and the importance of imperfect information. 1979b .

———. The choice of rental contract in peasant agriculture. In L. Reynolds,(ed.), *Agriculture in development theory.* New Haven, Conn.: Yale University Press, 1975.

Newberry, D. M. G., and J. E. Stiglitz. Sharecropping, risk-sharing and the importance of imperfect information. In J. A. Roumasset et al., *Risk, uncertainty and agricultural development*. New York: Agricultural Development Council, 1979.

Nogueira, Jorge Madeira. *O Estado e a conservação do solo agrícola: subsídio para formulação de políticas*. Brasília, Fundação Universidade de Brasília, 1984 (Texto para Discussão, 121).

Núcleo de Altos Estudos Amazônicos (NAEA). *Belém-Brasília: trabalho de campo*. Belém: NAEA/UFPa. 1975.

———. *Colonização não dirigida na Belém-Brasília*. Belém: NAEA/UFPa, 1976, 7 vols.

———. *Colonização e reprodução das estruturas sociais*. N.p., 1981.

OIT. Employment, income and equality: *A strategy for increasing productive employment in Kenya*. Geneva: OIT, 1972.

Oliveira, Adélia E. de. Ocupação humana. In Eneas Salatti et al., *Amazônia: desenvolvimento, integração e ecologia*. São Paulo: Brasiliense, 1983, pp. 144–327.

Oliveira, Francisco de. *A economia da dependência imperfeita*. Rio de Janeiro: Graal, 1977 (Biblioteca de Economia, 1).

Oliveira, Luiz Antônio Pinto de. O sertanejo, o brabo e o posseiro: a periferia da Rio Branco e os cem anos de andanças da população acreana. Master's thesis, Belo Horizonte, CEDEPLAR, 1982.

Oliveira, Orlandino de, and Cláudio Stern. Notas sobre a teoria da migração interna: aspectos sociológicos. In H. A. de Moura (coord.), *Migrações internas—textos selecionados* Fortaleza: n.p., 1980.

Osório, Carlos. Migrações recentes e desenvolvimento. *Revista Pernambucana de Desenvolvimento*, 5(2):217–233, July/December 1978.

———. A frente agrícola de Rondônia: algumas anotações. *Boletim Informativo PIPSA*, (3):29–33, October 1979.

Ozorio de Almeida, Anna Luiza. *Distribuição da renda e emprego em serviços*. Rio de Janeiro: IPEA/INPES, 1976 (Relatório de Pesquisa, 34).

———. Parceria e tamanho da família no Nordeste brasileiro. *Pesquisa e Planejamento Econômico*, 7(2):291–332, August 1977a.

———. Parceria e endividamento no Nordeste brasileiro. In *Seminário sobre desenvolvimento, planejamento e políticas agrícolas*. Rio de Janeiro: ETAP/FGV, 15–19, August 1977b.

———. *Migrações internas e pequena produção agrícola na Amazônia: uma análise da política de colonização do INCRA*. Vols. 1–6. Rio de Janeiro: IPEA/INCRA, 1981–1984.

———. From peasant to proletarian: capitalist development and agrarian transition: resenha bibliográfica. *Pesquisa e Planejamento Econômico*, 12(3):953–962, December 1982.

———. Colonização dirigida no Brasil: algumas questões. Rio de Janeiro: BNDES, 1984a.

———. A expansão da fronteira. *Ciência Hoje*, 2(10):38/42, January/February 1984b.

———. Seletividade perversa na ocupação da Amazônia. *Pesquisa e Planejamento Econômico*, 14(2):353–398, August1984c.

———. Atribulações de uma economista na Amazônia. *Ciência Hoje*, 3(16):65–

74, January/February 1985a.

———. Migrações internas e colonização na Amazônia: alguns resultados econométricos. In *Anais do XIII encontro nacional de economia*. Vol. 2. Vitória: ANPEC, December 1985b, pp.123–142.

———. O custo da fronteira. In *Encontro nacional da SOBER*. Rio de Janerio: UFRJ, 1987a.

———. A dinâmica econômica da fronteira brasileira. Thesis submitted to the Full Professorship Chair in Microeconomics, Federal University of Rio de Janeiro, 1987b.

———. Tecnologia agrícola moderna para o pequeno produtor na Amazônia. In *Seminário sobre tecnologia para os assentamentos humanos no trópico úmido*. Manaus: CEPAL, April 1987c.

———. A colonização oficial na Amazônia nos anos 80. Rio de Janerio: IPEA, December 1990 (Texto para Discussão, 207).

———. A colonização particular na Amazônia nos anos 80. Rio de Janeiro: IPEA, January 1991 (Texto para Discussão, 208).

Ozorio de Almeida, Anna Luiza, and Maria Beatriz de A. David. *Tipos de fronteira e modelos de colonização na Amazônia: revisão da literatura e especificação de uma pesquisa de campo*. Rio de Janeiro: IPEA/INPES, 1981 (Texto para Discussão Interna, 38).

Ozorio de Almeida, Anna Luiza, and Carlos Eduardo Rebello de Castro. A pequena produção: uma visão unificada. *Estudos Econômicos*, São Paulo: 19:9/23, 1989 (Número Especial).

———. O setor informal revisitado. *Anais da ANPEC*, Fortaleza, vol. 3, December 1989, pp. 1457–1473.

Ozorio de Almeida, Anna Luiza, et al. *Biotecnologia e agricultura: perspectivas para o caso brasileiro*. Petrópolis: Vozes, 1984.

———. *Desenvolvimento agropecuário do cerrado: agenda de pesquisas*. Rio de Janeiro: FEA/UFRJ, 1986.

———. Biotecnologia: situação atual e perspectivas. *Revista Vozes de Cultura*, Rio de Janeiro, December 1990, pp. 545–570.

———. *Biotecnologia: situação atual e perspectivas*. Rio de Janeiro: IPEA, 1990.

Pacheco, Maria Emília L. Circuitos de mercado e padrões de consumo alimentar entre camponeses de origem cearense numa região do Pará. In Otávio G. Velho (coord.), *Projeto hábitos alimentares em camadas de baixa renda*. Rio de Janeiro: Convênio FINEP-UnB-UFRJ,1977, pp. 50–137.

———. Colonização dirigida, estratégia de acumulação e legitimação de um estado autoritário. Master's thesis, Brasília, Faculdade de Ciênicas Sociais/UnB, 1979.

———. Pequena produção sob o domínio do capital comercial e usurário. Master's thesis, Rio de Janeiro, Museu Nacional, UFRJ, 1980.

Paci, Giovanni. *La estructura sociale italiana*. Bologna: Il Mulino, 1982.

Padis, Pedro Calil. A fronteira agrícola. *Revista de Economia Política*, 1(1):51–76, January/March 1981.

Paiva, Ruy Miller. *A agricultura no desenvolvimento econômico: suas limitações como fator dinâmico*. Rio de Janeiro: IPEA/INPES, 1979 (Série Monográfica, 30).

Paor, Jonathan. Fazendo movimento: conceptions of progress on the agricultural frontier in Brazil. Versão Preliminar, 1982.

Pastore, Afonso Celso. A oferta de produtos agrícolas no Brasil. *Estudos Econômicos*, USP, 1(3):35–70, 1971.

———. *A resposta da produção agrícola aos preços no Brasil.* São Paulo: APEC, 1973.

Patarra, Neide Lopes, and Otávio Ianni. Conceição do Araguaia; estudo de caso: dinâmica populacional, transformações sócio-econômicas, atuação das instituições. São Paulo: CEBRAP, 1979, mimeo.

Paulo, Nilson Maciel. Os camponeses e a intermediação comercial: um estudo sobre as relações mercantis dos pequenos produtores do sudoeste paranaense. Master's thesis, Rio de Janeiro, CPDA/UFRRJ, 1983.

Pena, M. *Notas sobre o estado e a organização da ciência.* Rio de Janeiro: CNPq, 1976.

Penna, J. A., and C. C. Mueller. Fronteira agrícola, tecnologia e margem intensiva. *Estudos Econômicos*, USP, 7(1):53–106, January/April 1977.

Pereira, Pedro Luiz Valls. Função de produção agrícola na fronteira Amazônica. N. p., 1985, mimeo.

Pessoa, D. Estudo da rentabilidade dos estabelecimentos agropecuários e das condições de arrendamento da terra nos Estados do Ceará e Pernambuco. Recife: SIRAC, 1974, mimeo.

Pinsky, Jaime (ed.). *Capital e trabalho no campo.* São Paulo: HUCITEC, 1977.

Pinto, Ernesto R. de Freitas. Os trabalhadores da juta: um estudo sobre a constituição da produção mercantil simples no médio Amazonas. Master's thesis, Porto Alegre, CPPGAPS/UFRGS, 1982.

Planejamento e Desenvolvimento. A conquista dos cerrados. Vol. 2, no. 22, March 1975, pp. 46–51.

———. Polocentro: os rumos da expansão agrícola na área dos cerrados. Vol. 6, no. 69, February 1979, pp. 20–25.

Platnner, S. Rural market networks. N.p., n.d., mimeo.

Possas, Mário Luis. *A dinâmica da economia capitalista: uma abordagem teórica.* São Paulo: Brasiliense, 1987.

Potter, J. M., M. N. Diaz, and G. M. Foster. *Peasant society: a reader.* Boston: Little, Brown, 1967.

Ramalho Filho, A. *Aptidão agrícola das terras de Goiás, Mato Grosso e Mato Grosso do Sul.* Rio de Janeiro: MA/CE-FGV, 1980.

Rangel, Ignácio de Mourão. Povoamento dos eixos rodoviários. CDEP, 1962, mimeo.

———. Características e perspectivas da integração das economias regionais. *Revista do BNDE*, 1968, pp. 43–71.

Ransom, R. L., and R. Sutch. Debt peonage in the cotton south after the civil war. *American Economic Review*, 62(1):77–86, March 1972.

———. The lock-in mechanism and over production of cotton in the post bellum South. *Agricultural History*, 59(2):405–425, April 1975.

———. *One kind of freedom: the economic consequences of emancipation.* New York: Cambridge University Press, 1977.

Raposo, Ben-Hur. *Reforma agrária para o Brasil.* Rio de Janeiro: Editora Fundo de Cultura, 1965.

Rebello de Mendonça, Carlos Eduardo. Integração de migrantes ao mercado de trabalho urbano: migrações internas no Brasil na década de '70. Master's thesis, Rio de Janeiro: IEI/UFRJ, 1987

Reid, Joseph D. Sharecropping as an understandable market response—the post bellum south. *Journal of Economic History*, 33(1):106–130, March 1973.

Resende, Eliseu. *Benefícios da redução dos custos de transporte*. Brasília: GEIPOT, 1981, p. 197.

Resenhas de Economia Brasileira. São Paulo: Saraiva, 1979.

Reynolds, L. (ed.). *Agriculture in development theory*. New Haven, Conn.: Yale University Press, 1975.

Rezende, Gervásio Castro de. Produção, emprego e estrutura agrária na região cacaueira da Bahia. *Pesquisa e Planejamento Econômico*, 8(1):83–116, April 1978.

———. Estrutura agrária, emprego e produção no nordeste. *Pesquisa e Planejamento Econômico*, 9(1):33–82, January/March. 1979.

———. Trabalho assalariado, agricultura de subsistência e estrutura agrária no Brasil. *Pesquisa e Planejamento Econômico*, 10(1):179–216, April 1980.

———. Crédito rural subsidiado e preço da terra no Brasil. Rio de Janeiro, IPEA/INPES, 1981 (Texto para Discussão Interna, 41).

Ribeiro, Ivan Otero (coord.). *Situação e evolução recente da agricultura brasileira: a produção familiar*. Rio de Janeiro: PERSAGRI II, Centro de Pós-Graduação em Desenvolvimento Agrícola/EIAP/FGV, 1981.

Ribeiro, Mário Audifax Pinto. Agroindústria e fronteira agrícola. Master's thesis, Rio de Janeiro: IEI/UFRJ, 1986.

Rofman, Alejandro. *Desigualdades regionales y concentración económica*. Buenos Aires: SIAP/PLANTEOS, 1974. 238p.

Romeiro, Ademar Ribeiro. Ciência e tecnologia na agricultura: algumas lições da história. *Cadernos de Difusão Tecnológica*, 4(1):59–95, January/April 1987.

Romeiro, Ademar Ribeiro, and Fernando José Abrantes. Meio-ambiente e modernização agrícola. *Revista Brasileira de Geografia*, 43(1):3–46, January/March 1981.

Rondônia, Secretaria de Agricultura. *Sistema agrícola de Rondônia para o pequeno produtor*. Porto Velho: 1980, 2 vols.

Rosa, Tereza Coelho C. Aspectos da industrialização na Amazônia; repercussões sobre o perfil da mão-de-obra. Master's thesis, Belém, UFPA, 1982.

Rosenzweig, Mark R. Neoclassical theory and the optimizing peasant: an econometric analysis of market family labour supply in a developing country. *Quarterly Journal of Economics*, 94(1)31–56, February 1980.

Roumasset, J. A., et al. *Risk, uncertainty and agricultural development*. New York: Agricultural Development Council, 1979.

Sá, Lais Mourão. O pão da terra, propriedade comunal e campesinato livre na Baixada Ocidental Maranhense. Master's thesis, Rio de Janeiro, Museu Nacional/UFRJ, 1975.

Saint, William S., and W. W. Goldsmith. Sistemas de lavoura, mudança estrutural e migração rural-urbana no Brasil. *Novos Estudos CEBRAP*, (25):135–164, 1979.

Salatti, Eneas, et al. *Amazônia: desenvolvimento, integração e ecologia*. São Paulo: Brasiliense, CNPq, n.d.

Sanchez, P. A., et al. Amazon basin soils: management for continuous crop production. *Science*, 216:821–827, May 1982.

Sanders Junior, John Houston, and Wilson Guedes Almeida. *Fontes de variação da renda 1973–1974, de pequenos proprietários e parceiros com sugestões políticas.* Fortaleza: DEA/CCA/UFPe, 1976a (Série Pesquisa, 14).

Sanders Junior, John Houston, and Frederich Been. Desenvolvimento agrícola na fronteira brasileira: Sul de Mato Grosso. *Estudos Econômicos*, USP, 6(2):85–108, 1976.

Sandroni, Paulo. O processo de diferenciação do campesinato: acumulação capitalista, acumulação camponesa e "preço camponês." *Boletim Informativo PIPSA*, (3):105–111, October 1979.

Santos, Angela Moulin S. Penalva. *Urbanização na fronteira: um subproduto da política de colonização.* Rio de Janeiro: IPEA, 1985 (Relatório 1–4).

Santos, Charley Francisconi. *O garimpo de ouro na Amazônia.* Rio de Janeiro: FEA/UFRJ, 1988 (Monografia de Economia).

Santos, Charley Francisconi V., Maria da Piedade Morais, and Leonardo Rangel Tura. *A colonização na Amazônia. Relatórios de Pesquisa de Campo*, Vols. 1, 2, and 3, 1988–1989. Rio de Janeiro: FEA/UFRJ, 1988, 1989, 1990.

Santos, José Vicente Tavares dos. *Colonos do vinho; estudo sobre a subordinação do trabalho camponês ao capital.* São Paulo: HUCITEC, 1978..

———. A produção subordinada do campesinato. *Ensaios FEE*, 2(2):109–117, 1981.

———. A política de colonização no Brasil contemporâneo. In *XXXVI Reunião Anual da SBPC.* São Paulo: ABRA, 1984.

———. A gestação da recusa: o colono retornando dos projetos de colonização da Amazônia. In *Revoluções camponesas na América Latina.* Campinas: UNICAMP, 1985 a.

———. Política de colonização agrícola e o protesto camponês. *Ensaios FEE*, 6(2):127–140, 1985b.

——— (coord.). *Revoluções camponesas na América Latina.* Campinas: UNICAMP, 1985c.

Santos, M. *O espaço dividido.* Rio de Janeiro: F. Alves, 1979.

Santos, Petrúcio Codá dos. *Capital mercantil e agricultura—Campanha de produção agropecuária—Maranhão (1946–1958).* Rio de Janeiro: CPDA/EIAP/FGV, 1981.

Santos, R. *História econômica da Amazônia (1800–1920).* São Paulo: T. A. Queiroz, 1980.

Sautchuk, Jaime, et al. *Projeto Jari: a invasão americana.* São Paulo: Brasil Debates, 1979 (Brasil Hoje, 1).

Sawyer, Donald Rolf. Colonização da Amazônia: migração de nordestinos para uma frente agrícola do Pará. *Revista Econômica do Nordeste*, 10(3):773–812, July/September, 1979a.

———. Peasants and capitalism on an Amazon frontier. PhD diss., Harvard University, 1979b.

———. Ocupação e desocupação da fronteira agrícola no Brasil; ensaio de interpretação estrutural e espacial. *Anais do Seminário Expansão da Fronteira Agropecuária, Meio Ambiente na América Latina.* Brasília: UnB, 1981.

———. A fronteira inacabada: industrialização da agricultura brasileira e debilitação da fronteira amazônica. Belo Horizonte, CEDEPLAR, 1983, mimeo.

Sawyer, Donald Rolf, et al. Política de desenvolvimento e expansão da fronteira na Amazônia: estudo do impacto em São Félix do Xingu. N.p., n.d.

Scheidt, Rogério S. *Rondônia. A questão da fronteira agrícola e o Estado capitalista autoritário.* São Paulo: PIPSA, 1985.

Scherer, Frederic M. *Industrial pricing: theory and evidence.* Chicago: Rand McNally, 1970.

Schmidt, C. B. *Técnicas agrícolas primitivas e tradicionais.* Brasília: Conselho Federal de Cultura/Departamento de Assuntos Culturais, 1976.

Schmink, Marianne, and Charles H. Wood. *Frontier expansion in Amazonia.* Gainesville: University of Florida Press, 1985.

Schmitz, Hubert. *Technology and employment practices: industrial labour process in developing countries.* Brighton: IDS/University of Sussex, 1983.

Schultz, T. W. *Transforming traditional agriculture.* New Haven, Conn.: Yale University Press, 1964.

Shanin, Theodor. *Peasants and peasant societies.* Middlesex: Penguin Books, 1971 (Penguin Modern Sociology Reading).

Sigaud, Lygia. Luta política e luta pela terra no Nordeste. *Dados—Revista de Ciências Sociais,* 26(1):77–97, 1983.

Silva, Fábio Carlos. Frentes pioneiras e campesinato na Amazônia oriental brasileira. Master's thesis, Belém, NAEA/UFPa, 1983.

Silva, Sérgio Santos. *Valor da renda da terra: o movimento do capitalismo no campo.* São Paulo: Polis, 1981.

Silva, Tatiana Lins e. Os curupiras foram embora: um estudo sobre alimentação e reprodução da força de trabalho entre camponeses paraenses. Rio de Janeiro: FINEP/FUB/Museu Nacional, 1977, mimeo.

Singer, Paul. *Economia política da urbanização.* 3d ed. São Paulo: Brasiliense, 1976.

——— (ed.). *Capital e trabalho no campo.* São Paulo: HUCITEC, 1977 (Coleção Estudos Brasileiros, 7).

———. *Dominação e desigualdade: estrutura de classes e repartição da renda no Brasil.* Rio de Janeiro: Paz e Terra, 1981.

Singh, L., L. Squire, and J. Strauss. *Agricultural household models.* New Haven, Conn.: Yale University, 1985 (Economic Growth Center Discussion Paper).

Sorj, B., and M. Pompermeyer. *Sociedade e política na fronteira amazônica: interpretação e contra-argumentos.* N.p.,1985.

Sousa, Ivan Sérgio Freire, and Michelangelo G. Trigueiro. A luta pela terra: considerações preliminares sobre suas características no Brasil. *Caderno de Difusão de Tecnologia,* 3(1):133–154, January/April 1986.

Southworth, H. M., and B. F. Johnston *Agricultural development and economic growth.* Ithaca N.Y.:, Cornell University Press, 1967.

Souza, Paulo Renato. A determinação do salário e do emprego em economias subdesenvolvidas. PhD diss., Campinas, IFCH/UNICAMP, 1980.

SPVEA. *Primeiro plano qüinqüenal.* Vol. 1. Belém: Setor de Coordenação e Divulgação, 1955.

Stark, N. *Biotropia*, 10, 1978.

Stein, J. L. The simultaneous determination of spot and futures prices. *American Economic Review*, 51(5):1 112–125, 1961.

Steindl, J. L. *Maturity and stagnation in American capitalism*. New York: Monthly Review Press, 1976.

Stiglitz, J. E. Incentives and risk sharing in sharecropping. *Review of Economic Studies*, 41, April 1974.

———. *Economics of information and the theory of economic development*. Stanford, Calif.: NBER, 1985 (Working Paper).

SUDENE/EMBRAPA. *Levantamento exploratório—reconhecimento de solos da área de atuação da SUDENE*. Recife: EMBRAPA/SNLCS (Boletim Técnico, 60) and SUDENE/DRN (Série Recursos Naturais, 12), 1973/1979.

Sweezy, Paul M. Demand under conditions of oligopoly. *Journal of Political Economy*, 47(4):568–573, August 1939.

Sylos-Labini, Paolo. *Oligopólio e progresso técnico*. Rio de Janeiro: Forense Universitária, 1980.

Szmercsányi, T. Notas sobre o complexo agroindustrial e a industrialização da agricultura no Brasil. *Revista de Economia Política*, 3(2):141–144, April/June 1983.

Tavares, Vânia Porto. *Colônia agrícola do Rio Preto*. Rio de Janeiro: IPEA/INPES, n.d.

———. *Núcleo de colonização Bela Vista*. Rio de Janeiro: IPEA/INPES, n.d.

Tavares, Vânia Porto, et al. *Colonização dirigida no Brasil: suas possibilidades na região amazônica*. Rio de Janeiro: IPEA/INPES, 1972 (Relatório de Pesquisa, 8).

Tcheyan, Nilo. A comparative study of the administration of two Amazonian projects: Alto Turi and Ouro Preto. Washington, D.C.: World Bank, 1979, mimeo.

Teixeira, Lindalva da Costa. Formas de organização da produção e condições de existência dos agricultores de pimenta do reino em Santa Isabel do Pará. *Boletim Informativo PIPSA* (2):177, July 1979.

Telser, Lester G. Futures trading and the storage of cotton and wheat. *Journal of Political Economy*, 66(3):233–255, June 1958.

Thorner, D. *Marx on India and the Asiatic mode of production*. N.p.: n.p., 1965.

Thorner D., and A. Thorner. *Land and labor in India*. New York: Asia Publishing House, 1962.

Tibhonv, V. On the industrialization of agriculture. *Problems of Economics*, 52(23):3–22, January 1978.

Tokman, Víctor. *El sector informal: quince años después*. Santiago: OIT/PREALC, 1985.

Tupiassu, Amilcar Alves. A Amazônia e a penetração do capitalismo. *Boletim Informativo PIPSA*, (1):22, April 1979.

Tura, Leonardo R. *O pequeno produtor agrícola da região de fronteira: uma análise do seu desempenho*. Rio de Janeiro: FEA/UFRJ, 1989 (Monografia de Graduação).

Valverde, Orlando. *Estudos de geografia agrária brasileira*. Petrópolis: Vozes, 1985.

Valverde, Orlando, and Catharina V. Dias. *A Rodovia Belém-Brasília: estudo de geografia regional.* Rio de Janeiro: IBGE, 1967.

Varese, S., and G. J. Martin. Eletricidad y produción en el trópico húmedo el desarrollo participativo no sostenido (México y Perú). *Seminário sobre tecnologia para assentamentos humanos no trópico úmido.* Manaus: CEPAL, 27–30 April 1987.

Veiga Júnior, V. D., C. B. Veiner, and O. G. Velho. Sete teses equivocadas sobre a Amazônia. *Religião e Sociedade.* Rio de Janeiro: ISER, (10):31–36, November 1983.

Velho, Otávio Guilherme. *Capitalismo autoritário e campesinato.* São Paulo: DIFEL, 1972.

———. Modes of capitalist development, peasantry and moving frontier. PhD diss., University of Manchester, 1973.

———. A fronteira e o pequeno produtor. *Boletim da ABRA,* 8(6), November/December 1978.

———. Antropologia para sueco ver. *Dados—Revista de Ciências Sociais,* 23(1):79–91, 1980.

———. *Frentes de expansão e estrutura agrária; estudo do processo de penetração numa área da transamazônia.* Rio de Janeiro: Zahar, 1981.

———. Fronteiras no Brasil. *Ciência Hoje,* 3(1): 69, January/February 1985.

Wagley, Charles (ed.). *Man in the Amazon.* Gainesville: Florida University Press, 1974.

Wagner, A. GETAT—A segurança nacional e o revigoramento do poder regional. In *Transformações econômicas e sociais no campo maranhense.* Vol. 7. São Luis: CPT-MA, 1981.

Wallerstein, Immanuel. *The modern world system.* New York: Academic Press, 1974–1980, 2 vols. (Studies in Social Discontinuity).

Whad, E. Cash or credit crops? An examination of some implications of peasant commercial production with special reference to the multiplicity of traders and middlemen. In J. M. Potter, M. N. Diaz, and G. M. Foster (eds.), *Peasant society: a reader.* Boston: Little, Brown, 1967.

Wharton, C. R. Marketing, merchandising and money-lending: a note on middle man monopsony in Malaya. *Malayan Economic Review,* 7, October1962.

———. *Subsistence agriculture and economic development.* Chicago: Aldine, 1969.

Wolf, E. Parentesco, amizade e relações patrono-cliente em sociedades complexas. *Cadernos de Antropologia,* (7), 1974.

Wood, Charles H. Peasant and capitalist production in the Brazilian Amazon: a conceptual framework for the study of frontier expansion. In E. F. Moran (ed.), *Developing the Amazon.* Bloomington: Indiana University Press, 1981.

Wood, Charles H., and M. Schmink. *Blaming the small farmer: production in an Amazon colonization project.* Gainesville: University of Florida Press, 1979 (Studies in Third World Societies).

World Bank. *Report.* May 1984.

Wright, Charles Leslie. Estado, reforma agrária e coletivização de terras rurais. Brasília: UnB, 1983 (Texto para Discussão, 97).

Yotopoulos, P. A., and J. B. Nugent. *Economics of development: empirical investigations.* New York: Harper & Row, 1976.

INDEX

Page numbers in boldface refer to maps and graphs.
Page numbers followed by "t" refer to tables and charts.

www.ingramcontent.com/pod-product-compliance
Lightning Source LLC
LaVergne TN
LVHW090024310826
846742LV00010B/21